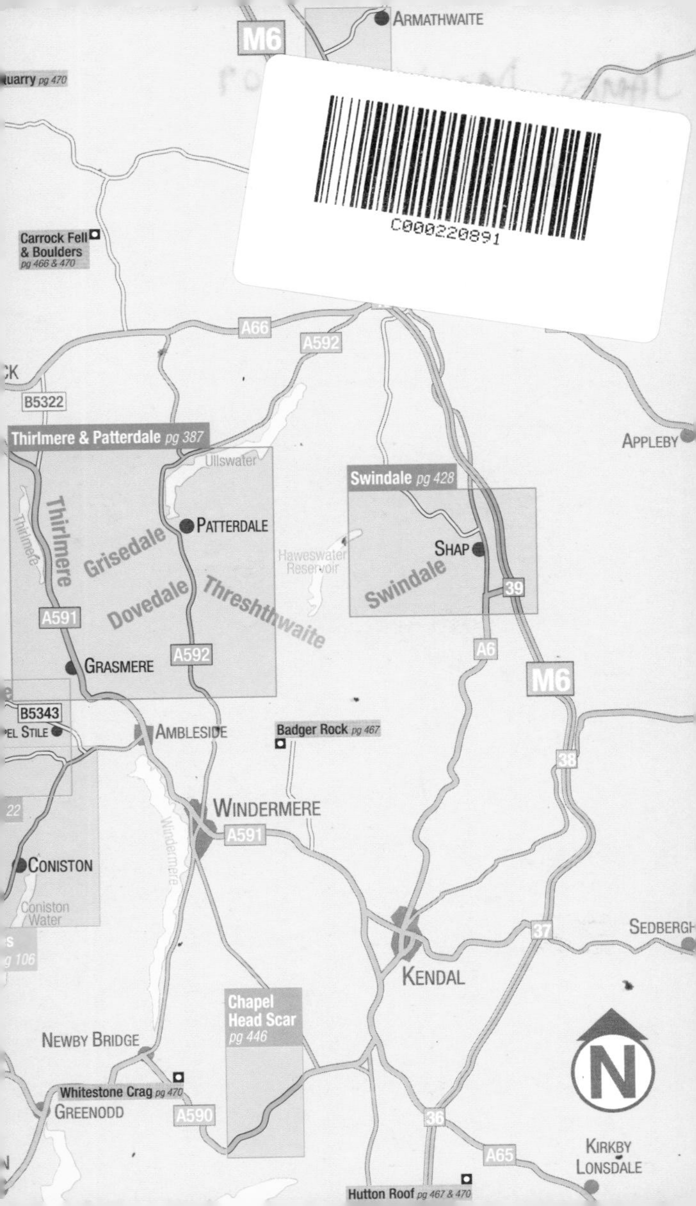

M6
ARMATHWAITE
uarry pg 470
C000220891
Carrock Fell & Boulders pg 466 & 470
A66
A592
B5322
Thirlmere & Patterdale pg 387
APPLEBY
Ullswater
Swindale pg 428
PATTERDALE
Thirlmere
Thirlmere
Grisedale
Haweswater Reservoir
SHAP
Swindale
Dovedale
Threshthwaite
39
A591
A592
A6
GRASMERE
M6
B5343
AMBLESIDE
Badger Rock pg 467
38
WINDERMERE
A591
Windermere
CONISTON
Coniston Water
SEDBERGH
37
KENDAL
Chapel Head Scar pg 446
NEWBY BRIDGE
N
Whitestone Crag pg 470
GREENODD
A590
36
A65
KIRKBY LONSDALE
Hutton Roof pg 467 & 470

JAMES DAVIDSON 6/09
07817939658

Lake District Rock

Selected Rock Climbs in the English Lake District

by Members of the FRCC Guidebooks Committee

Illustrated by Al Phizacklea

with additional illustrations
by other members of the
FRCC Guidebooks Committee

Edited by S.J.H. Reid

FRCC GUIDE

Published by
the Fell and Rock Climbing Club of the English Lake District

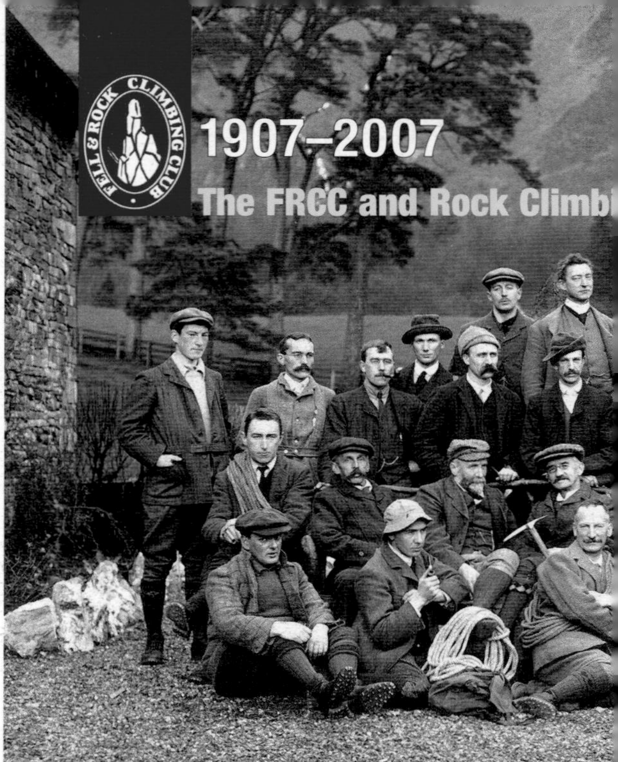

Above: The 2nd Annual Dinner of the FRCC at Coniston, 22nd November 1908

The formation of the **Fell and Rock Climbing Club** was proposed at Coniston in 1906 at the instigation of Edward Scantlebury and Alan Craig, two of a "coterie of keen young mountaineers living on the southern confines of the English Lake District". Before the end of the year the club had over 40 members enrolled and was officially founded in 1907 when Ashley Abraham accepted the office of President. The first Club Journal was produced that same year and many new climbs were reported therein and in further annual volumes.

The Club published its first rock climbing guidebook in 1922 (*Doe Crag* by George Bower) and since that date has produced a continuous series of definitive guidebooks to Lake District rock climbing.

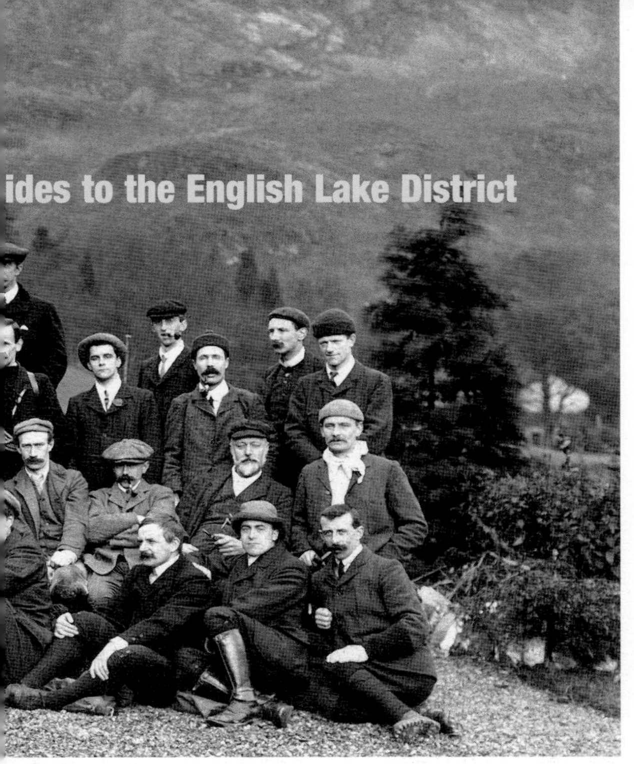

These guidebooks are written and published by volunteers who update the text and check new climbs, many of which have been, and continue to be, pioneered by Club members.

The Club now has over 1000 members and owns several club-huts both in the Lake District and elsewhere. Membership has always been open to applicants of either sex who can demonstrate an ongoing interest and enthusiasm for climbing in the Lake District. Enquiries regarding the FRCC and its guidebooks should be addressed to the current Club Secretary or Guidebooks Editor, whose addresses are available from the Club's website at www.frcc.co.uk or from the BMC.

This guide to a selection of the very best of the rock climbing of the English Lake District is the first of a number of publications and events commissioned to mark the centenary of the FRCC in 2006/7.

Dedication

This guidebook is dedicated to the founding members of the FRCC; George Harold Charter, Alan Craig, Sholto Hamilton Gordon, Charles Grayson and Edward Scantlebury, and also to the previous editors of FRCC Climbing Guides; Roger Chorley, Harry Kelly, John Wilkinson, David Miller, Dave Armstrong and Al Phizacklea.

First edition: 2003

ISBN 0-85028-045-1

Cover photo: Dominic Donnini and Tim Whitely on the magnificent ***Tophet Wall*** (HS), by Nick Wharton

Designed & typeset by **Vertebrate Graphics**, Sheffield.
www.v-graphics.co.uk

Manuscript preparation by
Synergy Consultants Ltd., Yewbarrow, Hampsfell Road, Grange-over-Sands, Cumbria, LA11 6BE.

Printed by the Ernest Press, Glasgow G44 5QD

Distributed by Cordee, 3a De Montfort Street, Leicester, LE1 7HD

Contents

The Borrowdale Area 316

Eastern Crags 386

Outlying Areas 436

Other Information 458

Key to diagrams

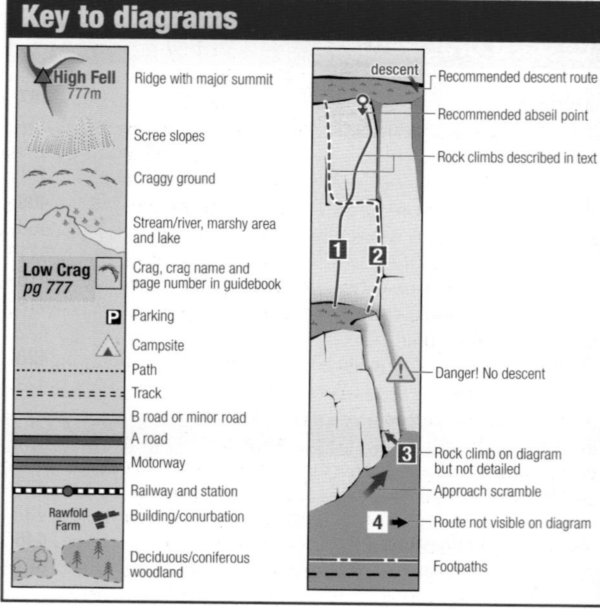

Introduction

Left: Traditional climbing on *Needle Ridge* (VD), The Napes
Photo: Stephen Reid

This guidebook gathers together a selection of the best rock-climbs in the Lake District, one of the most popular climbing areas in the British Isles. It is produced by the Fell and Rock Climbing Club of the English Lake District, a club that has been responsible for producing definitive guides to the area since 1922. The FRCC's current series of definitive guides form a complete record of rock climbing in the area. Work is on-going and the series is constantly under review. Details of the current guides are available from the FRCC website at www.frcc.co.uk. The writers and researchers of those definitive guides, climbers who know virtually every nook, cranny, rib, crack and groove of their crags, have written this guide.

This selected guide is aimed at the occasional visitor, the newcomer to the area, or the newcomer to the sport, who wishes to experience the classic climbs of the Lake District without the expense of investing in the full series of definitive guides. It covers all the major valleys, and in fact just about every crag of note. Well over 500 climbs are described in full, with more indicated in passing on Al Phizacklea's superb diagrams, and over 60 crags are covered. These include many popular 'roadside' venues like Shepherd's Crag in Borrowdale, Raven Crag in Langdale and Castle Rock in Thirlmere, as well as the classic high buttresses such as Scafell, Pillar Rock, Gimmer Crag and

Dow. Also included are a few of the best outlying crags (Chapel Head, Armathwaite and St Bees) that can provide a welcome haven in unsettled weather. There are also notes on bouldering, climbing walls and other information useful to the visitor. Whilst the bulk of the climbs described are in the VS to E2 range there are in fact over 100 routes of Severe or less, as well as over 100 of E3 and above.

In short, this is a guide to the very finest of Lake District rock climbing, described by those who know the area best.

General Notes

Grades

The standard British double-grade system is used. On first acquaintance, this may be puzzling to visitors from overseas used to climbs having a single grade, but in fact it is relatively simple and once understood, provides a great deal of information about the climbs. By far the majority of climbs in this guide require the use of leader-placed natural protection and on any route given an adjectival grade a full rack suitable to the climb being attempted should be carried. Grades are very personal, being influenced by an individual's stature and physique, their willingness to climb above protection, and their preference for a particular style of climbing.

Adjectival Grades

These give the overall grade of the climb in good weather conditions, taking into account such factors as technical difficulty, rock quality and protection. The grades are: Moderate, Difficult, Very Difficult, Mild Severe, Severe, Hard Severe, Mild Very Severe, Very Severe, Hard Very Severe, Extremely Severe, with the standard abbreviations being used in the text. The Extremely Severe grade is open ended and is currently divided into E1, E2, through to E10, though the hardest climb described in this book is E8.

Plus and Minus Grades

In this volume, adjectival grades have been further subdivided by use of a minus sign (-) to indicate routes that are considered easy for the grade, and a plus sign (+) for those thought to be hard. This system replaces the traditional graded list.

UK Adjectival Grade	UK Technical Grade (approx)	UIAA (alpine) Grade	European Equivalent	USA Equivalent	Australian Equivalent
Moderate		I, II	1	5.1, 5.2	4, 5
Difficult		II, III	1, 2, 2+	5.2, 5.3	5, 6, 7
Very Difficult		III, III+	2, 2+, 3–	5.2, 5.3, 5.4	6, 7, 8
Hard Very Difficult		III+, IV, IV+	2+, 3–, 3, 3+	5.4, 5.5, 5.6	8, 9, 10
Mild Severe		IV, IV+	3–, 3, 3+	5.5, 5.6	10, 11
Severe		IV, IV+, V–	3, 3+, 4	5.5, 5.6, 5.7	10, 11, 12
Hard Severe		IV+, V–, V	3, 3+, 4, 4+	5.6, 5.7	12, 13
Mild Very Severe	**4a, 4b, 4c**	IV+, V–, V	3+, 4, 4+	5.6, 5.7	12, 13, 14
Very Severe	**4a, 4b, 4c**	V–, V, V+	4, 4+, 5	5.7, 5.8	13, 14, 15
Hard Very Severe	**4c, 5a, 5b**	V+, VI-, VI	4+, 5, 5+, 6a	5.8, 5.9	15, 16, 17, 18
E1	**5a, 5b, 5c**	VI, VI+	5+, 6a, 6a+	5.9, 5.10a	18, 19, 20
E2	**5b, 5c, 6a**	VI+, VII–, VII	6a+, 6b, 6b+	5.10b, 5.10c	19, 20, 21
E3	**5c, 6a**	VII, VII+	6b, 6b+, 6c	5.10d, 5.11a, 5.11b	20, 21, 22
E4	**6a, 6b**	VII+, VIII–, VIII	6c, 6c+, 7a	5.11b, 5.11c, 5.11d	22, 23
E5	**6a, 6b 6c**	VIII, VIII+, IX–	7a, 7a+, 7b	5.11d, 5.12a, 5.12b	23, 24, 25
E6	**6b, 6c**	IX–, IX, IX+	7b, 7b+, 7c, 7c+	5.12b, 5.12c, 5.12d, 5.13a	25, 26, 27, 28
E7	**6c, 7a**	IX+, X–, X	7c+, 8a, 8a+	5.13a, 5.13b, 5.13c	28, 29, 30
E8	**6c, 7a**	X, X+	8a+, 8b, 8b+	5.13c, 5.13d, 5.14a	30, 31, 32

Technical Grades

These are included for each pitch of 4a and above on routes of VS and above. This grade is an attempt to assess the pure technical difficulty encountered on each pitch and once again is open-ended. The grades to date are: 4a, 4b, 4c, 5a, 5b, 5c, 6a, 6b, 6c, 7a.

French Grades

Fully bolt-protected 'sport' routes are given French grades overall. These grades, prefixed with an 'F', are comparable with the standard French/Spanish grades of 4, 5, 6a, 6b, 6c, 7a, 7b, 7c, and 8a. They are further subdivided with a (+) symbol.

Every attempt has been made to ensure that the grades given are as accurate as possible; however, caution should always be exercised and total reliance on a given grade avoided.

Terminology

A *wall* is almost vertical, or slightly overhanging. A *slab* is less than vertical. A *glacis* is a very easy-angled slab. An *arête* is a sharply-angled rib or ridge. *Climbs* and *pitches* are measured in metres (m).

Aid

None of the routes in this guide require the use of artificial aid.

Stars and Quality

All the routes in this selected guide are of high quality and consequently star ratings are not given.

Location of Crags

The location of each crag is indicated by its national grid reference. Beware those crags where the name on the map may be some way from the grid reference shown. The aspect of the main faces has been included to aid the choice of crags. The altitude given is based on a mean sea level of zero. The terms 'true left' and 'true right' are used to describe the position of a crag in a valley or gill relative to the direction of flow of the stream. The terms 'left' and 'right', unless otherwise stated, mean as the climber faces the climb. The terms *gill* and *ghyll* (meaning stream or gully) are interchangeable.

New Routes and Corrections

To aid writers of future guidebooks, please post comments, corrections, and details of all new climbs on the FRCC website www.frcc.co.uk. Traditionalists can still avail themselves of the New Routes Books at either *Rock and Run*, Ambleside or *Needle Sports*, Keswick.

Bolts & In-situ Protection

The placing of bolts is a subject which has aroused much emotive discussion during recent years.

In the interest of care and concern for crags and the mountain environment and a belief that British climbing in general should continue with the principle of leader-placed removable protection, the FRCC are generally in accord with the guidelines on the use of bolts for the protection of routes as set out by the BMC. It is agreed that in the Lake District bolts are only acceptable on certain quarried crags and some agreed limestone and sandstone outcrops. Climbers are asked to adhere to this policy and refrain from the temptation to place bolts on any natural crags.

Retro-bolting has taken place on a number of routes in the Lake District but only after consultation with the first ascentionist of that route. In order to avoid any conflict, please ensure that this policy is maintained.

A number of route descriptions in this guide contain references to in-situ protection including pegs, slings, bolts and wires. The history of these frequently dates back to the first ascent. There can be no guarantee that the fixed gear mentioned will still be in place when you climb the route or, more importantly, if it is there, that it will be of any use. It is well known that in-situ gear will deteriorate to a fraction of its original holding power due to the elements. This can occur in a matter of months rather than years, particularly where wires or hard steel blade pegs are concerned. Therefore it is for the individual climber to assess the reliability of any in-situ protection encountered. This is even more important on sea-cliffs such as St Bees where the corrosive action of the salt air can have a rapid detrimental effect. **Bolts have been known to fail in the past – they are not infallible.**

Fixed abseil points have been found around some of the crags over the years. They should be thoroughly inspected before use and, if found to be doubtful, backed up with new equipment.

Above: Flora Wharton checking the guidebook beneath Shepherd's Crag
Photo: Nick Wharton

History

First ascent details are given in the text. For a fuller history of Lakeland climbing the reader is referred to the FRCC series of definitive guidebooks.

Safety Advice

Climbing is a dangerous pastime that can seriously damage your health! Details of climbs recorded in this guidebook, together with their grades, reference to in-situ or natural protection, and locations, are made in good faith having been compiled from first ascent or past descriptions, checked and substantiated where possible with consensus comments.

Unfortunately climbs can change; holds fall off, rock becomes dirty, in-situ gear deteriorates or disappears. Even a minor alteration can have a dramatic effect on the grade or seriousness of a route. It is therefore essential that climbers judge the condition of any route before committing themselves.

The contents of this guidebook are believed to be correct. However, neither the FRCC nor its members and their friends involved with its production can be held responsible for any omissions or mistakes, nor liable for any personal or third party injuries or damage, howsoever caused, arising from its use. In this claims-conscious age, climbers are recommended to obtain suitable insurance cover. The BMC now provides third party liability cover for members and members of affiliated clubs.

Climbing in the Lake District

Left: Great Gable seen from Wasdale
Photo: Al Phizacklea

The Lake District National Park is situated entirely within the county of Cumbria in the North-West of England, not far from the Scottish border. It is a land of dramatic contrasts with rugged peaks, or fells as they are known locally, rising high over lush green valleys and the deep dark waters that give the area its name. Indeed it contains both the highest mountains and the most extensive lakes in England. However, unlike National Parks in many other parts of the world, the Lake District is a populated area, full of working hill farms, villages and market towns. It bears both the ancient scars of mining and quarrying and the modern ones of tourism and yet is still reckoned to be one of the most tranquil and beautiful areas in the British Isles. It is unsurprising therefore that the Lake District is popular not only with climbers, but also with hill walkers, fell runners, mountain bikers, canoeists and a host of other mountain and countryside users. Furthermore, it has an interesting history (as evidenced by such ancient monuments as the splendidly named Mediobogdum – the Roman Fort on Hardknott Pass, and the more recent Borrowdale wad mines), and is also especially renowned as a source of inspiration to many poets and artists, including Wordsworth, Coleridge, Ruskin, Beatrix Potter and three generations of the Heaton Cooper family. The unceasing efforts of a great number of people over many years have contributed toward keeping the Lake District as a place of great beauty to be enjoyed, not only by the outdoor enthusiasts, but also by the myriad of other visitors and also the locals, though it has to be said that the interests of these diverse groups do not always coincide. Not least among these efforts was the foresight of those who realised the dangers of unchecked development and campaigned long and hard for the area's special status. Now there are several bodies, statutory and otherwise, like the National Park Authority, the National Trust and the Friends of the Lake District, and their army of Wardens, Rangers and others, both paid and voluntary, who fight a daily battle to maintain the fragile fabric of this much loved landscape.

The valleys of the Central Lake District are arranged like the spokes of a wheel with the hub in the area of Great End, the northernmost outlier of the Scafell massif. The major valleys of this central area are in a clockwise direction, Langdale, the Duddon Valley, Eskdale, Wasdale, Ennerdale, Buttermere, Borrowdale and Thirlmere. East of Thirlmere lies the Helvellyn massif and the parallel valley of Patterdale with its subsidiary valleys of Grizedale, Deepdale and Dovedale. Eastwards again, the Far Eastern Fells have many small and relatively unfrequented valleys of which only Swindale features in this book. In addition, on the edges of the National Park, a few isolated crags provide good alternative venues in poor weather (not completely unknown in the region – after all, all those lakes have to come from somewhere!). Each of the main valleys has several crags and each of these crags has its own character and atmosphere, and indeed often its own special rock type, for within these few hundred square miles you may climb on limestone, sandstone, slate, granite, gabbro and, most widespread and varied, the complex andesites and pyroclastics of the 'Borrowdale Volcanic Group'. Virtually all these crags require leader-placed protection and belays, but a few quarries, limestone outcrops and the sandstone crags of St Bees are bolted. Whilst the bouldering on offer in the Lakes is not as extensive as that in some other areas of England, there is still plenty to go at if you know where to look. The major crags in terms of size are undoubtedly Scafell, Pillar, Gimmer and Dow; yet these are all situated at altitude and suffer the worst of the weather. Perseverance is needed to catch them at their best and it is more likely that most climbers will make their first acquaintance of Lakeland rock on the more easily accessed low-lying crags such as Raven's, Shepherd's, Reecastle or

Castle Rock of Triermain. Indeed, some folk never seem to climb anywhere else, but this is a shame, for the joy of Lakeland climbing lies in its variety. Here in this guide are gathered the very best of those routes on the very best of those crags, the bulk of them in the VS to E2 range that the majority of climbers seem to operate in these days. There are plenty of easier routes too, as well as a good introduction to some of the many superb hard climbs in the area. Certainly if you have climbed everything in this book, at least up to your top grade, you will have garnered an enviable wealth of climbing experience and memories.

Maps

The Lake District is well covered by maps. The Ordnance Survey Explorer Series 1:25000 sheets 4, 5, 6 and 7 cover the bulk of the area, whilst Explorer 303 is needed for St Bees. Harveys also produce an excellent set of maps at this scale (their Super Walker series), including the highly useful Central Lake District map - these have the advantage of being waterproof. At 1:50000, the Ordnance Survey's Landranger maps numbers 89, 90, 91, 96 and 97 cover the entire area except Armathwite which is on sheet 86. Sheet 90 which covers the central area is the most useful. As a general map of the area, the old Ordnance Survey's one inch to a mile Tourist Map, with its shaded contours and fine detail was very handy. Unfortunately is has been superceded by a modern version that is little more than a road map, though it is possible that the original may be updated and re-introduced.

Local Amenities – Accommodation & Information

The two major towns of the area of most interest to climbers are Ambleside in the south and Keswick in the north. The former may be considered the gateway to Langdale while the latter guards the entrance to Borrowdale, the two most popular climbing valleys in the Lake District. These two towns are linked via the A591 which runs through Grasmere and over Dunmail Raise into Thirlmere. They both have a great many B&Bs, Youth Hostels, pubs, takeaways, restaurants, cafés, grocery stores, and outdoor shops. Whilst they also have petrol stations, these are unlikely to be open 24 hours a day, for which a visit to Penrith or Kendal is necessary. The conglomeration of Windermere and Bowness, whilst popular with tourists, is too far away from the action to be of much interest to climbers though it does have the advantage of being connected by rail to Kendal. Those who prefer a quieter life will appreciate the many smaller towns and villages such as Coniston, Grasmere, Patterdale and Grange.

A list of useful telephone numbers and websites can be found on page 479.

Campsites, Bunkhouses, Camping Barns & Club Huts

Within the Lake District there are numerous camping barns, bunkhouses and campsites. In addition there are a great many superb climbing club huts, most of which are available to non-club members. To find out about these contact the British Mountaineering Council (BMC) in Manchester. To find out more about campsites and so on contact the tourist offices listed above or the campsites direct – details are given on page 481.

Wild Camping

Photo: Stephen Reid

Wild camping (ie camping outside of a proper campsite) is generally allowed on the fells above the 1000 foot (300 metre approx.) contour as long as one is above the final (intake) wall and not within 100 metres of habitation. Any campsite used should be left as it was found and all litter cleared.

Access & Conservation

Access to the crags described in this guide will be taken for granted by the majority of users but in fact in some cases it may have been achieved only through years of patient negotiation. Fortunately, the National Trust, Forestry Commission, United Utilities, or other private owners who are broadly sympathetic to climbers, own most of the crags described. In a few cases however, the situation remains delicate and increasing numbers of climbers are only likely to make it more so. Here is an area in which we can all help, not only by cherishing this region in the manner it deserves, parking thoughtfully, co-operating with farmers and landowners, following the country code, observing bird restrictions, picking up litter at crags and so on, but by ensuring that others do the same. Outsiders look on climbers as a group and inconsiderate behaviour by a few will be seen, rightly or

Above: Wasdale Campsite with Great Gable in the background **Photo:** Dave Willis

wrongly, as a reflection upon us all. The onus is on all of us to make certain that it doesn't happen in the first place.

Several of the crags described in this guide carry **Bird Restrictions** in the spring (typically from 1st March to 30th June), and crags that have been restricted regularly in the past are indicated in the text. However, the situation changes from year to year and climbers visiting any crag in the Lake District should make efforts beforehand to find out if there are *Schedule 1* birds or ravens in residence on the crag they intend to visit. Usually restricted crags will be signed, but this may not always be the case and all climbers should acquaint themselves with the latest known details which can be found on the BMC website at www.thebmc.co.uk or on the FRCC website at www.frcc.co.uk. Where birds have not nested in any particular year, the ban may be lifted earlier. If there are birds nesting, and there is an agreed restriction, then please be prepared to change your plans according to the agreement. It may be that only some parts of the crag are restricted, so other routes can be climbed. If this is the case it will be indicated on the signs. For more information on Bird Restrictions please see the notes on page 473.

Acknowledgements

Left: Matt Groves on *Needle Ridge* (VD)
Photo: Dave Willis

This guide is the product of many peoples' hard work and commitment, not the least of whom are the writers of all previous FRCC Climbing Guides.

In addition, the following guidebook writers, both past and future, have spent many arduous hours in beer-fume-filled pubs selecting routes before heading out into the fells on the onerous mission of checking and rewriting their descriptions. They are: Gary Baum, Max Biden, Al Davis, Rick Graham, Bill Hannah, Alan Hewison, Ron Kenyon, Al Phizacklea, Colin Read, Stephen Reid, Phil Rigby, Nick Wharton and Bill Young. Ron Kenyon, Max Biden and John Holden have further assisted way beyond the call of duty by checking the final text for errors, a seemingly endless task. Other members of the guidebook team have also assisted, in particular Chairman Alan Rowland and Treasurer John Barrett both of whom who had the vision to run with the idea. Latterly George Watkins has taken over from Alan, and has continued in supporting the project. The FRCC are also extremely grateful to Kevin Howett and Peter Davies for contributing to the notes on Bird Restrictions, and to Dr. John Ellerton of the Lake District Search and Mountain Rescue Association who wrote the section on Mountain Accidents. In addition the Lancashire Guidebook Committee are to be warmly thanked for giving their blessing for the inclusion of Chapel Head Scar. Our thanks are also due to the many other climbers who contributed

Above: Wastwater sunset **Photo:** Stephen Reid

with helpful comments and checking routes, in particular David Birkett and Alan Wilson, who greatly assisted with the bouldering section.

This guide would probably be just as accurate without photographs but many climbers would argue that they are by far the most important part of any guidebook. Our thanks are due to the photographers – their names are recorded in the text – and also to Nick Wharton who collected and collated hundreds of slides and pictures from all quarters of the country before making his final painstaking selection.

This guide also forms a unique homage to Al Phizacklea who over the last twenty years has produced what is quite possibly the finest collection of crag diagrams in the British Isles. For this guide, Al has excelled himself, drawing scores of new diagrams and updating and improving old ones, and, for the first time, the entire collection has been coloured – the results have astounded even Al himself. Within this book you have a large part of this extraordinary life's work.

We are grateful too to Susan Harvey of Harvey Maps, who has allowed Al to base his maps upon their excellent Lakeland series.

Thanks are also due to those responsible for producing these neatly typed lines from piles of illegible scrawl: Les and Jean Ainsworth of Synergy carried out the typesetting, Jon Barton and his gang at Vertebrate Graphics, the colour layout, and Peter Hodgkiss of the Ernest Press, the printing and binding.

Finally, on a personal note, I would like to thank my long-suffering family who have had to put up with "Dad's busy with his book" for far too long.

Stephen Reid,
September 2003

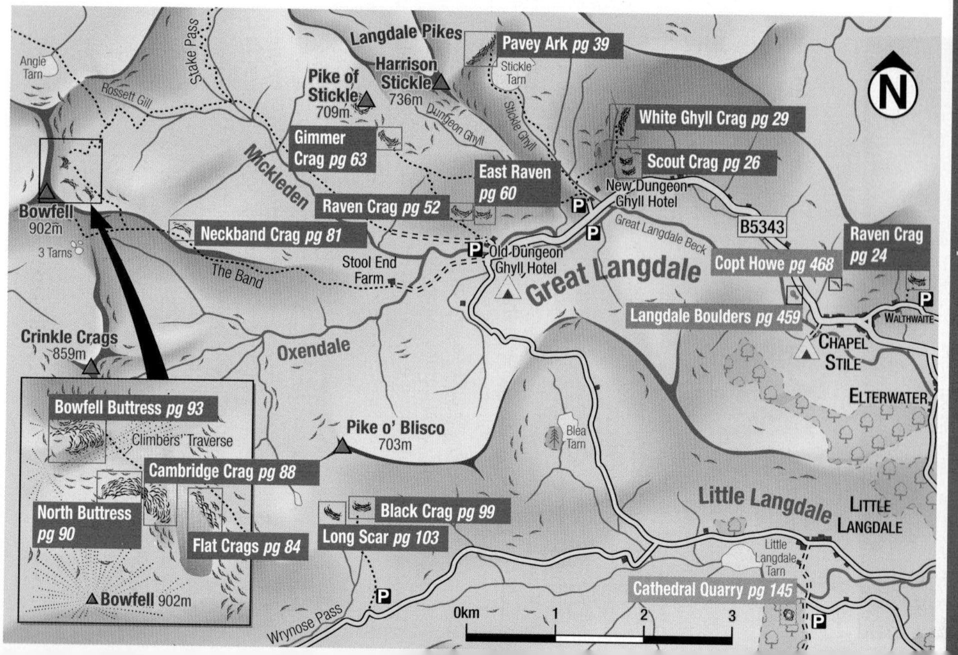
N
Angle Tarn
Stake Pass
Rossett Gill
Langdale Pikes
Pavey Ark pg 39
Stickle Tarn
Harrison Stickle 736m
Pike of Stickle 709m
Dungeon Ghyll
Stickle Ghyll
White Ghyll Crag pg 29
Gimmer Crag pg 63
Scout Crag pg 26
East Raven pg 60
Mickleden
Bowfell 902m
Raven Crag pg 52
New Dungeon Ghyll Hotel
B5343
Raven Crag pg 24
Neckband Crag pg 81
Great Langdale Beck
3 Tarns
Old Dungeon Ghyll Hotel
Stool End Farm
Copt Howe pg 468
The Band
Great Langdale
Langdale Boulders pg 459
Walthwaite
Crinkle Crags 859m
Oxendale
Chapel Stile
Elterwater
Bowfell Buttress pg 93
Pike o' Blisco 703m
Climbers' Traverse
Blea Tarn
Cambridge Crag pg 88
North Buttress pg 90
Black Crag pg 99
Little Langdale
Little Langdale
Flat Crags pg 84
Long Scar pg 103
Little Langdale Tarn
Cathedral Quarry pg 145
Bowfell 902m
Wrynose Pass
0km
1
2
3

Langdale

Left: Ian Hughes on *Gimmer Crack* (VS)
Photo: Dominic Donnini

Langdale

by Max Biden

The delightful **Langdale Valley** winds its brief passage westwards from Ambleside, served by the B5343 road from Skelwith Bridge to the Old Dungeon Ghyll Hotel. Here, the road turns sharply left to rise over the shoulder of Pike o' Blisco towards Little Langdale and the Wrynose Pass. The valley itself, now split into two by the ridge of The Band, continues on to culminate in headwalls containing the summits of Bowfell and the Crinkle Crags.

The Langdale Pikes, which form the valley's northern flank, lie almost at the geographical centre of the Lake District and their profile is one of its most recognisable mountain outlines. These slopes contain perhaps the best concentration of south-facing crags in the National Park, allowing climbing at most times of the year. The valley provides a good choice of high and low level venues, many of which are quick drying.

Ease of access from the population centres of Lancashire, Yorkshire and all points south conspires to increase the pressure on its somewhat limited parking facilities, and it pays to arrive early on a sunny Sunday. There is a bus service from Ambleside as far as the Old Dungeon Ghyll Hotel.

The crags are described **anti-clockwise** progressing up the valley.

Raven Crag, Walthwaite

Grid reference: **325 057**
Altitude: **180m**
Faces: **South**
Rock type: **Borrowdale Volcanic**
Approach time: **5 mins**

This crag provides an excellent selection of short routes. The rock is generally quick drying and sound. Belays tend to be well back from the top of the crag.

The crag is the conspicuous flat-topped outcrop lying behind the east side of Chapel Stile above the minor road to Grasmere. Access is from that road and there is limited parking in a small lay-by below the crag. A path leads from here diagonally up the hillside to the crag.

The path arrives at the lowest point of the crag, a fine buttress of clean rock taken by ***Route 2***. The crag is bounded on its left by a pronounced arête with the slab of ***Route 1*** to its left. Below and left again is an area of trees.

Descent: easily round either side of the crag.

The routes are described from **left** to **right**.

1 **Route 1**	22m	S–

Unknown – pre 1950

Pleasant climbing on good rock but without a generous helping of protection. Delicate, with its crux near the top. Start below a holly underneath the slab.

Scramble up to the holly and gain a ledge below the slab proper. Now follow the well marked way, first left then slightly right.

2 **Enterprize**	22m	VS–

D Wright, M Copley – Sept 1965

Excellent climbing up the fine arête. Start from the holly of ***Route 1***.

(4b). Climb up rightwards around the foot of the arête proper into a groove. Climb the slabby right side of the arête, moving left to gain its crest as soon as possible. Pull over a slight bulge onto the broader upper section, which is followed direct to the top.

1 Route 1	**S–**	**4 Tritus**	**HVS–**
2 Enterprize	**VS–**	**5 Walthwaite Gully**	**VS–**
3 Route 2	**HS**		

3 **Route 2**	37m	HS

Unknown

A little gem. Start below a shallow right-facing groove at the right side of the toe of the crag.

1 10m. Climb the groove until a move left leads onto the rib. Follow this to a spacious ledge and belay on the small ash or larger oak to the right.

2 27m. Climb the shallow square-cut groove immediately above the ash tree to some good pockets at 10 metres. Traverse right across the slab for 3 metres then up leftwards into a corner. Up this until a swing left gains the overhanging rib. Finish rightwards up the awkward chimney break.

4 **Tritus**	27m	HVS–

R M Biden, K Forsythe – c1977

An excellent steep and direct pitch on good rock up grooves in the nose where the crag bends round to the right. Start behind the large holly some 10 metres right of ***Route 2***.

(5a). Climb straight up the bulging wall on good juggy holds to a resting place beneath twin grooves. Enter the tapering right-hand groove awkwardly and climb it and the rib above to the top.

5 **Walthwaite Gully**	27m	VS–
J A Austin, J M Ruffe – May 1957		

Not a gully but a fine corner-flake giving pleasant sheltered climbing. Don't be put off by the trees, they are quite benevolent. Start at the bottom of the main angle, a few metres up from the holly of *Tritus*.

1 10m (4b). Climb the corner-crack to the large ledge.

2 17m (4c). Follow the fierce-looking flake-crack up the corner and rightwards round the roof to finish through the holly tree, fortunately of the not too prickly variety.

Scout Crags

Grid reference: **298 069**
Altitude: **275m**
Faces: **South**
Rock type: **Borrowdale Volcanic**
Approach time: **10 mins**

An excellent area for the beginner, these crags are reached by a short walk up the fellside behind a barn by the road, some two hundred metres east of the Stickle Barn/New Dungeon Ghyll car parks.

Lower Scout Crag

The first buttress is in the form of a left-facing corner formed by a steep wall to its left and narrower steep slab to its right. The left wall is split by a hand crack leading to a holly. The rock has been highly polished by generations of feet and the uncertain beginner should resist being put off by the resulting air of insecurity – things can only get better.

Descent: the path to the left of the crag.

The climbs are shown from **left** to **right**.

1	**Cub's Arête**	11m	S
2	**Cub's Groove**	13m	VD
3	**Cub's Crack**	13m	S+
4	**Cub's Wall**	13m	VD
5	**The Slab**	12m	MVS (used to be VD!)

Scout Crags

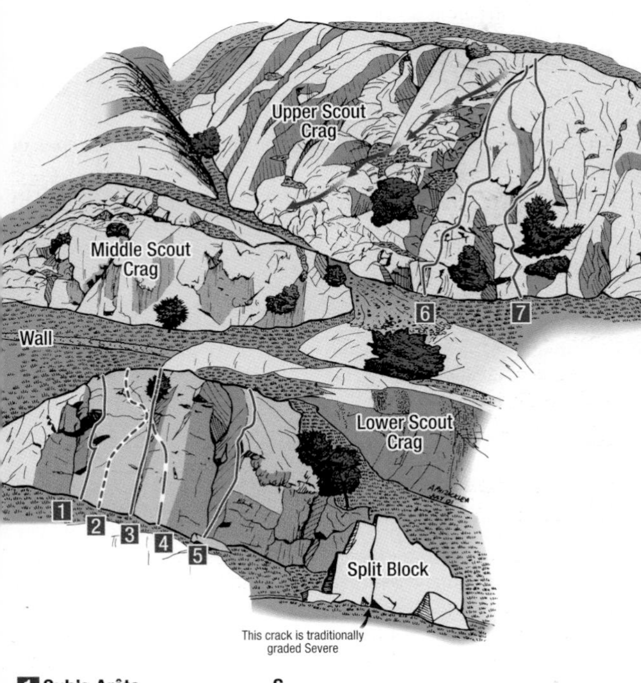

This crack is traditionally graded Severe

1 Cub's Arête	**S**		
2 Cub's Groove	**VD**	**5 The Slab**	**MVS**
3 Cub's Crack	**S+**	**6 Route 2**	**VD**
4 Cub's Wall	**VD**	**7 Route 1**	**VD+**

Upper Scout Crag

The largest of the crags lies above the stile behind the ***Lower Crag***. It is formed of rough, generally easy-angled rock, centred around a broad ridge to the right of an open corner. It is well supplied with good holds and pockets, but does not always lend itself to protection. **Descent:** from the highest point of the crag, an exposed but well worn path scrambles across and down leftwards (facing in), ending in a short crack down glaciated slabs into an easy scree gully.

The climbs are described from **left** to **right**.

6 **Route 2**	55m	VD
F Graham – Oct 1922		

Pleasant climbing left of the central rib. Start at a detached spur of rock, left of and slightly below the centre of the crag.

1 10m. A 6 metre stepped groove with a deceptively awkward start leads to a terrace. Belay at the back by an undercut crack.

2 13m. Avoid the crack (S if taken direct) by ascending on the left to a holly tree. Negotiate this rightwards to gain a ledge and oak tree belay just above.

3 13m. Traverse 3 metres right and make some interesting moves up and just left of the overhangs to belay in the groove on the right above them.

4 19m. Step back left and climb the easy-angled rib to the top.

7 **Route 1**	50m	VD+
F Graham – Oct 1922		

An excellent route following the line of the central rib above a large holly. The second pitch in particular is one of the best of its grade in the valley. Start to the left of a yew tree and below the large holly.

1 14m. Climb the short left-slanting ramp and pocketed, slabby grooves above to a good block belay at the base of the arête.

2 36m. Climb onto the block and traverse right onto the arête. Ascend this on wonderful pocketed rock in a delightfully exposed position to a ledge. Continue past flakes and easier slabs to chipped flake belays at the end of the difficulties. Adequate protection is available for the diligent leader.

White Ghyll Crag

Grid reference: **298 072**
Altitude: **400m**
Faces: **West**
Rock type: **Borrowdale Volcanic**
Approach time: **30 mins**

When viewed from the New Dungeon Ghyll car parks, ***White Ghyll Crag*** towers above the bed of the gill as a livid gash slicing the north-east horizon some half a kilometre east of Stickle Ghyll. It is a fine and compelling sight as the morning sun comes round into the gill, highlighting walls and flying arêtes, the red rock glowing warmly, whilst the ominous bulges of the upper crag still lurk in the shadows.

The crag is easily though steeply gained from the Stickle Barn car park. Behind and right of the Stickle Barn is a wooden bridge over the main beck. Cross this and a small slate bridge beyond, through a gate and onto an engineered path. Fifty metres up this a gate on the right leads to a path traversing the fellside above a wall, across the foot of a small larch plantation and into the gill itself (usually dry just here).

Turn into the gill and follow its relentless progress for what seems an age but is only about 350 metres (or 840 steps).

The sycamore tree in the centre of the gill, opposite the corner of *Slip Knot*, is the usual base for operations, but beware of scree dislodged by others higher up.

The crag forms the true left bank of the upper half of the gill and is divided into upper and lower sections by *Easy Rake*, the main descent route. The main feature of the *Lower Crag* is a series of open-book corners facing down the gill, the largest of which is capped by a huge overhang. *Slip Knot* climbs the slabby right wall of this corner, traversing left to avoid the roof. *Laugh Not* climbs the corner on the right. The *Upper Crag* begins at *Easy Rake* with an area of slabby walls and overhangs before developing leftwards into an aggressively impressive wall, protected at half height by formidable bands of overhangs. This buttress is terminated abruptly on its left by the beetling fissure of *White Ghyll Chimney*, left of which lies a fine sweep of slabs, merging gradually leftwards into the hillside.

Descent: *Easy Rake*. For routes on the *Upper Crag*, descend the hillside above the crag to two cairns marking the top of the *Rake*. Descend the shallow scree gully for about 30 metres (taking care to avoid dislodging scree as the fall-line is over routes on the *Lower Crag*) until two arrows scratched on rock ramps can be seen to the right (facing out). Scramble up past these to another cairn where an obvious rocky rake leads down left (facing in) to the foot of the *Upper Crag*. Do **not** follow the scree below the arrows as this leads directly over the top of the *Lower Crag*. For routes on the *Lower Crag*, scramble up broken rock above the top of ***Slip Knot*** and ascend the hillside to gain the cairns of ***Easy Rake***.

The routes right of ***Slip Knot*** are described from **left** to **right** up the scramble approach; the others are described from **right** to **left** as one ascends the gill.

Lower Crag

The following five routes are all reached by scrambling carefully up rightwards from the bed of the gill, starting adjacent to the sycamore and heading for ledges below the corner of ***Laugh Not***. They are described as one progresses from **left** to **right**.

1 Do Not Direct | 46m | E1-

P1: **L Brown, P Muscroft** (1 point of aid – now free) – Oct 1960 P2: **R J Birkett, L Muscroft** – June 1949

A first class route with varied climbing and a superbly positioned second pitch. Start below a broken groove set in the rib between *Slip Knot* and *Laugh Not*.

1 25m (5b). Climb the groove to a ledge and large spike on the right, below a fine crack in the south-facing wall. A small undercut impedes access to the crack but once started it is easier than it looks and gobbles protection. Belay on the spacious ledge above.

2 21m (5a). Climb the square-cut groove above the right edge of the belay ledge to an overhang. Traverse steeply up and left across the wall on large handholds, until a final awkward move round the nose gains a ledge. Easier climbing leads to belays well back.

White Ghyll – Lower Crag

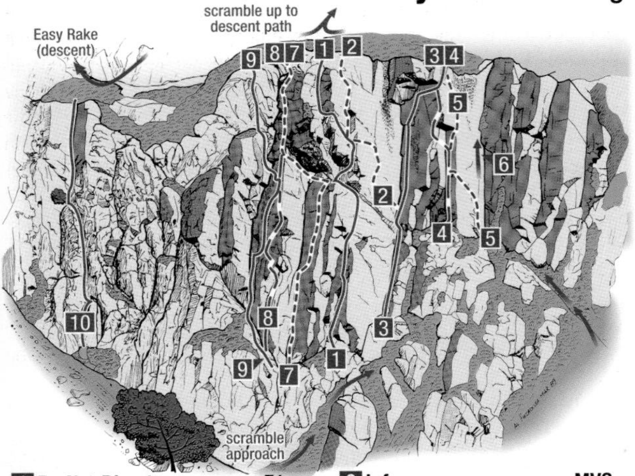

scramble up to descent path
Easy Rake (descent)
scramble approach

	Route	Grade		Route	Grade
1	Do Not Direct	E1–	6	Inferno	MVS
2	Waste Not Want Not	E1	7	Slip Knot	VS–
3	Laugh Not	HVS+	8	The Palestinians	E1+
4	Man of Straw	E1	9	Moss Wall	VS
5	Feet of Clay	E1+	10	Hollin Groove	S+

2 Waste Not, Want Not | 32m | E1

W Lounds, P Sanson – June 1977

Neat climbing based on an inverted left-facing, stepped faultline on the left wall of ***Laugh Not*** and starting as for that route.

(5b). From the start of the corner proper, climb the smooth section for 3 metres when a step left can be made. A further awkward step left gains the faultline. Climb this until pockets in the smooth wall below the overlap lead left again to a rib and groove (junction with ***Do Not*** which goes left here). Steady climbing up the groove and its left wall.

3 Laugh Not | 35m | HVS+

J Brown, R Moseley, T Waghorn (1 point of aid – now free) – Oct 1953

An excellent and clean-cut line up the smooth corner capped by an overhang right of ***Slip Knot***. Quite sustained, rather smooth in places,

but well protected and with enough good resting places. Start at a belay some 5 metres below the smooth part of the groove.

(5b). Climb the corner, which has an awkward overlap at 20 metres, and follow the wider crack more easily into the cave beneath the roof (good runners). Either step back down and traverse the shiny slab delicately right to gain the ledge on the rib and good nut belays or, more easily but spectacularly, reach out right to the prominent flat hold just above the overhang and, trying to keep your feet on the slab, continue right on big jugs to step onto the belay ledge. Go on, commit yourself – it's neither as hard nor as far as it looks!

4	**Man of Straw**	28m	E1

J A Austin, D G Roberts – April 1965

A delightful climb which is quite sustained but never desperate unless confidence in your feet starts to evaporate. It climbs the short slim groove in the rib right of ***Laugh Not***, exiting left to gain the arête above. Start beneath a boot-wide crack leading to the groove.

(5b). Climb the crack to a small ledge at the foot of the groove. Teeter up this almost to the roof when a short traverse left round two small ribs gains the ***Laugh Not*** slab and good runners in the thin diagonal crack above. From here a delightful two-step move back right above the roof leads to the arête and the nut belays of ***Laugh Not***.

5	**Feet of Clay**	25m	E1+

M G Mortimer, S Foster, M G Allen – June 1978

Essentially a right-hand start and finish to ***Man of Straw***, starting at the foot of the big corner to its right (**6 Inferno** MVS).

(5b). A short crack leads leftwards to the ledge at the foot of the ***Man of Straw*** groove. This time teeter all the way to the roof and pull out right onto the steep wall overlooking ***Inferno***. After a couple of committing moves up this, the difficulty eases gradually en route to the ***Laugh Not*** belays.

Returning again to the sycamore in the bed of the gill, the next feature is the large slabby corner capped by the biggest overhang. Routes are now described from **right** to **left**.

7 Slip Knot | 41m | VS–

R J Birkett, L Muscroft – May 1947

A justifiably popular route taking an excellent and varied line up the big slab, then left round the large triangular roof above. Pitch 2 gives an intimidating pitch and is a good introduction to the Very Severe grade. Start adjacent to the sycamore at the foot of the large right-facing corner and slab beneath the triangular roof.

1 21m (4a). Climb the corner for a couple of metres before traversing out onto the right wall where excellent holds lead up to a spacious ledge and belay under the roofs.

2 20m (4b). Traverse left into the corner and make a thought-provoking move across the left wall to gain the rib. Climb this with an exhilarating move over a bulge to a niche on the left. Continue up the steep wall on the right to easier climbing and the top. Belay well back.

8 The Palestinians | 37m | E1+

A Hewison, C Robinson – Aug 1981

A good line with interesting climbing up the big undercut rib left of the *Slip Knot* slab. Effectively a direct start to *Moss Wall/Slip Knot*. Start just left of *Slip Knot*, where a ramp runs up to the left.

(5b). From a few metres up the ramp, gain a large sloping foothold at three metres, either directly or via the short mossy groove on the left. Move up to the slanting overhangs and pull over leftwards onto the wall above (junction with *Moss Wall*). Step right below the next overlap and climb it by the big crack in its centre to gain the rib above. Climb this to finish as for *Slip Knot*.

9 Moss Wall | 43m | VS

G Oliver, D Laws – Aug 1959

An excellent route and considerably better than its appearance would suggest. It finds a way up the right wall of the big corner left of *Slip Knot*. Start as for that route.

1 13m. An easy pitch up the rampline leading leftwards to the foot of a shallow square-cut groove which forms the first part of the corner.

2 30m (4c). Climb this groove for 4 metres until a traverse can be made out onto the wall on the right. Good holds lead fairly directly up the wall to a resting place on the rib. (Just below ***Slip Knot***.) Good footholds lead leftwards into a steep groove which is climbed via a small overhang to a good ledge. Continue more easily to the top. Belay well back.

10 Hollin Groove	82m	S+

R J Birkett, L Muscroft – Aug 1945

A pleasant route taking in a fine corner groove at mid-height. Start at a crooked crack in a short corner with a small glacis at head height in its left rib. This is some 20 metres above the sycamore and just right of the main grooveline above.

1 23m. The crack in the corner has a mind of its own but can be persuaded to lead you to a ledge above, from which a step left gains the rib. This leads via another groove to a battered holly beneath the main corner.

2 24m. Climb the fine right-angle corner above to a terrace (the *Great Shelf*) and walk 13 metres back to belay at the rib ahead. (The ***Easy Rake*** descent route crosses here.)

3 12m. The steep rib leads to a spike belay.

4 23m. Continue pleasantly up the rib to the top.

Upper Crag

Between the Lower and Upper Crags is the well-trodden thoroughfare of ***Easy Rake***. 10 metres left of the foot of this is:

11 White Ghyll Wall	68m	VS–

R J Birkett, L Muscroft, T Hill – May 1946

A magnificent outing, weaving its way around the right-hand side of the armoury of overhangs. From the dank darkness of the gill, it ascends to reach open sunny rock and fine situations. Low in its grade, it is excellent introduction to the buttress and 'VS work'. Start at the foot of the prominent rib, right of the ash tree.

1 25m. Follow the rib and short wide crack to a ledge beneath the overhangs (optional belay) and traverse right for 8 metres to a stance beneath an undercut left-facing scoop.

White Ghyll – Upper Crag

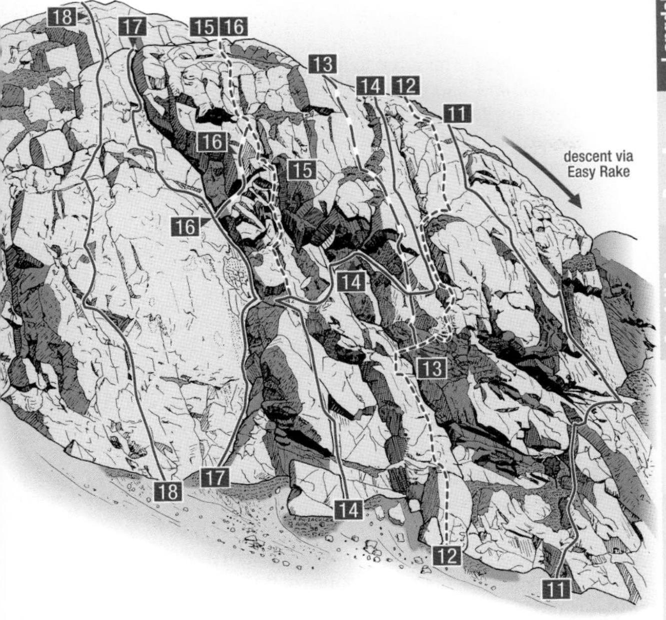

11 White Ghyll Wall	VS–	15 Paladin	E3–
12 The Gordian Knot	VS+	16 Chimney Variant	E1
13 White Ghyll Eliminate	E2	17 White Ghyll Chimney	S+
14 Haste Not	VS+	18 The Slabs, Route 1	S

2 15m (4c). Ascend the scoop and climb a problematical overlap (left or right side) to a small ledge at the foot of a large open corner. Move leftwards onto the steep wall and climb direct for 6 metres to an overhung ledge. Belay just down to the left in a slanting groove.

3 28m (4b). From below the belay, traverse delicately left for 2 metres out onto the slabs and then climb diagonally up left, passing a prominent ledge at 12 metres (optional belay) and another at 19 metres. Finish straight up the wall above.

12 The Gordian Knot | 56m | VS+

J W Haggas, E Bull – Sept 1940

A climb of great character following a natural line up the narrow slabby wall and hanging corner to its right. Sustained, with modest protection on the crux. Start at the foot of the slab which forms the right-hand side of a prominent rib running up to the overhangs.

1 20m (4b). A pleasant pitch. Climb the slab trending slightly rightwards until a steepening at 16 metres suggests a short traverse left, then up to a recess with an anvil-flake belay.

2 14m (4c). A teasing pitch on first acquaintance, with some suspect rock. Traverse easily right for 4 metres to an exposed ledge below the corner. Bridge through the bulge above via a small ledge on the right wall and move back leftwards into a corner, which is climbed to a ledge and belay just below its top.

3 22m (4b). Continue up the wide crack and exit right onto a long ledge. Climb pleasantly up the steep wall above the left side of this ledge to finish just left of ***White Ghyll Wall***.

13 White Ghyll Eliminate | 62m | E2

A Evans, D Parker, G Millar – May 1971

An exhilarating climb up the compellingly steep crack springing from the right-hand side of the first stance of the ***Gordian Knot***. Start as for that route.

1 20m (4b). As for the ***Gordian Knot*** to the anvil-flake belay.

2 15m (5c). Step right and survey the crack above. Translating desire into action, pull up steeply into the crack and follow it on an assortment of holds and jams to a stance in the 'coffin' groove on the ***Haste Not*** traverse. Debilitatingly well protected.

3 27m (5a). An awkward crack in the same line splits the roof above. Climb it to the foot of a bilberry rake, and finish up a thin crackline in the pleasant, rough white slabby wall above.

14 Haste Not | 59m | VS+

R J Birkett, L Muscroft – May 1948

An impertinent excursion for its grade which probes the monumental barrier of overhangs. Excellent climbing, featuring an exposed and enthralling traverse. Start in the right-facing corner, 5 metres left of the ***Gordian Knot*** and just right of a broad hanging rib.

1 22m (4b). Climb the slab to the inverted-V overhang. Cross the left wall with difficulty to gain a groove in the slab on the front. This leads via an awkward bulge to a large ledge and upstanding flake belay.

2 15m (4c). Traverse easily rightwards for 5 metres when a steep wall leads to the big roofs. A delicate step right gains a cramped gangway system running rightwards under the overhangs. Follow this and descend a bottomless coffin-like groove to a resting place in a short left-facing corner (optional belay). Step up the corner, swing right onto the rib and traverse right to belay in the next corner as for the ***Gordian Knot*** Pitch 2.

3 22m (4b). Step back left and climb awkwardly into a short groove at the right-hand end of an overlap. Pull out left and finish up the pleasant narrow rib, just right of a bilberry rake.

The next two routes breach the especially impressive area of overhangs which beetle out between ***Haste Not*** and ***White Ghyll Chimney***.

15 **Paladin**	49m	E3–
R Matheson (some aid) – Sept 1970	FFA: **R Matheson** – March 1971	

Climbs the biggest hanging groove in the overhangs. Low in the grade, it provides sustained, strenuous and exposed climbing. Definitely 'out there'.

1 15m. As for ***White Ghyll Chimney*** Pitch 1 to the upstanding flake belay.

2 25m (6a). Starting just left of the belay, climb the deceptively steep and fingery wall, trending rightwards into a corner. Step left and climb a slab and bulging wall until it is possible to move into the corner below the roof. Follow an ominous-looking block rightwards to get established in the main groove. Move up with difficulty and exit left into comparative calm below a subsidiary groove. Climb the left wall of this, via another awkward move.

3 9m. Easy ground to the top.

16 **Chimney Variant**	56m	E1
J A Austin, I Roper, D Miller – April 1966		

A justifiably popular climb, with excellent climbing and superb positions. It utilizes the obvious undercut gangway leading rightwards from the *Chimney* to a short but handsome square-cut hanging groove.

1 20m. *White Ghyll Chimney* Pitch 1.

2 28m (5b). Continue up the *Chimney* to the overhang. Pull over this and move right onto the gangway. Shimmy right to good runners in the base of the groove (beware of rope drag). Tricky moves up this lead to a step out right onto the rib. Stance and belay just above.

3 8m. Finish up the easier groove above.

17 **White Ghyll Chimney**	57m	S+
H B Lyon, J Herbert, H P Cain – Aug 1923		

A classic must for aficionados of this traditional genre. It climbs the impressive cleft formed by the junction of the central overhanging section and the slabs on its left. Start at the foot of the cleft where a ramp runs up into the initial groove.

1 20m. Easily up the groove to the large ledge and upstanding flake belay. Walk up to a thread belay in the *Sentry Box*, above which the chimney narrows to a crack.

2 25m. Climb the cave for 3 metres and then make a difficult move to gain a sloping hold on the left. Delicately reach some small handholds and continue more easily up a steep leftward-slanting diagonal groove to a ledge with a good belay 6 metres higher.

3 12m. Return 3 metres from the belay and climb the wall above for 5 metres. A delicate traverse then leads back into the *Chimney* which provides a fitting finish.

18 **The Slabs, Route 1**	69m	S
G Barker, A T Hargreaves – Sept 1930		

A really enjoyable excursion with some interesting moves up the fine sweep of slabs left of *White Ghyll Chimney*. Start at the lowest point of the slabs.

1 13m. A steady pitch straight up rough, worn rock to a ledge with a belay at its left end.

2 15m. Make a fine rising traverse across the wall on the left to a small ledge. The steep groove above leads to a step right onto a ledge with a satisfying spike belay on the right.

3 17m. Return to the point of arrival and attack the delicate wall. After an awkward start, better holds lead via the middle of three

grooves to a ledge, from which a further groove slightly right leads to the terrace rising from *White Ghyll Chimney*.

4 24m. There is a rib to the right. Start just right of this and then follow it pleasantly to the top.

Pavey Ark

Grid reference: **285 079**
Altitude: **570m**
Faces: **South-East & East**
Rock type: **Borrowdale Volcanic**
Approach time: **55 mins**

Above: Rob Fielding on *Bracken-clock* (E2)
Photo: Nick Wharton

Pavey Ark is one of the highest crags in Langdale and dominates the skyline right (north) of Harrison Stickle as one approaches the area from the south-east. The crag faces generally south-east and enjoys the sun from first light to mid-afternoon. It contains many excellent routes on good rock that has gained a legendary reputation for its roughness. Drainage lines can be slow to dry, especially early in the season, and vegetation can tend to the luxuriant.

The crag is quite complex in layout but the major climbing buttresses and other locational features can be identified from the initial crag diagram, when viewed from the dam on Stickle Tarn. *Jack's Rake* consists of a series of rocky troughs, scree covered ledges and short rocky scrambles running diagonally from bottom right to top left and divides the central part of the crag into upper and lower tiers. It is an excellent scramble and extremely popular which causes a real danger from dislodged scree falling over the lower tier. Any climbers who wish to base themselves beneath *Jack's Rake* should choose their position carefully, preferably out from the crag. Wearing a helmet is an even better idea than usual. By combining climbs on its lower and upper tiers, routes of over 160 metres (500 feet sounds better) can be made to the summit.

From the Stickle Barn, the top half of the crag can be seen peeping out above Stickle Ghyll. This provides the line of the main path, which starts behind the car park at Stickle Barn, and leads all the way to Stickle Tarn. The crag now dominates the view. From here, the shorter and drier route is clockwise round the edge of the tarn until an obvious path leads up towards the foot of *Jack's Rake* and *East Gully*.

Descent: for all routes finishing on or below *Jack's Rake*, it is easiest to descend the *Rake*. For climbs on the upper tier above *Jack's Rake*: (a) continue to the summit from where the top of *Jack's Rake* is 100 metres to the left. It can be located to the left (facing out) of a rock pinnacle, just below a short drystone wall. Now descend *Jack's Rake*; or (b) particularly for routes ending right of *Cook's Tour*, ascend until one can traverse right (various vague paths) into the scree filled depression of *North Gully*, which lies behind the *East Wall*. Descend this until the top of *East Gully* can be seen on the right and continue down this. Care is needed at the boulder choke at three-quarters height and with some scree-topped boulders near the bottom.

The climbs are divided into three areas and described thus: *Climbs below Jack's Rake*, *Climbs above Jack's Rake*, and the *East Wall*.

Climbs below Jack's Rake

These routes are described from **right** to **left**.

Walking round from the foot of the *Rake*, one comes to the impressive two-tier wall of *Arcturus* with a prominent overhang at half-height and defined on the right by a grassy rightward-slanting break with a holly at the bottom (**1 Deception** S).

2 Cruel Sister — 73m — E3

R Matheson, S Colvin (2 points of aid) – April 1972 FFA: **J Lamb, P Botterill** – Feb 1975

This brilliant climb follows the left-hand side of the superb undercut rib which forms the right edge of the upper *Arcturus* wall. The crux with its spaced protection commands respect. Start as for *Arcturus*.

1 30m (5b). Follow *Arcturus* to the juggy foothold level with the peg runner and move rightwards to a good ledge below the

Pavey Ark – South Face

	Route	Grade
1	Deception	S
2	Cruel Sister	E3
3	Arcturus	E1–
4	Capella	E1–
5	Crescent Slabs	S+
6	Stoat's Crack	HS
7	The Bracken-clock	E2
8	Rake End Wall	VS+
9	The Rib Pitch	HVS–
10	Rake End Chimney	D
11	Cook's Tour	VD+
12	Gwynne's Chimney	D
13	Aardvark	E1+
14	Poker Face	E1
15	Golden Slipper	HVS
17	Mother Courage	E4–

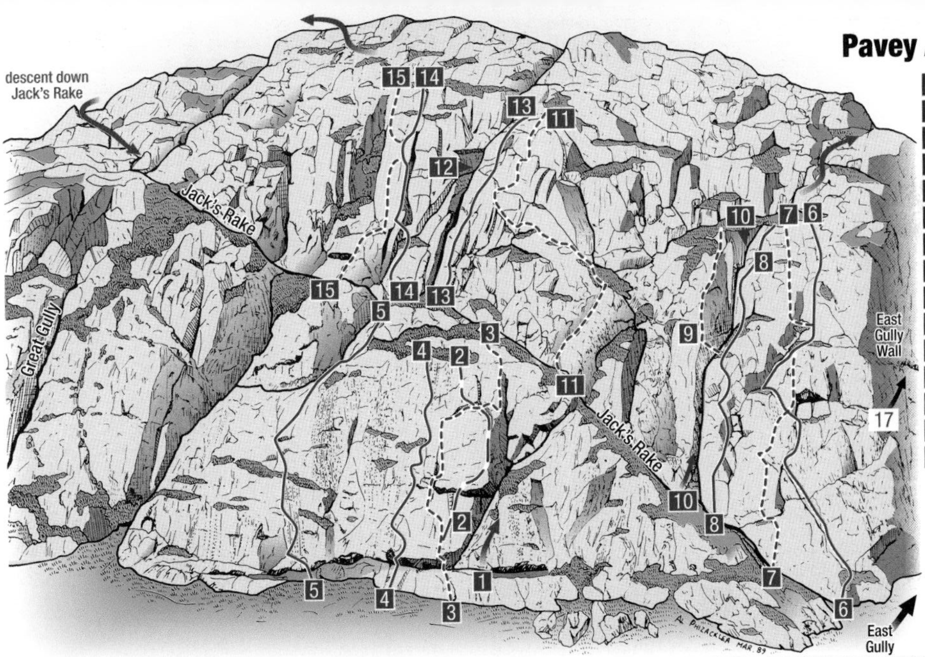

obvious shallow groove. Climb this to the ledge under the overhang and traverse right to belay.

2 25m (5c). Pull onto the wall behind the belay and traverse right to gain the wall above the overhang. Peg runner down right. Step up, traverse right to a block on the edge, and then go up to a good foothold. Climb the wall trending slightly left to a small overlap. Surmount this and gain a steep crackline which leads to the good ledge at the end of the ***Arcturus*** traverse. A magnificent pitch.

3 18m (5a). Reverse the ***Arcturus*** traverse leftwards for 3 metres and pull over the overlap above on widely space holds. Step left and climb the obvious corner to grass ledges. Move right and back left onto the second ledge for belays.

3	Arcturus	80m	E1–

J A Austin, E Metcalf – April 1962

This tremendous route gives fine open climbing in excellent situations and finds the easiest way up the impressive two-tier wall which dominates this part of the crag. The standard is well maintained at HVS, except for a short section on the first pitch which is both more serious and difficult; fortunately, it is also the least steep part. Start directly below the holly bush of ***Deception***. This is 12 metres right of a birch tree growing out of the overhangs which patrol the base of the crag.

1 33m (5b). Slabby rocks lead to the holly. Ascend the undercut rib 2 metres to the left, which guards access to the slab. After 2 metres move left to a jammed flake (thread runner) and pull right to reach and stand on a juggy foothold, just right of an old peg runner. A few delicate moves up the slab bring better holds and a runner in a quartz slot. Avoid the smooth section above by working left into a thin crack, which leads to a shallow niche and stance at a holly just above.

2 32m (5a). Pull over the small overlap on the right and climb a shallow groove to a small ledge. Step back into the line of the groove and climb the thin crack to a narrow ledge, with a large ledge a little higher (optional belay). Traverse right beneath the overlap, crossing a delicate and exposed little slab at the end. Step down to belay on the ledge below.

3 15m (4c). From the right end of the belay ledge, a tricky rib soon leads to easier ground and a belay. ***Jack's Rake*** is just off to the right.

4 **Capella**	70m	E1–

C Read, G L Swainbank – Aug 1997

Another excellent route which takes a good natural line up the slabby wall left of ***Arcturus***, finishing up a series of walls and corners. Low in its grade, with interesting, well protected climbing. In spite of its mossy appearance, it dries faster than ***Arcturus***. Start below the substantial birch tree growing out of the initial overhang.

1 **32m (5b).** Climb slabby rocks to gain an overhung glacis on the right side of the tree. Pull up and left behind the tree to gain the lip of the overhang. Follow a series of pockets trending rightwards up the wall for 4 metres, until a 2 metre traverse left can be made. Go straight up past a good flake and ledge, then diagonally right to beneath a steepening wall. Move right, climb the right side of this and pull up left to a ledge. Move up to the holly belay of *Arcturus*.

2 **38m (5b).** Starting left of the tree, bridge up a shallow groove to good holds on the left and gain the steep wall above. Move rightwards into a short left-facing corner and climb it to a good ledge on the right. Go up to another ledge. Move up rightwards and climb a fingery wall to a large flake. From its top, enter a shallow corner and follow it to the top. Step left to belay on nuts and a peg.

5 **Crescent Slabs**	60m	S+

G S Bower, A W Wakefield – June 1920

This very good climb follows a clean open line up the right-hand side of the slabs which lie some 30 metres left of ***Arcturus***. Start at a weakness at the right end of the slabs; a black groove just right of some bulging overhangs.

1 **12m.** Follow a rising gangway to the left. This is usually wet.

2 **12m.** Traverse obliquely right into a shallow groove. Ascend this for a couple of metres before working left over easier slabs to a spike belay.

3 **18m.** Go up steep slabs to a ledge and step back right below a block. Make a difficult move up from the block into a small scoop, then, after a couple of metres, move left to a small ledge.

4 **18m.** Pleasant slabs are climbed to a belay at the right end of the ***Crescent***, an overhanging barrier at the top of the slabs. Finish by scrambling up rightwards to ***Jack's Rake***.

Climbs above Jack's Rake

These routes are described from **right** to **left**.

6 **Stoat's Crack**	112m	HS

B R Record, J R Jenkins – June 1933

This pleasant route finds the easiest way up a very big area of steep rock and provides enjoyment with a mountaineering air. Quite bold and exposed in places. Start just right of the foot of ***Jack's Rake***, below a prominent left-slanting, right-facing corner-crack 16 metres up the crag.

1 16m. Scramble up blocks and ledges rightwards to gain the grassy ledge below the corner.
2 20m. Go up the crack for about 8 metres, break out left and ascend to a stance on the corner.
3 26m. Traverse to the groove on the left and follow this and the open corner above to a capacious overhung ledge.
4 24m. Step around to the left, along the grass terrace, and climb an open groove, finishing to the right. Traverse left along another ledge to a bilberry-filled groove. Climb this and grass above until it is possible to move right for 5 metres to belay below a sweep of slabs.
5 26m. Climb pleasant slabs, delicately at first, then a short wall and slabs lead leftwards to huge detached block. Thirty metres of scrambling finishes the climb.

7 **The Bracken-clock**	102m	E2

J A Austin, N J Soper, A Faller (1 point of aid) – June 1970 FFA: **R Valentine** – 1971

Excellent clean, open climbing up the steep, smooth walls left of ***Stoat's Crack***. Start below a shallow groove, about 20 metres up ***Jack's Rake***, where its bed contains a smooth slab split by a quartz vein.

1 18m (5a). Follow the shallow groove, past a difficult bulge, to the right end of a ledge. Belay at the left end.
2 14m (5c). Climb directly up the smooth slab to a good jug (runner). Continue straight up with some difficulty, to reach a traverse line.
3 20m (5b). Traverse right below the bulging wall for about 4 metres to a tiny platform on the edge of the smooth slabs. Climb

directly up over an awkward bulge, then go up to the right into an open groove overlooking ***Stoat's Crack***. Climb this to a ledge below a smooth little scoop.

4 24m (4a). Go up the scoop as for ***Stoat's Crack*** and walk to the right end of the ledge above. Follow slabs and ledges, trending right to a ledge below the final pitch of ***Stoat's Crack***.

5 26m. Finish up the pleasant rib about 6 metres to the left.

8 **Rake End Wall**	58m	VS+

H A Carsten, E H Phillips – Aug 1945

A splendid route finding the easiest way up the right rib of ***Rake End Chimney***. Enjoyable climbing on excellent rock, a well maintained standard and thought provoking crux can only be improved by finishing up the ***Rib Pitch***. Start below a rib 5 metres right of ***Rake End Chimney***.

1 21m (4b). Starting on the right, climb up past a wedged flake and go up an ill-defined crack until its steepening necessitates a move round the corner to the right. Follow a diagonal crack to a huge block beneath the overhanging corner-crack and belay on its right.

2 25m (4c). The imposing corner-crack above the block has some useful holds on the left wall and leads to a ledge. Step left from the left end of the ledge onto a fine slab. Climb up this into a small groove on the right of a slight overhang. Up the groove for a couple of metres until an awkward move left gains the arête. Follow this to the large terrace in ***Rake End Chimney***. (The start of the ***Rib Pitch***.)

3 12m (4b). From the top end of the terrace, climb the left edge of the wall to the right of the chimney, with a detour right to avoid its steepest section. A bold pitch.

9 **The Rib Pitch (Variation)**	36m	HVS–

J A Austin, J M Ruffe – June 1958

Half way up ***Rake End Chimney*** its right wall drops back for 6 metres or so, forming a terrace. The left-hand rib remains, standing out boldly in isolation and giving a superb pitch, steep and exposed.

3a (5a). Make an upward traverse left to the rib and climb it to the top.

10 Rake End Chimney | 70m | D

C W Barton – Oct 1898

A excellent climb which ascends the deep, often green, chimney located about 40 metres up *Jack's Rake*. A classic of its kind. Start at the foot of the chimney.

1 **10m.** Go up easy steps to the chimney proper.
2 **20m.** Climb the chimney past two ledges (optional belays) and over a chockstone.
3 **20m.** Walk up the gully.
4 **20m.** Climb up to and through the window and then go up the right wall to a small cave. Pass this on the left to finish easily.

11 Cook's Tour | 88m | VD+

J Cook, G B Elliot – March 1943

A good mountaineering route up the upper crag with some excellent pitches. Much harder if the rock is damp. Start at a leftward-facing, short easy chimney-crack, opposite a large rowan at the top of the long steep section of *Jack's Rake*.

1 **16m.** The open groove leads to a pinnacle platform; continue up the steep slabby corner, moving round to the right onto the top of a flake pinnacle.
2 **12m.** From the corner on the left, easy climbing is followed by steep bracken leading to a flake belay at the foot of an imposing slab.
3 **22m.** Move up to a large grass ledge 8 metres away on the left and walk along it for 14 metres to a flake belay below an open grassy gully.
4 **11m.** Climb the gully for 6 metres (this peters out onto easy ground if followed to its end); traverse right around the outside of a flake then up to a pleasant grassy corner. Ash-tree belay.
5 **27m.** Ascend the crack behind the tree to the top of the flake, then up left to a corner. Continue up the steep slab to a good ledge, Finish up the wall above, first slightly right, then straight up.

The level, half-way section of *Jack's Rake* is the starting point for the next routes. **12 Gwynne's Chimney**, a pleasant 25 metre D, starts at the middle of this level section, right of a prominent rowan tree.

13 **Aardvark**	55m	E1+
P Long, D J Harding (1 point of aid) – Sept 1972	FFA: **P Whillance, J Moore** – Aug 1975	

An excellent, exposed route with contrasting climbing up the steep arête right of ***Gwynne's Chimney***. Start 6 metres down to the right of ***Gwynne's Chimney*** on a small quartz glacis.

1 33m (5c). Climb straight up strenuously to a peg runner under a small overhang. Move left and up with difficulty, to gain a sloping ledge. From the ledge, make a delicate traverse up and rightwards across the wall to a small spike on the arête, which is then followed to a ledge and spike belay.

2 22m. Climb a short wall on the right to meet ***Cook's Tour***. Move right again and climb the obvious crack to slabs and the top.

14 **Poker Face**	82m	E1
J A Austin, K Wood – July 1966		

Excellent climbing up the slim, bottomless groove splitting the arête to the right of ***Golden Slipper***. The sense of exposure in the groove is offset by the superb protection. If the first pitch is damp, use ***Golden Slipper*** Pitch 1 instead. Start 5 metres left of ***Gwynne's Chimney***.

1 36m (4b). Go up easily to a ledge on the left. Climb the slabby corner, past a holly, to another ledge with a large block on the left. Climb straight up from the block and after about 5 metres traverse left to the belay of ***Golden Slipper***.

2 28m (5b). Slabby rock leads up right into the thin groove on the edge of the buttress. Climb the groove until it steepens considerably about 3 metres below the top. Make a difficult move left onto ***Golden Slipper*** and follow this to a large ledge. (The groove may be finished direct at a slightly higher standard.)

3 18m (4c). Climb the right-hand rib above the stance, with an awkward move to start its upper part.

15 **Golden Slipper**	60m	HVS
J A Austin, R B Evans – July 1958		

This splendid climb ascends the centre of the elegant pillar of perfect rock which sits above the horizontal middle section of ***Jack's Rake*** and to the left of an obvious dark corner. Protection is adequate for the diligent. Start at a gangway slanting right to a line of overhangs at 6 metres, 18 metres left of ***Gwynne's Chimney*** and just left of the top of the tricky step in the level section of ***Jack's Rake***.

1 18m (4c). Follow the gangway easily to the overhang and step right onto a grassy ledge. Climb directly up the steep wall above to another ledge and belay at the foot of the steepening slab.

2 24m (5a). Climb directly up a shallow left-facing corner in the slab on superbly rough rock. At its top where the slab becomes a wall, traverse across to the rib on the right and ascend to a large ledge and belay.

3 18m (4a). Traverse left and climb the rib to the top.

The East Wall

Above: The Dowthwaite brothers on *Astra* (E2) **Photo:** Al Phizacklea

The routes are described from **left** to **right** progressing up the gully. This is the steep, impressive wall above the scree filled gully of ***East Gully*** at the right-hand side of the crag. It contains some formidable pitches. The wall is divided into two parts by the right-to-left diagonal line of **16 Hobson's Choice** (MVS) which shares a common start with ***Astra***. The rock below and left of this is characterized by an unusual mottled appearance and has some loose holds. There is an obvious mossy, reddish groove-line up its centre, which contains a prominent holly. The rock to the right of ***Hobson's Choice*** is immaculately rough and sound. It is dominated by the leaning cleft of ***Fallen Angel*** with the attractive clean arête of ***Astra*** to its left, whilst to the right is yet another prominent corner which is taken by ***Cascade Direct***.

Pavey Ark – East Wall

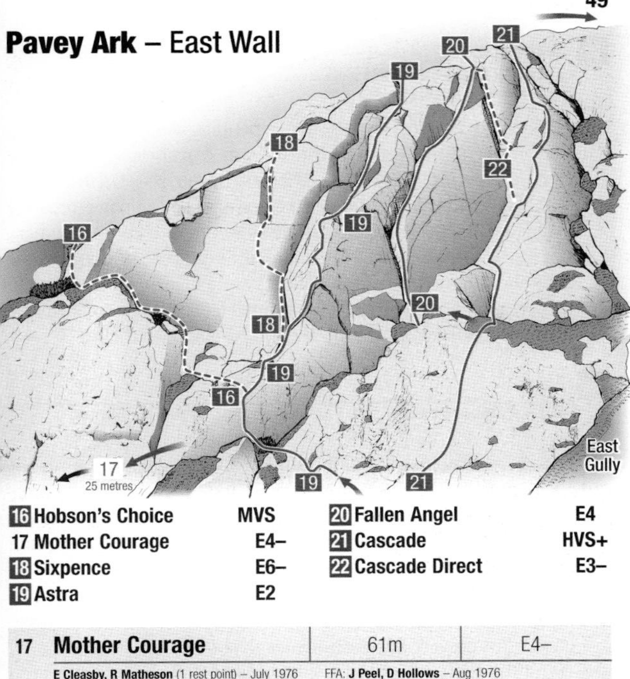

16 Hobson's Choice	MVS	20 Fallen Angel	E4
17 Mother Courage	E4–	21 Cascade	HVS+
18 Sixpence	E6–	22 Cascade Direct	E3–
19 Astra	E2		

17 **Mother Courage**	61m	E4–
E Cleasby, R Matheson (1 rest point) – July 1976	FFA: **J Peel, D Hollows** – Aug 1976	

Excellent, sustained and strenuous climbing up the steep mottled wall gives a memorable trip. Not too well protected. Start at the centre of the wall below and left of a prominent holly tree and just left of an obvious dirty groove. This can be reached by grassy scrambling from the bottom of the gully or, alternatively, by climbing Pitch 1 of *Astra* and descending carefully leftwards down a steep grassy ramp.

1 43m (6a). Climb the wall to a narrow ledge just left of the holly. The wall above the short steep gangway on the left leads strenuously to a flat hold. Continue direct to a bulge, pull over rightwards, then immediately back left to the foot of a steep groove and peg runner. Climb the groove and pull out right to a good hold. Climb towards a juniper up on the right then boldly up a rib on the left to a bay.

2 18m (4c). Step right onto the rib and climb this to the top. Belay well back.

18 Sixpence | 33m | E6–

A Atkinson, K Forsythe, R O Graham, T W Birkett (several rest points) – July 1981
FFA: **C Hamper, T W Birkett** – July 1983

A magnificent sustained line up the impending wall and audacious hanging groove in the headwall left of *Astra*. Start below the impressive open corner (**Eclipse,** E4 6a, 1976) as for Pitch 3 of *Astra*.

(6b). Climb the flake-crack and steep corner for 6 metres to a ledge on the right. Step up and into the groove above (runner), traverse left onto the wall and climb it direct to a good jug on the prominent horizontal break. Pull up and enter the groove. Initial progress is not easy; eventually a small ledge on the right can be reached, followed shortly by the top, strength permitting.

19 Astra | 88m | E2

J A Austin, E Metcalf, D G Roberts (1 point of aid) – May 1960 FFA: **E Grindley and party** – Aug 1971

A fabulous route which gains the superb slim groove in the rib left of *Fallen Angel* by way of some exposed and delicate wall climbing. Start from a subsidiary gully parallel to *East Gully* at a point almost directly below the slim groove, where a break allows access to an area of mossy slabs.

1 18m. Pull left onto the slab and follow a rising traverse leftwards until a large flake enables a long stride to be made into a grassy groove on the left. Belay on the ledge above.

2 10m (4b). Climb the steep awkward little wall on the left onto a slab which leads to a stance below the impressive open corner of *Eclipse*.

3 21m (5c). Cross the narrow easy-angled slab at the foot of the impending right wall of the corner to its right side. Make an exposed step round the rib and pull onto the steep undercut wall (useful hidden finger pocket out right) to gain the prominent flake on the right. Climb up and left delicately to where the angle eases. Move up and right to a thin crack and make a long reach right round the rib for a hidden pocket; swing round onto a slab and small stance.

4 34m (5a). Climb the narrowing slab right of the groove above on superb rock and continue in the same line to a ledge. The awkward V-groove ahead is climbed to another ledge and belay on the left.

5 5m. Finish up the short crack and easy scrambling above.

20	**Fallen Angel**	46m	E4

E Grindley, I Roper (1 point of aid) – Oct 1972 FFA: **J Lamb, P Botterill** – April 1974

A superb, technically demanding climb up the impressive right-slanting pea-pod groove. Start by traversing in from the gully along grass ledges, above the sweep of slabs, to a good ledge below the groove.

(6a). Climb the wide crack leading into the pod. Up this, over a difficult bulge (crux) and continue until the groove opens out and the slab on the right can be gained. Climb this rightwards to a crack and good foothold (possible belay). Follow the thin crack above for 6 metres and step right to another crack leading right to a bollard on the arête. Move left and into another groove which is climbed to the top.

21	**Cascade**	70m	HVS+

J A Austin, R B Evans – May 1957

An excellent climb up the right-leaning slab and cornerline to the right of *Fallen Angel*. Whilst lacking the fierceness of its more intimidating neighbours, it provides a fair taste of the problems of the *East Wall*. Start as for *Astra*.

1 21m (4c). Step across the steep wall and pull round onto the belt of slabs. Go up the right-hand side of these, almost overlooking the gully, to a grass ledge at the top with good belays below a 3 metre corner.

2 22m (5a). Climb the 3 metre corner and gain the slab above. This is topped in the main corner by a ledge. Climb almost to this ledge when steepening rock forces a few moves right and up on to a glacis. Belay here, level with the rock ledge.

3 27m (5a). A difficult wall immediately above leads up right to a grass ledge and bollard. Climb twin cracks in the chimney-groove above, passing a bulging flake en route to the top.

21	**Cascade Direct**	49m	E3–

P Long, A D Barley (3 points of aid) – Sept 1971 FFA: **P Whillance, J Moore** – May 1975

A splendid line up the hanging groove above Pitch 2 of Cascade, giving technical, fingery climbing, protected by small wires. Start as for *Fallen Angel*, traversing the ledges to belay below the 3 metre corner.

1 22m (5a). As for Pitch 2 and belay of *Cascade*.

2 27m (5c). From the ledge on the left, the hanging corner-groove is tantalisingly out of reach above a guarding wall. Gain it direct with difficulty, using the edge on the right before pulling into the corner. Continue to the capping overhang and pull leftwards round it to a ledge and belay.

Raven Crag

Grid reference: **285 064**
Altitude: **200m**
Faces: **South**
Rock type: **Borrowdale Volcanic**
Approach time: **15 mins**

Raven Crag is the line of buttresses and outcrops stretching across the fellside above the Old Dungeon Ghyll Hotel. ***Middlefell Buttress*** and ***Raven Crag Buttress*** are situated side by side directly above the hotel; ***East Raven Crag*** is the line of outcrops starting about 100 metres east of ***Raven Crag Buttress*** and slanting down towards the New Dungeon Ghyll Hotel.

The crags can all be reached by following the well marked, engineered path which starts at the rear of the Old Dungeon Ghyll Hotel and leads up to the foot of *Raven Crag Buttress*.

Middlefell Buttress

Middlefell Buttress is the prominent ridge forming the right-hand side of the wide, deep gully directly above the Old Dungeon Ghyll Hotel. **Descent:** for *Middlefell Buttress*, traverse left and cross the gully where a good path leads down a broad shoulder before entering the gully near the bottom. For *Mendes*, it is best to continue up Pitch 3 of *Middelfell Buttress* and descend as for that. **DO NOT descend *Raven Crag Gully* (the gully on the right) as a major rockfall has left it very unstable.**

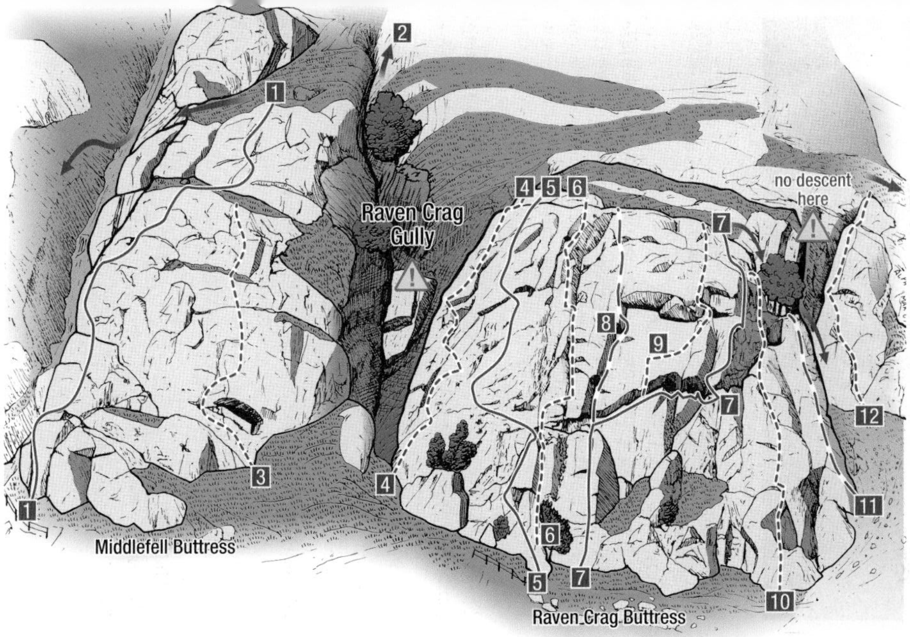

No.	Route	Grade
1	Middlefell Buttress	D
2	Curtain Wall	D
3	Mendes	VS
4	Evening Wall	S+
5	The Original Route	S–
6	Holly Tree Direct	HVS–
7	Pluto	HVS
8	Trilogy	E5
9	R 'n' S Special	E5
10	Bilberry Buttress	VS+
11	Revelation	HS
12	Centipede	S

Raven Crag Gully

no descent here

Middlefell Buttress

Raven Crag Buttress

Raven Crag

Above: *Middlefell Buttress* (D) **Photo:** Dave Willis

1 **Middlefell Buttress**	75m	D
J Laycock, S W Herford, A R Thomson – Sept 1911		

This fine, clean route provides an excellent (though polished) introduction to climbing, or a traditional mountaineering approach to *Gimmer Crag*, and takes a line up the crest of the buttress. Start just left of the lowest point of the crag, at a well-worn chimney.

1 **15m.** Climb the easy chimney and from the pinnacle above step across to a large terrace.

2 **45m.** Climb a short slabby wall and follow the well worn trail up the rounded rib to a large terrace, with intermittent belays if required.

3 **15m.** After re-belaying at the top of the terrace, start the wall above by traversing in from either the right (original) or left (harder), then up cracks and a final short corner, exiting right.

2 **Curtain Wall**	20m	D

An additional pitch can be obtained by climbing a short, steep slab higher up on the right. Further scrambling leads to the Gimmer path.

3 **Mendes**	47m	VS
P Woods, J Sutherland – Feb 1953		

A terrific main pitch up the centre of the slightly intimidating wall. Start some 50 metres up and right of ***Middlefell Buttress***, on slabby rock below a long overhang, above and right of a pinnacle and tree.

1 12m. Climb up easily leftwards beneath the overhang to gain a shallow groove. Follow this to a stance on the right.
2 26m (4c). Traverse right for a couple of metres and climb up on good holds until a pull up left gives access to easier angled rock. Continue up to a grassy terrace.
3 9m (4a). Climb the short steep wall via the obvious crack.

Raven Crag Buttress

This is the large dome-shaped buttress directly behind the Old Dungeon Ghyll Hotel. In the centre of the crag is a strikingly smooth wall, capped by a curving band of overhangs. Left of this is the fine long grooveline of ***Holly Tree Direct***, with an area of easier slabby walls left again. Right of the smooth wall, the crag bends round to give a series of ridges running up to ***Oak Tree Terrace***, just below the crag summit. This leads down towards a wet gully, right of which is the elegant triangular pillar of ***Centipede***.

Raven Crag Buttress provides excellent climbs in all grades. It has a sunny disposition with generally good quality, mainly clean, rock. **Descent:** a small and exposed path contours the foot of the rounded grassy summit of the buttress gently down leftwards (facing out) towards the trees on ***Oak Tree Terrace***. This is gained by a short tricky descent over some large split blocks and then back up left (still facing out). Follow the terrace down into the amphitheatre. Do **NOT** follow the path up right from the top of the climbs. The descent for ***Centipede*** is to contour horizontally right until across a stream and then follow a path down steep heathery rocks to the scree slope west of *East Raven Crag*. **Do NOT descend *Raven Crag Gully* (the gully on the left, between *Middlefell Buttress* and *Raven Crag Buttress*) as a major rockfall has left it very unstable.**

The routes are described from **left** to **right**.

4 **Evening Wall**	47m	S+
A Gregory, J W Tucker, J Woods – Oct 1947		

Start in the gully bed on the left of the crag, about 6 metres to the left of a large pinnacle which stands up on the right.
1 11m. Climb up for 4 metres until the wall steepens, make a traverse right into a shallow corner. Step right, and move up to a small stance.

2 **15m.** Climb up to a ledge, then traverse left to a short steep groove. Climb this, over a bulge, and traverse left again to a good ledge.

3 **21m.** Strenuously delicate moves lead up and right onto the exposed arête, which is followed to the top on good holds.

5 The Original Route	61m	S–

S Watson, D Usher, R Holmes, W Cowen, N Middleton – Aug 1930

An excellent route taking a clean natural line of weakness. Start at the lowest point of the buttress, 5 metres right of a large holly.

1 **12m.** Follow well-worn rock up leftwards and either pull into an awkward crack which is followed to a good ledge below a fine narrow pillar, or continue up left onto a ledge from where a quartzy wall leads to the same point.

2 **15m.** Climb the pillar on good holds and an awkward mantelshelf to a long ledge (optional belay just below), which leads left to a large pinnacle.

3 **14m.** Move back right 3 metres from the pinnacle and climb the steep wall above, trending slightly right to a group of ledges.

4 **20m.** Go straight up for 4 metres, then move left to a ledge under a bulge. Move left and step over the overlap. Continue directly up a steep section which gives access to easier ground and the top.

6 Holly Tree Direct	70m	HVS–

H Drasdo, E Mallinson – July 1952

A good route requiring an unexpectedly delicate touch. It takes one of the best lines on the crag, the long groove in the centre of the buttress, obvious even if the holly is no longer. Start as for the ***Original Route***.

1 **12m (4c).** Climb the wall on good holds to a ledge below an obvious corner.

2 **14m. (4b).** Climb the corner to a large ledge. Pinnacle belay just left of the steep upper section of the groove.

3 **21m (4c).** The main grooveline to the right is severely undercut, therefore, climb the parallel groove to its left and step right onto a small white-coloured slab (good runners higher up the groove). Make a long delicate step right to gain the recess in the main groove. Pull out to the right and climb up to a resting place. Continue up the groove, steep and delicate at first, to reach a belay

where the holly used to be (some 6 metres below an oak tree in the groove above).

4 23m (4c). Climb up a couple of metres and step out left onto the rib; follow it to the top.

7 **Pluto**	73m	HVS
A L Atkinson, J R Warner – Summer 1958		

A long, sustained climb of increasing difficulty with varied and interesting climbing. It weaves a line which probes the central wall before being forced off right to finish up a delicate rib. Start at a steep left-facing corner-crack at the foot of the crag, below the smooth central wall.

1 20m (4c). Climb the fine corner-crack to a good ledge and block belay below the corner.

2 27m (4c). Traverse rightwards below the overlap (some suspect holds) until an awkward move across a groove leads to the good ledge at the top of ***Bilberry Buttress***, Pitch 2.

3 26m (5a). Step back down left below the rib and climb its left-hand side on small holds, until it is possible to move right and go up to the traverse line of ***Bilberry Buttress***. Follow this left and finish on good holds.

8 **Trilogy**	31m	E5
Climbed as an aid-route **G West, J Hadfield, R Hughes** – Easter 1957 FFA: **J Lamb, E Cleasby** – May 1979		

A magnificent pitch up the great overhung corner which bounds the left side of the central wall. The initial section is poorly protected. Start from the large ledge beneath the corner, easily reached via the first two pitches of ***Original Route***, or by scrambling in from the left.

(6a). Climb the corner to a resting place below the large upper overhang. Pull through this to a tiny ledge on the left, step back right and continue directly to the top up a short steep groove.

9 **R 'n' S Special**	40m	E5
G Summers, E Cleasby (1 point of aid) – May 1977 FFA: **D Cuthbertson, M Hamilton** – July 1977		

A heart-stopping trip across the wall right of ***Trilogy***. Sustained, delicate climbing with minimal protection. Start as for ***Trilogy***.

(6a). Traverse rightwards under the overlap as for ***Pluto***, until it is possible to pull through the roofs to enter a shallow scoop.

Climb the wall to a peg runner on the right. Step down and traverse right to a good hold and climb directly to some sloping footholds. Reach blindly right round the rib then move up and right to better holds leading to the final roof. Pull leftwards through the overhang on good holds to finish up easy slabs.

10 **Bilberry Buttress**	76m	VS+
C F Rowland, J F Renwick – June 1941		

A classic climb with plenty of varied interest and a fine airy finish. Start at the lowest point of the right side of the crag below a curving hand-jam crack.

1 20m (4b). Scramble up to the foot of the crack and follow it to a ledge.

2 15m (4c). Climb the thin crack in the steep left wall past a bulge to a magnificent finishing hold. Follow the ridge to belay at the foot of a large sloping ledge.

3 41m (4b). Traverse the ledge rightwards a couple of metres to a shallow crack. Climb this to below a large detached block and make a short traverse left beneath it to a scoop. Continue traversing across a green groove to an easy finish.

11 **Revelation**	43m	HS
A Gregory, B Black, J Woods – March 1948		

A splendid gem, catching the morning sun, on clean rock up a prominent subsidiary buttress on the right-hand face of the crag. A prominent flake-crack just to the right of Pitch 2 is a good marker. Start at a small polished scoop at the foot of the buttress.

1 12m. Climb the scoop and follow the right edge of the buttress on well marked holds to a good ledge below an overhanging wall.

2 31m. Exciting climbing up the short overhanging wall and strenuous crack leads to a small ledge on the left (optional belay). Move up and then traverse right round a projecting nose. Climb its right-hand side to a sloping ledge at 15 metres. Continue straight up over bulging rocks to ***Oak Tree Terrace***.

The amphitheatre to the right is bounded on its right by a triangular-shaped buttress with an attractive undercut arête for its upper half.

Left: Neil Stabbs on the steep upper section of *Trilogy* (E5) **Photo:** Nick Wharton

12 Centipede	90m	S
A Gregory, C Peckett – July 1948		

A pleasant and varied route, taking the natural line of weakness up the triangular buttress. Start below and just right of a wide hanging crack which is just right of the base of a pinnacle on the lower section of the buttress.

1 **18m.** Climb the steep rib on good holds until a short traverse left enables the upper part of the crack to be reached by a tricky move. Follow this to a good ledge and belay on the giant flake.

2 **15m.** From the top of the flake, move rightwards and climb up to a mantleshelf. Continue until a traverse left under the overhang leads to a stance in the corner, below a diagonal crack.

3 **15m.** Step down and traverse horizontally across the wall on the right to a small ledge at the base of the arête, above the overhang. Follow the arête to a good ledge. Belay well back at the foot of the next pitch. (The diagonal crack can also be climbed but is not as satisfying.)

4 **42m.** Climb onto a rickety flake and continue up a series of slabs separated by steeper, trickier steps. Optional belay at 17 metres.

East Raven Crag

Grid reference: **287 065**
Altitude: **220m**
Faces: **South**
Rock type: **Borrowdale Volcanic**
Approach time: **15 mins**

This long line of outcrop-like buttresses starts some 100 metres to the right of ***Raven Crag Buttress*** and extends gently down towards the Stickle Barn car park. The buttresses are generally smooth with few features. The best markers are the fence about 20 metres in from the left and, further right, a deeply cut right-angled gully containing a large holly.

The rock is generally sound and quite compact, though rather dirty and vegetated in parts.

Descent: round the left end of the crag.

The climbs are described **left** to **right**.

East Raven Crag

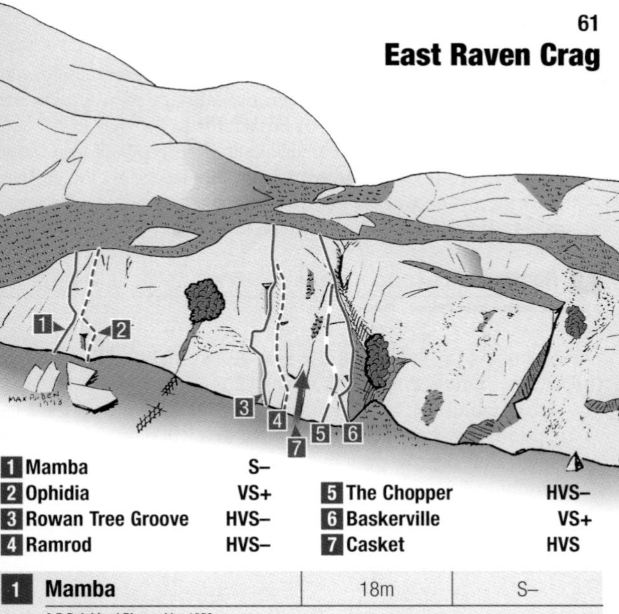

1 Mamba	S–	5 The Chopper	HVS–
2 Ophidia	VS+	6 Baskerville	VS+
3 Rowan Tree Groove	HVS–	7 Casket	HVS
4 Ramrod	HVS–		

1 Mamba | 18m | S–

A R Dolphin, J Bloor – May 1950

A steep and pleasant wall. Start at a rib just right of the broken rock forming the left end of the crag.

Climb the tapering slabby rib. Step left at its top and make a tricky move onto a ledge.

2 Ophidia | 18m | VS+

R M Biden, I Gray – July 1994

A pleasant direct variation on *Mamba*. Start a metre right of *Mamba*.

(4c). Climb the capped V-groove and wall to the top of *Mamba*'s rib. From the next ledge, step right and climb the bulging wall trending slightly right to finish at the right of two moss streaks.

3 Rowan Tree Groove | 36m | HVS–

J A Austin, J M Ruffe, R Jackson – May 1957

A good climb up the capped hanging groove containing a small rowan and overlooking the right end of a slabby area at mid-height.

Low in its grade, but entering the groove is quite committing and unprotected. Start below the upper groove, about half-way between the fence on the left and the rib of ***Baskerville*** to the right.

(4c). Climb the shallow flaky groove in the steep wall to a blunt pinnacle; step up and then left to gain the slab below the groove. Enter the groove with difficulty and climb it to overhangs. Traverse right to the rib and follow it to the top.

4	**Ramrod**	30m	HVS–
	J A Austin, I Roper, T Parker – Sept 1966		

Good climbing up the line of the slim groove right of ***Rowan Tree Groove***, and starting 2 metres to its right.

(4c). Climb up left to a blunt pinnacle and continue up the left-hand rib of a smooth little V-groove to a ledge below the overhangs. Pull directly over these into the slim groove above and climb it to the top.

5	**The Chopper**	30m	HVS–
	I Williamson, P Cornforth – 1983		

The steep, clean wall left of ***Baskerville*** gives a good, well protected, although rather contrived climb. Start below the middle of the wall, 4 metres left of ***Baskerville***, and just right of a slim impending corner-groove taken by **7 Casket** HVS (5a).

(5a). Climb the wall rightwards to the ledge on ***Baskerville***. Ascend the left-slanting crack almost into ***Casket***; gain the cracks in the wall above. Follow these to a ledge, and continue up the slim pillar above.

6	**Baskerville**	30m	VS+
	A R Dolphin, J Bloor – April 1949		

The steep rib immediately left of the deep, holly-filled right-angled gully gives a delightful, but fingery, pitch on lovely clean rock.

(4c). Starting on the right of the rib, climb round leftwards into and up a groove to a ledge at 5 metres. Step right and follow the rib, over an awkward bulge at 10 metres (good horizontal nut slot low on right), then easier ground to the top.

Gimmer Crag

Grid reference: **277 070**
Altitude: **525m**
Faces: **South-East to North-West**
Rock type: **Borrowdale Volcanic**
Approach time: **55 minutes**

Above: Adrian Ibertson on *Kipling Groove* (HVS) **Photo:** Dominic Donnini

This huge, barrel-shaped sweep of grey rock, with its fine situation is the jewel in Langdale's climbing crown. Set high above Mickleden, its profile is one of the most photographed in Lakeland, visible as it is from Windermere, 18 kilometres to the east, and all the way up the Langdale valley.

Its popularity is not surprising given the quality of both the rock and majority of its climbs, the potential for climbing in the sun all day and the generally quick-drying nature of many of its routes.

However, the climber should be prepared for a breeze; the crag is in an exposed position and those gearing-up on the sunny east side can be in for a chilly shock if they head off round to the north-west side without thinking ahead.

The easiest approach, although slightly longer in distance, is from the large car park beside the Stickle Barn. Take the main path for Pike of Stickle from the back of the car park. After 500 metres, cross the Dungeon Ghyll beck just above a stile, and follow a good path up the shoulder for a kilometre, passing above ***Raven Crags***, until the fellside falls back below the final mountain summits. Shortly after this, the crag comes into view directly ahead. When the main track steepens again, take a faint horizontal path leftwards. This leads straight to the main gearing-up point below the ***South-East Face***.

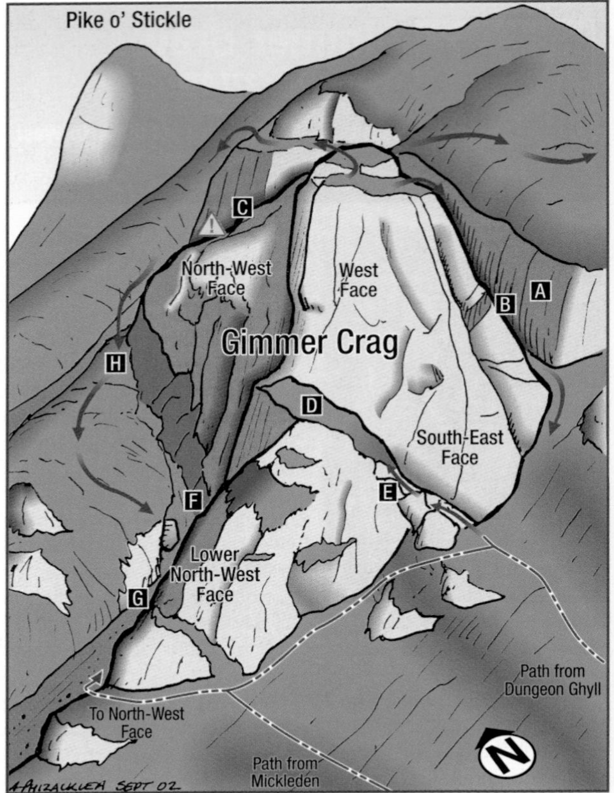

A **Main Wall**
B **South-East Gully** (descent)
C **Junipall Gully** (descent not recommended)
D **Ash Tree Ledge**
E **Bilberry Chute** (scramble)
F **Start of the Crack**
G **Start of Ash Tree Slabs**
H **North-West Gully**

From the car park at the Old Dungeon Ghyll Hotel, one can either take the main path up Mickleden for a kilometre and then follow a small steep path up the side of Grave Gill, which then contours leftwards to the toe of the crag (useful for the *North-West Face*); or, more directly, take the track to ***Raven Crag*** but branch off leftwards at about halfway, just after a stone slab bridge. Follow the small path, very steeply at first, for a kilometre until it contours directly to the main gearing-up point.

A traditional and most satisfying alternative is to start by climbing *Middlefell Buttress* and *Curtain Wall*, followed by further scrambling up the short outcrops above until a horizontal path is reached, the main route from the Stickle Barn. Follow this leftwards, as above.

Timewise, there is little to choose between any of these approaches.

The crag's topography is deceptively simple. It forms a somewhat conical pillar of rock protruding from the fellside. There are three main faces, the *South-East Face*, *West Face* and the *North-West Face*, which all provide excellent climbing. The front of the crag stands above a terraced slabby base, and the whole mass is defined by the faultline which separate it from the hillside. This gives the *South-East Gully*, which faces the usual direction of approach, and *Junipall Gully*, which extends down into the *North-West Gully* on the opposite side of the crag. Each face is given its own access details.

Descent: for access to the right of the crag, it is best to descend *South-East Gully* (Moderate). This is to be found a few yards behind and slightly right of, and almost level with, the top of the *West Face*. It is usually entered by an exposed straddling move and those not keen on this can find a way in higher up. The gully is quite narrow at first, with some suspect rock. About halfway down, cross the central rib and scramble down a series of short walls to finish down the far left-hand corner (facing out). An alternative to the gully is to traverse ledges rightwards from its top leading over the back of *Main Wall*, and then down into a grassy area above the main approach routes.

For descent to the left of the crag, it is best to avoid *Junipall Gully*. Instead, from the neck between the two gullies (behind the summit block), scramble up for some 15 metres and then trend leftwards to gradually descend into the upper open reaches of *North-West Gully*. After a short loose section, leave the gully for the heathery spur on the right (facing out) where a path winds down to the open scree area and large, flat boulder opposite the *Crack*.

The climbs are described from **right** to **left**.

Main Wall

The first route lies on the wall extending from the right-hand side of the lower part of *South-East Gully*.

1	**Main Wall Climb**	49m	VD
	G S Bower, F Graham – March 1921		

An excellent route on good rock. Start at an embedded flake at the foot of the wall, 6 metres below and right of a large detached flake.

1 **18m.** Pleasant climbing on satisfying holds leads up and slightly rightwards to a ledge and small belays.

2 **18m.** Move diagonally left to a ledge, then step right and continue directly up again to a good belay.

3 **13m.** Start the pitch on the left and climb direct to the top.

South-East Face

This is the wall facing the usual approach path from Dungeon Ghyll Hotel. It is easily identified by the long central twin-crack system of:

2	**Gimmer Chimney**	80m	VD+
	E Rigby, J Sandison, A S Thomson – Nov 1902		

This striking feature provides a classic route. Start at a broken rib under the main line, about 15 metres up from the gearing up point and 10 metres up and right of *Bracket and Slab Climb*.

1 **32m.** Climb the rib and ensuing easy chimney to a steep section at 23 metres which proves awkward. Easy climbing then leads to a good stance on the right.

2 **17m.** Traverse left for 3 metres into a tricky groove, which leads into a sentry box. Climb the deep crack, using good holds on its right rib, to a stance at the right end of the *Gangway*, beneath the black depths of the narrow chimney so obvious from below.

3 **11m.** Fortunately for the tyro, this MVS chimney is not compulsory, being Pitch 6 of *Bracket and Slab Climb*. Instead, traverse 5 metres right into the parallel chimney, which leads amenably to a belay in the open gully above.

4 **20m.** Start up the gully bed and finish up the rib on the right.

3	**Bracket and Slab Climb**	97m	S
	H B Lyon, J Herbert – Aug 1923		

An excellent, long and varied route, which is MVS if the strenuous chimney is included. Some 10 metres above the gearing-up ledge, is

Gimmer Crag – South-East Face

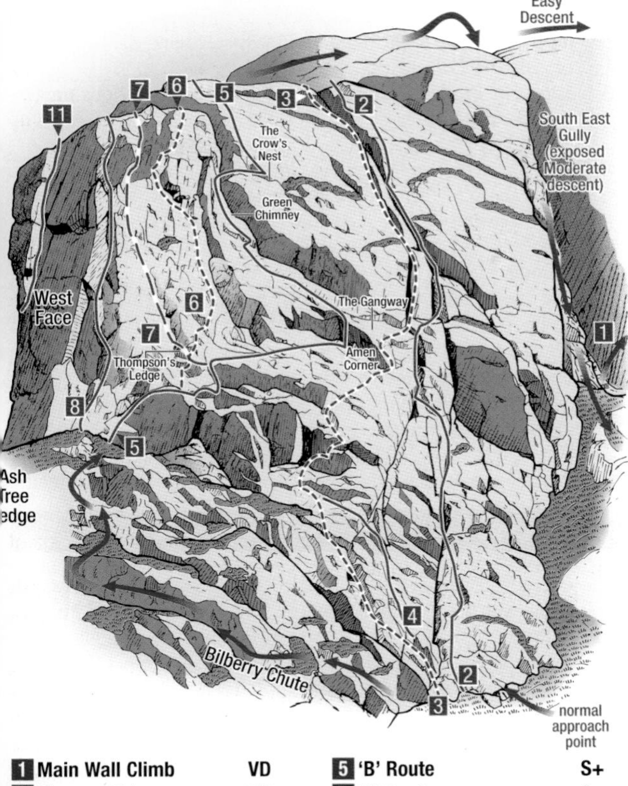

1 Main Wall Climb	**VD**	**5 'B' Route**	**S+**
2 Gimmer Chimney	**VD+**	**6 'C' Route**	**S+**
3 Bracket and Slab	**S**	**7 'A' Route**	**MS**
4 Bracket and Slab Direct Start	**VS**	**8 'D' Route**	**S+**
		11 'F' Route	**VS+**

the **4 Direct Start**, a clean slab split by a prominent right-to-left flake-crack, which is a good variation to Pitch 1 (VS 4b). Start in the bay 5 metres below this crack.

1 11m. Move left onto the easy-angled rib and climb up over its flake top to a ledge and then past an awkward slab to another ledge.

2 20m. Move right to a rib, which is followed for 10 metres to a grassy bank. Follow this to a belay in the rocky corner beneath an overhanging V-groove/niche (at the extreme right-hand end of *Ash Tree Ledge*).

3 12m. ***The Bracket***. Climb up a little and make a devious traverse right for 6 metres, past and over blocks, until a groove leads up to a stance.

4 26m. Traverse right over easy ground, under ***Amen Corner***, to reach the start of the ***Neat Bit***. Follow the leftwards-rising traverse 5 metres and then climb a crack which leads to the ***Gangway***. Traverse easily rightwards to the foot of the first of two chimneys (junction with ***Gimmer Chimney***).

5 9m. The narrow, slightly overhanging left-hand chimney is MVS and best suited to thin masochists who will bury themselves in it seeking security of sorts. It is most easily finished using holds on the right rib. Stouter individuals or those preferring a more consistent grade will opt for the easier chimney on the right (as for ***Gimmer Chimney***).

6 19m. Climb out of the gully leftwards to a ledge. Work back right to a point overlooking the chimney and continue up pleasant slabs.

The West Face

These routes start from the series of ledges collectively known as ***Ash Tree Ledge*** which are reached from the main arrival point via the ***Bilberry Chute***. A spindly rowan tree and large pointed flake block can be seen a few metres to the left. Traverse left behind a block, level with the top of the rowan, until a short exposed scramble over well worn rock leads onto a grassy terrace on the front of the crag. Follow this for 15 metres, then up to some large, flat, perched blocks. Go rightwards behind these and scramble up until you reach ***Ash Tree Ledge*** beneath the *ABCE* wall.

5 'B' Route — 69m — S+

H B Lyon, J Stables, A S Thomson – July 1907

An entertaining and popular climb. Towards the right end of ***Ash Tree Ledge***, where it slopes down to the right, a large platform can be seen up on the right, guarded by a short wall with the letters *ABCE* scratched on it. Start left of the letters at a good belay.

1 18m. Climb up and traverse right to the platform. Belay well to the right below a polished crack.
2 10m. Climb the crack to *Thompson's Ledge*. Easily right for 6 metres to the foot of the impending corner.
3 5m. *Amen Corner.* The overhanging and leaning corner succumbs to a positive approach; the polished holds requiring an equally polished technique for a stylish ascent. Belay on the left on the *Gangway*.
4 9m. Ascend the *Gangway* leftwards to a good ledge.
5 12m. Climb the left-facing corner above (*Green Chimney*) until a short traverse right leads round the corner into the *Crow's Nest*.
6 15m. Step right and follow pleasant slabs to the top.

6	**'C' Route**	62m	S+

A P Wilson, C H Jackson, A Brundritt – Aug 1918

A classic route giving some fine climbing in good positions and following a fairly direct line. Start as for *'B' Route*.
1 *18m.* Climb up and traverse right to the platform. Belay well to the right, below a polished crack.
2 27m. 3 metres left of the belay, a short but steep wall leads via a jammed flake into a steep recess, which is climbed with difficulty to *Thompson's Ledge*. Move right to a flake at the foot of a long groove leading up to a prominent square-cut overhang. Enter this groove via the right side of the flake and follow it to a small stance and good nut belays a few metres below the overhang.
3 17m. Climb up to the overhang and pull round left beneath it to gain a ledge. Follow the groove above, moving right at a flaky spike to finish direct in an exposed position.

7	**'A' Route**	75m	MS

E Rigby, D Leighton, J Sandison – April 1903

A great climb on excellent rock, so typical of this part of the crag. It takes a series of steps rising to the left from *Thompson's Ledge*. Start as for *'B' Route*.
1 18m. Climb up and traverse right to the platform. Belay well to the right below the polished crack.
2 5m. Climb the initial crack of *'B' Route* to belay immediately on *Thompson's Ledge*.

3 **9m.** Traverse left along ***Thompson's Ledge*** to the foot of the *Forty Foot Corner*.

4 **18m.** Climb the delightful corner to a good spike, and traverse left and slightly up to a ledge and belay at the foot of an open groove.

5 **11m.** Climb the groove (known as ***Lichen Chimney***). A good flake belay exists on the wall 2 metres above the finish.

6 **14m.** The rock staircase on the left leads across to a steep finishing crack.

8	**'D' Route**	31m	S+
	G S Bower, P R Masson – May 1919		

A brilliant pitch following a fine crackline, the initial section of which is quite delicate. Start some 12 metres above ***Ash Tree Ledge*** at some terraces with small blocky belays, below a triangular recess. This is just right of a smooth sweep of slabby walls, bisected by a square-cut overlap.

Climb up easily into the recess, make a dainty 5 metre traverse left to gain the right-slanting groove and crackline. Follow this for 9 metres to good ledge. Climb the ***Forked Lightning Crack*** above to join ***'A' Route*** below its final crack. Move up left into a sloping corner which is overcome via holds on the right wall.

9	**Spring Bank**	40m	E2–
	M G Mortimer, E Cleasby, M G Allen, M Lynch, J Lamb – June 1979		

A brilliant pitch up the middle of the smoothest piece of rock around. Excellent climbing on small holds and a testing roof in a fine position at two-thirds height. Very well protected. Start just left of ***'D' Route***.

(5c). Follow the rib just left of ***'D' Route***, then thin cracks in the slab to the roof. Pull over this on small holds, and continue more easily.

10	**Whit's End Direct**	40m	E1+
	J A Austin, R Valentine – Oct 1972		

Enjoyable slab climbing with a neat section through the roof. Start at the prominent left-slanting flake-crack, just left of ***'D' Route***.

Left: David Wareing in a typically amazing position on *'A' Route* (MS)
Photo: Barnaby Whiteside

(5b). Ascend the flake-crack and continue up thinner cracks to a resting point just below the overlap. Step right and climb up to enter the hanging corner from the right. (Entering it direct is much harder.) Exit back right onto the slab (reach helps) and finish up this on improving holds.

11 **'F' Route**	40m	VS+

R J Birkett, V Veevers – May 1941

A terrific pitch with the crux fittingly near the top. It takes the fine right-facing corner which separates the bulging front face from the slabby ***Spring Bank*** area. Start on ledges directly below the line of the main corner.

(4c). Scramble easily leftwards to a ledge below a barrier of overhangs (the ***Kipling Groove*** undercling pitch). Traverse right, under a rib, to gain a ledge which leads to an overhung recess. Follow a good flake back leftwards to a small ledge beneath the overhangs in the main corner. Move up right into the corner proper and follow it to a fine and bold finish.

For the complete experience, start the route by climbing the initial left-leaning flake-crack of ***Whit's End Direct*** to the overhung recess. This gives an even better pitch, sustained at VS+ (4c).

12 **Eastern Hammer**	38m	E3

P Livesey, A Manson – May 1974

Excellent fingery climbing up the centre of the bulging wall left of ***'F' Route***. Start by scrambling up to the ledge at the start of the ***Kipling Groove*** undercling traverse.

(6a). Pull over the overhang onto the steep wall and climb to a peg runner. Follow the crack to a good hold beneath the final bulges. Step up, move to the left end of the bulge and pull across it rightwards to a small ledge. Finish more easily up the final cracks of ***Kipling Groove***.

13 **Equus**	43m	E2+

To junction with *Kipling Groove*: **E Cleasby** – April 1976 Complete ascent: **M G Mortimer, M G Allen** – May 1976

An excellent and sustained pitch involving some difficult bridging up the slim groove between ***Eastern Hammer*** and ***Kipling Groove***. Start as for ***Eastern Hammer***. Very high in its grade.

Route	Grade
8 'D' Route	S+
9 Springbank	E2–
10 Whit's End Direct	E1+
11 'F' Route	VS+
12 Eastern Hammer	E3
13 Equus	E2+
14 Kipling Groove	HVS
19 Gimmer String	E1–

Gimmer Crag – West Face

(5c). Move up leftwards to the centre of the roof which forms the *Kipling Groove* undercling. Pull boldly over this and continue up the groove on small holds until forced left to a junction with *Kipling Groove*. Up this a short way to a resting place beneath a bulge and swing left to a small ledge. Climb the groove and exposed wall on the right to gain a horizontal crack, which is followed leftwards to finish.

14 **Kipling Groove**	52m	HVS

A R Dolphin, J B Lockwood – May 1948

A magnificent and popular classic route taking an impressive 'Rudyard' line up the steep front face of the buttress. Start as for *'F' Route*.

1 **10m.** Scramble up easily to a ledge below the overhangs.

2 **11m (4c).** The much photographed undercling pitch. Move up to and traverse left beneath the roof, to a crack which leads to an overhung recess. Care is required to avoid the rope snagging in the crack at the left end of the undercling.

3 **31m (5a).** Climb the right wall of the recess past a dubious block to the overhang, step right onto the edge and follow a crack to a resting place beneath the bulge. Pull up and across strenuously rightwards to reach a diagonal crack (crux) and continue to a horizontal crack. Traverse this right to a small ledge and ascend a crack to easier ground and the top. A first class pitch.

North-West Face

Traditionally known in less enlightened days as 'The Gentleman's Side' of *Gimmer*, this face provides some of the longer routes on the crag. The steep face containing *Kipling Groove* towers directly above the first four routes.

It can be reached most easily from the gearing-up point under *South-East Gully* by descending to the toe of the crag and up the other side into *North-West Gully* to a small level area before a final scramble onto the top of a giant boulder jammed in the gully bed. The flat top of this provides a good base camp, level with start of the *Crack*.

Left: Tracy Ward moving around the roof on *Whit's End Direct* (E1) **Photo:** Nick Wharton

15 Ash Tree Slabs | 48m | VD+

G S Bower, A W Wakefield – June 1920

A great climb up the handsome sweep of slabs overlooking the level area on the path, some 25 metres below the giant boulder. Start by scrambling up into a small bay at the foot of the slabs.

1 16m. Climb 3 metres up the corner and traverse diagonally left on good holds to the edge of the slab and follow this to a ledge.

2 32m. Climb 3 metres up to the left to a platform from which a groove leads up to the right. Follow this until it eases and continue up slabs to finish on ledges. ***'D' Route*** starts above and to the right.

16 Intern | 48m | E1+

P1 **P Fearnehough, J Oliver, J Hesmondhalgh** – May 1963 P2 **J A Austin, I Roper** – March 1966

A really worthwhile route which is sustained and varied, weaving a way up the bulging wall left of ***Ash Tree Slabs***. Start 8 metres left of this, below a steep, right-slanting crack.

1 18m (5b). Climb the crack for a few metres until it is possible to step left to gain the narrowing, left-slanting slab. Cross to its left edge which overlooks the gully using holds on the slab above. Pull up into a short groove and climb this to the foot of a left-slanting gangway. A technical and sustained pitch.

2 30m (5a). Climb the gangway for a short distance before moving back right to climb the wall above the belay. Crossing a bulge necessitates some bold moves which lead into a steep groove. Follow this to a rib, which leads in turn to the final steep crack of *North-West Arête*.

17 North-West Arête | 42m | VS–

R J Birkett, V Veevers – Sept 1940

A beautifully exposed route on good rock and generally excellent holds. Start at the left end of an obvious thin quartz ledge in the gully by the giant jammed boulder, a couple of metres below ***Asterisk***.

(4b). Climb easily up right to gain the wall. (The same point can be reached by climbing the obvious rampline starting lower to the right.) Climb the wall to a small overlap. Traverse right and up a crack to gain the foot of a groove which cuts through the left side of a large overhang. Climb the groove on good holds

Gimmer Crag – North-West Face

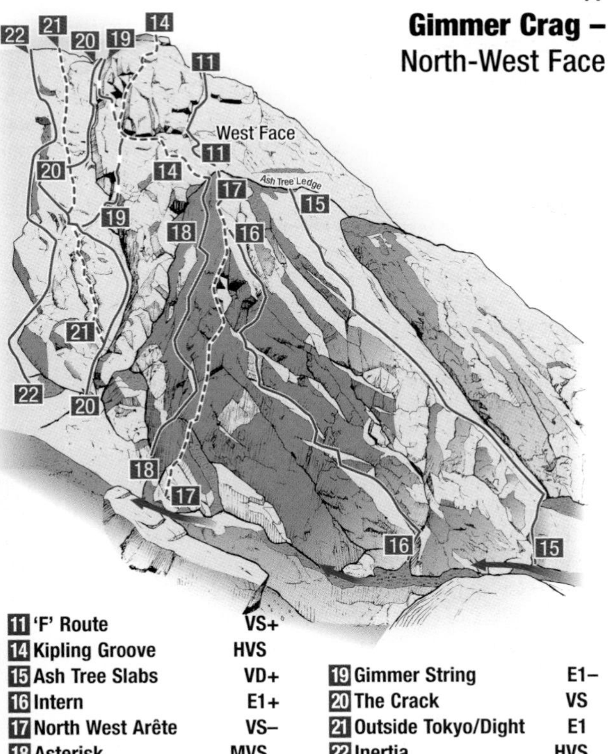

11 'F' Route	VS+		
14 Kipling Groove	HVS		
15 Ash Tree Slabs	VD+	19 Gimmer String	E1–
16 Intern	E1+	20 The Crack	VS
17 North West Arête	VS–	21 Outside Tokyo/Dight	E1
18 Asterisk	MVS	22 Inertia	HVS

and move right immediately above the overhang to gain the arête. Climb it more or less directly, finishing carefully up a thin, fragile looking flake-crack.

18 Asterisk | 38m | MVS

H S Gross, G Basterfield, B Tyson – May 1928

A splendid pitch, mostly on jugs, up the steep wall left of *North-West Arête*. Start at a rock ledge slanting up right, opposite the top of the giant jammed boulder in the gully bed.

(4b). There is an obvious crescent-shaped ledge 7 metres above the belay. Gain this by traversing right until good holds lead up slightly leftwards to its right-hand end. Follow the series of steps up to the right for 6 metres to a small niche and vertical crack in the centre of the wall. Climb this until the crack fades and leads back right to the arête. Step up left to the foot of a thin slanting crack which leads to the top, initially on small holds.

19 Gimmer String | 77m | E1–

The complete ascent: **J A Austin, E Metcalf, D Miller** – July 1963

A fine combination of pitches, strung together to provide varied and enjoyable climbing in exposed situations. Start as for the ***Crack***.

1 25m (4b). The first pitch of the ***Crack***.

2 25m (4c). Traverse right to the top of a pinnacle beneath a roof and step right to below an imposing wide crack. Pull awkwardly into it and continue to the stance on ***Kipling Groove***.

3 27m (5b). Climb straight up for a short way to some dubious blocks, then traverse left to a small ledge on the rib which is both undercut and overhung. Climb a thin crack on the right of the rib for about 5 metres, until a difficult pull leads round to the other side of the rib overlooking the ***Crack***. Climb the arête, trending left to a thin crack which leads up to a short problematic wall and an abrupt finish.

20 The Crack | 74m | VS

A B Reynolds, G G Macphee – May 1928

The obvious great corner cleaving the crag from top to bottom. A combination of a fine natural line, exposed and sustained climbing and excellent rock make this one of Lakeland's grandest crack climbs. Start about 10 metres above the start of ***Asterisk*** at the foot of an easy angled corner, which leads up to the foot of the crack proper.

1 26m (4b). Scramble into the corner and climb the clean-cut crack until a delicate traverse left leads to the foot of a short groove. Climb this to a ledge and pedestal belay.

2 26m (4c). Thin cracks above the belay lead to a horizontal break. Stand in this by some tricky moves and traverse left to a large ledge at 8 metres. A hard pull up on the steep ridge leads to better holds, followed by an easy traverse back right into the crack at the ***Sentry Box***. A strenuous pull out of this gains a good ledge – the ***Bower***.

3 22m (4c). The deep crack gives a sustained pitch, with a problematic overhang en route.

21 **Outside Tokyo/Dight**	68m	E1

P1 and part P2: **G Gibson, D Beetlestone** – Aug 1979 Part P2 and P3: **J A Austin, E Metcalf** – May 1963
Part P2: **R Moseley, R Greenall** – Oct 1953

This excellent route takes a fairly direct line up the sweeping slabby wall left of the *Crack*, starting as for that route.

1 21m (5b). Climb to a crack in the left wall which bends left to the foot of two grooves. Climb the right-hand one, which comprises a series of slanting steps.

2 31m (5b). Follow the *Crack* onto the horizontal break. Step right and climb a tricky crack to ledges beneath some overlaps. Pull over the first one with difficulty, stepping right into the thin crack. Follow this past a second smaller overlap, and then climb more easily leftwards into a sentry box. Ascend the crack on its left to yet more overhangs, and move right to a small stance (as for *Inertia*).

3 16m (5a). Climb the corner above the stance for a couple of metres before pulling up strenuously round a small rib into the groove on the right. Finish up this.

22 **Inertia**	71m	HVS

P2 **L Brown, R G Wilson, C E M Yates** – Aug 1959 P3 **E Metcalf, J A Austin** – May 1963

This climb approaches the slabs left of the *Crack* via a steep groove in the rib bounding their left side. Start in the corner/gully left of the slabs and level with the large ledge mentioned on Pitch 2 of the *Crack*.

1 20m. Climb easily up the corner/gully to a ledge at the foot of a prominent corner-groove in the right wall.

2 27m (5a). The groove is awkward to start. Gain the top of a small pedestal in the corner and pull round the overhang into the groove on the right. Ascend this for a short way and traverse out to the rib on the right. Make a difficult move up this and go up and across right to a sentry box. Climb the crack on the left until stopped by the overhang and step right to a small stance.

3 24m (5a). Above on the left, a long narrow slab slanting up to the left finishes against a line of small, square-cut overhangs. Climb the slab, then the corner-crack where it steepens, to the end of these overhangs. Finish rightwards up a groove.

Bowfell

Above: The Climbers' Traverse on Bowfell, with Flat Crags and Bowfell Buttress in the background **Photo:** Nick Wharton

Bowfell is the highest summit of the Langdale horseshoe and its crags offer some excellent climbing in a wonderful mountain setting. Its long approach (by Lakeland standards) filters out the crag rats and creates a Mecca for enthusiasts who are well rewarded for their efforts. The main climbing is on four separate crags which lie in a rough semi-circle high on the north-east side of the mountain overlooking the upper reaches of Mickleden. Most of the climbs are on good rock (brilliant in places) but care should be taken, as on all mountain crags, to watch for loose flakes and blocks.

The easiest approach is from the Old Dungeon Ghyll car park. Follow the road to Stool End Farm (no parking allowed here), then up the long ridge of the Band which separates Mickleden from Oxendale. After about 60mins, the path levels out, passing above ***Neckband Crag*** which lies out of sight on the northern side. The main track can now been seen to contour the fellside leftwards to the col of Three Tarns. Quit this in favour of the path running up the ridge on the right which, after a steep scree covered section, leads to an exposed undulating path known as the **Climbers' Traverse**. This contours rightwards below a line of broken outcrops to the foot of ***Flat Crags***. Avoid a false track which leads straight on by keeping close under the right end of ***Flat Crags*** and the foot of the ***Great Slab*** to arrive at an ever-flowing spring, the **Waterspout**, at the base of ***Cambridge Crag***. ***North Buttress*** lies up on the right just around the corner and ***Bowfell Buttress*** across the wide scree fan to the right.

Neckband Crag

Grid reference: **256 062**
Altitude: **550m**
Faces: **North**
Rock type: **Borrowdale Volcanic**
Approach time: **1 hr 15 mins**

This superb little crag is tucked away in a cove overlooking Grunting Gill on the right flank of the Band and below the level area some two-thirds of the way up it. (Marked as *Earing Crag* on the large scale Ordnance Survey map.)

The crag is compact with an outcrop atmosphere and comprises a series of three main left-facing corners. Its left side in particular hosts a concentration of immaculate pitches up excellent grooves and cracks on rough, solid rock. Some areas are mossy and with its northerly aspect, it does take a few days to dry out, particularly at the beginning of the season; but it is a cool haven on a hot summer's day.

Approach as for Bowfell until, at the beginning of the level area, a vague path branches right, passes right of a knoll and descends steeply leftwards towards the left end of the crag. This branch off the main track is easily missed which will be realised as the ridge steepens again, but by dropping down into the gill on the right, it is possible to double back to the base of the crag.

Descent: from the belay terrace, walk left and scramble, first up, then down, steep ground leading back to the foot of the crag.

The routes are described from **left** to **right**.

1 Cravat	35m	VS

H Drasdo, N Drasdo – 1950

An excellent route up exposed rock at a reasonable grade. Start at a short corner below the east-facing wall at the left end of the crag.

(4b). Climb the corner to a ledge. From its right end, climb a short crack until a line of holds lead rightwards to a scoop in the arête. Move up this to a ledge. Go round the rib on the right and follow a thin crack in the slab diagonally right to reach a good crack 2 metres left of the corner. Finish up this crack.

2 Aragorn	40m	E2

A Evans, D Parker – Sept 1971

An excellent pitch with interesting, exposed and varied climbing. Start in the corner as for *Mithrandir*.

(5c). Follow the corner for about 4 metres. Traverse the undercut slab left to a spike at the base of a large niche on the arête. Pull into the niche and either exit direct up into an easier groove or move left round the rib and climb it to the same point. Climb the groove and finish up the thought-provoking continuation crack which slants left to the top.

3 Gandalf's Groove Direct	36m	E2–

J A Austin, F P Jenkinson – July 1964 Direct finish: **I Williamson, J White** – July 1983

Described here with the direct finish, this is a magnificent outing across the left wall of ***Mithrandir*** and up the left arête. Delicate balance climbing on beautiful rock, requiring steadiness on the upper section. Start as for *Mithrandir*.

(5b). Ascend the corner for about 6 metres, until a descending traverse leads easily out left to a very shallow right-facing corner near the rib. Climb delicately up this and step left onto the rib (junction with ***Cravat***). Fortified by a runner in the crack on the right, continue boldly up the right-hand side of the rib, the difficulty slowly easing towards the top.

4 Mithrandir	33m	HVS+

J Hartley, R Sager – Aug 1972

A classic line up the first large left-facing corner. Unfortunately, the seepage line from the overhang near the top is slow to dry and the moves round the overhang are much harder if this is damp. Start at the foot of the corner.

(5a). Climb it!

If the groove is wet, the **5 Glorfindel** variation (HVS) gives an excellent finish creating the easiest way up an uncompromising piece of rock: halfway up the corner, gain ledges on the right wall (junction with ***Gillette Direct***), From the top one of these, traverse right to the arête and enter the crack round the corner. Finish up this.

Neckband Crag

	Route	Grade
1	Cravat	VS
2	Aragorn	E2
3	Gandalf's Groove Direct	E2–
4	Mithrandir	HVS+
5	Glorfindel (variation)	HVS
6	Gillette Direct	E2
7	Razor Crack	E1–

6	**Gillette Direct**	35m	E2

K Wood, J A Austin – July 1968 Direct finish: **W Lounds and party** – 1969

A brilliant, well protected route up the compelling line of narrow, hanging grooves in the right wall of *Mithrandir*. Start right of the line at a ragged crack below a band of overhangs at 3 metres.

(5c). Climb the crack to the overhang and good runners (thread). Protected by these, traverse left onto the slab and enter the groove with difficulty. Continue delicately to a small ledge. Gain a better ledge and climb the steepening groove above to good finishing cracks in the final bulge.

7 **Razor Crack**	35m	E1–

J A Austin, K Wood – Aug 1966

A classic pitch which climbs the superb crackline up the slabby left wall of the central corner and takes in several impressive overlaps. Technically low in the grade but giving strenuous and sustained climbing; good protection and resting places. Start as for *Gillette Direct* at the ragged crack.

(5a). The crack is immediately strenuous to the overhang at 3 metres. Traverse right beneath this until a thin crack enables a pull over and moves back left into the wider, main crack. Follow this over several overlaps and the odd jammed flake to the top where you can sink thankfully amongst the bilberries.

Flat Crags

Grid reference: **249 064**
Altitude: **750m**
Faces: **East-North-East**
Rock type: **Borrowdale Volcanic**
Approach time: **1 hr 35 mins**

Flat Crags lies above the right end of the **Climbers' Traverse** and is easily identified by the very pronounced sloping strata of the rock. This creates an illusion that the crag is not as steep as it really is. The rock is excellent and compact, and dries quite quickly.

A tapering rock terrace rises from right to left beneath the severely overhanging central section, home to some desperate routes, and leads to a wide bay. The narrow section of the terrace is particularly exposed. **Descents:** either down the *Great Slab* behind the crag to the Climbers' Traverse, or scramble down leftwards onto the upper reaches of the rock terrace for further routes.

The climbs are described from **right** to **left**.

1 Flat Crags Climb	43m	S–
Unknown possibly pre-1926		

Although artificial in line at times, this route contains some amazingly exposed climbing when it makes a cheeky excursion into the hidden upper reaches of the crag. Start at slabs some 10 metres right of the rock terrace, and just right of the top of the huge block at its base.

1 16m. Climb direct up the excellent slab for 7 metres when a short traverse left gains a ledge. Traverse rightwards and up past another ledge to reach the large grassy terrace.

2 27m. Walk up the terrace to where it steepens. Re-belay and look left. A sloping ledge can be seen leading to the edge of the crag in a very exposed position. Follow this easily and move delicately round the edge to discover a fine deep crack. Climb this, either direct or on its left, and then the corner above finishing steeply. Further scrambling leads up a pleasant ridge to an obvious summit.

The next three routes start from the bay at the top of the rock terrace.

2 Fastburn	36m	E2
E Cleasby, I Greenwood – June 1979		

A superb pitch which goes directly up the centre of the ***Flat Iron Wall***. It provides a contrasting combination of strenuous crack and delicate wall climbing. Start at a hanging crack 5 metres right of ***Flat Iron Wall***.

(5b). Climb the crack and hollow flake above to a good ledge (junction with ***Flat Iron Wall***). Continue delicately up the wall, trending left to join the obvious thin slanting crack. Follow the crack, moving out right at the top to a good ledge. Move immediately back left and climb the wall to easier ground above.

3 Flat Iron Wall	43m	E1
J A Austin, F Wilkinson – July 1971		

An excellent first pitch which finds the easiest way up the undercut, white, wrinkled wall so prominently visible from the approach walk. The wall looks holdless, but is just off-vertical and covered in little edges. Protection is better than might be expected – sufficient to allow one to savour the excursion. Start below a mossy corner defining the left side of the wall.

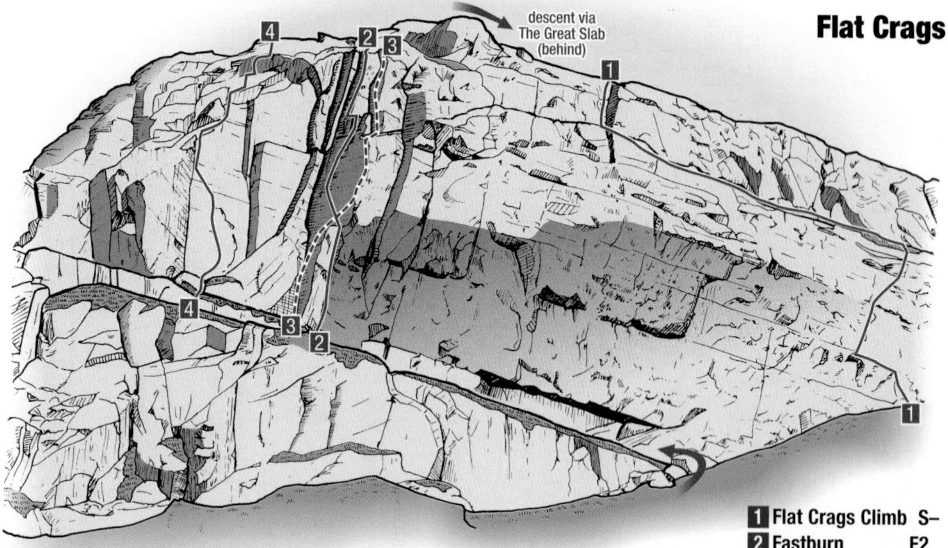

descent via
The Great Slab
(behind)

1 Flat Crags Climb S–
2 Fastburn E2
3 Flat Iron Wall E1
4 Slowburn E2–

1 22m (5a). Make a rising traverse rightwards to gain a small ledge above the overhangs (junction with ***Fastburn***). Step right and climb directly up the wall, over a slight bulge near the top, to a ledge on the right arête. Move up to a stance on the larger ledge above.

2 21m (5a). On the left, a succession of three little corners prove to be disproportionately awkward for their size, and are difficult to protect. Alternatively, it is more pleasant to move right from the belay and up into a shallow, laid-back groove. Ascend this to a large ledge and climb a short steep crack above.

4 **Slowburn**	33m	E2–

B Berzins, M Berzins – July 1979

A good route, steeper than it looks, which follows the left-bounding wall of the bay on sloping holds. Start just below the toe of the slab at a short corner.

(5b). Climb up easily to an obvious small pocket in the left wall. Pull out left to a cracked spike. Follow a ramp that leads rightwards, to its top. Traverse delicately up and leftwards to a ledge on the arête. Pull up and follow the edge of the wall up and right in an exposed position until a steep move gives access to easy slabs leading to the top.

Cambridge Crag

Grid reference: **246 066**
Altitude: **775m**
Faces: **East**
Rock type: **Borrowdale Volcanic**
Approach time: **1 hr 40 mins**

Cambridge Crag rises up leftwards from the Waterspout and overlooks the ***Great Slab***, an obvious expanse of very easy-angled, sparsely vegetated rock. The crag is a mass of jumbled pinnacles, short walls and ribs.

Descent: Walk off left to join and descend the path beneath the crag.

1 The Cambridge Climb	77m	VD
W T Elmslie, A de St C Walsh – Sept 1922		

A very good climb, a classic of its era and genre, with some excellent positions. The grade increases exponentially in the wet, even in nailed boots. Start about 10 metres left of the Waterspout at the foot of a broad slab sloping upwards to the right.

1 11m. Climb the slab to corner.
2 9m. Step round the rib on the right and climb up to a good ledge equipped with an overhanging block belay.
3 14m. Traverse left to the second of two grass niches, above which a sharp jutting flake is climbed to another grassy corner.
4 15m. Climb the pleasant flake chimney to a ledge on the right.
5 11m. Step back left into the chimney and climb to a large terrace.
6 17m. A giant's three-step staircase leads up and rightwards with increasing difficulty to an exit on the ridge. Easy scrambling leads to the main ridge.

Right: Lovely climbing on the *Cambridge Climb* (VD) leads almost to the summit of Bowfell
Photo: Nick Wharton

North Buttress

Grid reference: **246 066**
Altitude: **785m**
Faces: **North-East**
Rock type: **Borrowdale Volcanic**
Approach time: **1 hr 45 mins**

North Buttress stands above and to the right of ***Cambridge Crag***, facing across to ***Bowfell Buttress*** on the opposite side of the wide scree shoot. Rambling and vegetated on the left, its steep right-hand side presents an obvious series of three fine grooves climbed by (from left to right) **3 Gnomon** E1(5b), ***Mindbender*** and ***Sword of Damocles***. These all give excellent climbing on rock as rough as anything on the mountain. An excellent venue for a hot day, when you will probably still have the crag to yourselves.

Descent: Down the wide scree shoot between the crag and *Bowfell Buttress*.

The routes are described from **left** to **right**.

2 Riboletto	43m	E4–

P Rigby, A Greig – June 1988

A brilliant pitch, perhaps the highest finishing in Langdale. Graded for its bold start. Well to the left of the top of the buttress can be seen a fine arête rising to its own summit. The best approach is to abseil down its right-hand side from the summit blocks; care is needed to make sure the bottom of the rope reaches the start. It is also possible to scramble up the ground below; a maze of heavily vegetated grooves and broken rock. Start below the smooth groove on the right side of the rib.

1 33m (6a). Climb the groove for 5 metres to a grassy incut hold (skyhook runner for the trusting), then make some delicate moves left to gain the narrow hanging slab below the rib which leads left round the corner to a good rest below a thin groove and crack with lots of runners. Continue up the left side of the rib (crux), useful small hidden hold right of the rib, to reach a good ledge. Follow the rib past another small ledge to belay below a short wall.

	Route	Grade
1	The Cambridge Climb	VD
2	Riboletto	E4–
3	Gnomon	E1
4	Mindbender	E2
5	Sword of Damocles	E1

Bowfell, Cambridge Crag, North Buttress

2 10m (4c). Climb the wall. The summit of the mountain lies just behind for those traditionally inclined.

4	Mindbender	28m	E2
	R J Kenyon, R Bennett – June 1979		

A fantastic pitch up the central V-groove, with better protection than appears from below. There is a large ledge directly below the groove. Start at a crack beneath this, gained by scrambling left from ***Sword of Damocles***.

(5b). The start is a bit of a shock, but a fist crack up on the right provides a good home for a large friend. (Alternatively, traverse further left and climb a more civilised crack to the ledge above. Climb the groove on immaculate rock, past a difficult bulge, to a steep airy finish. Scramble to the top.

5	Sword of Damocles	56m	E1
	P J Greenwood, A R Dolphin, D Hopkin – Aug 1952		

A classic route of its day, which climbs the right-hand and largest of the three grooves. The ***Sword***, a wedged rock spike which gave the climb its name, has long since gone. Start from the ledge below the groove beneath a prominent, overhung curved crack, actually the base of a huge pinnacle.

1 23m (4c). Climb the crack to enter the groove on the right. Move up easily to the foot of a corner behind the pinnacle. Climb this until a long stride right can be made to gain a ledge on the edge of the buttress; move up a little until a dramatic semi-hand-traverse can be made leftwards back into the main corner, to a stance on the left wall.

2 15m (5b). Climb the groove (where the ***Sword*** was) passing to the left of an awkward bulge. Move right above this to a small stance.

3 18m (5a). Climb the steep impressive flake-crack to a resting place; continue up the crack, until a move right leads to easier climbing and the top.

Bowfell Buttress

Grid reference: **246 067**
Altitude: **750m**
Faces: **North and East**
Rock type: **Borrowdale Volcanic**
Approach time: **1 hr 45 mins**

Above: Neil Stabbs climbing *Air on a Bowstring* (E3–) **Photo:** Tim Whiteley

This is the northern most of the cirque of crags flanking the north-east side of Bowfell. When viewed from the valley, it stands out prominently as a triangular buttress, right of a wide fan-shaped scree shoot, itself just right of the mountain summit. The upper right quarter of the crag comprises an impressive smooth white wall, visible from afar. ***North Gully*** is the deep cleft on the right of the crag. The rock is generally excellent, apart from the usual perched flakes and blocks found on the ledges of mountain crags.

Descent: walk over the summit of the buttress (*Low Man*) down into the col and descend the loose cleft on the left, traversing right (facing out) towards the bottom. It is not as bad as it looks. Alternatively, climb up the other side of the col onto the main fellside and walk left (south) to descend the wide scree shoot.

The routes are described from **left** to **right**.

Bowfell Buttress

1 Bowfell Buttress (top section only)	**VD+**
2 Air on a Bowstring	**E3–**
3 Ledge and Groove	**VD+**
4 Woolly Jumper	**E1–**

Left: Neil Stabbs in full control on the upper section of *Bowfell Buttress* (VD+)
Photo: Nick Wharton

1 Bowfell Buttress | 106m | VD+

T Shaw, G H Craig, G R West, C Hargreaves, L J Oppenheimer – May 1902

A classic mountain route which picks the easiest way up the centre of the buttress. Book early to avoid the queues. Pitch 5 becomes much harder in the wet. Start below a small ridge 3 metres left from the edge of the smooth wall forming the foot of the crag.

1 14m. Climb the ridge to a good belay.
2 9m. Climb the short smooth chimney on the right, then easy ground to a terrace.
3 12m. Climb the steep wall above moving diagonally leftwards to a sentry box in a chimney.
4 18m. Follow the chimney for about 12 metres and continue up easy ledges to a large terrace sloping down to the right; follow this for about 7 metres and belay at the foot of a highly polished crack.
5 17m. The *Slippery Crack*. This crack is very steep and awkward and would be given a higher grade if it were not for tradition and the comforting, ample grass terrace below. Once standing on the rock ledges above, slabby rock leads back left to a pinnacle belay.
6 18m. Move left and ascend a groove leading to a chimney. Go up to a slab and continue up the wall above until a short traverse left across the corner leads to a platform and large belay.
7 18m. Step back to the right and follow a groove and its left-hand branch to the finish.

2 Air on a Bowstring | 112m | E3–

P1: **Unknown** – 1964 P2 and 3: **R B Evans, A H Greenbank** – 1964 P4 and 5: **J Cooper, T Walkington** – 1992

A magnificent final pitch, just warranting its grade, up the centre of the *White Wall*. The climbing is varied, bold in places, and with the crux at the top. Described here starting from the base of the crag, it is possible to scramble up the ridge left of *North Gully* and across left directly to the foot of Pitch 3. Start below the right-hand of the cracks in the smooth wall forming the foot of the crag.

1 25m (5b). The crack is harder than it looks and has no protection until the difficulties ease at a niche after 5 metres. Step right and continue more easily to a grassy ledge 5 metres left of a slim groove.
2 25m (4c). Climb the groove direct to a belay below the polished crack of *Bowfell Buttress*.
3 12m (4c). Step down right and climb the deep V-groove to a terrace below the *White Wall* at a crack 3 metres right of a corner.

4 15m (5c). Climb the crack which leans slightly right and is very stubborn for a couple of metres. Either continue up the crack above and step right to a block belay or move right into a corner and climb it to the same point.

5 35m (5c). Climb the short corner to ledges at its top below an impending wall which guards entry to a continuation corner above. Move left for 2 metres (runners) and boldly work up right to gain the foot of this corner. Climb it more easily to a good rest. At the top of the groove, step left round a neat triangular rib into a slim groove and from its top, use a small upside down spike on the left to pull onto the final headwall. Climb this to the top.

3 **Ledge and Groove**	102m	VD+

R D Stevens, G Stoneley – May 1945

A fine mountaineering route which audaciously attacks the right-bounding arête of the *White Wall* only to be forced out right, from where it gradually works its way back left again. To call it 'rambling' would be to neglect the traditional aspiration of seeking out the line of least resistance up an uncompromising piece of rock! Start about 20 metres right of the right-hand crack in the smooth wall forming the foot of the crag.

1 17m. A short wall and groove lead to a large ledge at 5 metres from where a rib leads to another ledge; belay at its right-hand end.

2 21m. A short wall is followed by a staircase to the right to a ledge at 9 metres. (This is the right end of the terrace below the *Slippery Crack* of *Bowfell Buttress* Pitch 5.) Above is a right-facing corner with an overhanging right wall. Just round the corner on the left, a line of good holds leads up left for 4 metres and then back right across the top of the groove to a stance overlooking the chockstone of *North Gully*.

3 12m. Step up, traverse right to a short groove which is climbed to a sloping ledge. From the left end of this, climb the ridge to a stance.

4 15m. Crux. Make a delicate traverse right into a chimney/corner formed by a small subsidiary buttress. Climb this to a ledge and large belay on top of this buttress.

5 20m. A shallow groove on the right leads to an awkward landing on a grass ledge at 7 metres. Traverse easily left for 6 metres to the foot of a steep crack in a corner. Up this for 2 metres, make

an awkward move onto a small ledge on the left, followed by further awkward moves past a projecting boulder guarding entry to a large grassy terrace.

6 17m. Move left along the terrace and climb a crack to a ledge and up the short wall above to the top.

4 **Woolly Jumper**	60m	E1–

J Cooper (with back rope) – Aug 1990 Start of P1: **R M Biden, G Halliwell** – Sept 1998

Excellent; a minor classic which climbs the right arête of the ***White Wall*** by its right-hand side. Modest protection makes the exposure well felt. Named after a sheep with short-lived aeronautic ambitions. Start at the right-hand end of the big terrace, which is halfway up ***Bowfell Buttress*** but easily reached by scrambling up ***North Gully*** for 25 metres, then out left onto the ridge to below the first of two short grooves in the arête. Its right wall is heavily undercut.

1 30m (5a). There is an obvious layaway hold on the lip of the overhung right wall. Gain this from the left and use it to pull confidently round onto the slab above. Continue more easily up left to the next groove. Climb this to a ledge at the foot of the main arête.

2 30m (5b). Starting below the left side of the arête, make an awkward move round it to gain a niche in the right wall. Delicate moves up the right rib of the niche gain a ledge above. Step left and climb up to a small quartz ledge on the arête. Stand on this and follow a shallow flake rightwards to a narrow ledge. Step back left and layaway up the arête on superbly rough rock, and with great exposure down the ***White Wall***, until the angle eases below a wide crack. Climb this to a large ledge and belay. Scramble off to the left.

Above: Tim Whiteley and Charlotte Walmsley on *Woolly Jumper* (HVS+) **Photo:** Dominic Donnini

Pike o' Blisco

Pike o' Blisco is the attractive rugged mountain on the left (south) side of the upper valley of Great Langdale, although the climbing described is most easily reached from the top of Wrynose Pass at the head of Little Langdale.

Black Crag

Grid reference: **274 037**
Altitude: **580m**
Faces: **South and West**
Rock type: **Borrowdale Volcanic**
Approach time: **25 mins**

A marvellous outcrop of excellent clean, rough rock on the southern slopes of Pike o' Blisco. Although the routes are only short, they get the sun from early morning until sunset and dry very quickly. The base of the crag is L-shaped and has a wonderful outlook around three-quarters of the compass. It can provide a delightful day or evening's climbing, even in winter if the wind is quiet.

The crag is reached by following the Red Tarn path north from the top of Wrynose Pass for just over ½ kilometre, then striking rightwards up a vague track (past a fenced off boulder) generally in the direction of the summit of the mountain. Turn left towards the crag when it comes into view and head up to the pleasant terraced platform which lies beneath the *Needle*.

The routes are described from **left** to **right**.

Descent: there are numerous easy scrambles down from routes on the *South Face*. All the routes on the *West Face* end on a terrace which leads leftwards and down to the north end of the crag.

West Face

A slim terrace runs rightwards from about the middle of the face to the platform beneath the *Needle*. Care is needed around the undercut nose itself, where the terrace is cut away by a corner in the tier of rock below.

Black Crag – West Face

	Route	Grade
1	Slipshod	HVS
2	Yellow Fever	E2–
3	The First Touch	E1
4	The Needle	VD
5	Needle Arête	E3

1 Slipshod	16m	HVS
R Greenwood, R Cooper, P Donnelly – July 1984		

The fine crack above a triangular niche in a small bay just left of the slim terrace. Start below the niche.

(5a). Climb the wall direct through the niche to gain the crack. Follow it to a block-lined ledge, step right and finish up a short wall.

2 Yellow Fever	16m	E2–
R Greenwood, C Ensoll, P Donnelly – July 1984		

Superb climbing up the thin cracks in the smooth wall left of the ***First Touch***. Start 2 metres left of that route where the slim terrace meets the hillside and the undercut wall starts to curve up leftwards.

(5b). Pull up onto the wall and step left to climb the line of thin cracks, passing the right end of a block-lined ledge near the top.

3 The First Touch	16m	E1
R Greenwood, C Ensoll, P Donnelly – July 1984		

Attractive line, elegant climbing. Start below the obvious right-facing hanging grooveline above the left end of the slim terrace.

(5b). Climb the wall to gain the groove and then leftwards to the top.

South Face

The left-hand end of this overlooks the gearing-up point on the terraced platform.

4 The Needle	12m	VD
E J Hodge, J Lynam – 1955		

This is a striking 8 metre javelin of rock which appears to have slipped on its base so that it overhangs its lower 4 metre wall on the west side. This route starts in the angle on that west side.

Climb the wide corner-crack to gain the gap between the pinnacle and the crag. Climb the chimney above, and up to the pointed summit.

Black Crag – South Face

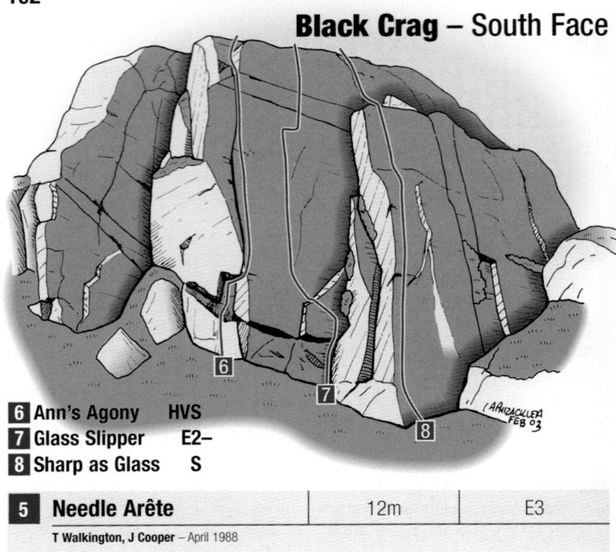

5	Needle Arête	12m	E3

T Walkington, J Cooper – April 1988

The south-west outside arête of the *Needle*. There is a protection peg tucked under a tiny overlap halfway up the upper part.

(6a). Climb the wall below the arête to a ledge at 4 metres. Move left to gain the arête and climb it using holds on either side as required.

To the right the crag again becomes disjointed until after about 50 metres there is the impressive slab taken by *Glass Slipper*, with an obvious undercut crack in its left arête, **6 Ann's Agony** (HVS 5b).

7	Glass Slipper	16m	E2–

T Walkington, A Cammack – Oct 1987

Beautiful, deliciously delicate climbing; never desperate, it can be memorable beyond its size. If you stray into the crack on the left for runners, go back to HVS. Start in the corner on the right of the slab.

(5b). Climb the corner to a nut runner at 3 metres. Step left above the overhung base. Work left and upwards to climb the slab slightly left of its centre until beneath the short headwall. Step right and finish direct.

To the right is a further slab of diminishing height. Its left arête gives:

8 **Sharp as Glass**	16m	S
N Franklin, N Reid – Aug 1989		

Float up the right-hand side of the arête overlooking *Glass Slipper*.

Long Scar

Grid reference:	**272 036**
Altitude:	**560m**
Faces:	**South-West**
Rock type:	**Borrowdale Volcanic**
Approach time:	**25 mins**

This long low outcrop compliments ***Black Crag*** by providing a selection of quick drying routes of modest grade on similar rock. It is situated above the main Red Tarn track from Wrynose Pass, about 200 metres beyond the turn off to ***Black Crag***. The most prominent feature is the ***Central Gully*** and its slabby right wall.

Descent: round the right-hand side of the crag.

The climbs are described from **right** to **left**.

1 **Old Holborn**	14m	M
D Worrall – 1982		

A very pleasant scramble. Start from the base of the easy ramp at the toe of *Central Gully's* right-hand wall.

Ascend the ramp to below a block on a ledge. Step right around it to another ledge and continue up broken rock to the top.

2 **Intruder's Corner**	18m	VD
D Worrall, R Linton – 1982		

Start 4 metres right of *Central Gully*, below the left end of an easy ramp.

Up slightly rightwards to a grass ledge. Finish up the fine corner-groove above.

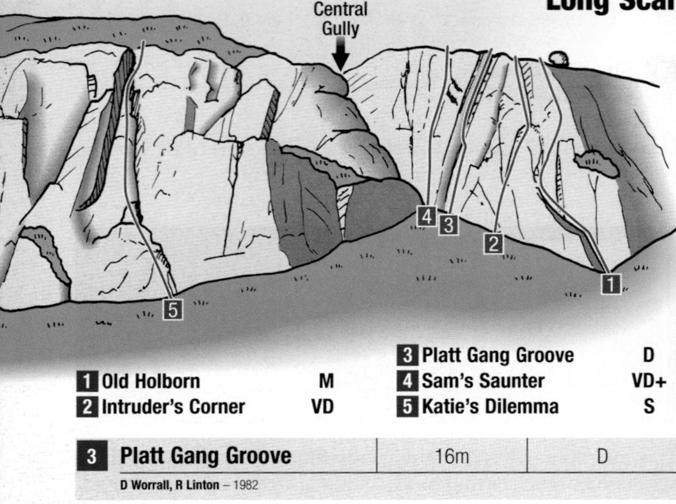

1	Old Holborn	M
2	Intruder's Corner	VD
3	Platt Gang Groove	D
4	Sam's Saunter	VD+
5	Katie's Dilemma	S

3 Platt Gang Groove	16m	D
D Worrall, R Linton – 1982		

Start 2 metres right of the foot of *Central Gully*.

Climb the right-slanting, shattered-looking grooveline in the centre of the wall, avoiding a ledge on the right near the top.

4 Sam's Saunter	15m	VD+
R Linton, D Worrall – 1982		

Start at the foot of *Central Gully* and climb the clean right wall, following a series of indefinite cracks and slight grooves direct.

5 Katie's Dilemma	20m	S
R Linton, D Worrall – 1982		

Twenty-five metres left of *Central Gully* is an obvious groove at the left side of the wall.

Gain the groove from the right and continue up the right-hand corner above a large perched block.

There are plenty of other good lines up to VS in grade.

Right: Langdale from Gimmer Crag **Photo:** Stephen Reid

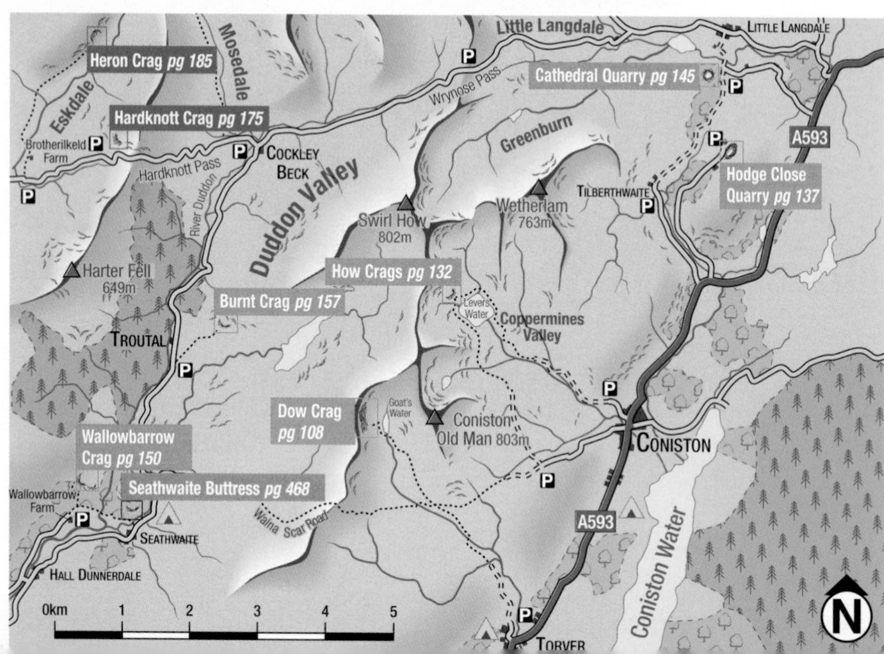
Heron Crag pg 185
Mosedale
Little Langdale
Little Langdale
Eskdale
Hardknott Crag pg 175
Wrynose Pass
Cathedral Quarry pg 145
A593
Brotherilkeld Farm
Cockley Beck
Hardknott Pass
Greenburn
Hodge Close Quarry pg 137
Tilberthwaite
River Duddon
Duddon Valley
Swirl How 802m
Wetherlam 763m
Harter Fell 649m
How Crags pg 132
Burnt Crag pg 157
Levers Water
Coppermines Valley
Troutal
Dow Crag pg 108
Goat's Water
Coniston Old Man 803m
Coniston
Wallowbarrow Crag pg 150
Seathwaite Buttress pg 468
Wallowbarrow Farm
Walna Scar Road
Seathwaite
A593
Coniston Water
Hall Dunnerdale
0km
1
2
3
4
5
Torver
N

Dow Area

Dow, Coppermines, Slate & Duddon

Left: Jeremy Wilson on *'C' Ordinary* (D)
Photo: Nick Wharton

Dow

by Al Phizacklea

Dow Crag is the largest crag in the southern Lake District, and is easily reached by those approaching from the south. The crag contains 'three star' routes right through the grades from D to E6, making it a firm favourite with many climbers. For those looking for solitude, the Coppermines Valley is the place, and for a quick fix, the slate quarries are literally a stone's throw from the car park.

The centre for those climbing in this area is the village of Coniston, which has a fine selection of pubs, cafes and shops. The easiest approach from the motorway is via the A590 Barrow-in-Furness road, before turning north at Greenodd towards Coniston. The alternative route, through Windermere and Ambleside, is often slow and jammed with tourists in the summer months. For the harder climbers, the best piece of advice from the locals is this: if the afternoon feels too cold on Dow Crag, get down to Coniston, (which only takes 40mins), have a brew and then go to the more sheltered slate quarries. As there are no easy routes in the quarries, the only advice for others is to take an extra jacket!

Dow Crag

Grid reference: **264 977**
Altitude: **610m**
Faces: **East**
Rock type: **Borrowdale Volcanic**
Approach time: **1 hr 5 mins**

Above: Dom Donnini on *Isengard* (HVS+)
Photo: Nick Wharton

An excellent crag which provides a rich variety of first class climbing throughout the grading spectrum. It has a special atmosphere, with extensive scree slopes sweeping down to the steely blue depths of Goat's Water, backed by enchanting views of the lowlands and estuaries to the south.

The rock is high quality rhyolite which is generally very sound and gives good friction when dry, but can resemble verglas in the wet, particularly on the more polished routes. *Dow* catches the morning sun and is a fast drying crag, but some of the chimney and cracklines can take a while to dry out. Be warned that the crag has a cold reputation amongst climbers who are not regular visitors.

The most popular approach is from Coniston, where a road leads up the hill opposite the petrol station (signposted Walna Scar track) to an even steeper section. Follow this to a gate at 1½ kilometres, where the metalled road becomes a track. Park here, then follow the direct continuation for 2 kilometres, passing through two rocky 'gateways', to a very large cairn which marks the junction with the Torver to Goat's Water track. Walk rightwards up the steep grassy bank and after 1½ kilometres the tarn is reached. The crag is gained by following any one of a variety of paths up the extensive scree slope.

The crag has five main buttresses, *'A'*, *'B'*, *'C'*, *'D'* and *'E'*, separated by fine gullies and chimneys. Only on *'A' Buttress* do the climbs continue to the top of the mountain. Climbs on the other buttresses usually finish on a 'half-way' ledge called *Easy Terrace*, which affords the most convenient means of descent. There is a rescue box at the foot of *'B' Buttress* (renewed in 2000).

Each buttress is described from **left** to **right**. The details for the descents are given under their respective headings. The descriptions of the routes are also in order from **left** to **right**.

'A' Buttress

This is the tall, narrowing buttress on the left, bounded on both sides by large gullies, the left-hand one being *Easy Gully*, the deeper right-hand one is *Great Gully*.

Descent: the easiest descent involves scrambling to the main ridge of the mountain, then turning left, passing the head of *Easy Gully* to reach the top of a shallower diagonal gully after 150 metres. This leads down to the foot of the crag.

1 Arête, Chimney and Crack | 97m | MS

T C Ormiston-Chant, T H G Parker, S H Gordon – Sept 1910

An excellent and popular route up *'A' Buttress* which combines all three elements of its name. Start about 10 metres right of the bed of *Easy Gully*, below the clean left-hand arête of *'A' Buttress*. This curves slightly rightwards towards its foot and is marked by an edging of quartz.

1 27m. Climb the arête using the quartz edging to start until a good rock ledge is reached at 12 metres. The wall above is steeper and the holds smaller. Climb up and slightly right, then continue directly up an exposed crack above to grass ledges.

2 21m. A broken grooveline can be seen running up and slightly right from here. Climb up, passing a couple of large flakes, then step right into the grooveline. Follow this, passing to the left of a prominent pinnacle to belay on a well-worn ledge in a recess below the steeper rocks.

3 15m. Using the flake-crack below the bulging rock, climb up and right until a short hand-traverse leads into an open chimney on the right. Climb straight up and over a bulging chockstone to belay on a ledge immediately above.

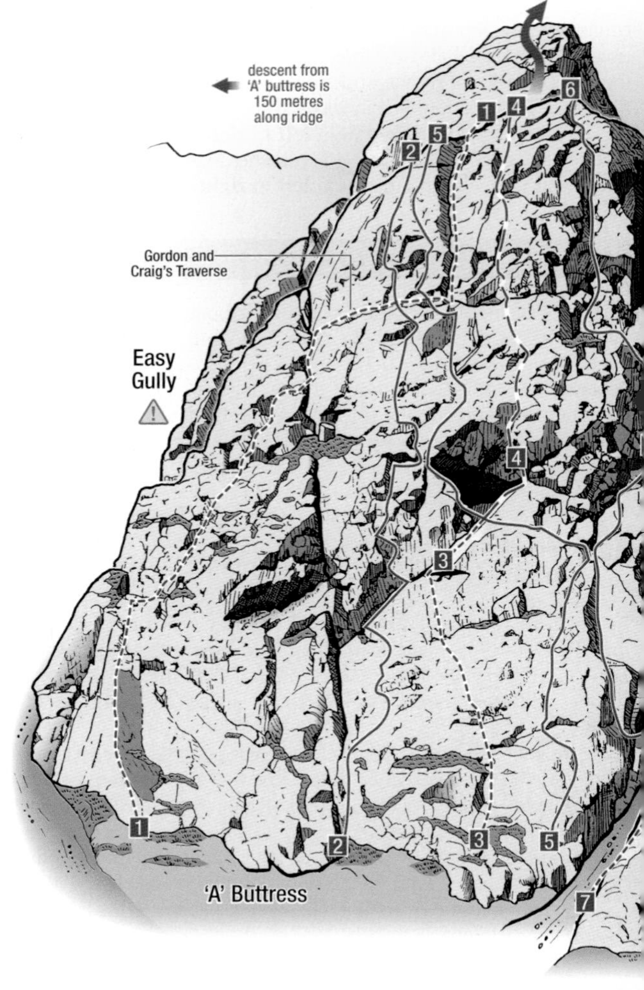

1 Arête, Chimney & Crack	MS	4 Samba Pa Ti	E2
2 Abraxas	E3+	5 Eliminate 'A'	VS
3 Isengard	HVS+	6 Side Walk	E2–

Dow Crag – 'A' Buttress & 'B' Buttress (Upper)

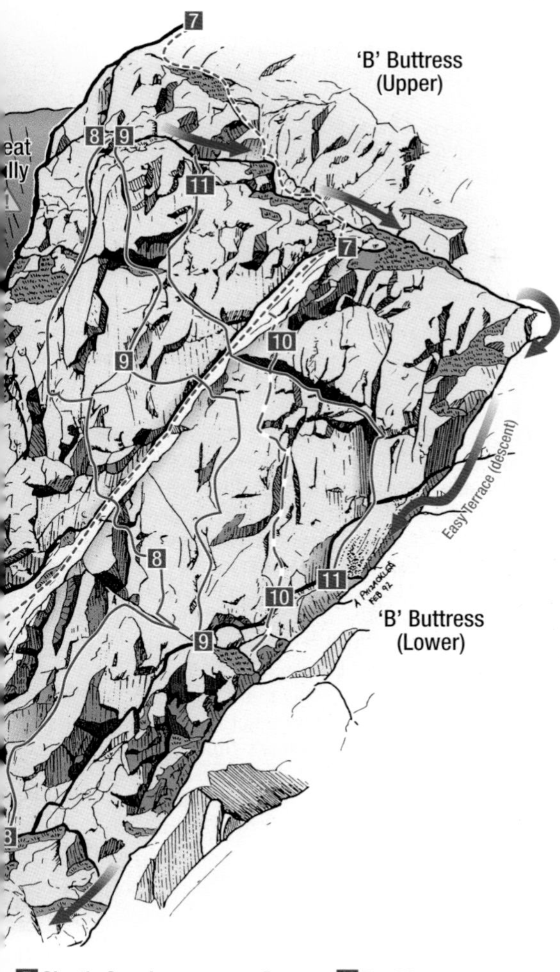

7 Giant's Crawl	D	10 Tumble	E4
8 Nimrod	E1	11 Catacomb	E1
9 Holocaust	E4		

4 10m. To the right is ***Gordon and Craig's Traverse***, which is followed horizontally right across the exposed narrow ledge into the centre of the buttress. A couple of metres before a tiny grass ledge is reached an obvious crack rises steeply above. Belay below this.

5 24m. The crack is climbed for its full length to easy ground at the top of the buttress. The belays are set well back. The start is the hardest section, but it maintains its interest throughout. Scramble up to the summit ridge to finish.

2	**Abraxas**	85m	E3+

R Matheson, J R Martindale (1 point of aid) – June 1975
FFA: **M Berzins, R H Berzins, P Botterill** – Aug 1976

An impressively steep route, with a serious first pitch and a strenuous crack for the second pitch, which is notorious for stopping a lot of people! Start below the long right-facing corner just left of the centre of the buttress.

1 18m (5c). Move right for 3 metres to a flake, then climb the steep wall above to a shallow recess. Pull over the bulge and gain the mossy slab above with difficulty. This leads leftwards to a stance below the overhanging wall. A bold pitch with scant protection.

2 25m (5c). Climb the wall above until beneath the overhang, then pull right into the groove above which leads to a resting place on the right. Step back left and climb the crackline with difficulty, to reach an undercut flake, where an exhilarating move right leads up into a groove above the steepest section. Climb this to a roof, then traverse right to join ***Eliminate 'A'***.

3 12m (4c). Climb the steep groove just left of the block, then directly up the wall and pull over a bulge into a short V-groove. Go up this to the ***Gordon and Craig's Traverse***.

4 30m (5b). Approach the steep shallow groove directly, just to the left of the hanging arête, and climb it on small holds. Move left and follow the grooveline and easier walls to the grassy ledge.

3	**Isengard**	48m	HVS+

L Brown, A McHardy – April 1962

A fine route in its own right, but when combined with ***Samba Pa Ti***, it creates an excellent direct way up ***'A' Buttress***. Technical but well protected climbing. Begin on a ledge a couple of metres left of ***Eliminate 'A'***, below a short right-facing corner crack.

1 9m (4b). Climb the crack and move up right to a stance.
2 39m (5b). Move across the slab on the left and follow the obvious diagonal line, passing an awkward bulge, to a long horizontal ledge. Step right a couple of metres and climb the steep crack to the overhang, which is breached at the weakness. Follow the slab to the large cave.

Originally ***Isengard*** followed ***Eliminate 'A'*** (Pitches 4, 5 and 6) to the top. For those who relish very exposed situations, take the following:

4 **Samba Pa Ti**	54m	E2
A Hyslop, R O Graham – Aug 1977		

A rather bold route with steep and strenuous climbing starting from the cave at the top of Pitch 2 of ***Isengard***.

1 30m (5b). Climb the right edge of the slab to the overhangs and boldly pull over the first bulge on excellent holds. Move up the groove 2 metres and pull out rightwards onto the steep wall above. Climb directly to the bulge and skirt it on the right, moving left to easier ground and belays on ***Gordon and Craig's Traverse*** below a crack.
2 24m (4b). Climb the faultline, 9 metres right of the main crack. This leads to the narrow neck at the top of the buttress.

5 **Eliminate 'A'**	110m	VS
H S Gross, G Basterfield – June 1923	P5: **D Miller, J A Austin** – April 1965	

An absolute classic route which follows a cunning line through the steeper sections of ***'A' Buttress***. The climbing is continually interesting and the atmosphere is superb. Start from a well worn grass ledge at the lower right-hand edge of the buttress, about 6 metres up from the scree at the base of ***Great Gully***.

1 13m (4b). Traverse delicately rightwards, round the edge, onto a steep wall overlooking ***Great Gully***. Move into a short groove which leads to a grass ledge.
2 23m (4b). Climb into a shallow depression in the steep wall above. At around 6 metres an awkward move right and a mantelshelf enables a little ledge to be reached. Follow the groove above and exit delicately left onto a slab. The recess above is the ***Raven's Nest*** where a belay is possible. From here either traverse right round the exposed corner and up a wide crack to a sloping

ledge, or, more difficult, climb the V-groove above directly to the same ledge (4c).

3 15m (4c). The ***Rochers Perchés*** pitch. From the left end of the ledge step onto the exposed wall and move delicately up to the sloping shelf in the corner, where the perched blocks used to sit. Step delicately down and round the rib on the left (excellent thin thread), where an easy ledge runs across a sloping slab to a belay in a large cave.

4 16m (4a). The impressive diagonal 'crevasse' line is followed up and left beneath the roof, until an exposed bulge at the far end leads to a recess. Belay on the large blocks above.

5 18m (4c). Move right from the block and step down to a slab. Traverse the slab rightwards, beneath the overhang, until a bold and very exposed ascent leads into a groove. Up this to ***Gordon and Craig's Traverse***.

6 25m (4b). Above lies the wide upper crack of ***Arête, Chimney and Crack***. Move 3 metres left of this until below a steep shallow corner. Climb this and traverse right using a flake beneath a little overhang to a rib just left of the wide crack. Pull leftwards over this overhang and follow a clean shallow groove slightly leftwards to a grass terrace.

6 **Side Walk**	91m	E2–

L Brown, B Stevens (1 rest point – now free) – April 1960

A magnificent expedition offering exposed climbing up the steep grooves and walls overlooking ***Great Gully***. Start just below the first chockstone of ***Great Gully***.

1 16m (5b). Climb the crack on the left of the boulder to the top of the pillar. Make an intimidating traverse left on small holds to a small ledge, where a hard move up the wall leads to a grass ledge below a large corner.

2 9m (5a). The sustained corner is climbed to the large sloping ledge on ***Eliminate 'A'***.

3 12m (5b). Traverse right on to a slab, beneath an impressive steep wall overlooking the gully. Climb a small overhang into a corner containing a thin crack. Climb to another overhang, pulling out rightwards to a large ledge.

Left: Stephen Reid on Pitch 5 of the immaculate *Eliminate A* (VS) **Photo:** Oliver Turnbull

4 27m (4b). The rock requires care. Climb above the belay to some perched blocks, slightly to the right. Move above these, trending first left, then right until a large triangular grass ledge is reached. Climb up to the right for 3 metres to some blocks.

5 27m (5a). Climb to the right to beneath a large bulging groove. The groove is climbed direct to an overhang at 12 metres, passing a large insecure flake. The overhang is turned on the left by climbing an awkward crack past some doubtful blocks to the top.

'B' Buttress (Upper Section)

This is the section of the crag lying to the right of *Great Gully* above the slanting descent rake of *Easy Terrace*. The most obvious line is that of *Giant's Crawl*, a large diagonal slab cutting across the buttress from the foot of *Great Gully*.

Descent: the upper section of *Giant's Crawl*, which follows a grassy terrace back left above the main mass of the buttress to a point overlooking *Great Gully*, is the descent route for most of the climbs here. Reverse this to descend via *Easy Terrace*.

7 **Giant's Crawl**	115m	D

E T W Addyman, O T Addyman, Stobart – April 1909

An excellent route for its grade and inescapable. It follows the wide slabby gangway running diagonally rightwards from the foot of *Great Gully*. Start at the foot of *Great Gully*, where easy rocks run up to the slab.

1 **18m.** Climb the easy slabs and move left to a sloping ledge at the foot of a crack.

2 **15m.** Climb the crack, passing a final quartz section to a good ledge. The quartzy slabs to the right give a bolder variation at VD.

3 **14m.** Traverse the ledge and easy ground diagonally rightwards to a stance on the edge.

4 **20m.** A short wall leads to a ledge at the *Narrows*. Continue up slabs to a ledge beneath a good crack (possible belay). Climb this to easy ground. *Easy Terrace* is gained from here by scrambling down to the right – an option taken by those who do not wish to continue to the summit ridge.

5 **18m.** Follow a well marked grassy terrace leftwards to an awkward corner crack. This leads to a large ledge on the edge of the buttress overlooking ***Great Gully***.
6 **12m.** Round to the left is a groove. Climb the crack up this and exit on the right.
7 **18m.** Easier climbing leads to a scrambling finish to the summit.

8 Nimrod | 84m | E1

D Miller, D Kirby (1 point of aid – now free) – June 1962

A brilliant route which gets progressively harder. Start about 12 metres right of the foot of ***Giant's Crawl***, on a large grass ledge. This is at the foot of a cracked blocky ramp which runs parallel to, but 8 metres higher than, ***Easy Terrace***.
1 **30m (5a).** Climb the wall to flakes below a shallow groove. Enter this and pull over the left-hand side of a small overhang to a flake. Traverse right, at first horizontally, then diagonally up to small ledges beneath a bulging wall. Climb down these ledges to a large grassy terrace for a comfortable belay. (This terrace is at the top of the ramp from where the pitch started).
2 **15m (5b).** Move back up to the ledges and climb the steep wall on the right until an awkward traverse left leads into the main groove. Move up to a small spike, and exit left on large finishing holds. Belay on ***Giant's Crawl***.
3 **26m (5c).** Behind the belay is an open, left-facing corner. Climb up to a small ledge below this and move up to a thin light-coloured crack in the left wall. Traverse delicately left across the steep wall to reach a prominent small blocky ledge on the arête. Turn the bulge above on the right to reach easier ground and a grass ledge.
4 **13m.** A short wall above leads rightwards to a large ledge at the top of Pitch 5 of ***Giant's Crawl***. Descend rightwards to reach ***Easy Terrace***.

9 Holocaust | 72m | E4

R Matheson, G Fleming, J Poole (2 points of aid) – July 1971 FFA: **R Matheson** – Aug 1975

A great climb, requiring confidence and impetus on the crux – the most fallen from piece of rock on the crag. Start below the centre of the steep wall, by an embedded flake on the grass ledge just to the right of *Nimrod*'s second pitch. This ledge is easily reached by scrambling across from half-way up ***Easy Terrace***.

1 36m (6a). Climb the shallow groove above the belay to good runners by a down-pointing fang. Pull up to a thin diagonal crack on the right (Micro-Friend), before leaping boldly right across the leaning wall to excellent side holds, which lead up into a shallow depression above. Follow a steep slab diagonally right (poorly protected), to a runner below steeper rock. Traverse delicately left to reach ***Giant's Crawl***.

2 21m (5b). Above is a smooth overhanging wall. Follow the groove on the right of this, until a swing left around a rib leads to a quartz-riddled slabby gangway. Climb this to a recessed grass ledge.

3 15m (5b). From the left end of the ledge climb a steep wide crack direct to a good ledge. Descend right down this to ***Easy Terrace***.

10 **Tumble**	36m	E4

P Livesey, J Lawrence – June 1975

One of the best single pitch wall climbs in the area, providing sustained, rather than technically exacting climbing. Climbs the slim groove in the steep wall right of ***Holocaust***, start directly below the groove.

(6a). Step up left and continue to a slight bulge, then traverse rightwards and enter the groove. Climb to the top of the groove to a short crack. Traverse left to a nose, and climb directly up past the left end of the bulge to reach the traverse line of ***Catacomb***. Climb directly over the capping roof above the thread on huge holds and continue to ***Giant's Crawl***.

11 **Catacomb**	60m	E1

R Matheson, M R Matheson – April 1972

An extremely enjoyable and varied outing which traverses below the line of overhangs capping the ***Holocaust*** wall. Start at the right-hand end of the grass ledge, at the foot of a mossy slab, below a wide steep crack. (Easily reached from half-way up ***Easy Terrace***).

1 36m (5a). Climb the short slab and wide crack to a chockstone where a committing move left on flakes leads to the obvious rising traverse line below the overhangs. Follow this all the way to ***Giant's Crawl***. Belay up on the right.

2 24m (5b). The obvious left-slanting line in the steep wall behind *Giant's Crawl* is followed strenuously to reach the right-hand side of a grass ledge. Step up right and surmount the overhang with difficulty, to enter a groove. Follow broken cracks out right to reach a grass terrace. Descend down this to reach *Easy Terrace*.

'B' Buttress (Lower Section)

This section of the crag lies below *Easy Terrace*, which is used for **descent** from all routes on this wall. The first route starts about 20 metres right of the foot of *Easy Terrace*, where a fragile spike leans against the wall.

12 **Pink Panther**	40m	E2
R Matheson, M R Matheson – June 1973		

An excellent diagonal line up the immaculate wall, with fingery climbing and adequate protection (take a sling with something to weigh it down!).

(5c). From the spike, step right onto the wall and climb a scoop to reach a slight depression in the middle of the face. Move right beneath steeper rocks to reach a truncated spike below a rounded bulge. Stand on this with difficulty and enter a groove on the right. Climb this to its top and then pull out left on to a slab below an impressive overhang. Skirt round the right-hand end of this and climb a scoop to easier ground.

13 **Leopard's Crawl**	48m	HVS+
R J Birkett, L Muscroft, T Hill – Sept 1947	P2: **D Miller, D G Roberts** – July 1968	

Superb open climbing on perfect rock. A masterpiece of its generation and one of Jim Birkett's finest routes. It starts 4 metres right of *Pink Panther*, where a large flake is bridged against the wall.

1 28m (5a). Step up from the block and traverse right to better holds. A short ascent then leads to a crack on the left of a brown crinkly wall. Cross this delicately rightwards and enter the base of a scoop, which is awkward and not well protected. Climb the scoop to a ledge below the top corner crack of *Murray's Route*.

2 20m (4c). Traverse right along the flake system and then climb a shallow groove in the wall above to easier ground.

14 Tarkus | 53m | E1

R Matheson, M R Matheson – April 1972

A thoroughly enjoyable route, with a variety of delicate, strenuous and exposed climbing up the wall right of ***Leopard's Crawl***. Start from a little ledge a couple of metres below and to the right of the bridged block of ***Leopard's Crawl***.

1 33m (5b). Traverse boldly right on to the steep wall to step onto a small flat-topped flake in a shallow groove, then move up with haste to a horizontal break. Traverse right to a little ledge below an obvious steep crack. Climb this and the wall above, trending leftwards to reach the ledge below the top corner of ***Murray's Route***.

2 20m (4c). Pitch 2 of ***Leopard's Crawl***.

15 Murray's Direct | 48m | VS

P1: **G H Mackereth, B Tyson, A H Griffin** – Sept 1931
P2: **J A Mullan** – Aug 1945 P3: **E H Prior, J B Meldrum** – Oct 1922

An excellent route which finishes up the capped, right-facing corner high above the rescue box. It is a combination of three old variations on ***Murray's Route***, each pitch retaining its own history and character, creating a justly popular climb. Start at a vertical embedded flake 10 metres down and right of the bridged block, and about 14 metres left of the rescue box.

1 12m (4c). ***Tiger Traverse***. From the top of the flake, move right on sloping holds until an outward shelving slab can be gained and followed delicately rightwards to a ledge below an open corner.

2 10m (4b). ***The Link Pitch***. Step right and climb the wall above the perched flake until the horizontal hand-traverse flake on ***Murray's Route*** is reached. Move left to belay on a small ledge below the final steep corner.

3 26m (4c). Climb the crack, using a good old-fashioned strenuous layback, until a diagonal line can be followed rightwards below the overhang. Keep moving right until an exit can be made up cracks to easier ground. Scramble diagonally left to reach ***Easy Terrace***.

16 Murray's Route | 74m | S

D G Murray, W J Borrowman, B L Martin – April 1918

A popular classic which weaves its way up an impressive area of rock with the most delightful situations. Start just left of the rescue box at an open V-chimney.

Dow Crag – 'B' Buttress (Lower)

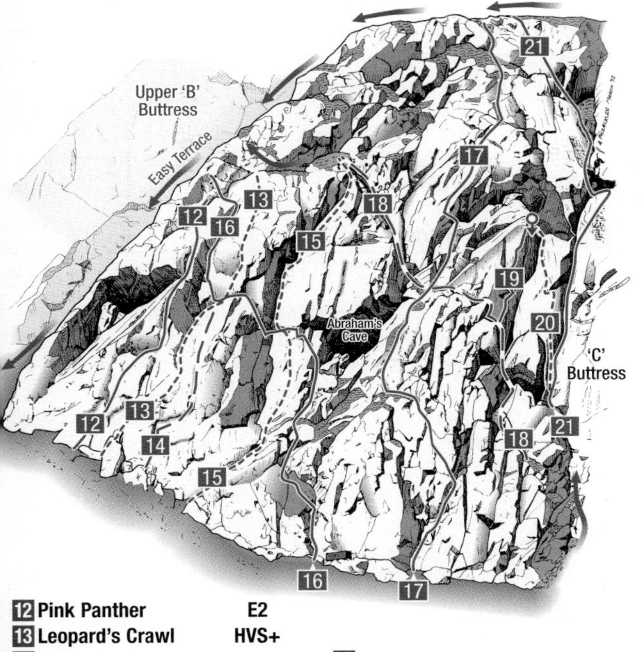

12 Pink Panther	**E2**		
13 Leopard's Crawl	**HVS+**		
14 Tarkus	**E1**	**18 Woodhouse's Route**	**VD+**
15 Murray's Direct	**VS**	**19 Woodhouse's Arête**	**E6**
16 Murray's Route	**S**	**20 The Shining Path**	**E5**
17 Abraham's Route	**HS**	**21 Central Chimney**	**S+**

1 23m. Climb the chimney to an overhanging wall, and then cross the polished slab on the left with difficulty (crux) to a crack. Continue under the bulging rock, round a corner and up to a ledge. The best belays are to be found on the large ledge directly below the corner.

2 12m. Traverse rightwards over the obvious detached flake and follow the arête above for a few moves before stepping right into a short chimney. Climb this and the blocks above to a comfortable stance in a large cave (*Abraham's Cave*).

3 **21m.** Exit leftwards up the fine steep crack and traverse horizontally to a possible belay below the steep final corner of ***Murray's Direct***. Climb the short flake chimney in the left wall and swing along the exposed flakeline, descending slightly to a stance below a flake, about 2 metres right of a steep corner.

4 **18m.** Move up the good flake above which is followed leftwards into the corner. Climb the wide crack above which leads awkwardly to a ledge. From there a V-groove on the left leads towards ***Easy Terrace***.

17 **Abraham's Route**	62m	HS
G D Abraham, A P Abraham, F T Phillipson – March 1903		

A fine route of increasing interest. Start up a wide broken groove, which is the first easy break right of the rescue box.

1 **13m.** Climb the rightwards-trending groove to some grass ledges. Continue up the groove to a recess. Belay on the right.

2 **12m.** Step onto a rock ledge on the right and stride back left across the recess to follow fairly easy rocks up and leftwards to the middle of a long grassy ledge.

3 **13m.** Climb the very shallow open groove on the left side of the steep wall above. Easier rocks then lead to the grass terrace on *Woodhouse's Route*.

4 **24m (4a).** Climb directly up a series of short grooves and walls to a ledge below a blocky spike, towards the left end of the diagonal overhanging wall above. The step left onto a slab above is not easy, but good small holds lead to a spike, where a gangway/groove continues rightwards to the crest of the buttress, and a belay. Easier climbing leads up to ***Easy Terrace***.

The next three routes start below the long corner between *'B'* and *'C' Buttresses*. (This is the line of ***Central Chimney***).

18 **Woodhouse's Route**	42m	VD+
G F Woodhouse, A J Woodhouse – Aug 1905		

A good old-fashioned route, which is very efficient at removing skin from exposed knees! It follows a diagonal line leftwards across the buttress. Start by scrambling up from the foot of ***Central Chimney*** for 25 metres to a well-worn platform below and left of the large pinnacle, directly below a wide groove.

1 20m. The easy groove leads to a steep crack on the left, which is climbed to the crevasse behind the pinnacle (possible belay). The slanting chimney is entered awkwardly and climbed to a ledge and belays. The ledge system is followed leftwards to a deep recess.

2 22m. The wall on the left is climbed, with the right foot in the deep crack, to a grass ledge. Climb the arête on the left to a large terrace. ***Easy Terrace*** is reached by scrambling.

19 **Woodhouse's Arête**	26m	E6

K Phizacklea, R Matheson – May 1998

A spectacular route up the overhanging arête at the right-hand side of ***'B' Buttress***, which is guaranteed to clock up the air miles. Start as for ***Woodhouse's Route***.

(6b). Follow ***Woodhouse's Route*** to stand on a good flake in the slanting chimney to the left of the large pinnacle. Reach right around the arête to a good jug, pull up on this (Friend 2) and continue steeply to a small ledge below an open groove. Move up to a short flake, then step right beneath the overhang to gain the upper arête (peg). Gain a pocket on the right and climb to the top using a brilliant sequence of exposed moves.

20 **The Shining Path**	25m	E5

A Hyslop, D Kells – June 1992

A superb route in a sport climbing mode up the steep wall above the right-hand edge of ***Woodhouse's Pinnacle***. Five pegs (which should be backed up with wires) show the line, a Friend 2 and a Rock 6 are also required. The first peg is very low and could easily be overlooked.

(6b). Bridge up the right edge of the pinnacle until it is possible to establish oneself on the wall. Climb up, with a particularly desperate move past the fourth peg, to reach a small fragile pocket. Follow the corner above pulling out awkwardly leftwards onto a large sloping ledge. Abseil off.

21 **Central Chimney**	53m	S+

O G Jones, G Ellis – April 1897

An old classic climb which remains popular. Takes the obvious right-facing corner/crackline between ***'B'*** and ***'C' Buttresses***. Start by

Keith Phizacklea poised beneath the blank crux of the magnificent *Woodhouse's Arête* (E6) during his first ascent, and (**inset**) the fall
Photos: Rob Matheson

scrambling up easy ground to a large ledge on the right of *Woodhouse's Pinnacle*.

1 **25m**. Climb the initial crack using holds on the right wall, with an awkward smooth section at 9 metres. Continue up the chimney, over a slight bulge to a belay in a recess above some wedged blocks.

2 **10m**. Follow the rib on the right wall, then back left into a conspicuous cave left of a line of overhangs, where care with loose rock is needed.

3 **18m**. Exit awkwardly leftwards out of the cave to ledges above (belay possible). Follow grass leftwards to more suitable belays. *Easy Terrace* is reached by scrambling further up and left.

'C' Buttress

This is the rounded slabby buttress right of *'B' Buttress*. The foot of the buttress is actually the lowest point of *Dow Crag*. (Water is usually available just a few metres right of this point - a small but constant flow out of a crack in the rock). All the routes end on *Easy Terrace*, which is followed leftwards for the **descent**.

22 'C' Ordinary Route | 76m | D

G F Woodhouse, A J Woodhouse – Aug 1904

This is probably the most popular route on the crag, and rightly so. However, the climb becomes much more difficult under cold and wet conditions, and it has been known for ill-equipped parties to get into trouble. Start just left of the lowest point of the buttress.

1 **15m**. Follow the flake-crack up to a protruding block and then pass just left of three small triangular overhangs up the crest of the buttress to the top of a long flake. The slab on the left is a pleasant variation.

2 **9m**. Follow the slabby scoop, leading to easier ground. Scrambling leads to a big ledge with a fallen flake lying on it, below a steep wall.

3 **7m**. From the left end of the ledge, follow a scoop up right to a ledge (the steep wall can be climbed direct but is harder).

4 **12m**. Trend back left across the slabs to reach a ledge on the edge of the buttress. Follow this directly to another large ledge.

5 10m. Step onto a large slab above, which leads rightwards to ledges. Continue to the one which has spectacular views into *Intermediate Gully*.

6 13m. The flake system in the steeper wall on the left is obvious. This leads leftwards, under a prow, followed by an awkward and exposed crack to its top. A stance and belay exist up and right.

7 10m. Move right along the slabs to a good ledge. Follow a gangway rightwards round a bulge to another ledge. Pull up to the left and traverse horizontally left until easy rocks lead to ***Easy Terrace***.

23 **Eliminate 'C'**	46m	VS+
H S Gross, G Basterfield – July 1922		

A very enjoyable route, providing delicate climbing in an exposed position high on the left of ***Intermediate Gully***. Start from the large ledge at the top of Pitch 1 of the ***Intermediate Gully***.

1 14m (4c). Climb the slab out leftwards, using a diagonal (often greasy) crack beneath an overlap to start. Step left onto the wall to reach a small ledge. An awkward traverse left leads to an exposed ledge on the arête. Climb a crack above to reach a grass ledge.

2 12m (4a). A shallow groove on the right leads up the wall above and around the arête on the right. Follow this easily to reach the large ledge on ***'C' Ordinary Route***, which overlooks ***Intermediate Gully***.

3 20m (4c). Move into the steep corner on the right. Traverse delicately right across the rough wall to reach an obvious (and slightly loose) spike on the arête overlooking ***Intermediate Gully*** – an exciting position! Climb up the arête to a gangway which runs back left towards easier ground and ledges. Scramble up ***'C' Ordinary Route*** to ***Easy Terrace***.

24 **Intermediate Gully**	52m	MVS
E A Hopkinson, J H Hopkinson, Campbell – April 1895		

The deep cut crack separating ***'C'*** and ***'D' Buttresses*** becomes a titanic struggle in damp or greasy conditions. Despite the advances in equipment over the last two centuries, the gully still retains its reputation for difficulty. Begin by scrambling about 30 metres up the lower section of the gully to a cave beneath the first pitch.

Dow Crag – 'C' Buttress & 'D' Buttress

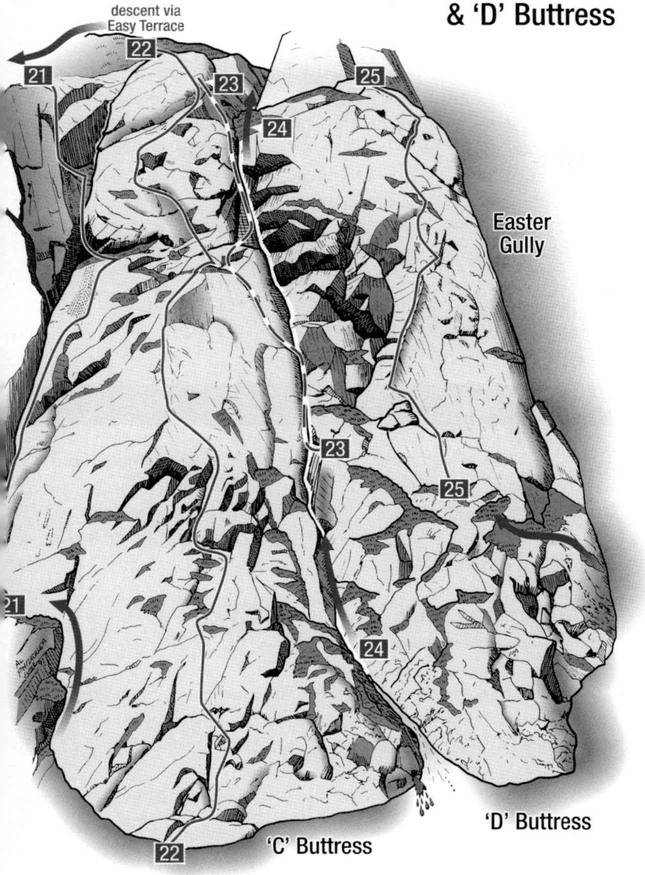

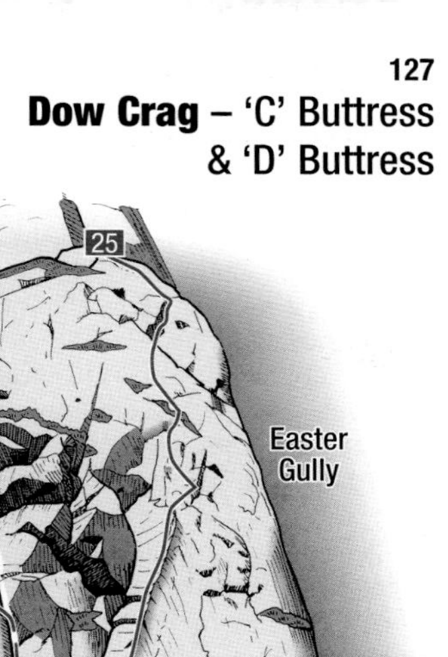

21 Central Chimney	S+	23 Eliminate 'C'	VS+
22 'C' Ordinary Route	D	24 Intermediate Gully	MVS
		25 'D' Ordinary Route	VD

1 9m (4a). Climb the awkward crack and the right wall of a short chimney to a large ledge.
2 8m (4b). The troublesome chockstone above is climbed direct. Continue more easily to a ledge and a belay on the right.
3 21m (4a). The wide crack leads strenuously to easier ground. When it steepens again, climb the left wall to a recess below a jammed chockstone.
4 5m (4b). Another unsympathetic chockstone leads with considerable difficulty to a deep cave.
5 9m. From a small ledge on the right, stride left into a groove on the left wall. Follow a crack to *Easy Terrace*.

The gully can be continued to the summit of the mountain, however this is of little interest to the climber.

'D' Buttress

This is the conical buttress which swings round at the right-hand end to form part of *Easter Gully*.
Descent: the easiest descent is made by striking across leftwards to reach a well worn platform at the right-hand end of *Easy Terrace*, which is followed leftwards.

25 **'D' Ordinary Route**	52m	VD
G F Woodhouse, A J Woodhouse – Aug 1904		

A good buttress climb, open and clean. Start on a grass shelf in the centre of the buttress, below some steep slabs. This is reached by scrambling 30 metres from the foot of the buttress. Excellent flake belay.
1 10m. Climb the steep slab on the left, moving further left to belay behind a large detached block.
2 20m. Step off the large block with difficulty and continue up the right side of the arête to a ledge. Climb the slab above, and move right to ledges and belays a few metres higher in a recess.
3 12m. Climb a shallow groove on good holds for 7 metres, then traverse horizontally right along ledges and up to a stance overlooking *Easter Gully*.
4 10m. Scramble up and left to *Easy Terrace*.

Easter Gully (The Amphitheatre)

Easter Gully divides *'D'* and *'E' Buttresses* and is, in section, like a vast funnel. At about 35 metres above the scree it is spanned by a huge chockstone, beyond which is the *Amphitheatre*, the starting point of many excellent routes. This chockstone is surmounted on the left and is known as the *Cave Pitch* (M). Care should be taken not to send loose stones or dead sheep (of which there are plenty) from the *Amphitheatre* onto climbers approaching from below. At the back of the *Amphitheatre* are two obvious corners: the left-hand is **26 Broadrick's Crack** (HS) and the right-hand is *Hopkinson's Crack*.
Descent: scramble up and left until a shallow grassy chimney leads down onto a broad grassy dome (the true top of *'D' Buttress*). Continue into the easy top section of *Intermediate Gully*, and descend this to a well-worn platform on the right (looking out). This is the end of *Easy Terrace* which can be followed to the bottom of the crag.

27 **Great Central Route**	60m	HVS+

J I Roper, G S Bower, G Jackson, A P Wilson (using combined tactics on P2) – Sept 1919
FFA: **C F Kirkus** – 1931

A climb of great character up the imposing pillar in the centre of *The Amphitheatre* between the two obvious corners. A major breakthrough for its time – even with the use of combined tactics (a method still occasionally employed today!). A superb blend of strenuous and delicate climbing in a position of great exposure. Start at the foot of the pillar.

1 24m (5a). Climb the nose and the pleasant slabs rightwards to a ledge below a steep crack, 3 metres left of *Hopkinson's Crack*. This is the infamous *South America Crack*. Climb it strenuously, exiting left onto the *Bandstand* ledge.

2 24m (5b). As delicate as the previous pitch was strenuous. Start from the sloping left edge of the ledge, just left of a slight nose. Climb the thin crinkly wall to slightly better holds, move right, and up to a good little ledge (crux). Follow the crackline above to the large diagonal overhang. Traverse left under this, across the mossy slab to join *Broadrick's Crack*. Up this for a couple of metres, then step right onto a ledge on the front face of the pillar.

3 12m (4b). Traverse rightwards along the ledge and move round the grossly exposed corner (look down!). Finish up the pleasant slabs above.

Dow Crag – Easter Gully

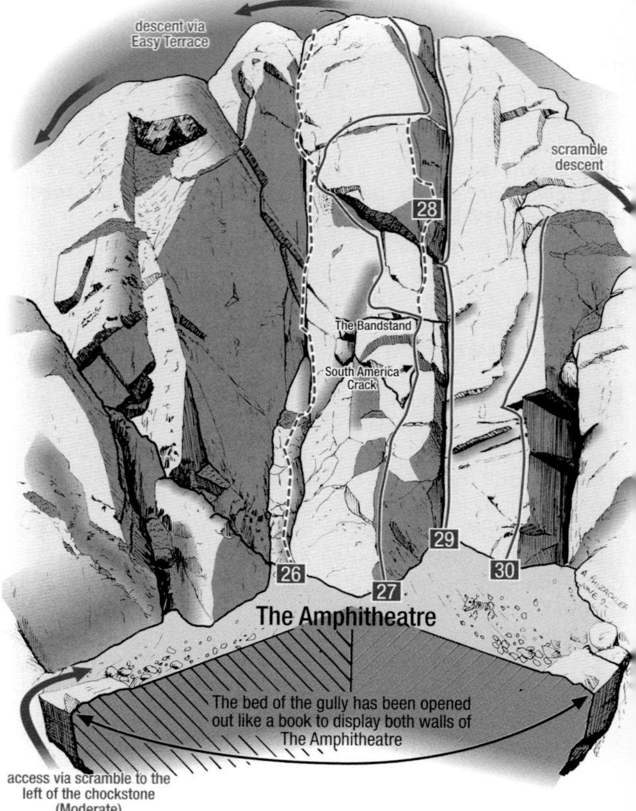

26 Broadrick's Crack	**HS**	**29 Hopkinson's Crack**	**HS**
27 Great Central Route	**HVS+**	**30 Black Wall**	**HVS**
28 The Norseman	**E4**		

28 **The Norseman**	57m	E4
I Greenwood, P McVey – June 1979		

Difficult climbing in a fine situation up the arête at the top of the central pillar. Start as for *Great Central Route*.

1 24m (5a). Pitch 1 of *Great Central Route*.

2 33m (6a). From the right end of the ledge a thin crack is followed to the diagonal overhang. Pull over this rightwards to a good rock ledge. The wall above to the peg runner is very committing. Move up again and step left around the arête. Climb the crack on the left side to easier ground.

29 **Hopkinson's Crack**	45m	HS
C Hopkinson, O Koecher – April 1895		

A superb old-fashioned crack climb taking the big corner on the right of *The Amphitheatre*.

1 15m. The crack is climbed directly to a good ledge on the left, below the *South America Crack*. Thread belay.

2 12m. Step back into the crack and continue with greater difficulty, exiting left onto the *Bandstand* ledge.

3 18m. Follow the wider crack directly to easier ground. (Some of the flake holds are not above suspicion).

30 **Black Wall**	30m	HVS
J I Roper, G Basterfield – June 1920		

An enjoyable wall climb on a sunny day, which follows the steep right-hand edge of the wall to the right of *Hopkinson's Crack*. Start just left of the entrance to a dark chimney.

(5a). Climb the steep little buttress on well-spaced holds to a rock ledge below an overhang. Move up to beneath the overhang and pull round the left side onto the wall above. Continue directly to ledges.

The Coppermines Valley

by Al Phizacklea

The Coppermines Valley is the name commonly given to the area drained by Church Beck, to the north-west of Coniston village.

The easiest approach is to drive up to the first gate on the Walna Scar road and park there. Walk up the right-hand fork in the road, crossing the tourist trail up the mountain to reach an area of large boulders. Continue rightwards to reach Levers Water, from where the crags can be seen - easy and very pleasant.

Little How Crag

Grid reference: **274 996**
Altitude: **550m**
Faces: **South-East**
Rock type: **Borrowdale Volcanic**
Approach time: **1 hr**

A beautifully positioned crag, above the north-western shore of Levers Water, with some wonderful routes, which are all recommended, being on rough sound rock which catches the sun for most of the day.

In the centre of the crag is a sweep of slabs bounded on its right by a corner. The routes are described from this feature.
Descent: is down a gully well to the left.

1 **Sunshine Arête**	41m	D

G S Bower, W J Borrowman, T C Ormiston-Chant – May 1919

The easiest, but none the less an enjoyable line up the arête right of the corner. Start at the base of the corner.

1 8m. Make a rising traverse onto the arête and up to a ledge and block belay.
2 21m. Climb the left edge of the steep slab to a large grass ledge.
3 12m. Traverse left across the ledge and follow a slab up to the left.

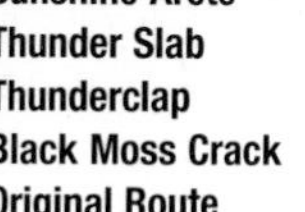

Route	Grade
1 Sunshine Arête	D
2 Thunder Slab	HS
3 Thunderclap	VS
4 Black Moss Crack	HS
5 Original Route	VD+
6 Misty Slabs	VD

5 6
500 metres

Little How Crag

2 **Thunder Slab**	42m	HS

G S Bower, W J Borrowman, T C Ormiston-Chant – May 1919

An enjoyable open climb, taking the easiest line up the right-hand side of the slab. Start at the base of the corner.

1 30m. From the chockstone, climb the corner for a couple of metres and move left up a thin diagonal crack until a few moves back right lead to the base of a short shallow corner, 3 metres left of the main corner. Climb it, exiting left and move up to the line of bulges. These are avoided on the right by following the main corner to grass ledges.

2 12m. Follow the easy line leftwards to the top. The left-hand crack in the steep wall above is a most entertaining alternative.

3 **Thunderclap**	30m	VS

R Matheson – July 1983

A good, well protected route taking a direct line up the centre of the slabs. A pitch of sustained interest. Start a couple of metres left of *Thunder Slab* at the base of the curving crackline.

(4c). Climb the wall directly, passing to the left of a grass ledge at 9 metres, and taking the line of bulges at the top by the groove-line on the left.

4 **Black Moss Crack**	39m	HS

First ascentionist unknown

The obvious curving line, well named! Start as for ***Thunderclap***.

1 30m. Move up the crack and follow it in its entirety, finishing up a steep wider section. Belay on the right.

2 9m. Climb leftwards up a scoop, then rightwards to the top.

Great How Crag

Grid reference: **277 998** Altitude: **540m**
Faces: **South to East** Rock type: **Borrowdale Volcanic**
Approach time: **1 hr 05 mins**

These extensive but broken-looking rocks are situated above the north-western bank of Levers Water, and about 500 metres right of *Little How Crag*. The crag is well worth a visit; the climbing is on rough sound rock with excellent positions.

Descend: to the right, down a grassy rake (care needed if wet).

5 **Original Route**	60m	VD+
D Copley, W L Barnes, I R Currie – Sept 1961		

Follows the prominent sharp-edged ridge starting from the lowest point of the crag. An interesting route with a mountaineering feel to it.

1 15m. Starting from the foot of the ridge, climb its left side to a ledge. Move round to the right and back through a window to a large block ledge.

2 6m. Step onto the wall from the top of the lower block and move up to the right to a grass ledge. (Using the upper block is more gymnastic).

3 12m. Climb the slab, behind the block at the back of the ledge, to the foot of the steep crack. Ascend the crack with difficulty and continue to a grass ledge above.

4 15m. Ascend the big flake and descend to a block bridge in the gap beyond. Climb the wall ahead for about 5 metres to a grass ledge and block belay on the right.

5 12m. Step left from the ledge and climb up to the left to another ledge. Ascend the grooves above to large grass ledges.

6 **Misty Slabs**	78m	VD
A W Gough, H McDonald, H Turner – Oct 1961		

A thoroughly enjoyable climb. Start 100 metres left of *Original Route* at the foot of a slab running up to the right.

1 30m. Traverse diagonally right across the slab for about 20 metres, to the edge. Move up onto the easier-angled slab above and climb it leftwards to a large grass ledge.

2 18m. Move left on to a steeper buttress and climb up to easier rock, which leads to a stance and belay at the foot of a crack.

3 30m. Climb the crack (taller people have the advantage), to the easier slabs above. Continue up the arête on the right edge of the slabs to the top (belays at 15 metres).

Tilberthwaite Slate

by Al Phizacklea

The Tilberthwaite valley is a beautiful and peaceful backwater between Tilberthwaite and Little Langdale, about 4 kilometres north of Coniston. This area contains no natural crags, but to many climbers this is their Mecca; for it contains some of the best slate quarries in the country.

Hodge Close Quarry

Grid reference: **316 017**
Altitude: **170m**
Faces: **West**
Rock type: **Quarried Slate**
Approach time: **5 mins**

Hodge Close is an impressive quarry hole which has become the focal point of Lake District slate climbing. It offers a wide variety of climbing styles for the extreme leader, from unprotected run-outs for cool cats to well bolted routes for those who have gone to the dogs. The quality of the rock varies too; generally it is very solid with reasonable friction (for slate) with fewer of the friable edges found in other slate areas. However, several areas of the quarry are unstable, and rockfalls do occasionally happen.

Hodge Close Quarry is reached from a junction on the A593 Coniston - Ambleside road, 3 kilometres north of Coniston. A minor road signposted "Hodge Close only" is followed for 2 kilometres to where it finally emerges from the woods directly in front of the huge quarry hole. There is ample parking space here.

The Main Wall

This is the impressive wall rising above the pool opposite the car parking area. The first route starts from behind the pool, its base is

Left: Nick Wharton taking the plunge at Hodge Close **Photo:** John Wilson

reached through the archway from the adjacent quarry. This is entered by walking past the houses at the end of the road and trending rightwards.

1	First Night Nerves	55m	E5
	R O Graham, A Phizacklea – Sept 1987		6 bolts

An excellent route which provides sustained, well protected climbing up the steep black wall right of the rockfall scar, before taking a bold direct line up the left side of the ***Main Wall***. Start about 10 metres right of the highest point of the scree, below a little alcove sporting an iron spike at shoulder height.

1 48m (6b). Stand on the spike (bolt) then climb up the two sloping niches on the left to gain the traverse line below the steeper rock. Move left into a hanging groove (nuts and Friend 2), then step up and right to gain twin bolts. Climb up and right precariously across a quartzy band (bolts) to reach a good hold below an undercut flake. Climb the flake (wires) passing a bolt and further delicate climbing which leads directly to a blunt spike, above and left of a slender groove. Continue directly to another bolt, then traverse left to reach a large sloping ledge and bolt belay.

2 7m (5a). Continue up the corner to the top.

About 20 metres above the pool are a series of grassy ledges just right of a steep black wall, which marks the lower edge of the main slab. The next three routes start from this ledge, which is reached by abseil.

2	The Main Event	45m	E5+
	P Whillance, R Parker, P Botterill, D Armstrong, A Murray – March 1980		

The original slate frightener has now become a classic test of cool. Start at the left edge of the ledge.

(6a). Traverse leftwards along an overhung ramp below the steep wall for 4 metres, then pull up onto the upper slab with difficulty to reach a peg (the first protection on the route). Follow the thin flake up leftwards, then move up to a large ledge and good runners (junction with ***Ten Years After***). A long, shallow groove leads up and slightly left to a ledge and bolt runners. Climb straight up for a few metres before stepping right to finish directly.

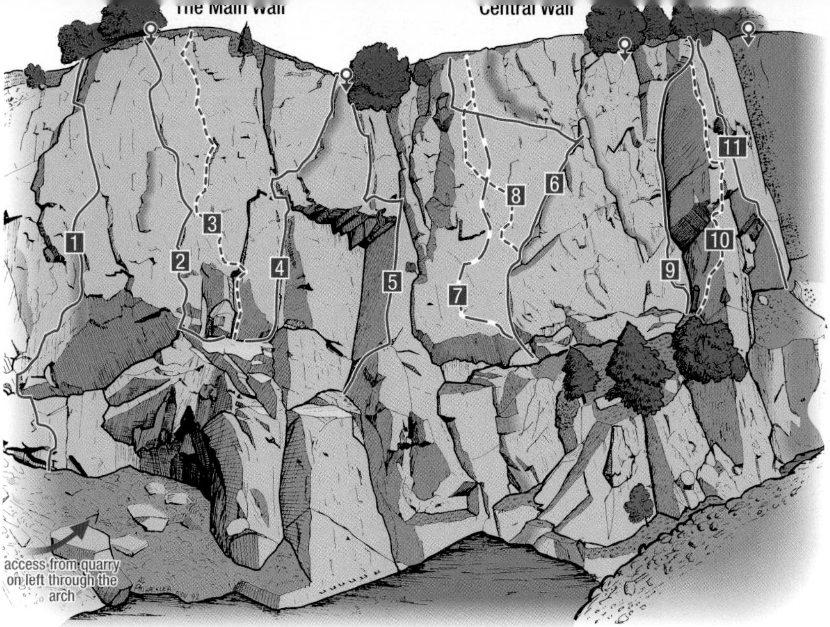

	Route	Grade
1	First Night Nerves	E5
2	The Main Event	E5+
3	Ten Years After	E4
4	Sky	*F6b+*
5	Life in the Fast Lane	E5
6	Big Dipper/ Mirrormere	E2
7	Beef Jerky	*F7b+*
8	Limited Edition	*F6c*
9	Behind the Lines	HVS–
10	Malice in Wonderland	E3+
11	Through the Looking Glass	E2+

3	**Ten Years After**	45m	E4
	R Matheson, E Cleasby – April 1980		

A beautiful modern slate classic combining sustained elegant climbing with well-spaced gear. It is strongly advised that the protection in the initial groove is pre-placed. Start from the centre of the ledge, beside a perched flake at the foot of a tapering slim groove.

(5c). Climb the large flake and enter the groove for the pre-placed protection then pull out leftwards onto the undercut wall. Step delicately left, then climb up to better holds by a peg and wire runner, then rock over leftwards to reach some ledges (good wires). Step right from here, and use a hollow flake to reach a shallow stepped groove which is climbed to a peg. Continue directly up the wall to a small groove: this has a good wire at its top to protect the awkward finishing move.

4	**Sky**	47m	*F6b+* (E2 5c)
	E Cleasby, R Matheson – April 1980 (Retrobolted 1996)		**6 bolts**

A superb route up the thin flake to the left of the prominent roof. Start at the right-hand end of the ledge of ***Ten Years After***.

Climb the short corner and follow the thin flake to where it peters out level with the roof. Step left into a short corner (small wires required), then pull out right onto the headwall. Follow the ledge system rightwards to finish.

5	**Life in the Fast Lane**	45m	E5
	P Whillance, A Murray, R Parker – April 1980		

Another fine route renowned for its boldness, which climbs above the large roof at the right-hand side of the ***Main Wall***. Start from a ledge at the foot of the groove which runs up to the roof.

(6b). From the foot of the groove, a shattered flake runs up right to the base of a prominent, bold arête (Friend). A very difficult smear leads to easier climbing directly up the rib to the right-hand side of the overhang. Step right into a dirty corner (runners), then traverse back left directly above the roof with difficulty (poor peg to start) to reach a shallow grooveline. This leads past a peg runner directly to the top.

The Central Wall

All these routes start from the large tree-covered terrace reached by abseil from the large sycamore tree at the top.

6 **Big Dipper/Mirrormere**	64m	E2
P1: **P Whillance, R Parker** – March 1980	P2: **E Cleasby, A Phizacklea, R Matheson** – April 1980	

A pleasant combination, initially climbing a rightward-leaning diagonal ramp up the wall, followed by a delicate traverse leftwards to reach the top. Start on the large terrace below a steep flake-crack, towards the left end of the ledge.

1 34m (5b). Climb the flake which leads strenuously to the ramp system. Follow this right, past the bolt belay of ***Limited Edition***, and the continuation groove to a bollard and bolt belay at its top.

2 30m (5b). Traverse the wall on the left for 8 metres, then climb up to a ring bolt. Continue leftwards to gain the top bolt on ***Limited Edition***, then step down, and traverse delicately left onto the arête which is followed directly to the top.

7 **Beef Jerky**	42m	*F7b+* (E5 6c)
K Phizacklea, C Matheson – July 1998		**8 bolts**

A tremendous route providing exceedingly sustained climbing - so called because "there ain't nothin' tougher than Beef Jerky". Start up *Big Dipper*.

Pull into the initial flake of ***Big Dipper***, then traverse left just above the roof (2 bolts) before climbing up to a large bracket bolt on a slight crease in the slab. Traverse right to a very vague scoop, then climb straight up, through a small break in the overlap to gain the traverse line of ***Limited Edition***. Clip the bolt on the left before moving rightwards on to the blank wall, where a direct line leads to the final bolt and finish of ***Limited Edition***.

8 **Limited Edition**	33m	*F6c* (E4– 6a)
P Carling, P Noble – May 1986 (Rebolted 1992)		**5 bolts**

An excellent route which climbs the left side of the wall. Start from the bolt belay at the top of the ramp on ***Big Dipper***, usually reached by abseil.

From the lower left point of the ramp, step across left (bolt) to gain a shallow right-facing scoop and climb this delicately past a bolt to an excellent hold. Traverse diagonally left across the wall to reach a flake and a bolt, then up and slightly right, past another bolt, to better holds below the slight steepening of the headwall. A hard move on quartz holds past the top bolt leads to a tiny right-facing flake, finish up this.

9	**Behind the Lines**	33m	HVS–

R Parker, A Murray, P Whillance – March 1980

A classic of the quarry, this route takes the prominent slabby corner which forms the angle between the ***Central Wall*** and the arête of *Malice in Wonderland*. Start by a large pine tree growing at the right end of the ledge.

(5a). Climb delicately left from the tree to reach a short corner. A few bold moves up this enables the main cornerline to be entered. Follow this, with good protection, to the bulge just below the top. Traverse right to finish.

10	**Malice in Wonderland**	43m	E3+

P Whillance, R Parker, E Cleasby – April 1980

A beautiful route requiring a bold but graceful approach to climb the smooth arête right of ***Behind the Lines***. Start at the pine tree, as for *Behind the Lines*.

(5c). Climb the rib on the right to the overhang. Step right, past a bolt, and pull directly through the overhang on good, but widely spaced holds, to land on the slab above. Traverse back left, just above the roof to reach the main arête. Climb the left side of this, passing a good diagonal crack, to a tree on its right flank. Step back onto the arête and climb it with conviction, past a thin RP crack on the left, to a delicate and gripping finish.

11	**Through the Looking Glass**	42m	E2+

E Cleasby, R Matheson – April 1980

Another excellent route which takes a shallow grooveline in the face right of *Malice in Wonderland*. Start at the same level as the terrace

Left: Helen Davies delicately balanced on *Limited Edition* (*F6c*) **Photo:** Dominic Donnini

below *Central Wall*, but from the floor of the quarry to its right, below a short rib which leads to the right-hand side of a low blocky overhang.

(5c). Climb the rib to a runner where it merges into the wall above. Step left below the roof, and stand up to clip a peg in the clean wall above it. Cross the lip of the roof leftwards to gain a good ledge, where good gear can be arranged for the next section. (An upward pulling nut prevents it from lifting out.) Climb the fine flake-crack above to enter a long shallow groove, which snakes upwards to a tricky finish.

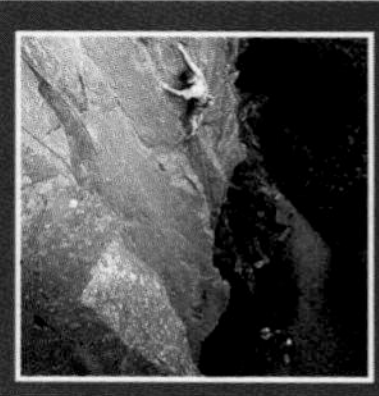

Cathedral Quarry

Grid reference:	**314 028**
Altitude:	**150m**
Faces:	**West to North**
Rock type:	**Quarried Slate**
Approach time:	**5–25 mins**

This impressive hole of high quality slate lies on the south side of the River Brathay in Little Langdale. It contains some spectacular climbing in a sunny location and it is often pleasantly sheltered from the wind (a fact not lost on the local midges).

The quarry is adjacent to the ford where the Tilberthwaite–Little Langdale track crosses the River Brathay. This ford is reached from the A593 Coniston–Ambleside road along a minor road (signposted High Park) which is ½ kilometre south of the Little Langdale road junction. Take the right fork of this minor road alongside the woods, through two farmyards, to where it drops down to the river, 2 kilometres from the main road. There is limited parking here (strictly no minibuses).

From the ford, follow the lane upstream for 100 metres where a steep little path leads to a flat topped spoil heap. At the far end of this, walk around the top to find the slippery descent route.

The routes start in the open part of the quarry by the large cave 'window', and are described from **left** to **right**.

Left: Rob Matheson, cool as ever, on *Malice in Wonderland* (E3+) **Photo:** Nick Wharton

1 **Night of the Hot Pies**	30m	E1+
R Brookes, M Dale – July 1987		

An excellent route which follows the straight crackline on the right of the hanging slab above the hole. Start up the protruding arête on the right of the cave.

(5b). Climb the arête to steeper rock at 9 metres (bolt). Move left and swing round a bulge to enter a smooth grooveline (bolt). Climb the prominent crack on the left, which runs directly up the side of the slab to the top (wires).

2 **An Alabuse**	32m	E3–
R Brookes, S Alden, N Toledo, A Warrington – July 1987		

A superb route up to the right of the cave.

(5c). Start up the initial rib of *Night of the Hot Pies*, then step left and climb directly up a short square-cut groove to reach a prominent hanging flake at the top end of the smooth groove on *Hot Pies* (bolts). Layback around this to stand on a good hold on the rib. Continue directly, passing a spike runner to finish delicately up the top slab (bolt).

3 **Going Underground**	40m	*F6a+* (E2 5c)
P Clarke, R Brookes – Aug 1981 (Retrobolted 1996)		**8 bolts**

This route follows the diagonal ramp to give a pleasant, well protected climb. Start up *Night of the Hot Pies*.

After a few metres up the rib, step right and follow the ramp past a loose flake and sapling to its end. An awkward move leads to the top.

4 **Darklands**	38m	E3
M Dale, R Kirby – Aug 1988		

A spectacular route which forces an improbable line straight through the impressive, stacked overhangs. Start at a slabby recess 6 metres right of *Night of the Hot Pies*. Nuts required.

(5c). Climb the slab to the overhang at 6 metres, where a move past a V-notch leads into a scoop (bolt). Cross the red wall on the right to reach a large bollard on a ledge at 10 metres (possible belay). Take the slab on the left to below the large roof, then

1 Night of the Hot Pies E1+
2 An Alabuse E3–
3 Going Underground *F6a+*
4 Darklands E3
5 China Crisis *F7a+*
6 Basilica *F7a*
1
2
3
4
5
6

pull up right into a bottomless V-groove (bolt). Step rightwards airily (bolt) to below a second large jagged overhang, where a hidden pocket above enables a bolt to be clipped. Make a wild pull over the roof onto a hanging slab, then follow the groove up right to a projecting flake. Climb past this on the right (wires) and continue up a shallow groove to a sapling, finishing left.

5	**China Crisis**	26m	*F7a+* (E4 6b)

D Bates – June 1989 **K Phizacklea, R Matheson** (New start and finish) – May 1996 **6 bolts**

A brilliant route, giving sustained technical climbing with an extremely precarious finish. Start by two trees on the ground, 5 metres right of a slimy corner, below and left of the impressively smooth hanging slab.

From an upstanding flake, climb up to an arched niche and pull directly up to jugs, and a good hold by the second bolt. Using a shot hole on the left, swing leftwards around the rib and stand on the ledge. Use an undercut to pull directly into a slabby recess above, then step right and move up to a hanging flake on the left of an easy groove. Layback the flake to finish - if you can!

6	**Basilica**	45m	*F7a* (E4 6a)

R Matheson, D Donnini, K Phizacklea – April 1993
Upper Section: **R Graham** – June 1989 Lower Section: **A Hyslop, I Williamson** – Summer 1989 **9 bolts**

Another brilliant route which traverses above the cave mouth to finish up a notorious line of chipped holds in the centre of the smooth wall. Start below a smooth clean wall at the right-hand arête of the huge cave mouth.

Climb the steep arête, until a line of shot-holes on the right wall leads to a ledge and an old abseil point. Pull up to a bulge, where fingery climbing (often damp) leads to a good handrail. From here, traverse left into the centre of the wall and make a very hard move to gain the first chipped hole. Follow the shallow groove above to good ledges, where sustained climbing on widely spaced pockets leads directly to the top.

Left: Brian McKinley amidst the overhangs on *Darklands* (E3) **Photo:** Al Phizacklea

The Duddon Valley

by Al Phizacklea

This peaceful valley in the south-west corner of the Lakes, is an area of great natural beauty which surrounds the River Duddon on its 20 kilometre journey from Wrynose Pass to the Duddon Estuary.

Access is possible from the north via the Hardknott–Wrynose Pass road; the easiest approach from the south is from Broughton-in-Furness, where a branch road leaves the A595 (T) at Duddon Bridge. This narrow tortuous road runs the length of the valley, through Ulpha and Seathwaite to join the Hardknott Pass road at Cockley Beck.

The crags are described in order as one moves northwards up the valley.

Wallowbarrow Crag

Grid reference: **222 967**
Altitude: **210m**
Faces: **South-West**
Rock type: **Borrowdale Volcanic**
Approach time: **15 mins**

Wallowbarrow is a splendid valley crag providing a good selection of routes to accommodate low to middle grade climbers. It gives fast-drying wall climbing on clean and solid rhyolite, and is a popular refuge for climbers when the higher crags are wet.

There may be a **Bird Restriction** on part or all of *Wallowbarrow Crag* from 1st March to 30th June or part thereof. Signs at the crag should inform you, but if in doubt contact details for further information are given in the Access and Conservation section.

The most popular approach is from High Wallowbarrow Farm – reached by following a minor road from the bridge over the River Duddon, about 1½ kilometres south of Seathwaite. This leads along

Right: The beautiful, secluded Duddon Valley – Wallowbarrow Crag is in the top left corner
Photo: Al Phizacklea

Above: Julie Bowbly on *Thomas* (S)
Photo: Nick Wharton

the west side of the river to the farm, above which the crag is clearly seen (reached by a winding track up the wooded hillside). The farmer allows parking by the farm, though expects a small donation for this facility.

The crag consists of two main buttresses separated by the obvious *Red Gully*.

West Buttress

The rock is generally good though belays invariably prove scarce near the top of the crag. **Descent:** to the left (certainly NOT down *Red Gully*).

1 **Western Wall**	33m	MVS+
L G Sullivan, P E Wilson, J Jenkinson – May 1963		

A little gem, exposed and satisfying. It climbs the grey wall on the left-hand side of the buttress in a rising diagonal line. Start 5 metres below and right of a large perched flake, beside a detached-looking block.

1 15m (4b). Stepping from the block, gain the narrow ramp and traverse diagonally rightwards (delicate), stopping just short of the crackline. Climb the steep wall to a ledge.

2 18m (4a). Trend rightwards up a slabby ramp to a large flake, step right and move steeply up impending rock on good holds.

2 **Malediction Direct**	49m	VS
A J Simpkin, A H Greenbank – March 1959		

A fine little climb with some steep moves, following the distinct incut groove of pale coloured rock to the right of ***Western Wall***. Start below the middle of the buttress where a broken rib points towards a dry-stone wall.

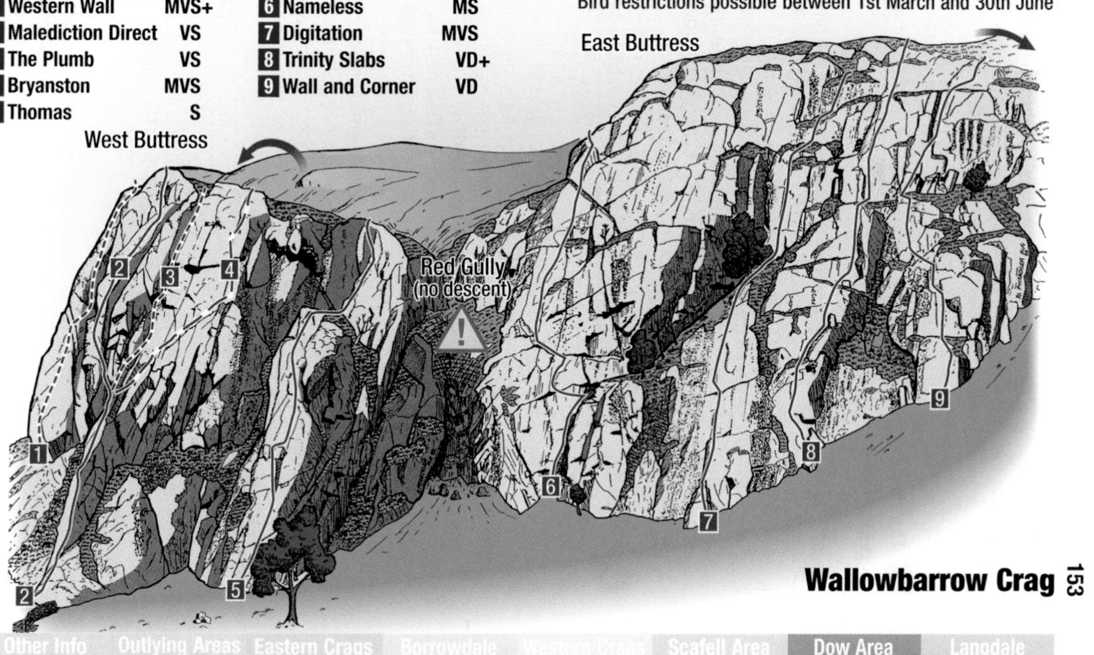
1 Western Wall MVS+
2 Malediction Direct VS
3 The Plumb VS
4 Bryanston MVS
5 Thomas S
6 Nameless MS
7 Digitation MVS
8 Trinity Slabs VD+
9 Wall and Corner VD
Bird restrictions possible between 1st March and 30th June
East Buttress
West Buttress
Red Gully
(no descent)
1
2
3
4
5
6
7
8
9
2

1 24m. Climb the rib to an obvious niche and flake belay.
2 25m (4c). Climb the bulge to the left of the small roof, pulling into the open grooveline and following it steeply, trending left at the top up impending rock.

3 **The Plumb**	51m	VS
D Miller, J A Austin – June 1967		

This is the obvious line to the right of *Malediction Direct*, its steep chimney-crack offering an uncompromising line and a suspenseful finish.
1 24m. Climb the rib of *Malediction Direct*, Pitch 1.
2 27m (4c). Move a couple of metres right of the niche and climb the open grooveline to the obvious chimney-crack. Take this, surmounting the hanging flake with difficulty, from where improving holds lead to easy ground directly above.

4 **Bryanston**	53m	MVS
J Smith, W F Dowlen – April 1956		

A good climb of increasing difficulty with an exhilarating final pitch up the obvious wide crack near the right-hand side of the headwall, right of *The Plumb*. Start as for *Malediction Direct*.
1 24m. Climb the rib of *Malediction Direct*, Pitch 1.
2 16m. Go diagonally right, following an obvious weakness, for 9 metres. Traverse horizontally right and ascend to a small stance next to a detached block.
3 13m (4b). Climb the crack, making an awkward entry move from the left. Continue to a recess, then step left and climb the wall directly to the top. Belay well back.

5 **Thomas**	57m	S
W F Dowlen, D Stroud – June 1955		

Fine climbing and deservedly popular. ***Thomas*** climbs the clean pillar of rock that forms the right-hand profile of the ***West Buttress***. It begins three metres left of the large oak tree at a well worn patch on the ground.
1 *21m.* Climb the obvious crackline slanting steeply up to the right, then move directly upwards to below some perched blocks, moving right under these and up to a ledge and tree belay.

2 18m. Move back right on to the face and climb the steep cracked wall to a large ledge at the top of the pillar. Block belay.

3 18m. Make an awkward move right and climb the wall into the exposed and shallow grooves above. Good holds lead to the top. Belay well back.

East Buttress

Descent: to the right.

6 **Nameless**	63m	MS
W F Dowlen, J Hollin – June 1956		

A very good climb, exposed and satisfying. It begins up a prominent groove, a few metres right of the foot of ***Red Gully***.

1 12m. Climb the groove to a decidedly awkward final steepening. Protection is sparse and the exit is difficult. Belay on the ledge immediately above, below a triangular roof.

2 20m. Step down and left across the face to a definite impasse. Make a move upwards and swing out on to the steep face on the left, directly above the overhang. Climb this slightly left for 3 metres, then more delicately, turn a bulge on the right up a shallow groove. Easy rocks lead to a stance.

3 18m. Climb the shallow groove on the right, to a grass ledge, then step left across a slab and follow the cracked wall to a good ledge with a flake belay.

4 13m. From the higher rock ledge on the right, climb leftwards across the wall to easier ground.

7 **Digitation**	48m	MVS
D G Heap, J R Amatt, C B Greenhalgh – April 1963 P2: **J Walmsley, J Rostron, D P Davies** – 1959		

One of the most popular routes on the crag, starting from the three poised blocks below a clean slab overlooked by a large oak tree. It climbs directly up the slab and breaches the distinctive overlap above.

1 30m (4b). Step right off the topmost block and climb the wall to a small ledge. Move left, and climb the shallow right-facing corner to the overlap. Pull boldly over leftwards and continue, more or less directly, to the oak tree.

2 18m (4b). Climb a thin crack in the centre of the steep wall at the back of the ledge to the horizontal flake. Follow pleasant walls to the top.

8	**Trinity Slabs**	60m	VD+

Unknown – 1951

An excellent climb, following the stepped buttress to the right of *Digitation*, starting by a flake capped with an overhang 15 metres right of *Digitation*.

1 18m. Climb the wall, just left of the flake, and where it steepens move leftwards to below a short shallow corner. Continue directly to a large flake belay.

2 12m. The bouldery wall on the left of the flake leads to a leaning block. Step off this onto a short wall leading to a large ledge and belays over to the right.

3 15m. The grooveline on the right is awkward and leads to the next ledge system and nut belays.

4 15m. Make a difficult pull into an incipient groove above, then step right onto the final arête.

9	**Wall and Corner**	58m	VD

Unknown – 1951

An absorbing climb and of no mean difficulty in its first 30 metres. Begin up a short smooth wall near the right-hand end of the crag and about 20 metres right of *Trinity Slabs*.

1 10m. Climb onto a small rock ledge and continue up the centre of the wall on small polished holds to a large ledge below the large flake overhang.

2 15m. Climb the shallow groove and crack (crux) past the left side of the overhang, until easier rocks lead leftwards to a large flake.

3 12m. The wall above the flake is climbed for 5 metres until a step left arrives at a dry-stone wall. Climb past this on the right to a belay by a bridged block on the right.

4 21m. Step left off the block, up the steep wall, and bridge back right across the corner to a grassy recess. Follow the right-hand wall of the large corner above to the top.

Burnt Crag

Grid reference: **243 991**
Altitude: **350m**
Faces: **South**
Rock type: **Borrowdale Volcanic**
Approach time: **20 mins**

Properly called ***Little Blake Rigg*** (the true ***Burnt Crag*** lies 500 metres south-east), this is definitely the best crag in the area for the hard climber. It offers fine lines on steep, compact rock and being south-facing it dries quickly, except for a couple of short-lived seepage lines in the grooves. ***Burnt Crag*** is the largest wall of rock found on the rugged hillside to the east of Troutal Farm, (this is the only building found next to the road, 3 kilometres north of Seathwaite).

The best approach is to park by the cattle grid south of Troutal, (235 985) and follow the track alongside the wall through several gates then strike rightwards up the hillside, aiming for a gate in the wall which is hidden by a small knoll. The crag lies diagonally leftwards up the fellside from here.

The main feature of the crag is a slanting, right-facing corner in the centre, which is the line of *Shifter*. The routes are described from **left** to **right**. There is an easy **descent** on both sides of the crag.

1 **Breaker**	24m	E2+

R O Graham, G Smith – July 1983

A good strenuous route up the steep left wall of the crag.

(5c). Climb the left-slanting diagonal crack, then the wall via breaks to a chockstone below a prow of rock. Traverse right along a ledge to a small cave. Pull back left using the large flake above to finish up a groove.

2 **Double Trouble**	27m	E3+

I Greenwood, A Hyslop, A Phizacklea – Oct 1979

A fine but unyielding climb that starts below the right arête of the overhanging left-hand wall of the crag, about 9 metres left of *Shifter*.

Burnt Crag

	Route	Grade
1	Breaker	E2+
2	Double Trouble	E3+
3	Innocenti	E3
4	Shifter	E3
5	Burning Desire	E5–
6	An Alien Heat	E5

A Phizacklea Sept 92

(6a). Step off the boulder and climb across the steep wall, past two horizontal slots (Friends) to a niche. Up this, then a difficult groove above leads to the top.

3 **Innocenti**	30m	E3
R O Graham, A Hyslop – Oct 1979		

A good sustained climb up a thin left-trending flake which starts below a square-cut corner, capped by an overhang, 2 metres left of ***Shifter***.

(6a). Using a flake, awkwardly enter a shallow niche, then follow the strenuous flake-crack out leftwards until a resting foothold can be reached on the left wall. Move up to a patch of heather, then follow a slanting line back right above the big overhang; where a good sharp flake continues in the same direction through the final bulge.

4 **Shifter**	30m	E3
R O Graham, I Greenwood – Sept 1979		

An excellent climb, strenuous but well protected. Start below the central rightwards-facing corner.

(6a). A steep crack leads to a small ledge at the foot of the corner. Burn up this, passing a thin section to reach the upper bulge, pull out left and finish up the final groove.

5 **Burning Desire**	30m	E5–
A Phizacklea, J L Holden – April 1989		

A scorcher! Start below a steep pink groove 8 metres right of ***Shifter***.

(6b). Enter the groove using a large flake, and climb it to good holds where it peters out. Traverse slightly left and move up to the overhang (peg), then step right and stretch up for a flat hold in the small groove immediately to the right. Stand on this and finally drift delicately right to enter the prominent bottomless groove which leads easily to the top.

6 An Alien Heat	26m	E5
M Radtke, J Cooksey – July 1989		

Another blistering route starting below the left-hand end of a sloping glacis, which is about 6 metres up the crag. A large selection of small wires is essential.

(6b). Climb the groove to the glacis and follow a shallow corner above its left end to where the rock bulges. Difficult climbing slightly rightwards leads to a jug at the foot of a right-facing groove, finish up this.

Left: Andy Rowell stops briefly to place gear on *Shifter* (E3) **Photo:** Al Phizacklea

Scafell Area Map

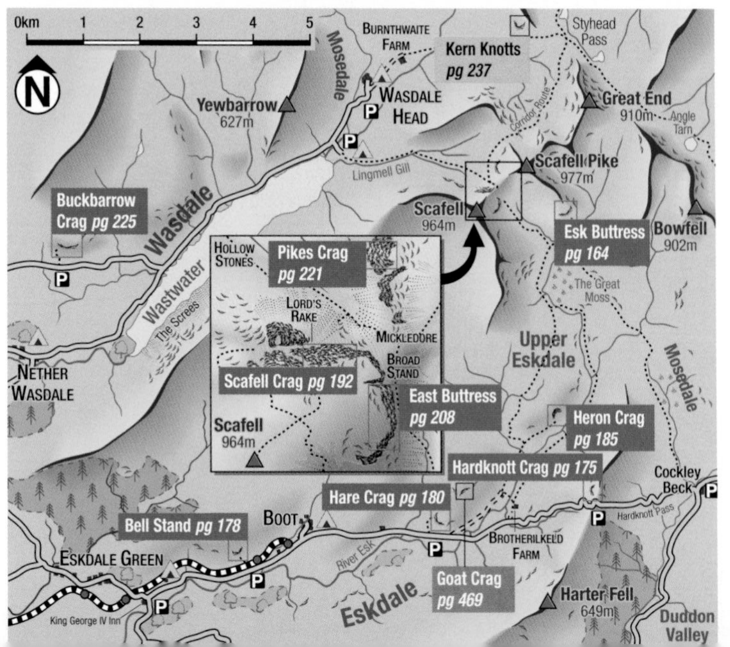

Scafell Area

Eskdale, Scafell & Wasdale

Above: Scafell **Photo:** Ron Kenyon

Eskdale

by Al Phizacklea

This beautiful valley, hidden in the west of the Lake District, offers a great deal of variety for the climber.

The lower section of the valley, containing the road, holds many small outcrops of excellent quality granite which can be easily reached a few minutes from the car. A unique feature of Eskdale is the miniature railway linking Ravenglass and Boot, known as "T' La'l Ratty". The upper stretches of Eskdale, defined as the area north of Brotherilkeld (the last farm in the valley bottom), is by contrast a wild, treeless setting for one of the finest crags in the Lake District, Esk Buttress.

Esk Buttress

Grid reference: **223 065**
Altitude: **490m**
Faces: **South-East**
Rock type: **Borrowdale Volcanic**
Approach time: **1 hr 30 mins**

Shown as ***Dow Crag*** on OS Maps. Without doubt, one of the finest and most impressive crags in the district. The situation is idyllic; the large open walls look out over the wild expanse of Upper Eskdale. Although close to the Scafell massif, it lies at an altitude of less than 500 metres and enjoys a reputation for drying rapidly. This coupled with a south-easterly aspect makes it a pleasant place to climb. It remains a place where the climber, whatever his standard, can enjoy predominantly wall climbs of the highest quality.

Despite its apparent remoteness the crag can be reached fairly painlessly by a variety of highly scenic routes. For those based in Langdale, Coniston, or the South Lakes the easiest and most popular approach is to drive to Cockley Beck (246 017), from where a path, often wet, leads up Mosedale and over to Lingcove Beck. Beyond the beck a narrow path contours under a long, broken crag and eventually descends to the Great Moss. Esk Buttress is directly ahead, and is reached by skirting the wet area and fording the river.

Alternatively from Brotherilkeld in Eskdale, follow the path alongside the River Esk to eventually arrive at the outlet of the Great Moss. *Esk Buttress* is 1 kilometre ahead, and is reached by skirting the wet areas on the left.

The crag is a series of steep walls, gradually rising in size from the left to culminate in the inspiring *Central Pillar*. Defining the right side of the *Central Pillar* is the deep corner of *Trespasser Groove*; further right again more broken walls run into *Esk Chimney*. Beneath the crag, especially on the left, is steep broken ground, which has to be negotiated to reach the foot of many of the climbs. With a little forethought it only amounts to easy scrambling and the starts of the climbs are easily located.

Descent: the best descent from all routes is to move back beyond the top of the cliff a short distance, then gradually descend broken ground towards the left side of the crag (right looking out) using a sketchy path. A short wall is descended to reach a small stream.

The Gargoyle Wall

The first three routes lie on the lower left-hand wall of the crag, known as the *Gargoyle Wall*. This is easily identified by a curious perched block at its top, the *Gargoyle*.

1 Gargoyle Groove — 55m — VS

A R Dolphin, L J Griffin – Aug 1947

A good route which gives better and harder climbing than its apparently broken appearance would suggest. It follows the long, well defined groove at the left end of the wall, to finish just left of the *Gargoyle*. Start at the foot of a small buttress directly below and left of the groove, at a triangular wedged block.

1 19m (4b). Climb the buttress to ledges and scramble up to the foot of the main groove.

2 18m (4c). Go up the groove until forced onto the left wall by an overhanging nose. After a strenuous move on the left, move right to the tip of the nose above the overhang; easier climbing leads to a pinnacle belay on the left.

3 18m (4c). Step back right and follow the remarkably sustained groove to the top, finishing just left of the *Gargoyle*.

2 Gargoyle Direct — 81m — HVS

D W English, M McKenzie, K Brannon – June 1962

The main pitch offers delightful, open wall climbing with good protection. Start at a narrow rock rib directly beneath the *Gargoyle*. This is the only continuous line of rock leading to the foot of the wall.

1 42m (4a). Climb easily up the clean rib to grass and heather ledges. Steep scrambling, passing a rock crevasse, leads to a spike belay directly below the *Gargoyle*.

2 39m (5a). Climb the wall, trending left slightly to reach a large spike at 8 metres, then move back right to below a shallow groove. Follow the strenuous crack in the groove for 5 metres, when a move left enables a rest to be taken. Continue left to a rib

and follow it to a ledge beneath the *Gargoyle*. A short crack on the left leads to a block belay.

3 **Grand Slam**	39m	E1
W Young, I Singleton – Aug 1973		

An excellent pitch up the centre of the wall, which contains a strenuous fingery crux above the overhang. Start by climbing Pitch 1 of *Gargoyle Direct*, then walking right to below a thin vertical crack in the centre of the clean wall.

(5b). Move up to the base of the crack and climb the initial flake until it steepens, then follow a rising line up right to a spike. The wall above leads to a square-cut overhang, pull out of the left side of this on small holds to thankfully gain a ledge. The wall on the right leads to the top.

The Red Edge Area

This section of the crag is the steep clean wall below and left of the *Central Pillar*.

The next route starts below a prominent deep chimney at the left-hand end of this wall. Scramble approach.

4 **The Red Edge**	60m	HVS+
J A Austin, N J Soper, E Metcalf (1 point of aid – now free) – June 1962		

Superb climbing up the exposed, grooved rib forming the right edge of the chimney. The difficulties are continuous but nowhere excessive and protection is good throughout.

1 39m (5a). Ascend the chimney for 5 metres, until a thin flake/crack on the right wall leads to the rib. Follow the rib for a short distance until a shallow groove on the left can be entered. Climb the steep groove to an overhang which is turned on the right; an easier groove above leads to a belay on the right.

2 21m (4c). Move back left and follow a crack and then large flakes, slightly leftwards, towards the top.

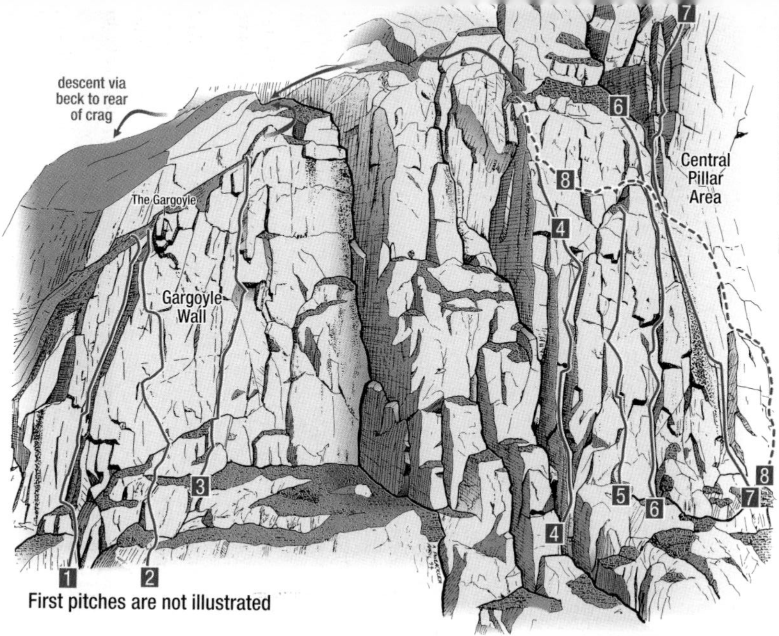

	Route	Grade
1	Gargoyle Groove	VS
2	Gargoyle Direct	HVS
3	Grand Slam	E1
4	The Red Edge	HVS+
5	Humdrum	E3
6	Black Sunday	HVS
7	Square Chimney/ Medusa Wall	VS
8	Bridge's Route	HS

descent via beck to rear of crag

The Gargoyle

Gargoyle Wall

Central Pillar Area

First pitches are not illustrated

Esk Buttress
– Red Edge Area

5 Humdrum	38m	E3

R H Berzins, M Berzins – Aug 1977

A tremendous climb which boasts the best pitch of its standard on the cliff. Scramble up to the highest grass ledge, mid-way between the chimney of ***The Red Edge*** and the ***Square Chimney***, and belay 3 metres left of a small tree.

(5c). Climb steeply up towards some stepped grooves and follow these, with several bold moves, to a resting position. Go diagonally up leftwards to the top of a groove on the left. After a couple of metres of ascent, traverse the wall on the right to a flat hold in the middle of the wall. Follow a thin crack above into a groove, pull directly over the square-cut overhang above to finish at a grass ledge. Abseil descent.

6 Black Sunday	63m	HVS

J A Austin, E Metcalf, N J Soper – June 1962

A justifiably popular climb up the steep groove/crack system parallel and to the left of ***Square Chimney*** route. The lower sections are rather mossy and need time to dry out after rain. Scramble up to a small tree by the start of ***Humdrum***.

1 33m (5a). Move up to a prominent mossy crack and climb it to a slab on the right. Regain the crack and follow it for a couple of metres to where it fades, where a step left leads to a thin slanting crack. Follow this to a resting place beneath an overhang. Traverse right, back into the main crackline, and pull rightwards round an overhang, then ascend a short wall to a ledge.

2 17m (5a). Climb the corner crack above until more broken rocks lead to a belay on the left (junction with ***Bridge's Route***).

3 13m (4b). The wall to the left of a mossy scoop is climbed; belay well back.

The Central Pillar Area

The ***Central Pillar*** is the unmistakable towering wall in the centre of the crag. It is bounded on its right by the deep corner of ***Trespasser Groove***, and on the left by a mossy grooveline. The lower part of this groove forms a distinctive shallow square-cut chimney, the starting point for the next route.

Esk Buttress – Central Pillar Area

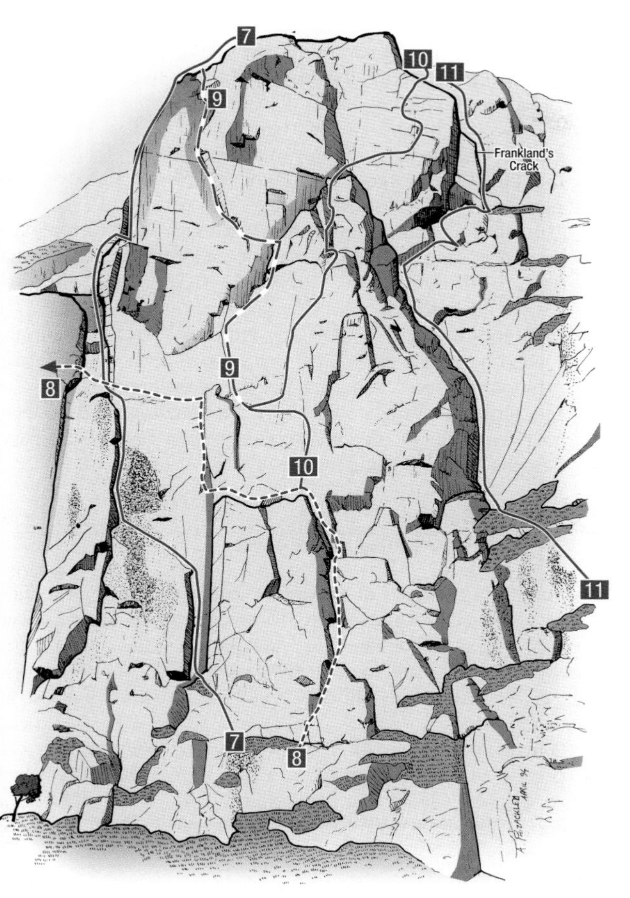

7 Square Chimney/ Medusa Wall	VS	9 The Cumbrian	E5–
8 Bridge's Route	HS	10 The Central Pillar	E2
		11 Trespasser Groove	HVS

7 Square Chimney/Medusa Wall Combination | 80m | VS

P1-3: **R J Birkett, L Muscroft** – Aug 1947 P4,5: **A R Dolphin, L J Griffin** – Aug 1947

An excellent combination, starting up the square-cut chimney and finishing in a superb position up the left side of the main headwall. The extensive moss around the lower half is purely cosmetic, as the holds used for climbing are clean. Start by scrambling with care up broken rocks to a ledge below the chimney.

1 15m (4c). Climb the chimney to a sloping ledge on the left.

2 15m (4b). Cross a mossy slab on the left to enter a groove with a crack in the back; follow this to a small stance.

3 21m (4c). Continue up the groove which widens to form a shallow gully. Climb this until a clean rock ledge on the right can be reached. This ledge forms a distinct step in the huge left-hand arête of the headwall.

4 13m (4c). Climb the shallow groove up the left side of the wall, about 3 metres left of the arête, to the top of a pinnacle. Traverse right to an exposed stance on the edge of the headwall.

5 16m (4b). Go up the groove above the belay for 5 metres, then traverse right to the edge, which is followed to a good ledge. Easy climbing and scrambling remains.

8 Bridge's Route | 76m | HS

A W Bridge, A B Hargreaves, M Linnell, W S Dyson – July 1932

One of the classic routes of the district, providing a great introduction to the crag. The route initially follows a direct line up the lower part of the pillar, before traversing leftwards across the crag to finish above the ***Red Edge***. Start by scrambling up vegetation and short rock walls to a cleaned ledge, just below, and 9 metres right of the base of *Square Chimney*.

1 26m. Move slightly right from the belay, and follow steep cracks passing an awkward pinnacle to gain a very shallow cracked corner, which leads to a grass ledge. Climb a crack above to a good flake which leads leftwards to a ledge overlooking ***Square*** *Chimney*.

Right: John Ellis on the traverse pitch of the delightful *Bridge's Route* (HS)
Photo: Stephen Reid

2 13m. Climb a steep groove above the left-hand side of the ledge and continue directly to a spike belay directly below the looming headwall.
3 12m. Traverse delicately left to a mossy ledge below an open chimney. A groove on the left leads onto the front face and a block belay.
4 9m. Continue traversing left along the sloping shelves to a small stance by a pile of flakes on the edge of the buttress.
5 16m. Climb a mossy groove to a large grass shelf; belay well back.

9 **The Cumbrian**	80m	E5–

R Valentine, P Braithwaite (3 points of aid) – May 1974
FFA: **M Berzins** – Aug 1977 P1: **R O Graham, A Hyslop** – July 1977

This climb boasts an awe-inspiring main pitch which takes the sensationally positioned left-slanting corner high on the front face. Technically sustained and strenuous on the crux, but the protection is good. It starts as for ***Bridge's Route***.

1 36m (5a). Follow Pitch 1 of the ***Central Pillar***.
2 44m (6a), but (6b) for the short. Continue up the slab above, in the same line, to a triangular overhang in the crease formed by the junction of the headwall and the lower slabs. Pull over the overhang to some small wires a couple of metres above. Step left onto the impending wall to reach a shallow groove. Move up and left again with increasing difficulty, to enter the base of the slim corner. Climb the corner, surmounting a bulge near the top, and follow a slabby groove rightwards to a final bulge. Overcome this with difficulty.

10 **The Central Pillar**	98m	E2

P Crew, M Owen – June 1962 P1: **R O Graham, A Hyslop** – July 1977

A superb climb with some exciting positions, taking a devious line around the right-hand side of the pillar headwall. Protection is reasonable but a bold approach helps on Pitch 2. Start up ***Bridge's Route***.

1 36m (5a). Follow Pitch 1 of ***Bridge's Route*** to the top of the large flake-crack. Climb a thin crack directly up the wall for 9 metres and step left to a belay close to the pinnacle on ***Bridge's Route***.
2 32m (5b). A good pitch to second. Climb the crack above and right of the belay for a couple of metres, until a traverse, on small

holds, leads diagonally rightwards across the wall to a narrow ledge. Move up left, then step airily right around a nose to a small ledge on the light-coloured rib (peg). A shallow groove is climbed for 5 metres, then step right into a second small groove (Friend 1½). Continue up this groove to reach a sloping ledge below an open corner.

3 21m (5b). Traverse delicately across the exposed wall on the right and pull up to a small ledge (peg runner). Move left to a doubtful block, where a long reach leads to a higher ledge, then move right and climb up to reach a grassy bay on the right.

4 9m (4c). Climb the undercut flake-crack on the right of the bay.

11 **Trespasser Groove**	111m	HVS

A R Dolphin, D Hopkins – Sept 1952

A deservedly popular route which offers well protected climbing, often of a strenuous nature. It follows the deep corner, bounding the ***Central Pillar*** on the right, before steepening rocks force the climb out right to finish. Start below a sweep of slabs reached by scrambling 16 metres up an easy rake, from scree at the right-hand side of the crag.

1 25m. Climb the centre of the clean slabs to finish rightwards onto a sloping heather terrace.

2 15m. Traverse up to the left to a ledge and then follow a groove above to the foot of the main corner.

3 27m (4c). Ascend a slab for a short distance until moves left lead into the main corner which is followed to a recess. Go over a bulge to a second recess and continue steeply to a tiny ledge and spike belay.

4 10m (5a). Climb onto a ledge on the right wall of the corner, then continue up a thin crack in the wall above to a large flake. Move up right to a good ledge.

5 10m (5a). A corner on the left is followed to an overhang. Pull awkwardly up to the right and step across rightwards to better holds. Climb directly to a good ledge (***The Waiting Room***).

6 24m (5a). ***Frankland's Crack***. The slightly overhanging crack leads, with interest, onto a slab. Follow the slab up to the left and finish up a steep crack in the left corner.

Hardknott Crag

Grid reference: **228 016**
Altitude: **440m**
Faces: **West**
Rock type: **Borrowdale Volcanic**
Approach time: **5 mins**

A relatively small but impressive crag, (shown as ***Raven Crag*** on OS maps), that lies a few minutes walk from the Eskdale side of the top of Hardknott Pass. It faces west, dries quickly, and offers some excellent climbing, often of a strenuous nature. The centre of the crag consists of steep grooves and cracks, whilst on the right, a blank-looking wall gives climbing of a bolder ilk.

Descent: to the right of the crag.

The routes are described from **right** to **left**.

1 **Copenhagen**	27m	E2

R Matheson – July 1976

A tremendous line up the centre of the clean right-hand wall, with excellent climbing throughout. Start a couple of metres right of *Powerglide*.

(5c). Climb a short wall for a couple of metres then follow a shallow groove that slants slightly right to good holds in the centre of the wall. Continue into the shallow inverted V directly above, then struggle onto a sloping ledge and second niche above this. Climb boldly leftwards over the roof, finishing slightly leftwards.

2 **Powerglide**	30m	E3+

E Cleasby – June 1982

A superb, sustained pitch directly up the left side of the steep wall. Start at the left-hand side of the wall below a slim bottomless groove 6 metres above the ground.

Left: Caroline Fanshawe beneath the roof on Pitch 5 of *Trespasser Groove* (HVS)
Photo: Stephen Reid

(5c). Climb the wall on the right for a couple of metres (wire), then step left to a sloping ledge below the groove. Enter the groove with difficulty, and continue boldly to gain a good hold out left. Climb directly up the wall, passing a good spike, to where a long reach gains an obvious undercut, below a left-facing flake. Step left to a thin crack and follow this to better holds by the left arête: finish easily above.

3 **Not Hard**	30m	HVS+
C J S Bonington, M Thompson – 1964		

An excellent pitch up the long green groove immediately left of the steep wall. Rather unpleasant if the line is greasy.

(5b). Climb the initial groove with difficulty to reach the main corner. Despite its green appearance, it provides sustained climbing with a technical finish.

4 **Intrusion**	34m	HVS
B Smith, J D Wilson – July 1969		

Start at a rounded, shattered nose 3 metres left of *Not Hard*.

1 9m (4c). Climb the steep buttress to a small ledge on the left.

2 25m (5a). Traverse right, and pull over an overhang into a shallow green scoop. Climb straight up to a narrow ledge, and finish up the rib above.

5 **Earl Boethar**	33m	E2+
E Cleasby, M Lynch – May 1982		

A very strenuous route for its grade, but the good protection makes this an excellent test of a climber's fitness - or lack of it! It takes the largest of the square-cut grooves in the centre of the crag. Start at a platform below a wide corner, 6 metres left of *Intrusion*.

(5c). Climb a wide crack in the right wall of the corner to a broken ledge. Ascend the corner above, passing a rectangular block to reach a bulge, overcome this with difficulty to gain a good jam and a 'cheeky' rest below the final roof. Pass this on the left and climb the final short corner.

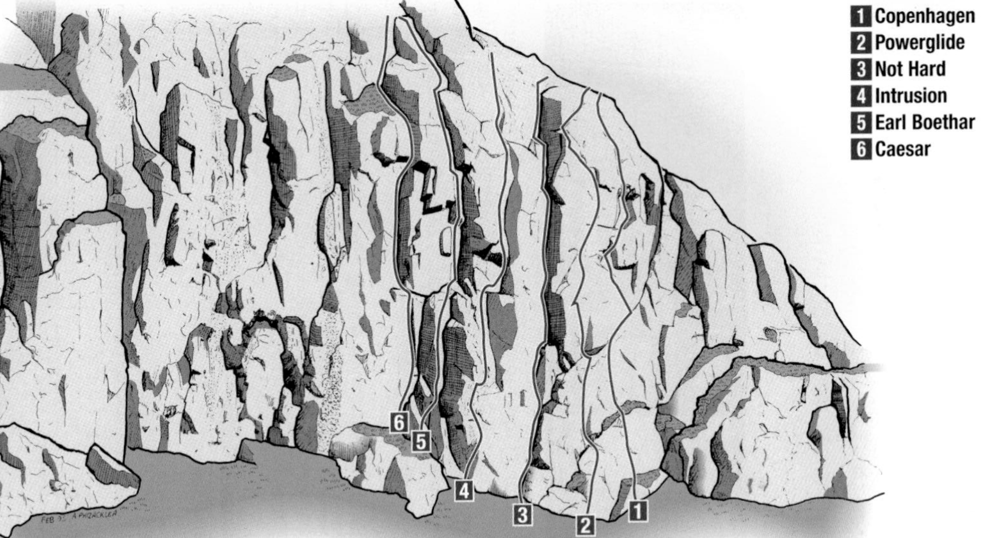

	Route	Grade
1	Copenhagen	E2
2	Powerglide	E3+
3	Not Hard	HVS+
4	Intrusion	HVS
5	Earl Boethar	E2+
6	Caesar	E4–

6	Caesar	30m	E4–
	T Rogers, R O Graham – Sept 1989		

An excellent route up the slim corner to the left of ***Earl Boethar***. The best protection comes with the skilled use of small wires. Begin as for *Earl Boethar*.

(6a). Climb the wide initial corner using the narrow flared V-slot to reach a ledge. The slim corner is followed with escalating difficulty, and only relents once the top groove is reached. Finish up the groove above.

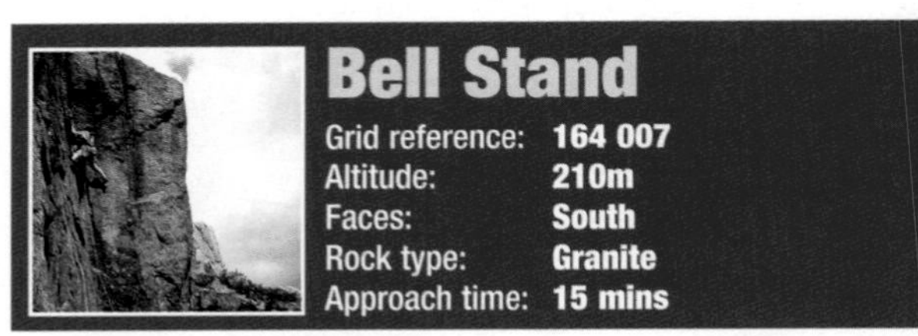

This little granite outcrop is situated high on the hillside above Beckfoot railway station and is clearly visible from the King George IV pub, although from here it looks deceptively small. It is a sunny, quick-drying face of rough rock which bears a close resemblance to a natural gritstone edge.

Park at Beckfoot station (near Stanley Ghyll House, 2 kilometres up the valley from the King George IV pub) and walk back down the road to a quarry. A sketchy path leads just left of the quarry to the crag in 15mins.

1	Innocuous Corner	12m	HVS
	P Whillance – April 1991		

A pleasant route if dry.

(5a). Climb the slim right-facing cornerline directly.

2	Sideslip	17m	E2–
	P Whillance, C Fanshawe – Dec 1991		

A good route starting 2 metres left of the prominent holly.

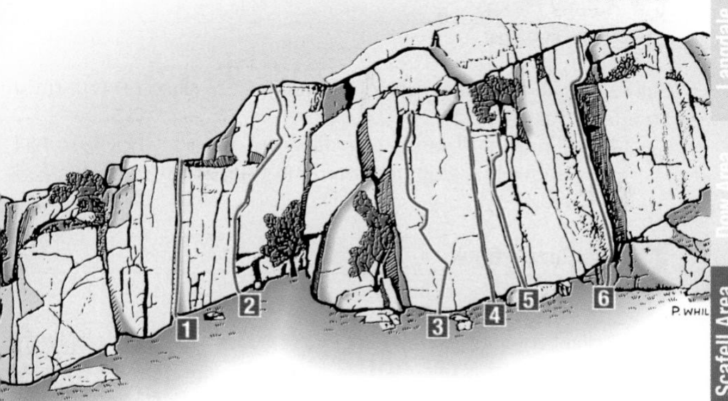

1 Innocuous Corner	HVS	4 Plumbline	VS–
2 Sideslip	E2–	5 Hollow Flakes	MVS
3 Anniversary Waltz	E1+	6 The Puzzle Book	E2

(5c). Climb up to a small triangular overhang, then follow the slim groove on its left and continue up cracks to below the nose. Traverse right to reach a ledge, then step up left and climb a thin crack to the top.

3	**Anniversary Waltz**	16m	E1+

P Whillance – April 1991

A very fine route up the left-hand side of the steep clean wall. Start below the centre of the wall at a thin crack.

(5c). Climb the crack and move left to a ledge on the arête. (This can be easily gained by a direct, but inferior start.) Step up right to a thin crack with difficulty and follow this to the top on better holds.

4	**Plumbline**	15m	VS–

P Whillance – April 1991

(4c). The obvious direct crackline forming the right-hand side of the wall, exiting leftwards above the sloping ledge.

5 **Hollow Flakes**	15m	MVS
P Whillance – April 1991		

Start a couple of metres right of ***Plumbline*** at a slim corner formed by a large flake.

(4b). Climb the flake to a small overhang. Use the horizontal break above to swing right and pull up to a sloping ledge. Exit leftwards.

6 **The Puzzle Book**	14m	E2
P Whillance – April 1991		

An excellent route up the large open cornerline which is deceptively awkward. The start is often wet.

(5c). Follow the corner with escalating interest directly to the top.

Hare Crag

Grid reference: **200 013**
Altitude: **170m**
Faces: **South-West**
Rock type: **Granite**
Approach time: **10 mins**

This crag is a fine collection of steep buttresses and blank open slabs formed of delightfully rough granite. The routes, although short, are clean, fast drying and sunny, allowing a pleasurable afternoon's climbing at all grades. Many of the routes follow cracklines, but these are frequently found to be shallow rounded affairs offering only poor protection.

The crag is prominently displayed on the fellside behind the Youth Hostel as one drives up the valley. Park just off the road directly opposite Wha House Farm, where a 10 minute walk over a low hill leads to the crag. There are several separate buttresses which are described in order as they are approached, working from right to left.

Descents: are obvious.

The routes are accordingly described in order from **right** to **left**.

Right-Hand Slabs

The triangular clean slabs on the right of the crag.

1 **Easy Slab**	24m	VD
Unknown		

A lovely route, not too well protected, starting 5 metres right of the ***Rib***.
Follow the jagged 'lightning crack' up the centre of the slab to a triangular niche, then trend leftwards to reach the top of the ***Rib***.

2 **The Rib**	22m	D
Unknown		

A pleasant open route starting from a well trodden patch immediately below the left-hand rib of the slabs.
Follow the crest of the rib to a thread belay in the grass gully on the left. Abseil from the tree or scramble to the top.

The Lower Buttress

This is a steep wall capped by a slab about 40 metres left of the ***Right-Hand Slabs***.

3 **International Rescue**	16m	E3
A Phizacklea, B McKinley – April 1990		

A great little problem, starting just left of the jagged overhang, 3 metres right of the ***Groove***.
(6a). Gain a diamond-shaped hanging slab from the left, then pull leftwards with difficulty into a short groove to reach a small spike (thin sling). Exit rightwards onto the cracked slab above and finish easily.

4 **The Groove**	15m	E1
E Cleasby, A Phizacklea – Nov 1981		

A sustained little pitch with good protection which follows the obvious dark left-facing groove in the centre of the buttress.

(5b). Climb the groove, pulling out right at the top and finish up the wide crack.

5	Fireball XL5	20m	MVS
	J Daly – Nov 1987		

A very fine route starting at the left side of a large finger of rock, about 6 metres left of the *Groove*.

(4b). Climb the crack to the top of the flake, then follow short, rounded cracks above to a sloping ledge. The slabby corner above leads to the top and a bolt belay. (Gasp!)

The Central Slabs

These magnificent smooth slabs are the main feature of the crag.

6	Slit Wall	23m	HVS
	Unknown		

The prominent central crack in the steep lower wall.

(5a). Climb the crack with a difficult move to reach the slabs above. Follow the easy cracks to the top.

7	Hareless Heart	24m	E1
	A Phizacklea, E Cleasby – Nov 1981		

Good slab climbing which can be quite hare-raising! Start at a large flake on the left-hand side of the steep lower wall.

(5b). Climb the flake and wall above to reach the slab. Climb directly up this until a faint diagonal crease runs up right. Follow this to a tiny overlap (runner), then step back left and finish directly up the rippled slab.

8	Slab Route	28m	S
	D N Greenop, T Baldwin, M Woods – Jan 1971		

A pleasant, delicate route running diagonally rightwards across the slab. Start from the grass ledge above the left side of the steep wall at the top of Pitch 1 of *Jugged Hare*.

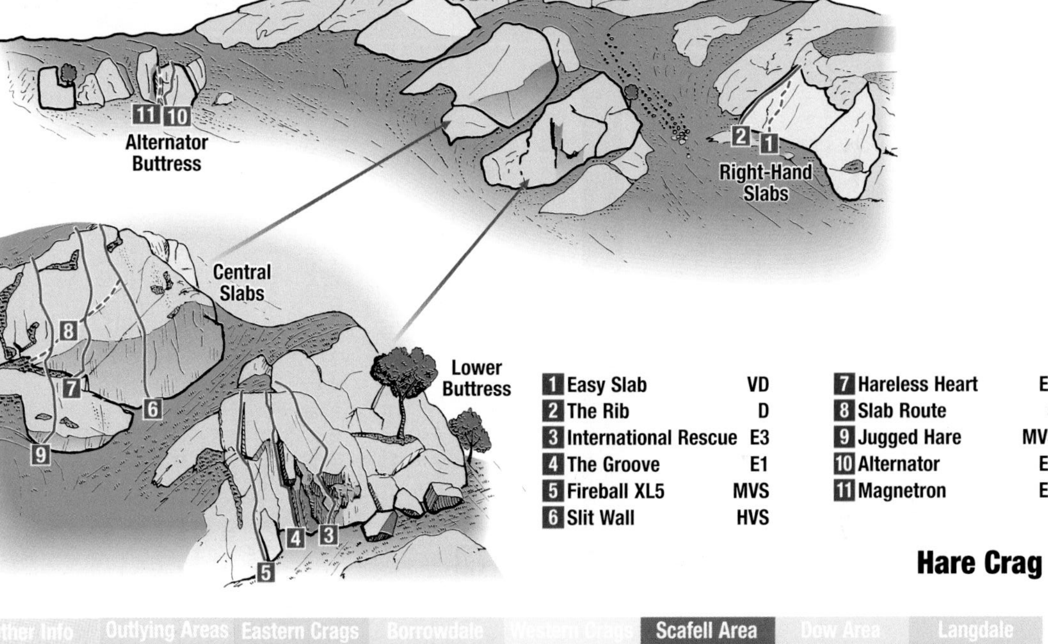

	Route	Grade
1	Easy Slab	VD
2	The Rib	D
3	International Rescue	E3
4	The Groove	E1
5	Fireball XL5	MVS
6	Slit Wall	HVS
7	Hareless Heart	E1
8	Slab Route	S
9	Jugged Hare	MVS
10	Alternator	E3+
11	Magnetron	E2+

Hare Crag

Climb the obvious crack slanting rightwards across the slab to reach a ledge in its centre, where a crackline running to the highest point of the slabs is followed to the top.

9 **Jugged Hare**	28m	MVS
D N Greenop, T Baldwin, M Woods – Jan 1971		

Below the left-hand end of the slabs is a lower subsidiary slab. This fine varied route starts just left of the lowest point of this at a line of small steps in the initial wall.

1 10m (4b). Climb the centre of the slab, passing a poor nut runner, to the grass ledge below the main slab.

2 18m (4a). Gain the obvious curving flake above and climb it, continuing up the rounded cracks to finish.

Alternator Buttress

The steep wall 120 metres left of the ***Central Slabs*** is identified by a large holly on its right-hand side.

10 **Alternator**	17m	E3+
K Phizacklea, J Daly – Nov 1987		

A superb strenuous pitch up the centre of the face, starting just right of *Magnetron*.

(6a). Climb a faint rib to an amazing blocky foothold, then balance across right to finish up a shallow hanging corner.

11 **Magnetron**	15m	E2+
J Daly, K Daly – Nov 1987		

A good sustained line starting in a shallow groove just left of the centre of the wall.

(5c). Climb directly up the shallow groove and follow the increasingly strenuous crack above to good finishing holds out right.

Heron Crag

Grid reference: **222 030**
Altitude: **250m**
Faces: **South-East**
Rock type: **Borrowdale Volcanic**
Approach time: **30 mins**

An excellent valley crag which dries quickly and offers many impressive routes, often of a strenuous nature. The focal point of the crag is the central pillar containing the classic ***Gormenghast***. The right wall looks unappealing at first sight due to a copious tapestry of moss and lichen. Many of the routes, however, retain clean holds and can be enjoyed in spite of their dirty surroundings.

There may be a **Bird Restriction** on part or all of *Heron Crag* from 1st March to 30th June or part thereof. Signs at the crag should inform you, but if in doubt contact details for further information are given in the Access and Conservation section.

The crag is reached from the foot of Hardknott Pass. The steep profile of the buttress is easily seen on the hillside; the best of several approaches being to cross the river at Brotherilkeld and go via Taw House and Scale Beck Bridge. A good, narrow path contours along the hillside to eventually arrive at the foot of the crag.

Descent: traverse leftwards from the top of the crag to reach a wide scree gully.

The routes are described from **left** to **right**.

1 **Sidetrack**	55m	VS

R B Evans, I F Holliwell – Aug 1960

A popular route with an enjoyable main pitch, which makes an ascending traverse beneath the overhangs on the left-hand wall of the crag. Start 6 metres left of a vegetated, dirty gully.

1 8m (4b). Climb a stepped groove and slabs rightwards to a belay in the gully.

2 35m (4c). Gain a ledge, above on the left, and make an ascending leftward traverse until beneath a steep wall, which leads to a groove beneath the overhangs. Continue delicately up left to a sloping ledge and second groove; follow this over a small overhang and pass a second overhang on the right. An easy wall leads to an oak tree.
3 12m (4a). Climb the rib above.

2 Gormenghast | 53m | E1–

L Brown, A L Atkinson – March 1960 P3: **D D Whillans, A Ashworth** – 1961

A classic climb of great character which ascends the front face of the central pillar. The rock is delightfully clean and solid, and the protection is good, except for the start of the second pitch. Start 6 metres right of the dirty gully.
1 10m (4c). Climb the steep clean grey wall directly to a ledge below the main crack.
2 18m (5a). Climb the steep wall a couple of metres left of the main crack on flat holds to where it eases slightly, then traverse right to a good niche. (The main crack can be climbed directly to the niche and is well protected 5b.) From the niche, move up then step left into a groove which leads to a flake belay 6 metres below the holly tree. (A belay can be taken at the tree, but if the peregrine has been nesting, the smell is overpowering.)
3 25m (5a). Climb up to the tree, then step to the right and climb up on good holds past a prominent block. A crack leads to the centre of the headwall, where a thin crack is followed directly up the wall until better holds lead right to a good ledge and tree. Climb straight up to the top.

3 Iago/Titus Combination | 51m | E3

I Singleton, A Jackman (2 points of aid) – July 1965 P3: **A Phizacklea, D R Lampard** – May 1989

This exacting climb takes a direct line up the crag, starting 6 metres right of *Gormenghast*.
1 12m (5b). Climb the obvious clean groove between ***Gormenghast*** and ***Bellerophon***, until a crack near the top of the groove allows a large hold to be reached. Move up to a large grass ledge.
2 21m (6a). Climb the very steep wall boldly to an overhang below a slim groove (peg) then climb the crack in the groove with

Bird restrictions possible between
1st March and 30th June

1	Sidetrack	VS
2	Gormenghast	E1–
3	Iago/Titus	E3
4	Bellerophon	VS+
5	Spec Crack	E1
6	Mean Feat	E3+

difficulty, to reach good holds before moving up to a ledge. Follow the obvious crack first right, then left, to the top of the needle.

3 18m (5c). Stand on a musical (very fragile) flake on the right and step up to obvious undercuts, where a long reach above the overhang reveals a good flake. Step left and climb directly to a tree, finishing as for *Gormenghast*.

4 **Bellerophon**	57m	VS+
O R D Pritchard, B S Schofield – May 1958		

An excellent route taking the long, deep groove defining the right side of the main pillar. The route contains good positive holds, good protection and an inescapable line. Unfortunately, it is extremely mossy and frequently wet, although the holds are always clean. Start at the toe of the arête, 9 metres right of *Gormenghast*.

1 10m (4b). Climb the shallow groove in the arête, left of a square-cut chimney, to a large grass ledge.

2 12m (4c). Make a delicate move to the right to the foot of a steep crack. Ascend the crack to a large grass ledge.

3 13m (4c). Climb the groove until it is possible to step left and belay on the pinnacle at its top.

4 22m (5a). Either step off the top of the pinnacle, or move round a nose on the right and work up a crack until good holds permit a strenuous pull-up. Easier climbing leads to a ledge. Finish up an overhanging crack on small holds and pull out right at the top.

5 **Spec Crack**	58m	E1
J A Austin, E Metcalf – Aug 1961		

An interesting route which breaks through the overhangs 8 metres right of ***Bellerophon***. Worthwhile despite the vegetation.

1 22m (5a). Climb the wall to the overhang, pull strenuously through this and follow the crack past heather patches to a holly tree.

2 12m (4b). The crack on the right leads to a small stance below an overhanging crack.

3 24m (5a). Climb the crack until it is choked with rock; break onto the left wall and ascend to a small ledge. Follow the crack above to the top.

Above: Upper Eskdale, Esk Buttress and Scafell Pike **Photo:** Al Phizacklea

6 **Mean Feat**	54m	E3+

P1: **T W Birkett, R O Graham** – May 1977 P2: **T W Birkett, R O Graham** (one point aid) – July 1977
FFA: **J Lamb, P Botterill** – Sept 1977

An excellent route of absorbing technical interest, climbing the line of the prominent clean streak high in the centre of the wall. Start in a large capped scoop, 20 metres right of ***Bellerophon***.

1 26m (5c). Climb to a ledge at 6 metres, where awkward moves lead into a scoop above on the left (peg runner). Traverse the undercut wall leftwards to the edge, then steeply up until easier moves lead left to a junction with ***Spec Crack***. Follow the thinner, left-hand crack directly above the holly tree to a peg belay, below a long roof.

2 28m (5c). Ascend the wall just left of the belay, moving slightly right to a short bulging section (poor RP runner). A few bold moves lead to a resting place. Step right, and climb the wall above directly to the centre of a long square overhang; pull over this and continue more easily to the top.

Scafell (pronounced Scawfell)

by Al Phizacklea

Left: Luke Steer on *Moss Ghyll Grooves* (MVS–)
Photo: Bill Birkett

Scafell is the second highest mountain in England and its two main crags provide the focal point of Lake District climbing. Throughout the past hundred years these crags have been a forcing ground for standards, and many of the routes are rich in history and legend. The only drawback of these crags is their position, high on the mountain, and therefore subject to the worst conditions that the weather can produce. When it is dry and warm, there is no finer place to climb in England.

Scafell lies close to the central hub of the Lake District and is easily accessible from Wasdale, although it may also be reached from the head of Borrowdale.

The shortest and easiest approach to the crag is from the car park and campsite at the head of Wastwater (182 076), 1 kilometre southwest of Wasdale Head. A good path leaves the valley near Brackenclose (FRCC hut) and follows Lingmell Gill to where it emerges at a broad, grassy boulder-strewn area known as Hollow Stones. Continue up to to a large conspicuous boulder below the crags, a good place to rest and study the topography of the area. (The last reliable water source lies a hundred metres to the left from here.)

On the right is ***Scafell Shamrock***, a lower, subsidiary buttress separated from the main crag by a diagonal gully known as ***Lord's Rake***.

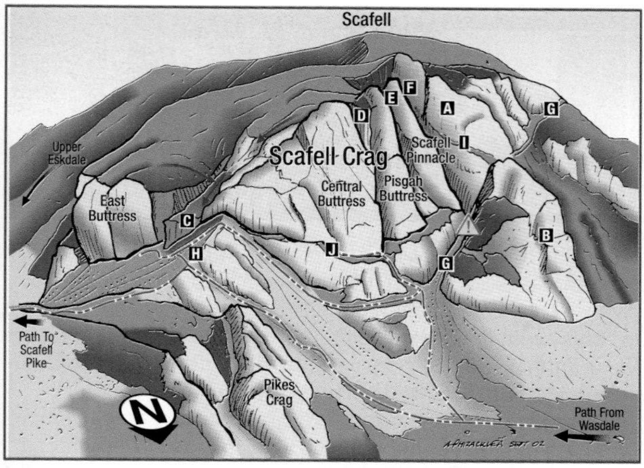

A Deep Ghyll Buttress
B Shamrock
C Broad Stand (descent)
D Moss Ghyll (no descent)
E Steep Ghyll (no descent)
F Deep Ghyll
(no descent down lower half)
G Lord's Rake
(descent not recommended)
H Mickledore
I West Wall Traverse
J Rake's Progress

Straight ahead lies ***Scafell Crag***, with its four main buttresses separated by deeply cut gullies. Left of Scafell Crag is a low col called Mickledore, which must be crossed if the ***East Buttress*** is your goal: from here it is hidden on the other side of the mountain. Finally, to the left of Mickledore lies ***Pikes Crag***, often known by the name of its main buttress as ***Pulpit Rock***.

It takes no more than an hour to reach the large boulder, and all the crags can be reached in a further 20–30mins steep walking up the scree.

The approach from Seathwaite in Borrowdale is made by taking the track to Styhead Pass. Here, a path known as the Corridor Route rises across the hillside on the left, crossing the broad col between Scafell Pike and Lingmell and continues as a faint horizontal path below ***Pikes Crag*** to reach Mickledore. This approach takes 2 to 2½hrs to complete.

Scafell Crag

Grid reference: **209 068**
Altitude: **790m**
Faces: **North**
Rock type: **Borrowdale Volcanic**
Approach time: **1 hr 20 mins**

This is the magnificent large face of rock overlooking the approach walk from Wasdale. At first, the topography of the crag seems complicated, but there are four individual buttresses which are (from left to right): *Central Buttress*, *Pisgah Buttress*, *Scafell Pinnacle* and *Deep Ghyll Buttress*. These are separated by prominent gullies which are named *Moss Ghyll*, *Steep Ghyll* and *Deep Ghyll*.

A good path runs horizontally below the entire crag to link up with the foot of *Lord's Rake*. About 10 to 15 metres above this path is a narrow grassy shelf, called *Rake's Progress*, which runs below the main crag providing access to all the routes. *Rake's Progress* can be gained easily from the foot of *Moss Ghyll*.

Descents: most climbers descend leftwards to reach Mickledore, by scrambling down an awkward rockstep called *Broad Stand* (D, 1802). From the top of the crag, walk down leftwards until a large shelving platform on the right (looking out) can be reached. This is followed to its lower left corner, where a series of polished steps lead to an exit via a squeeze chimney on to the scree on the Eskdale side of Mickledore. This can be treacherous in slippery conditions, when great care should be exercised. (For descents down *Deep Ghyll*, see the notes in the section on *Scafell Pinnacle*.)

The routes are described from **left** to **right**.

Central Buttress

This is the first clean wall right of *Mickledore*, which is identified by the prominent feature of the *Great Flake* in its centre. This entire face provides brilliant steep climbing in an exposed position on good rock.

Scafell Crag – Central Buttress

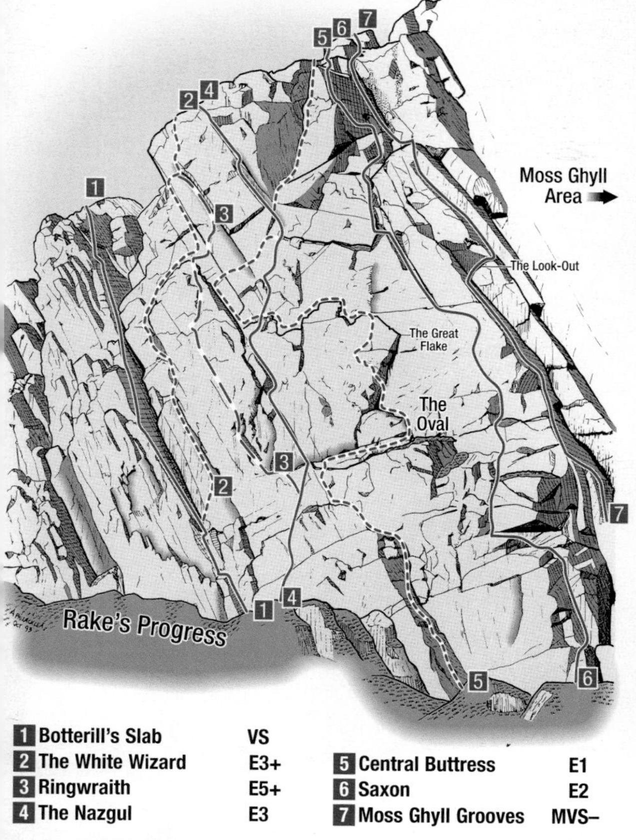

1 Botterill's Slab	VS			
2 The White Wizard	E3+		5 Central Buttress	E1
3 Ringwraith	E5+		6 Saxon	E2
4 The Nazgul	E3		7 Moss Ghyll Grooves	MVS–

1	Botterill's Slab	87m	VS

F W Botterill, H Williamson, J E Grant – June 1903

A compelling line up the narrow light-coloured slab slanting across on the left side of the *Central Buttress*. A fast-drying and deservedly popular route. Start below the foot of the slab.

1 15m (4b). Climb up a short chimney and continue in the same line to the foot of the slab.
2 36m (4c). Climb the slab by its left edge to a platform on the arête. Continue up a thin crack to belay in a recess on the left at the top of the slab. An outstanding pitch.
3 36m. Climb up into the gully on the right and continue up it easily, or choose a line up the left wall to the arête.

2	**The White Wizard**	96m	E3+

C J S Bonington, N Estcourt (6 points of aid) – Sept 1971 FFA: **M Berzins, G Higginson** – 1976

A magical route with varied and interesting climbing, culminating in a tremendous final pitch which leaves you spellbound till the very end. It follows a line of steep grooves and cracks up the wall right of *Botterill's Slab*.
1 15m (4b). Pitch 1 of *Botterill's Slab*.
2 24m (5c). Climb the corner of *Botterill's Slab* for a few metres until a long step right and a steep crack lead to a ledge (peg runner). Climb the shallow corner on the right, until a move left and a crack lead to a ledge.
3 20m (5c). Climb the continuation of the groove with moves on the left wall at half-height, and then an overhanging crack to a good ledge.
4 15m (5b). From the right end of the ledge, move across and up to gain the bottom of a prominent crack. Climb this to a ledge.
5 22m (5c). Pull up round the arête on the right (peg runner) and climb the awkward groove on the right to a small ledge. Step up delicately round the bulge to the right to easy ground.

3	**Ringwraith**	94m	E5+

M Berzins, R H Berzins, C Sowden – May 1977

An excellent route providing sustained climbing up the leaning wall and the slim hanging corner right of the *White Wizard*.
1 18m (4a). Pitch 1 of the *Nazgul*.
2 30m (6b). Climb the short ramp on the left to a bulge and nut runner, where a long reach gains a series of layaway holds above, which lead to a peg. Climb directly up the smooth wall on small holds until a long reach leads to a jug. Step left to a runner and

Left: Luke Steer on one of the classic routes of Scafell, *Botterill's Slab* (VS)
Photo: Bill Birkett

a small ledge above, then continue directly on better holds to a pinnacle belay.

3 10m. Easily up the ramp to belay below Pitch 4 of the ***White Wizard***.

4 36m (6a). Traverse right into the obvious overhanging corner and follow this strenuously to join the ***White Wizard*** at the groove on Pitch 5. Finish up this.

4 **The Nazgul**	84m	E3
L Brown, K Jackson (3 points of aid) – July 1966	FFA: **P Botterill, S Clegg** – June 1975	

A direct line to the left of ***Central Buttress***. A superb, strenuous second pitch contrasts with the delightful, airy last pitch. Start at a short crack just right of ***Botterill's Slab***.

1 18m (4a). Climb the crack and ascend easily rightwards to a flake belay below an obvious thin green crack slanting leftwards.

2 24m (5c). Step left and climb the arduous crack to a resting place in a niche. Swing out left on to a narrow slab and follow it for a few metres until it is possible to climb the wall on the right into the obvious deep corner. Belay by the large flakes above (on ***Central Buttress***).

3 12m (5b). Move right along the flake to a detached pinnacle. Stand on this, then step right into a surprisingly delicate scoop and climb up to a good ledge.

4 30m (5a). Climb the thin crack/ramp on the left to where it widens. Continue up to a bulge then pull over rightwards to gain the higher parallel rampline. Follow this in a superb situation to the top.

5 **Central Buttress**	122m	E1
S W Herford, G S Sansom, C F Holland (using combined tactics) – April 1914 P3: **A Marr, M Tooke** – July 1990 P6: **F G Balcombe, J Wright, J R Files** – June 1934		

This route which weaves its way up the centre of the main face can justifiably claim to be one of the most famous rock climbs in the country. The traditional crux of the route was the ascent of the ***Great Flake***, but following the loss of the crucial chockstone this is avoided by an exposed variation onto the face of the flake. Start just right of a short rocky step in the path below the crag, about 10 metres left of the deep chimney of ***Moss Ghyll***.

1 15m (4b). Climb a narrow slanting ramp up leftwards to a belay at its top.

2 25m (4b). Climb up easily and traverse leftwards to a crack which leads to the left end of a narrow ledge. Traverse right to a larger ledge (the ***Oval***) and belay below the obvious flake-crack.

3 25m (5b). Climb easily to the foot of the ***Great Flake***, and continue for 5 metres to a sloping ledge on the left. An exposed traverse, using a horizontal crack, leads leftwards for 2 metres onto the front face of the flake (runners). Make a difficult move up and then climb more easily to the crest of the flake. Follow the flake leftwards to reach a spacious ledge. The original line directly up the ***Great Flake*** is now E3 (5c).

4 18m. Walk along the ledge and climb an easy ramp to block belays.

5 15m (4c). Descend a little and traverse delicately right past a small pinnacle into a corner. Climb the corner and traverse easily right to a spacious ledge.

6 24m (5a). Climb the thin crack and gangway above the left end of the ledge for about 5 metres and traverse rightwards into a corner. Climb the corner to the top and exit leftwards.

6 **Saxon**	120m	E2
J Eastham, E Cleasby – July 1976	P1: **A Mullan, H Thompson** – July 1939	

Another magnificent climb which has achieved the status of a modern classic. The main pitch climbs the wall and slanting crack right of the ***Great Flake***. Start just left of the foot of the deep chimney of ***Moss Ghyll***.

1 42m (5a). Start up the corner; then climb the rib and go up to a large ledge below a triangular roof. Traverse left for 4 metres to a corner and climb this and the wall above, bearing left, to the ***Oval***. Belay 10 metres right of the ***Great Flake*** below a short corner.

2 39m (5c). Climb the corner and move left a little. Continue up the wall and then climb diagonally right to the arête and a small ledge (runner). Traverse back left on tiny stepped ledges; then climb straight up to the obvious crack. Climb the crack (awkward when wet) and the groove above, then step left to a ledge.

3 39m (5b). Climb the mossy corner-crack behind and continue to a second short corner, climb this and pull out right. Step left onto the headwall above the overhang and climb up leftwards to the arête and follow this to the top.

7 Moss Ghyll Grooves | 79m | MVS–

H M Kelly, B Eden-Smith, J B Kilshaw – July 1926

A delicate climb of outstanding interest following the slanting groove system just right of the main face. The crucial sections are short and well protected, although they are probably as difficult as anything on ***Botterill's Slab***. Start about 25 metres above ***Rake's Progress***, from a grass ledge which runs from the right into ***Moss Ghyll***. A slanting groove runs up to the left.

1 17m. The groove leads to a good ledge at the same horizontal level as the ***Oval***. The overhanging block on the right is then climbed to a ledge below the main corner.

2 20m (4c). Climb 3 metres up the corner and traverse delicately left to a small ledge overlooking the main wall of ***Central Buttress***. Ascend the arête, leading back to the groove. Go up this and the narrow slab, then traverse right into the next groove (the *Look-Out*).

3 24m (4a). The slab ahead is climbed first on its right side, then on the left, and finally straight up.

4 18m. Climb the left wall of the gully for 5 metres and break out to a large ledge on the left. The steep wall above is delicate at its start and leads to the summit ridge.

8 Slab and Groove Route | 72m | VS+

R J Birkett, L Muscroft – Aug 1948

A fine route with a superb first pitch which starts up the big slab, capped by an overhang, on the left side of ***Moss Ghyll***, opposite ***Tennis Court Wall***. Start at the top of Pitch 1 of ***Moss Ghyll***.

1 33m (4c). Climb the groove on the right side of the slab for 6 metres; then traverse left to the foot of a thin crack which is climbed to a pocket near the arête. Follow the edge for a couple of metres and traverse left into a groove, which is climbed until level with a recess on the left. Go back right into a corner immediately above the overhangs that cap the slab.

2 39m (4a). Climb the groove; then easily to the top.

Scafell Crag – Moss Ghyll Area

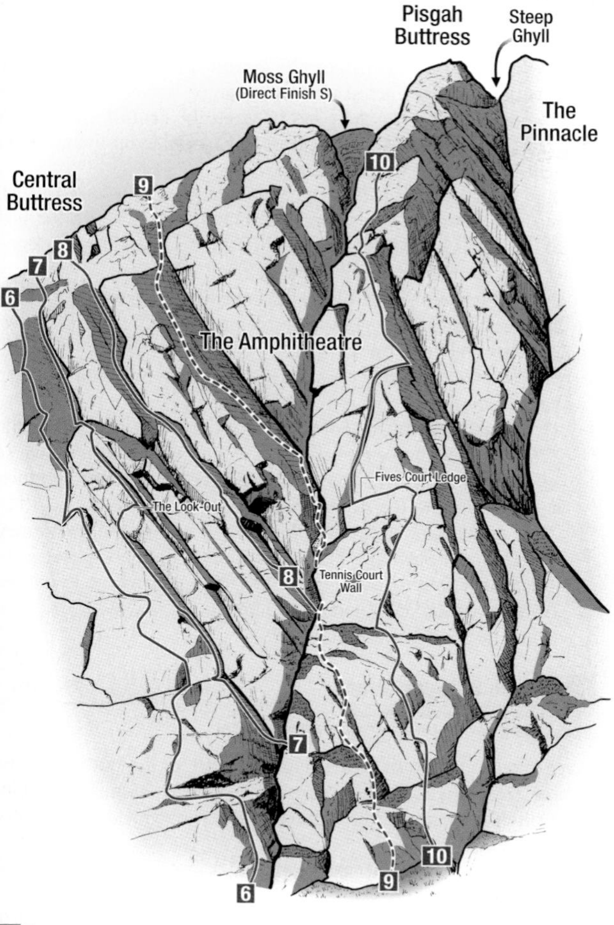

6 Saxon	**E2**		
7 Moss Ghyll Grooves	**MVS–**	**9 Moss Ghyll**	**S**
8 Slab and Groove Route	**VS+**	**10 Pisgah Buttress Direct**	**S**

9 Moss Ghyll | 120m | S

J N Collie, G Hastings, J W Robinson – Dec 1892

A route for all seasons, which can be ascended in any conditions, by many variations. The interest is most sustained in wet conditions, or under snow and ice. The gully lies between the ***Central*** and ***Pisgah Buttresses***. Start from ***Rake's Progress***, and scramble up the grass on the right of the lower chimneys.

1 50m. Although this is one of the finest gullies in the Lake District, most parties avoid the several short chimney pitches in the bed of the ghyll and instead scramble up the easier and much cleaner slabs on the right flank. Only Difficult.

2 8m. *Tennis Court Wall*. Climb the impending broken crack in the steep right wall of the gully, about 5 metres right of a mossy cave. Belay on the ledge on the right.

3 8m. Traverse delicately back left into the ghyll and walk into the back of a cave.

4 17m. Climb into the roof of the cave and traverse left through the ***Attic Window*** above the large chockstone, where a thin traverse left (the ***Collie Step***) leads to a dirty grooveline. Step left and then continue up into the ***Amphitheatre***.

5 27m. At the back of the ***Amphitheatre*** is a deep, black chimney (***Direct Finish*** S), with a blunt rib rising up the slabs 5 metres to its left. This rib is followed by a crack to large blocks at 15 metres. Traverse left and climb an easy chimney.

6 10m. The short corner on the left.

10 Pisgah Buttress Direct | 101m | S

P1–3: **C D Frankland, V W Brown** – April 1920
P4–5: **O G Jones, G D Abraham, A P Abraham** – April 1898

A very fine route which weaves up the centre of the buttress to the right of ***Moss Ghyll***. Start from a grass shelf about 15 metres right of ***Moss Ghyll*** near the middle of the buttress at a right-facing, shallow corner.

1 24m. Climb the corner and continue delicately in the same line for 12 metres. Work right and over an awkward bulge to a little slab, which leads to an easier groove slanting from right to left. Up the groove to a ledge and flake belay.

2 21m. Climb the slab above the belay, followed by a short upward traverse to the right under some doubtful looking blocks. Continue

up a corner, then a staircase leads to a deep crevasse on the right overlooking *Steep Ghyll*.

3 10m. Traverse left along a horizontal ledge to the ***Fives Court*** ledge and belay beneath a corner-crack.

4 19m. Climb the awkward corner-crack followed by an easy slab-by groove which leads to blocks on the edge of the buttress overlooking *Steep Ghyll*.

5 27m. Starting with a difficult pull-up to a ledge, follow the ridge above to its end. Scramble up easy-angled slabs.

Scafell Pinnacle

This is the conical buttress between ***Steep Ghyll*** and ***Deep Ghyll***. The ***Pinnacle*** has two summits, ***High Man*** and ***Low Man***. Most of the routes lead to ***Low Man***, from which the ***High Man*** is reached by the *Knife-Edge Arête*.

The rock of the ***Pinnacle*** is generally very clean and solid, and most of the routes up the front face are fast drying. Few climbers appreciate the sunny nature of the ***Pinnacle***. Those routes facing ***Deep Ghyll*** receive the sun after mid-day, and in the early evening sunshine, the slabs on the front face provide some of the most enjoyable climbing on the mountain. The ***Pinnacle Terrace*** is the highest in the series of grassy ledges below the ***Pinnacle***, which is easily reached by scrambling. Most routes start from this feature.

Descents: the summit plateau is reached from ***High Man*** by descending into ***Jordan Gap*** (10m, M), the cleft which separates ***High Man*** from the top of ***Pisgah Buttress***. Traverse easily around to the left to reach the top of the mountain. To descend to Mickledore, trend leftwards to pick up a faint track which leads down to ***Broad Stand*** (see the description on page 192 in the ***Scafell Crag*** introduction). In the past, most climbers would have descended down ***Deep Ghyll*** which is to the right of the ***Pinnacle***. Descend the eroded funnel until it opens out by an impressive chimney on the left (looking out). Here a small cairned hump on the left side of the gully bed indicates the start of the ***West Wall Traverse***, which leads down across the left wall until it meets ***Lord's Rake***. This has always been loose, and recently a large rockfall has left it even looser. ***Broad Stand*** is probably preferable.

The first route starts from the bed of ***Steep Ghyll***, which is easily reached by scrambling up the lower rocks.

11 Slingsby's Chimney Route | 103m | VD

W C Slingsby, G Hastings, E Hopkinson, W P Haskett-Smith (with combined tactics) – July 1888

The easiest way up the ***Pinnacle***, this route has a fine, classic atmosphere and good situations. Only Very Difficult for a few metres at the start of Pitch 3, the rest is Moderate. Start about 60 metres up the bed of ***Steep Ghyll***, just below where it steepens and narrows.

1 22m. Easy rocks, ledges and slabs on the right wall of the gill lead to the ***Crevasse***.

2 12m. Step awkwardly across the ***Crevasse*** and climb a short slab to the foot of ***Slingsby's Chimney***.

3 36m. The undercut chimney is very difficult to start but soon relents. Follow the continuation of the chimney and scramble to the top of ***Low Man***.

4 33m. The ***Knife-Edge Arête*** is ascended, followed by fine climbing up the crest to the top of ***High Man***.

12 Hopkinson's Gully | 78m | MVS

S W Herford, G S Sansom – June 1912

An excellent, delicate route which follows the shallow, open corner running up the centre of the buttress. Start from the extreme left end of the ***Pinnacle Terrace*** about 10 metres from ***Steep Ghyll***. The foot of the corner is guarded by a 2 metre wall, which has a little pyramid of rock to its left.

1 24m (4b). Climb the short wall to the right of the small pyramid of rock. The corner above is followed, finishing with a square chimney which is climbed to a ledge on the right. Sustained and not too well protected.

2 21m (4a). Continue leftwards up the shallow bed of the groove finishing up a wide crack which splits the slab.

3 9m. The chimney above leads to the ***Crevasse*** on ***Slingsby's Chimney Route***.

4 24m (4a). Ascend the cracked slab to the left of ***Slingsby's Chimney***, followed by a corner crack on the right, to the top. Move down left; then climb up and to the right to ***Low Man***.

Scafell Crag – Pinnacle Face

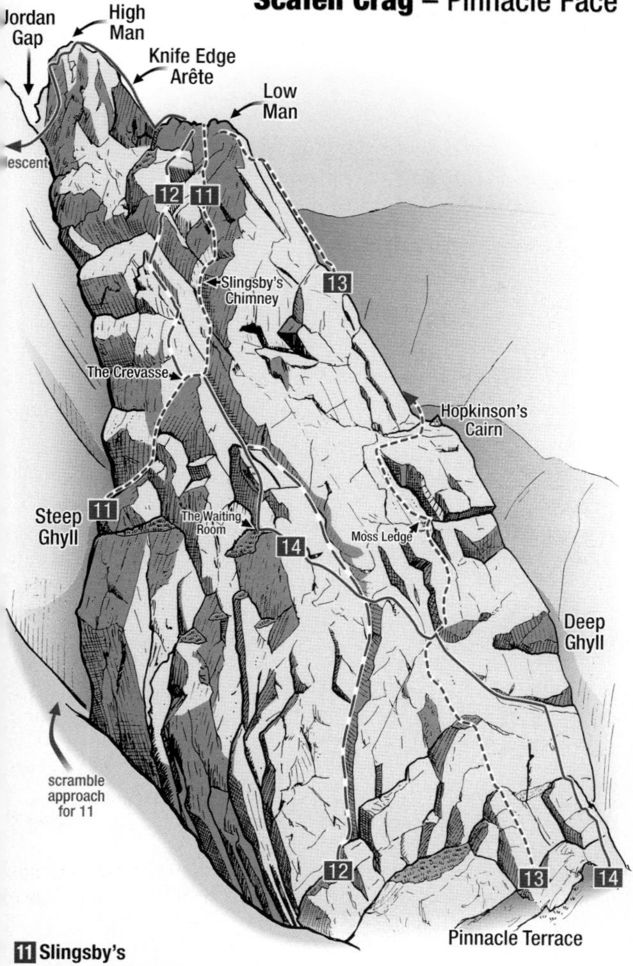

Jordan Gap
High Man
Knife Edge Arête
Low Man
escent
12 11
Slingsby's Chimney
13
The Crevasse
Hopkinson's Cairn
Steep Ghyll 11
The Waiting Room
14
Moss Ledge
Deep Ghyll
scramble approach for 11
12
13
14
Pinnacle Terrace

11	**Slingsby's Chimney Route**	**VD**
12	**Hopkinson's Gully**	**MVS**
13	**Moss Ledge Direct & Jones's Arête**	**MVS**
14	**Jones's Route Direct from Lord's Rake**	**HS**

13 Moss Ledge Direct and Jones's Arête | 93m | MVS

F Graham, G M Wellburn – Sept 1925 P7: **O G Jones, G P Abraham, A D Abraham** – April 1896

A superb route with slab and rib climbing that gives one of the finest outings of its standard in the Lake District. Start 6 metres left of the edge of ***Deep Ghyll*** at the top of a grassy trod, at the foot of a small buttress lying against the slabs directly below some grass ledges.

1 12m. The face of the small buttress is climbed to reach a grass ledge.

2 9m (4c). A couple of metres to the left, a rib on the wall leads, with difficulty, to the grassy niche at the end of Pitch 1 of ***Jones's Route Direct***.

3 15m (4b). Follow a diagonal fault cutting up through a nose on the right and step onto slabs which are followed to ***Moss Ledge***, below a left-facing corner

4 12m (4a). Climb the steep slab ahead, bearing slightly left, which leads to ***Hopkinson's Cairn*** ledge, the best belay being on its left side.

5 21m (4a). The rock on the extreme edge of the ***Pinnacle*** overlooking ***Deep Ghyll*** is climbed to a ledge. Several possible lines.

6 6m (4c). *Bad Corner*. This is a shallow slabby left-facing corner which has a notorious sloping ledge at mid-height. Either go directly up the corner on the left, or climb the slab on its right, moving rightwards.

7 18m (4a). ***Jones's Arête***. Go straight up, usually on the left side. A second steepening soon eases and leads to the top of ***Low Man***.

14 Jones's Route Direct from Lord's Rake | 54m+ | HS

O G Jones, G T Walker – April 1898

A diagonal line running leftwards from the bottom right of the ***Pinnacle***. It is reached by scrambling up slabs and ledges, from the right-hand end of ***Pinnacle Terrace***, to some detached blocks and a good thread on the edge overlooking ***Deep Ghyll***.

1 15m. The *Gangway*. Go delicately up to stand on the slabby ramp, then follow this leftwards and continue up a slab to a grassy niche. Care is needed to protect the second.

2 21m. Go straight up, making for a rock scar at 9 metres. Step left into the shallow groove of ***Hopkinson's Gully***, up it to a vibrating flake, then diagonally left to a recess called the ***Waiting Room***.

Left: Sunrise over Scafell as seen from Wasdale **Photo:** Al Phizacklea

Langdale Dow Area Scafell Area Western Crags Borrowdale Eastern Crags Outlying Areas Other Info

Scafell Pinnacle – Deep Ghyll Face

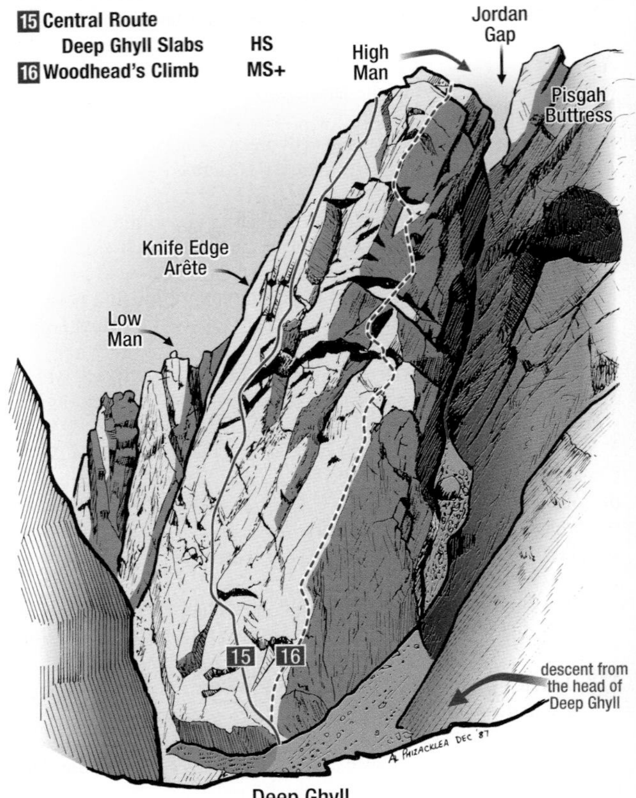

3 **9m.** Climb up into the cave on the right. From its roof a triangular ledge projects. This is the ***Mantelshelf***, which gives the traditional, precarious crux. It is followed by the ***Toe Traverse***, rightwards, to join the wide crack on Pitch 2 of ***Hopkinson's Gully***.

4 **9m.** The chimney above leads to the ***Crevasse***.

5 Finish up either Pitches 3 and 4 of ***Slingsby's Chimney Route***, or Pitch 4 of ***Hopkinson's Gully***.

The next two routes climb the slabby upper face of the *Pinnacle*, which overlooks *Deep Ghyll* directly opposite the *Great Chimney*. This point is easily reached from the descent down *Deep Ghyll*.

15 **Central Route – Deep Ghyll Slabs**	51m	HS

H M Kelly, G S Bower, R E W Pritchard – Aug 1920

A fine route which starts as for *Woodhead's Climb*.

1 18m. Go diagonally left across the slab, crossing a little overlap to reach a pile of blocks.

2 18m. Climb straight up the slab to a niche, in the line of overhangs, at 9 metres. An awkward pull over this is followed by a narrow slab on the face on the right which leads to a grass ledge.

3 15m. The steep overlapping slabs immediately left of the grassy gully give an interesting finish.

16 **Woodhead's Climb**	45m	MS+

P1: **A G Woodhead, W L Collinson** – Aug 1907 P2: **S W Herford, S F Jeffcoat** – July 1913

One of the best climbs of its length in the area. Start at the base of the blunt arête, formed where the *Deep Ghyll* slabs meets the wall coming down from *Professor's Chimney*. (This is the dirty chimney separating the *Pinnacle* from the main hillside).

1 24m. Follow the arête, very delicately at first, (easier on the *Deep Ghyll* side) to a possible stance at 9 metres. Continue up the poorly protected arête to a large grassy recess beneath the huge overhangs.

2 21m. Climb into a corner on the left and cross the slabs above to the right to a small ledge. Continue straight up for a few metres, over a bulge, and trend left to turn the next overhang (steep and exposed, but well protected). Follow easier rocks up the crest to *High Man*.

East Buttress

Grid reference: **210 067**
Altitude: **750m**
Faces: **East and South-East**
Rock type: **Borrowdale Volcanic**
Approach time: **1 hr 30 mins**

Left: Joe Grinbergs on *Centaur* (HVS+)
Photo: Stephen Reid

The ***East Buttress*** is a formidable crag found on the Eskdale side of Mickledore, where the sheer size and steepness of its structure forms an impressive sight. The rock is excellent, being both sound and rough, with few loose sections, although perched blocks at the top of the crag do pose a potential hazard. The crag has a wet reputation as many of the natural lines carry drainage from the hillside above, but the exposed walls dry fairly quickly. An early start is recommended as the left end of the crag stays in the sun until early afternoon.

For approach details, see the **Scafell Introduction** on page 190. Those climbers approaching from Wasdale or Borrowdale will have to cross over the col of Mickledore from where the crag can be reached in 2mins. Sacks are usually left on Mickledore (in the sun) or below the right-hand side of the crag, at a small walled enclosure.

Descents: those climbers who wish to return to the left-hand side of the crag (for ***Ichabod***, etc) should trend left above the crag and descend an easy gully, returning along a good path running horizontally below the crag.

The normal descent is by striking up and slightly rightwards from the top of the crag, where an easy rock chimney leads down into the upper part of ***Mickledore Chimney***, which should not be

East Buttress – Right Hand Side

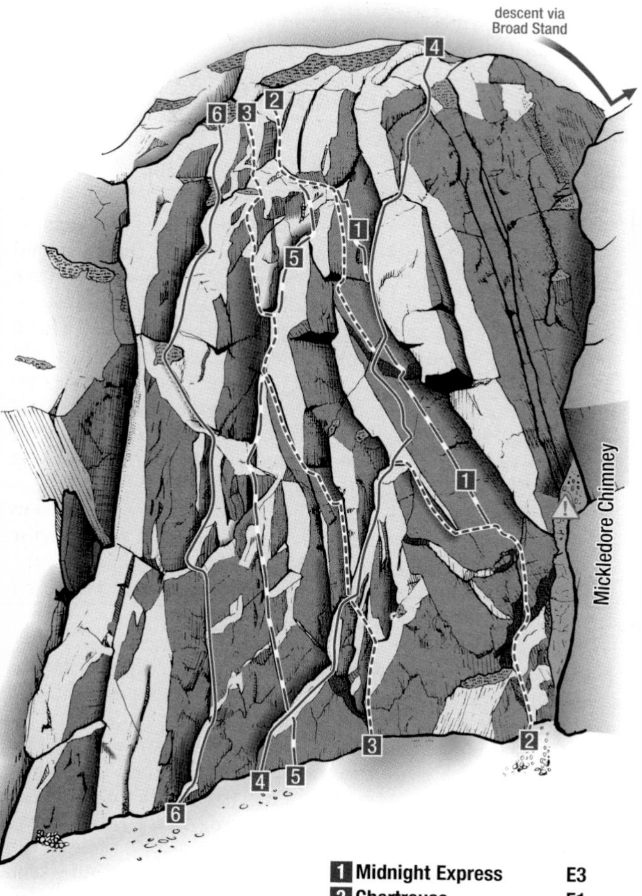

	Route	Grade
1	Midnight Express	E3
2	Chartreuse	E1
3	The Fulcrum	VS+
4	Mickledore Grooves	VS
5	Leverage	E1–
6	Dyad	E3

descended. The path continues on the other side of this and leads down and left to ***Broad Stand***; follow this to Mickledore. Care should be exercised to prevent loose stones from being dislodged down *Mickledore Chimney*.

The first prominent feature of the crag is a large, smooth slab which starts at the bottom of ***Mickledore Chimney***.

1 Midnight Express	45m	E3
P Botterill, J Lamb – July 1979		

A superb route with two contrasting pitches, a long and very committing slab followed by a short, technical but well-protected top pitch. Start at the foot of ***Mickledore Chimney***.

1 36m (5b). Climb up ***Chartreuse*** to the grass ledge and then climb the centre of the slab to stand in an obvious triangular hold. Move awkwardly left for a couple of metres and climb up over a small overlap to the second, larger overlap. Move back right and pull through the bulge to join ***Mickledore Grooves*** (Pitch 2) at the diagonal crack above the bulge. Climb directly to a large block and step right to belay in the corner.

2 9m (6a). Move back left to the block and climb the shallow groove above, moving left to the top of the crack on ***Chartreuse***.

2 Chartreuse	54m	E1
R Smith, D Leaver – May 1958		

Good climbing with some memorable situations. The serious first pitch across the clean slab is contrasted by a strenuous and awkward top crack. Start at the foot of ***Mickledore Chimney***.

1 27m (5a). Climb rightwards up a diagonal break parallel with the gully bed to a grass ledge where an obvious hand-ledge runs leftwards across the slab. Make a thin move left from its end and climb the shallow groove to the large ledge at the end of Pitch 1 ***Mickledore Grooves***.

2 27m (5b). Step onto a ledge on the slab to the right. After stepping left follow a diagonal crack over a bulge (as for ***Mickledore Grooves***). Step back left and climb up to a resting place on the left of the huge block. Traverse right and climb the brutal crack to the top.

3 The Fulcrum

54m	VS+

K Jackson, J Adams – June 1968

A pleasant climb which winds its way through an area of steep rock. Start about 15 metres left of ***Mickledore Chimney*** at the first break in the wall below a short, open chimney.

1 15m (4c). Climb up for 5 metres until a sloping ramp on the right can be entered. Climb the groove to where ***Mickledore Grooves*** (Pitch 1) crosses it. Small stance.

2 18m (4c). Ascend the recessed wall on the left to awkwardly gain a slab. Traverse horizontally left across the slab, under an overhang, to a pair of cracks. Climb these to the base of a groove and follow this to a stance on its left rib.

3 21m (4b). Continue up the groove to the overhang and take the steep crack on the left. Pull out right at the top, then move left and climb to the top.

4 Mickledore Grooves

67m	VS

C F Kirkus, I M Waller, M Pallis – May 1931

One of the best routes of its standard in the Lakes, following a sustained diagonal line to finish with a long pitch across the top of the large slab. Start about 8 metres left of the ***Fulcrum*** at the foot of a rightward slanting gangway.

1 25m (4c). A short overhanging wall leads to a slab on the right which is ascended to the foot of twin grooves. Climb the left-hand groove for 5 metres and make an awkward step right into the right-hand groove. This is climbed to a ledge with a large block.

2 42m (4c). Move onto a ledge on the slab to the right. Step left and follow a diagonal crack to the right, over a bulge, on good holds. Climb up and right to a groove; follow it until it steepens and traverse right to a sloping ledge. Move around the corner on the right and continue horizontally for 9 metres to a mossy opening which leads to the top.

5 Leverage

48m	E1–

R Smith, D Leaver – May 1958

A couple of metres right of the start of ***Mickledore Grooves***, a line of thin cracks goes up the crag. These provide good, steep and sustained climbing with excellent protection. Start just right of ***Mickledore Grooves***.

1 22m (5b). Climb the initial crack, crossing the ramp of ***Mickledore Grooves***, and follow the steep crack above to a slab on the right. Step left onto a bulge and follow the cracks over two more bulges to an easier chimney and a stance.

2 26m (5a). Take the groove above and move right into the corner. Climb this, traverse right under the obvious roof and climb up onto a slab. Continue to the top.

6 **Dyad**	63m	E3
K Jackson, C Read (some aid) – June 1968	FFA: **J Lamb, P Botterill** – June 1974	

A good, strenuous climb, following an entertaining crack on Pitch 1. Start 5 metres left of ***Mickledore Grooves*** at a small steep ramp.

1 21m (6a). Climb the delicate ramp and pull out right. Climb the crack above to a poor ledge and follow the thin crack above to a ledge on the left with a peg and low nut belays.

2 18m (5c). Move up to the groove above and follow it until a step right can be made onto the rib. Climb this for 3 metres, then step left and follow a slab to a ledge.

3 24m (4b). The easy crack on the right.

To the left of ***Dyad*** is a small walled enclosure. Beyond this, the ground drops away and the crag becomes incredibly steep and often wet. At the left-hand side of the overhanging wall is a series of impressive leaning cornerlines. ***Lost Horizons*** is the largest, central groove in this area.

7 **Shere Khan**	99m	E5
E Cleasby, R Matheson (one rest point) – May 1977 FFA: **R Fawcett** – 1979 P4: **E Cleasby, R Matheson** – Aug 1983		

This magnificent bold climb takes the rightward-slanting groove and rampline, right of ***Lost Horizons***. Scramble up the lower rocks right of ***Lost Horizons*** to a ledge below a steep groove with 2 peg runners at 6 metres.

1 24m (6a). Climb the groove and pull out rightwards with difficulty to gain the sloping ramp. Follow this to its end, where a low runner can be placed, and climb the serious groove above to pull out right onto a sloping ledge.

East Buttress – Central Area

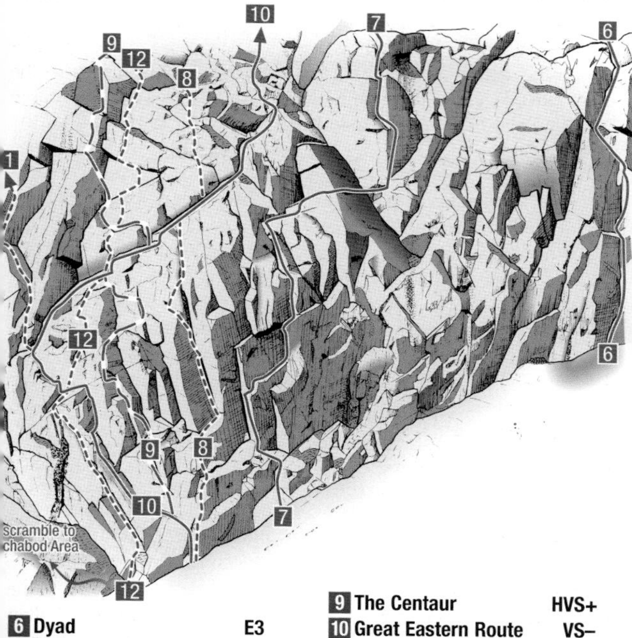

6 Dyad	**E3**	**9 The Centaur**	**HVS+**
7 Shere Khan	**E5**	**10 Great Eastern Route**	**VS–**
8 Lost Horizons	**E4+**	**11 The Yellow Slab**	**HVS–**
		12 Chiron	**E3**

2 21m (5c). Climb the obvious steep groove above and continue up a mossy crack to belay on the ledge system.

3 27m (5a). Move across to the obvious mossy steep corner. Climb this and break out rightwards at its top. Alternatively, for a better finish, traverse right around the wall to a white slab, which can be crossed to reach the base of a steep prow hanging above the slab.

4 27m (6a). Climb easily to the foot of the prow. Gain a thin crack on the right wall of the rib and follow it until a move left leads into the base of a shallow niche on the edge. Climb up to a sloping ledge on the left and follow the long broad groove to finish on the right. This pitch only applies if the alternative Pitch 3 is climbed.

8 **Lost Horizons**	69m	E4+

P Livesey, J Lawrence (one point of aid) – Sept 1976 FFA: **R H Berzins, M Browell** – June 1982

This is the central and largest leaning groove on this section of the crag, which gives superb and varied climbing in very impressive positions. Start at an opening 5 metres right of the lowest part of the crag.

1 17m (4c). Climb up then trend rightwards up slabs to a short wall. Up this and the slab above to belay on a slab, at the foot of the largest corner.

2 37m (6b). Climb the strenuous corner to a ledge which is deceptively unbalancing. Continue up (peg runner) to below the narrow V-niche and traverse left to a ledge (crux). Move back right to regain the crackline above the corner with difficulty, and climb up to the ramp of *Great Eastern*. Block belay on the right.

3 15m (5c). Climb the crack which splits the overhanging wall above.

9 **The Centaur**	90m	HVS+

L Brown, S Read – June 1960

A magnificent climb, which weaves its way up the left-hand set of grooves just at the point where the whole crag bends round to form the left-hand face. An intricate line which can be awkward to follow. Start as for *Lost Horizons*.

1 18m (4b). Climb up *Great Eastern* to the ledge on the left, then step up right and follow a light-coloured, left-trending groove to a good ledge. Continue up the cracked wall to a stance.

2 14m (5a). Climb the corner for 3 metres and move left onto the very edge of the buttress. Follow this for 5 metres then traverse back right crossing the groove to a stance.

3 15m (5a). Move right and climb a short corner parallel to the main groove until a ledge on the left can be gained. Traverse left along the ledge to rejoin the main groove and climb this to join *Great Eastern*. Go up the step in the slab above and belay.

4 18m (4c). Traverse 5 metres right and climb a short groove to a ledge which runs across an impending wall just above. Follow this leftwards and upwards to a large green slab near the corner.

5 25m (4c). Climb steeply up to the left and traverse behind the detached pinnacle to a ledge. Step up to the left and climb back right to two more poised pinnacles and a ledge. Layback the spectacular crack to the top.

10 Great Eastern Route | 88m | VS–

M Linnell, S H Cross – Aug 1932

A fine climb that wanders up the buttress in an impressive setting. The technical difficulty is not great but care should be taken to protect the second. Start at an opening 5 metres to the right of the lowest part of the crag, as for *Lost Horizons*.

1 12m. Easy rocks are followed by a walk to the left.

2 28m (4c). Ascend the cracked slab slanting up to the left to bulging rocks at 6 metres. An overhang is passed by using a layback move; a little higher is a ledge. Traverse left across the slab and climb the corner. Step round left onto the face and climb up onto a good stance.

3 9m (4b). The steep cracks ahead lead to a stance below a nook.

4 24m (4b). Cross the slab on the right and go up the step. Ascend a little on good holds and continue the rising traverse rightwards to a crevasse.

5 15m (4a). Three metres higher is a shelf below a corner, climb either the left wall or the chimney on the right to a ledge. Climb up and round the corner on the right to a ledge at the top of a large white slab.

11 The Yellow Slab | 90m | HVS–

M Linnell, H Pearson (1 point of aid) – Sept 1933 FFA: **R J Birkett, L Muscroft** – Aug 1938

Superb climbing in a magnificent situation, taking a long leftward rising traverse from the toe of the buttress to the top of *Ichabod*. Start as for *Great Eastern Route*.

1 40m (4c). Pitches 1 and 2 of *Great Eastern Route*.

2 30m (4c). The crack on the left is climbed to a ledge at the foot of the *Yellow Slab*. Climb this directly at first, then leftwards until it ends. Move left and follow an exposed crack until a belay can be taken on an obvious shelf on the left.

3 20m (4c). Move left round the corner, carefully using a doubtful flake, then working diagonally leftwards across the exposed wall, keeping a few metres below the overhangs, to the top.

East Buttress – Left Hand Side

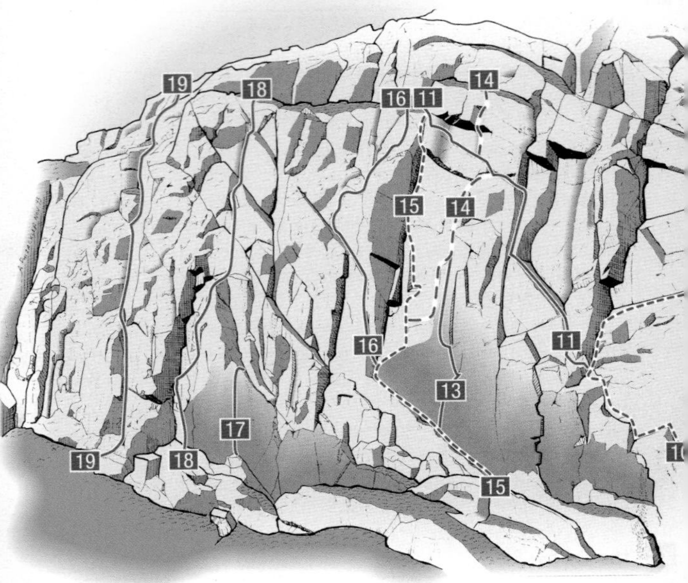

10 Great Eastern Route	VS–			
11 The Yellow Slab	HVS–		16 Phoenix	E1
13 Borderline	E7–		17 The Almighty	E5+
14 Roaring Silence	E3–		18 Hell's Groove	E1–
15 Ichabod	E2		19 Trinity	HVS+

12 Chiron | 77m | E3

A Phizacklea, A Rowell, J L Holden – May 1990

An excellent route taking in the clean wall left of the *Centaur* in its lower half. Start just left of *Great Eastern Route*.

1 25m (5b). Scramble leftwards to reach a thin flake system in the steep wall just left of the initial groove of *Great Eastern*. Follow the flake, past a hollow section, then traverse leftwards above a vegetated waterfall. Pull up to belay in a sloping recess on *Great Eastern*.

2 16m (5c). Move right to the apex of the slab, then pull up strenuously to reach a narrow sloping ledge system. Climb into a shallow recess above (Friend ½ on left) and climb the wall on the left on small holds to exit precariously onto a smooth glacis. Step left and up to a belay on the slab of ***Great Eastern***.

3 9m (5c). Above a step on the belay slab is a short steep wall. Climb this to a horizontal ledge on Pitch 4 of the ***Centaur***, and overcome the bulge above on the right to another large sloping slab.

4 27m (5c). Walk right and pull up to a crack running diagonally leftwards in the overhanging wall above. Follow this strenuously to a point 3 metres short of the corner on the left. A short steep flake and crack above leads to a grass ledge. Follow the corner behind to the top.

From the lowest point of the crag, where ***Great Eastern*** starts, the crag bends leftwards to form the South-East Face of the buttress.

The climbs to the left of ***Great Eastern*** start from a system of ledges and terraces above a broken mass of rock and vegetation. This is reached by unpleasant scrambling, diagonally up and leftwards across steep grassy steps from the lowest point of the crag. From here, a path runs along a terrace below the rest of the crag.

13 **Borderline**	36m	E7–

C Sowden, M Berzins – June 1986

An awe-inspiring route which climbs the incredible curving flake up the centre of the overhanging wall. Start on the easy ramp leading to the start of ***Ichabod***, below the rightward-arching flake.

(6c). Gain the flake and climb it boldly to a peg runner. Step left and climb across with difficulty to a second peg and good nut. Continue up moving right then diagonally left to a thread and resting ledge. Move up to join ***Roaring Silence***, which is followed to belay below the overhangs. Finish across leftwards, as for ***Yellow Slab***.

The first easy break beyond the impressive overhanging wall is an easy ramp. The next three routes start by scrambling up the ramp to a belay below a steep cornerline.

14 **Roaring Silence**	54m	E3–

R H Berzins, M Berzins, J Lamb – June 1979

Excellent airy climbing up the immaculate walls and overhang to the right of *Ichabod*.

1 36m (5c). Follow the first pitch of ***Ichabod*** into the shallow corner. Traverse right to a thin crack and climb it until it steepens. Traverse right again to a good crack and follow it, and the slab above, to belay below the overhangs.

2 18m (5c). Climb up to the niche which splits the right-hand side of the overhangs and follow it to the top.

15 **Ichabod**	45m	E2

G Oliver, G Arkless, L Willis (3 points of aid – now free) – May 1960

Superb classic climbing on excellent rock taking a line just right of the large corner at the left side of the overhanging wall.

1 30m (5c). Climb the right-hand of the two cracks, passing below a protruding nose, and from the niche traverse delicately right into a shallow corner. Climb the corner to a small ledge at the foot of a V-chimney. Follow this to an awkward exit left into the larger corner which leads more easily to belay beneath a steep crack.

2 15m (5a). Climb the crack to the top.

16 **Phoenix**	48m	E1

P1: **R Moseley, D M Adcock** (1 point of aid) – Aug 1957 FFA: P1: **D Miller** – June 1962
P2: **A G Cram, W Young** (1 point of aid – now free) – June 1967

A superb, well protected climb, following a cracked groove up the front of the tower to the left of Ichabod.

1 27m (5b). Enter the groove by the obvious jamming crack, just left of ***Ichabod*** then climb the cracked corner above and pull out left with difficulty to a poor resting place. Continue up the crack and pull out onto a ramp. Follow this to a belay.

2 21m (5b). Descend slightly from the belay and climb a bold wall to good holds. Continue up for 6 metres then traverse right to the arête. Finish up this.

Left: Jim Roberts in a splendid position on the second pitch of *Phoenix* (E1)
Photo: Stephen Reid

17 **The Almighty**	18m	E5+
P Botterill, J Lamb – Aug 1981		

The thin, fierce overhanging crack between ***Phoenix*** and ***Hell's Groove***, provides a thankfully short but sensational climb. Start from a large block 8 metres right of ***Hell's Groove***.

(6b). Climb the very strenuous crack on small layaways to a blunt spike, where improving holds lead to a belay on a rampline. Abseil descent.

18 **Hell's Groove**	66m	E1–
P J Greenwood, A R Dolphin – May 1952		

A superb climb of great character, which follows the cracked wall just right of the large open corner forming the left side of the overhanging wall, about 30 metres left of ***Ichabod***. Start below the crack.

1 8m (5b). The problematic crack leads to a belay in the groove.

2 22m (5a). From the sloping ledge in the groove, climb out rightwards to a crack and ascend to another sloping ledge. Continue to a further ledge with a block at its right edge. A short wall and crack lead to a belay with a poor stance.

3 21m (4b). Climb a crack in the wall to the right of the overhang to ledges. Traverse the steep wall on the left to an open chimney; climb this to the left end of an amphitheatre. Thread belays.

4 15m (4a). Climb up a slab to the left and traverse back rightwards along the block to an easy chimney. Climb this and its continuation to the top.

19 **Trinity**	67m	HVS+
D D Whillans, J Sutherland – June 1955		

The obvious fine groove system 10 metres left of ***Hell's Groove*** gives interesting and enjoyable climbing.

1 30m (5a). Climb up to the groove and follow it to an overhang. Climb this on its left to a ledge.

2 28m (5b). Climb the bulge in the corner onto a slab. Follow the slab and layback crack above to step left onto a slab. Move diagonally left to the foot of a short wall and belay on the large grass ledge above.

3 9m (4c). The corner above.

Pikes Crag

Grid reference: **210 071**
Altitude: **760m**
Faces: **West**
Rock type: **Borrowdale Volcanic**
Approach time: **1 hr 10 mins**

This is the large slabby crag to the left of ***Mickledore***, which has the benefit of catching the sun for most of the day, and drying more quickly than Scafell. The rock is clean and rough on the better routes, but many contain large ledges and a number of loose blocks. The main mass of ***Pikes Crag*** is called ***Pulpit Rock***, which forms an independent summit cut off from the rest of the mountain by deep clefts.

Descent: from the top of *Pulpit Rock* involves a short, steep scramble on the Scafell side of the col, but in bad weather an abseil may be required.

1 Grooved Arête	120m	VD

C F Holland, G R Speaker – April 1924

A good route with varied situations up the prominent arête on the right of the main face, which falls from the highest point of the crag. Start in a V-shaped hollow below a large overhang, just to the right of the arête.

1 18m. Move off to the right and enter an easy grassy groove running back to the left. Follow this to the foot of a steep crack.

2 15m. The left-hand crack is climbed for 8 metres, when a traverse is taken to the arête on the left, which is climbed past the end of the overhang to a grass ledge. Belay in the chimney a little distance back.

3 24m. The chimney is climbed, passing over a bulge at 8 metres. Continue up a broken groove until grassy ledges lead rightwards into a rectangular corner.

4 20m. The crack in the right-hand corner is hard to start. Continue up to a pile of blocks, pass them, and make a pleasant traverse to the right, to a prominent block on the edge of the ridge.

5 18m. Climb the slab ahead, work to the left, and then cross over to a series of ledges on the edge.

6 12m. Step over the corner on the left and continue up a slab to a ledge below a huge block. Climb the chimney on the left of the block.

7 13m. Go along a ledge, running down to the left, on the wall above the gap, and regain the slabby front of the buttress, which is climbed direct to the summit of ***Pulpit Rock***.

2 **The Nave**	129m	HVS
W Young, J Wilkinson – June 1974		

This adventurous climb runs up the sweep of slabs left of ***Grooved Arête***. Start just right of the lowest point of the crag, 6 metres below ***Grooved Arête***.

1 30m (4c). Climb the arête to some doubtful blocks. Move over these with trepidation, and up the wall above on small holds, to a large comfortable ledge.

2 39m (5a). A good pitch. Go left across the ledge for 5 metres and climb diagonally leftwards for 7 metres up the slabs to a black mossy streak. Move back rightwards and straight up the centre of the slabby pillar to a bold finish.

3 30m (4b). The slabs, starting on the left, lead more easily to a stance.

4 30m (4b). Climb the slabs and cracks above, heading for a conspicuous notch in the skyline, right of a large overhang and finish on the summit of the crag.

3 **The Sentinel**	77m	VS+
P L Fearnehough, J Wright – April 1960		

This route is easily identified by the striking face crack which splits the central square-cut pillar 20 metres up the crag. Start at the right-hand edge of the steep rib, which lies immediately to the left of a green mossy gully.

1 18m (4c). Steep delicate climbing, first up the rib, then trending left, leads to a grass ledge.

2 24m (4c). Climb the corner above the ledge for 5 metres to an overhang split by a crack. Climb the bulging crack, with a move right by some loose flakes, to the top of the pillar.

3 20m. Easier climbing straight up to a stance below and to the left of an obvious overhanging crack which can be seen on the skyline.

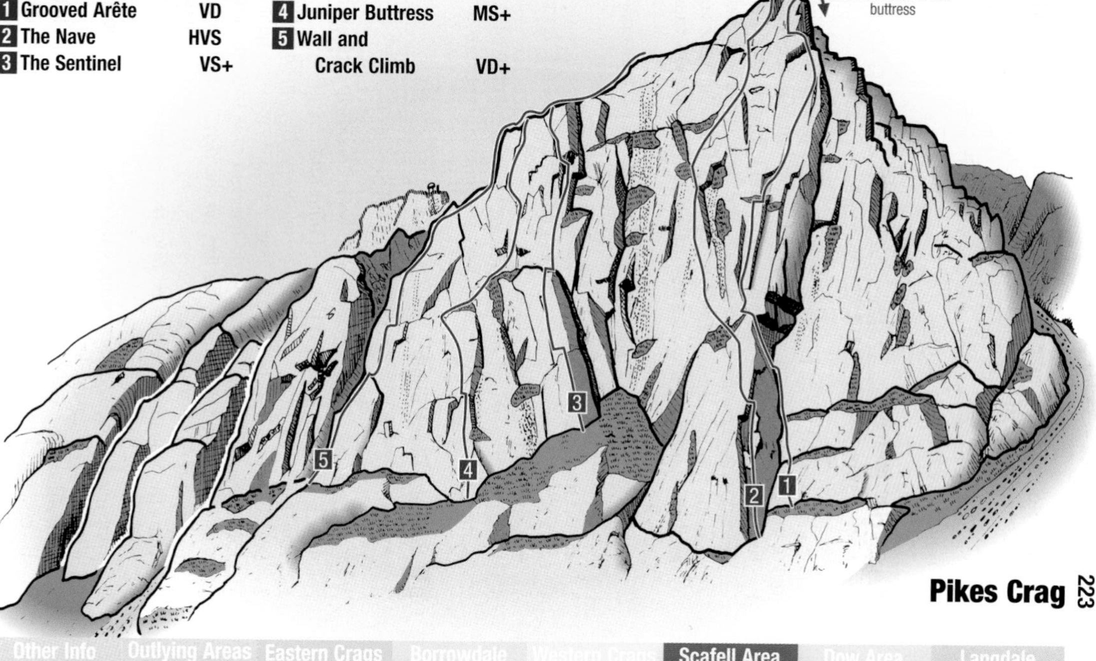
1 Grooved Arête VD
2 The Nave HVS
3 The Sentinel VS+
4 Juniper Buttress MS+
5 Wall and Crack Climb VD+
down the back of the buttress
1
2
3
4
5

4 15m (4c). Climb carefully up doubtful rock to the overhang and pull over it strenuously. Continue straight up the crack to a stance. Alternatively, the overhang may be avoided by climbing the corner above the stance, and traversing right across the clean wall above to rejoin the route.

4 Juniper Buttress | 75m | MS+

H M Kelly, R E W Pritchard, N L Eden-Smith, W Eden-Smith – April 1924

A popular route with fine climbing. Start at a detached block at the foot of the crag about 13 metres to the right of *Wall and Crack Climb*.

1 **18m.** From the block a ledge is reached and a traverse made to the right into a corner below a crack. The crack is climbed, and near the top it is left in favour of the arête. From the ledge so reached, climb a furrow slanting up the wall to the right to a grass ledge.

2 **10m.** Climb a series of blocks to the left, finishing up a rather difficult crack.

3 **15m.** Ascend rightwards to the edge of a grassy gully.

4 **17m.** A groove, above and to the left, followed by a crack, leads to a shelf with a recess at its back.

5 **15m.** The exposed wall above is climbed by a difficult thin crack, starting at a rib just to the right. Easy scrambling to the top.

5 Wall and Crack Climb | 80m | VD+

H M Kelly, R E W Pritchard, B Eden-Smith, G Wilson – April 1924

A clean route on very good rock, with some polished problems. Follows the apparent left-hand ridge of *Pulpit Rock*.

1 **10m.** Climb the ridge.

2 **9m.** A steep wall is climbed to a ledge.

3 **15m.** A vertical crack, or the face to the right of it, is climbed to a rock platform from which, starting on the right, a staircase of rock is ascended to a terrace.

4 **10m.** The wall above is climbed from right to left on improving holds.

5 **10m.** Climb a zig-zag crack running up to the right in three risers.

6 **11m.** A rock staircase leads to a ledge.

7 **15m.** The almost vertical crack, or the wall on its left, is followed by easier rocks to the top.

Wasdale

by Al Phizacklea

The tiny hamlet of Wasdale Head, snuggled at the end of the Wasdale valley, is the birthplace of rock climbing in England. The old hotel has been the preserve of climbers since the legendary days of Haskett-Smith, Jones and Collie, and the two campsites at the valley head can be very busy during the holiday period. Although close to the geographical centre of The Lake District, it is a rather remote centre, as the only major road access is from the west coast of Cumbria via the A595. The major crags of ***Scafell***, ***Gable*** and ***Pillar*** are all accessible from Wasdale Head, whilst ***Buckbarrow***, ***Eskdale*** and ***St Bees*** provide convenient wet-weather alternatives.

Buckbarrow

Grid reference:	**135 057**
Altitude:	**350m**
Faces:	**South-East**
Rock type:	**Borrowdale Volcanic**
Approach time:	**20 mins**

Buckbarrow is the large, broken crag that can be clearly seen on the left when travelling towards Wasdale Head, on the opposite side of the valley to the Screes above Wastwater. It yields some excellent climbing on rock that is generally fast drying and provides a real alternative within the Wasdale Valley to the often wet higher crags. It holds the sun all day and occupies a pleasant situation overlooking the west end of Wastwater.

Approaching from Gosforth, the Wasdale road reaches a high point after approximately 7 kilometres at Harrow Head Farm. The crags can now be seen up on the left. If approaching from Wasdale Head, take the right-hand fork in the road which is half-way down the side of the lake.

Witch Buttress

The most obvious and cleanest piece of rock on the hillside being easily identified by its fine central detached pillar with a pleasant grassy ledge below. Just above *Witch Buttress* lies the long outcrop of *Pike Crag*. Approach by ascending directly up the scree run above the road.

Descent: follow the rake down right until reaching a small path that leads back left and down over a rock step to the base of the central pillar.

The routes are described from **left** to **right**.

1 The Mysteron	35m	HVS+

W S Lounds, J C Eilbeck – early 1960s

A good climb, with the second pitch providing a safe introduction to the harder routes on the crag. Start below a large corner left of the central detached pillar.

1 10m. Climb up and left to a large flake below the large overhanging corner of *Imagine*.

2 25m (5b). Traverse left below a green wall to a groove. Climb this then make a committing move (crux) onto a small ledge high on the left. Continue straight up the crack until it is possible to step left into a crack that leads to an easy ridge. Finish up this.

2 Imagine	38m	E1+

A Stephenson, J Wilson – April 1981

An excellent route giving steep and sustained climbing up the overhanging groove and continuation corner right of the *Mysteron*.

1 25m (5b). Climb the large flake as for the *Mysteron* and pull into the steep groove on the right. Difficult moves up the groove lead to the roof (thread runner). Pull over on undercuts and good jugs into the easier continuation corner which is followed, trending right, to below an undercut crack.

2 13m (5a). Awkward moves give access to the crack that leads to the top.

1 The Mysteron HVS+
2 Imagine E1+
3 Witch VS
4 Too Many Hands E2
5 Pace Maker VS+
6 Needless Eliminate E1–
7 The Buckbarrow Needle VS
8 Last of the Summer Wine E1

Buckbarrow Crag – Witch Buttress

3 **Witch**	40m	VS
P Walsh, M Burke – March 1961		

A justifiably popular route of traditional style taking the obvious chimney line on the right-hand side of the central pillar.

1 27m (4c). Climb the chimney for 10 metres then move right with difficulty into a small niche. Good holds lead up the wall to regain the chimney/crackline above the overhang. Follow the crack to the top of the pillar.

2 13m (4c). Step up and left into the open groove that leads to the top.

4 **Too Many Hands**	40m	E2
A Stephenson, C Sice, J Wilson, W Young, A Edwards – May 1981		

An excellent steep pitch with spaced protection. Four metres right of *Witch* and 15 metres from the ground is a large wedged block. A thin crack runs up the right-hand side of this block and through the overhang above. Start just left of the crackline.

(5b). Enter the fault/crackline from the left and follow it to the large wedged block. Climb the continuation crack above to a pinnacle, then step off this into the hanging corner. A long reach gives access to the next short corner which is exited left onto a ledge at its top. Exposed moves now lead out right across the steep slab to the arête where easier climbing leads to the top.

5 **Pace Maker**	40m	VS+
J Wilson, A Stephenson, C Sice – May 1981		

A surprisingly enjoyable pitch climbing the obvious corner 5 metres right of *Too Many Hands*. Start at the bottom of the corner.

(4c). Climb the corner to a bulge, step left into the next corner and follow this until forced out right to the rib that leads up to a ledge. Step diagonally left to a spike then up to a ledge below a steep corner. Climb the corner, which is difficult to start, up to the top.

Pike Crag

The line of crags above ***Witch Buttress***, starting on the right of a prominent pinnacle climbed by the ***Buckbarrow Needle***.
Descent: down the rake on the left.

Routes are described from **right** to **left**.

6	Needless Eliminate	22m	E1–
	P Stewart, J W Earl – June 1979		

A fine pitch climbing the groove and crack just right of the ***Buckbarrow Needle***. Start in the corner just right of the crack of the right-hand start of the ***Buckbarrow Needle***.

(5b). Hand-traverse diagonally left to a large spike, then pull onto a ledge on the right. Step back left and climb the well protected crack direct to the top.

7	The Buckbarrow Needle	23m	VS
	A H Greenbank, P Moffat – 1957		

An interesting climb of traditional character, the first pitch climbing the obvious crack on either the right or left-hand side of the ***Needle***.

1 13m (4b). Climb either of the cracks to the top of the ***Needle***.

2 10m (4c). Step off the ***Needle*** onto the wall above and make a bold move up on small holds to easier ground above.

8	Last of the Summer Wine	22m	E1
	J Wilson, B Smith – May 1982		

Good climbing up the steep wall just left of the ***Buckbarrow Needle*** finishing with an intimidating crack up the overhanging wall. Start just left of the ***Buckbarrow Needle*** left-hand start at some small grassy ledges.

(5b). Climb the groove and step right onto a flake. Continue up the wall trending right until it is possible to swing across left into the base of the overhanging crack (good runner). Straight up the crack to the top.

Western Crags Area Map

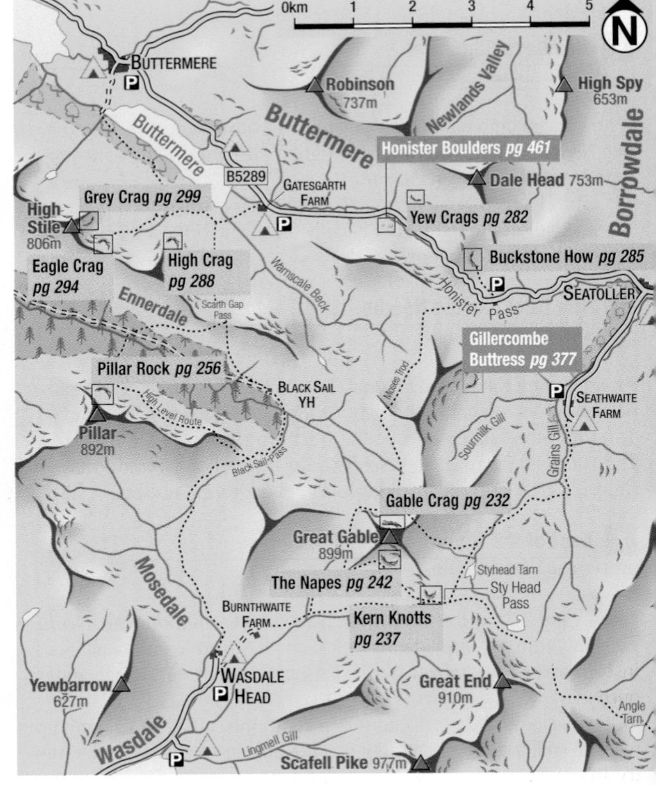

Western Crags

Gable, Pillar, Buttermere & St Bees

Left: The *Sphinx*, Great Gable
Photo: Nick Wharton

Great Gable

by Bill Young & Phil Rigby

Great Gable is the distinctive pyramid-shaped mountain which dominates the head of Wasdale, a scene which has been adopted as the logo for the Lake District National Park.

The climbing is easily accessible, and is divided into three main areas. ***Gable Crag*** lies just below the summit of Great Gable, facing north to the head of the Ennerdale valley. The ***Napes Ridges/Tophet Wall*** group and ***Kern Knotts*** both lie on the Wasdale side of Great Gable, overlooking the path to Sty Head Pass; both these crags face generally south and come into condition quickly after bad weather.

The Gable Memorial

In 1923, after considerable search and effort, the FRCC succeeded in purchasing some 3000 acres of hill land above the 1500 foot contour in the vicinity of Styhead and presented it to the National Trust as a memorial to those of its members who gave their lives for their country in the First World War. Included in this area lie the summits of Lingmell, Broad Crag, Great End, Allen Crags, Glaramara, Seathwaite Fell, Kirkfell, Green Gable, and Great Gable where a bronze memorial tablet was fixed and where a simple memorial ceremony is conducted every Remembrance Sunday.

Gable Crag

Grid reference: **213 105**
Altitude: **800m**
Faces: **North**
Rock type: **Borrowdale Volcanic**
Approach time: **1 hr 15 mins**

Gable Crag is the large, broken crag on the Ennerdale side of the summit of Great Gable. The best climbing is centred around ***Engineer's Slab***, the magnificent clean, steep wall high in the centre of the crag. In spite of the terminology 'slab', the wall provides sustained climbing which generally follows well-protected cracklines or the blank walls in between them.

As the crag has a northerly aspect, the sun only falls on it late in the day, and this can result in cold conditions on all but the calmest of days, with some lines holding water well into a dry spell.

The crag can be approached from Wasdale or Honister Pass. From Wasdale Head, follow the valley path towards Great Gable, then ascend the rounded ridge rising above the footbridge. Half-way up this steep ridge, follow a traverse line rising leftwards across the scree to the col at Beck Head. Go up the shoulder of Great Gable for 200 metres, where a vague narrow track leads off left under *Gable Crag*.

The easiest approach is from the north, from the summit of Honister Pass. Follow the old quarry track steeply up the hillside behind the quarry buildings for 1 kilometre then turn south onto a well marked track that runs south into Stone Cove below *Gable Crag*.

The foot of the wall is reached by scrambling up steep, broken ground to the right of a broken buttress directly below the wall.

Descent: The easiest descent is either east or west down the walker's paths around either end of the crag. This involves a long walk, and the steep approach scramble has to be re-ascended. For teams wishing to climb a second route on the wall, the best descent is to scramble with care down steep broken ground to the left of the wall (on the right if facing out), where a short gully leads back down to the foot of *Engineer's Chimney*. It is quicker still to abseil from gear (not in place) from a ledge above the left side of the face (right of *Engineer's Chimney*), any gear used for this purpose can be retrieved at the end of the day.

Gable Crag – Engineer's Slab

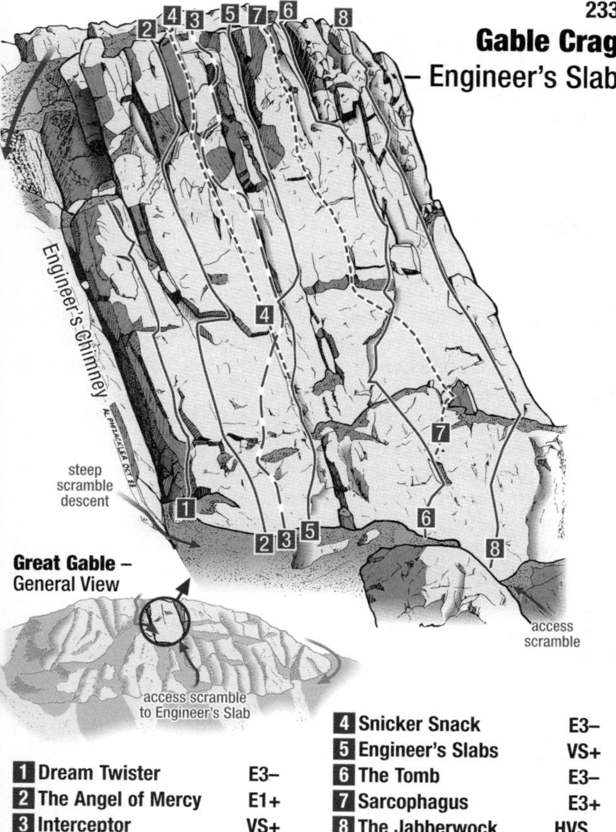

	Route	Grade
1	**Dream Twister**	**E3–**
2	**The Angel of Mercy**	**E1+**
3	**Interceptor**	**VS+**
4	**Snicker Snack**	**E3–**
5	**Engineer's Slabs**	**VS+**
6	**The Tomb**	**E3–**
7	**Sarcophagus**	**E3+**
8	**The Jabberwock**	**HVS**

The routes are described from **left** to **right**, the deeply-cut chimney on the left (*Engineer's Chimney*) is an obvious landmark.

1	**Dream Twister**	45m	E3–

C Downer, A Hall – July 1987

A good, well protected line, with the overhang and crack above providing a sustained crux section. Start from a grass ledge 4 metres right of *Engineer's Chimney*.

(5c). Easy rocks lead to a ledge and loose blocks. Pull into the groove on the left, exiting right at the top onto a good ledge below the wall. Climb the wall direct to the overhang. Pull over this using the crack above, moving left at its top into a wider crack, curving rightwards to a good ledge. The short crack above leads to a large grass ledge and thread belay.

2 The Angel of Mercy	60m	E1+
J Lamb, P Botterill – June 1979		

To the right of ***Dream Twister*** is a chimney/niche with a capping block about 25 metres up the face. To the right of the niche is a steep wall split by a crack which provides the crux pitch of this fine route. Start directly below the niche.

1 25m (5a). Climb the wall on small but good holds to the niche. Peg and nut belays below the block.

2 35m (5b). Move up and make difficult moves across the sandwiched slab on the right to gain the crack. Follow the crack, which gives excellent climbing to where the angle eases, then climb the ramp up and right to below an overhanging crack splitting the headwall. Difficult moves lead up the crack to the top (large Friend useful).

3 Interceptor	65m	VS+
P L Fearnehough, N J Soper – June 1967		

An excellent companion climb to ***Engineer's Slabs***. It works its way through the overhangs left of ***Engineer's Slabs***, starting about 5 metres left of that route.

1 30m (4c). An awkward pitch with difficult route finding. Climb diagonally left to the left end of a grass ledge, then straight up to another grass ledge at its right end. An ascending traverse right on small holds leads across the wall to the twin cracks of ***Engineer's Slabs*** and the sentry box. (Care should be taken to protect the second.)

2 15m (4c). Climb straight up the grooveline above to the overhangs, traverse left into two parallel cracks (***Snicker Snack***) and climb these to a stance by a huge flake.

3 20m (4c). Layback the flake and traverse right to a groove and climb it until a prominent spike on the right can be reached. Climb the rib to the top.

4	Snicker Snack	57m	E3–

C Downer, A Hall – July 1986

A superb, modern classic, taking the obvious direct crackline up the steep wall left of ***Engineer's Slabs***. The climbing, which is both difficult and sustained, gives one of the best routes on the crag. Start in the middle of the wall, as for ***Engineer's Slabs***.

1 45m (5c). Climb the wall of ***Engineer's Slabs*** for 12 metres, then continue straight up the superb sustained thin crackline above to belay at the huge flake of ***Interceptor***.

2 12m (5b). Climb the flake and traverse right, surmount a small overhang to gain a thin crack (about 3 metres left of the finishing groove of ***Interceptor***) and follow this to an awkward finish.

5	Engineer's Slabs	60m	VS+

F G Balcombe, J A Shepherd, C J A Cooper – June 1934

A magnificent climb of great character, taking the obvious crack and grooveline up the centre of the wall. The last pitch, which is often damp, can prove to be a little intimidating but this does not detract in any way from the quality of the climbing below. Start just left of a groove in the middle of the face.

1 26m (4c). The wall leads past a small pinnacle to the foot of a crack. Climb the crack for 5 metres then step into twin cracks on the right which lead to a chimney and sentry box.

2 34m (4c). Traverse right for 2 metres into a crack, and climb this for 8 metres to a ledge, followed by a layback crack to a good ledge. The chimney above gives access to a groove that leads to the top. If the final groove is wet, move left and climb the crack and rib to the top.

6	The Tomb	68m	E3–

A G Cram, W Young (1 point of aid – now free) – Sept 1966

A superb route that climbs the wall right of ***Engineer's Slabs*** by utilizing the obvious curved overlap. The climbing is never too hard, but the crux pitch requires a confident approach, with widely spaced but good protection. Start 6 metres right of ***Engineer's Slabs***.

1 18m (4c). Traverse right and up to gain the obvious sentry box. Climb this and the wall above, leftwards to a ledge, then step left to belay below a break.

2 20m (5c). The wall on the left is climbed on small holds for 6 metres to a rest point below the left end of the curving overlap (protection slot above). Move right under the overlap to its end, where protection can be strenuous to place. Pull through the next overlap onto a small ledge, and traverse right into a steep crack which leads to a good stance.

3 30m (5a). Climb the groove above to the overhang, and step left into the open groove which leads to the top.

7 **Sarcophagus**	64m	E3+

P Whillance, D Armstrong – July 1977

A technically absorbing face route at the top of its grade, climbing the blank wall below the traverse of the ***Tomb***, then the overhang and break above. The route requires steady nerves on its poorly protected second pitch but the quality is there all the way. Start as for the ***Tomb***.

1 18m (4c). As for Pitch 1 of the ***Tomb*** to the sentry box. Climb up then right across the wall above to a large flake.

2 18m (5c). Step up left to a small block at the right end of a grass ledge. Step off the block and make a series of committing moves up the wall to join the ***Tomb*** at the right end of the curving overlap. Move left to a thin crack, climb up to the overlap (good runners), and pull over strenuously, stepping right onto a narrow ledge. Small nut belays. An exciting pitch.

3 28m (5b). Move up and left into a groove/crackline. Follow this, and jam the crack above to finish up a groove, left of the deep groove on the ***Tomb***.

8 **The Jabberwock**	75m	HVS

R Valentine, J Wilkinson – June 1970

The obvious steep crack and grooved headwall at the right end of the face provide a route of high quality with an exposed top pitch. Start from the lowest point below the right side of the face.

1 22m (4c). Climb the cracked wall to ledges on the right of a large flake.

2 28m (5a). Climb the crack, passing a large ledge at 18 metres, to a sloping ledge and shattered blocks.

3 25m (4c). The short slab on the left leads to a very exposed groove which is climbed to the top on good holds. Some suspect blocks.

Kern Knotts

Grid reference: **215 096**
Altitude: **520m**
Faces: **South-West**
Rock type: **Borrowdale Volcanic**
Approach time: **1hr – 1 hr 15 mins**

Above: John Pattison on the traverse of *Buttonhook Route* (HVS+) **Photo:** Phil Rigby

Kern Knotts Crag holds a commanding position overlooking the upper Wasdale Valley and Scafell Range. It is very steep and compact, and provides climbing of high quality and character, on sound, rough rock which dries quickly.

The routes range from traditional, to the more modern athletic variety and provide many classic lines. The older routes should not be considered as soft options, with the polished nature of some of these classics providing additional spice.

Kern Knotts is easy to reach. Starting from either Wasdale Head or Seathwaite, Borrowdale, take the path to Sty Head Pass, and from its highest point, follow the **Climbers' Traverse**, a gently rising track which crosses the south-west flank of Great Gable. This path is rather vague at first, but soon becomes better defined and passes under *Kern Knotts* before continuing on to the *Napes*.

Descent: is easiest to the left.

The routes are described from **right** to **left**.

The main feature of the crag is a steep wall at its right-hand end, set at right angles to the rest of the crag. Pitch 2 of *Kern Knotts Chimney* (see Route **4** overleaf) provides access to the top of the crag for the first three routes.

1 Innominate Crack	20m	VS
G S Bower, B Beetham, J B Wilton – April 1921		

The best single-pitch crack climb of its grade in the valley. It follows the thin cracks in the centre of the smooth wall which faces towards Sty Head Pass.

(4b). Follow the twin cracks until forced into the right-hand one, which is followed to the top, passing a sloping ledge at 15 metres.

2 Kern Knotts Crack	22m	VS
O G Jones, H C Bowden – April 1897		

Takes the obvious break in the left side of this wall. A route of great character, its grade being set by the mirror finish of the crux sentry box.

(4c). Climb the crack to a sentry box at 8 metres. Either climb the sentry box direct by some very precarious antics, or bypass it on the right wall using small holds followed by a long step back left. The upper section of the crack is easier.

3 The Buttonhook Route	30m	HVS+
F G Balcombe, C J A Cooper – June 1934		

A very steep, exposed and classic climb that threads its way up the corner of the prominent buttress. Start at the foot of the buttress around the corner to the left of *Kern Knotts Crack*.

(5a). Climb a short, cracked slab to the overhang. Pull out right to reach a good jug and climb the steep rock above to a small ledge. Traverse left to another small ledge at 5 metres, then climb very steep rock above, trending left. The angle eases after 7 metres. Trend right to a pinnacle on the right edge of the buttress, then go direct to the top on sloping holds.

4 Kern Knotts Chimney	60m	HS
O G Jones, W H Fowler, J W Robinson – Dec 1893		

This is the prominent chimney facing down Wasdale, on the left side of the lowest point of the buttress. A classic which has become a victim of its own popularity, now being very polished, especially on its second pitch which should be approached with care.

1 30m. Easy rocks lead to a large platform. Climb the chimney, passing a chockstone en route. Pass under a block to belay on the other side of the buttress.

Kern Knotts – Right Hand Side

1 Innominate Crack VS
2 Kern Knotts Crack VS
3 The Buttonhook Route HVS+
4 Kern Knotts Chimney (top pitch) HS

2 30m. Step from the top of the block onto the slab using polished, sloping holds. Easier rocks then lead to the top. (The slab may be avoided by going left but that would spoil the fun.)

5	Central Climb South Face	37m	MVS

H M Kelly, R E W Pritchard, A P Wilson – Aug 1919

Start 4 metres left of *Kern Knotts Chimney*, just right of parallel grassy cracks.

1 25m (4b). Easy rocks lead up right, following the line of the right-hand crack to a pinnacle. Climb steeply above for 12 metres, then traverse left to belay as for Pitch 1 of *Crysalid*.

2 12m (4b). Continue left to the base of a steep scoop which is climbed with a good finishing hold.

Kern Knotts – Left Hand Side

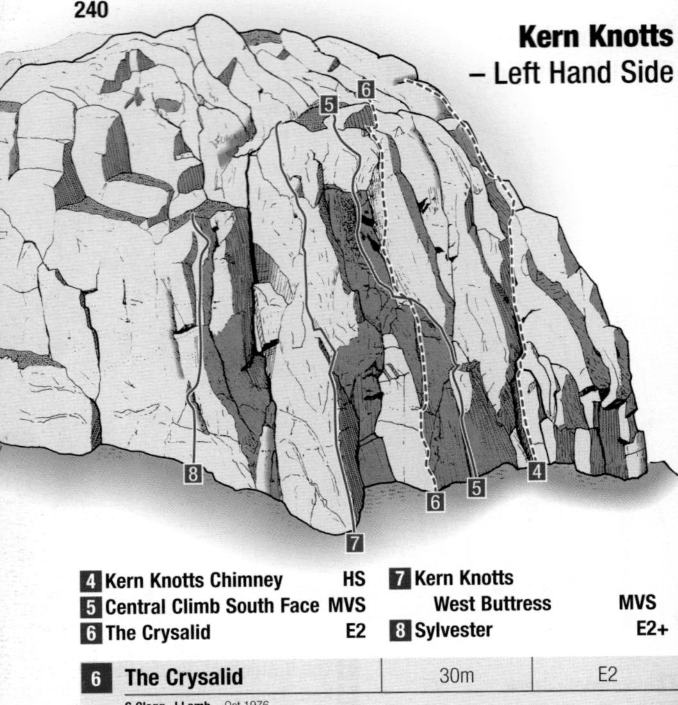

4 Kern Knotts Chimney **HS**
5 Central Climb South Face **MVS**
6 The Crysalid **E2**
7 Kern Knotts West Buttress **MVS**
8 Sylvester **E2+**

6	**The Crysalid**	30m	E2

S Clegg, J Lamb – Oct 1976

An excellent exercise in steep, fingery climbing, with the crux at the top. Start 2 metres left of *Central Climb South Face* at a blunt arête.

(5c). Climb the arête to below a faint crack in the steep slab. Follow this and a short wall to the base of a steep groove. Climb the steep groove on small holds to a good but doubtful flake. Step left onto a slab and follow this to the top.

7	**Kern Knotts West Buttress**	33m	MVS

G S Sansom, S W Herford – April 1912

Climbs the steep buttress 8 metres left of the *Crysalid* giving good, open situations. Start just left of the lowest point of the left-hand end of the buttress.

Right: Kevin Avery checks his gear on *Sylvester* (E2+) **Photo:** Phil Rigby

1 16m (4b). Easy rocks are followed by a short steep section to a spike. Climb the V-groove above, swing left at the top and continue steeply to a large ledge.

2 17m. The easier rocks on the left are followed to the top.

8	**Sylvester**	25m	E2+

T Furniss, P Rigby – June 1981

A very good pitch that requires a bold approach. Start 8 metres left of ***Kern Knotts West Buttress***, and left of a chimneyline, at a steep wall seamed by thin cracks leading to a shallow groove.

(5c). Easy rocks lead to a good spike runner; step right onto the cracked wall to gain a ledge on the arête (runners up and right of here – get them while you can). Step back left and climb the shallow protectionless groove above using sloping holds.

The Napes

Grid reference: **210 099**
Altitude: **650m**
Faces: **South-West**
Rock type: **Borrowdale Volcanic**
Approach time: **1 hr 15 mins – 1 hr 30 mins**

Above: *Napes Needle*
Photo: Stephen Reid

The birthplace of English rock climbing. This excellent crag, although rather broken, provides climbing of all grades in superb surroundings with its splendid ridges and steep walls overlooking the upper Wasdale Valley and the Scafell Range.

The *Napes* is quite unique with its classic ridge climbs and the famous pinnacle of *Napes Needle*. Its relatively easy access and fine climbs has resulted in this being a popular stamping ground for the lower grade climber and beginner, but it also provides some high quality testpieces. The majority of the crag is fast drying and holds the sun late into the day.

Great Gable – General View

- **A** **Needle Ridge**
- **B** **Eagle's Nest Ridge**
- **C** **Arrowhead Ridge**
- **D** **Napes Needle**
- **E** **Westmorland Crag**
- **F** **Great Hell Gate** (descent)
- **G** **Needle Gully** (no descent)
- **H** **Eagle's Nest Gully** (no descent)
- **I** **Arrowhead Gully** (no descent)
- **J** **Little Hell Gate** (descent)
- **K** **The Sphinx Rock**

Langdale
Dow Area
Scafell Area
Western Crags
Borrowdale
Eastern Crags
Outlying Areas
Other Info

Although most of the climbs are on sound rock, care should be taken when on the ridges as any stonefall will rake the gullies and their walls, eventually crossing the busy path at the bottom.

Starting from either Wasdale Head, or Seathwaite, Borrowdale, take the path to Sty Head Pass, and from its highest point, follow the **Climbers' Traverse**, a gently rising track that crosses the south-west flank of Great Gable. This path is rather vague at first, but soon becomes better defined and passes under ***Kern Knotts*** before continuing on to the *Napes*.

The first large wall to be reached, across a wide scree chute called Great Hell Gate, is *Tophet Wall*, an impressively steep rockface. The next prominent feature is the characteristic shape of *Napes Needle*, which stands directly below the classic ridge climb of *Needle Ridge*. Beyond *Needle Gully* stands the imposing *Eagle's Nest Ridge* and *Abbey Buttress*, which is immediately followed by *Eagle's Nest Gully* and the final major ridge, *Arrowhead Ridge*. The track below the crag then continues to *Sphinx Rock*, a shapely detached block at the extreme left-hand end of the crag.

Descents: From *Tophet Wall*, *Needle Ridge* and *Eagle's Nest Ridge* scramble up to a junction with, then go down Great Hell Gate. This scree descent is worn and requires caution. Descent from *Arrowhead Ridge* is by scrambling up, then going west to meet the top of the steep, rocky path that leads down towards the *Sphinx Rock*. The general descents described are lengthy, but on no account try to ascend or descend the gullies, as they are loose and dangerous.

The climbs are described from **right** to **left** starting from Great Hell Gate at *Tophet Wall*.

Tophet Wall

Facing east, this superb wall repays an early start.

1	Tophet Wall	75m	HS+
	H M Kelly, R E W Pritchard – July 1923	P1: **M de Selincourt** (solo) – Aug 1925	

A true classic, winding its way through some very impressive rock architecture. Start right of a rightward-leaning crack/corner in the centre of the wall.

1 20m. Climb the wall just right of the crack, until a step left can be made into the crack, which is followed to a ledge. An ascending traverse right leads to a ledge at the foot of a wall.

1	**Tophet Wall**	**HS+**
2	**Supernatural**	**E5+**
3	**The Vikings**	**E3+**
4	**Tophet Grooves Direct**	**HVS+**
5	**Tophet Bastion** (upper part)	**VD**

2 **17m.** The wall above is climbed to a broken ledge and corner on the left. Climb the crack in the corner followed by the right wall, to a slab that leads to a corner.

3 **15m.** Semi-hand-traverse 10 metres right in a sensational position to a corner. Climb the rib on the right to a ledge.

4 **23m.** Ascend the small pinnacle on the right, then step left into the crack which is followed to a rock ledge. Easy climbing leads to the top of the ridge.

2 **Supernatural**	82m	E5+

P Whillance, D Armstrong – July 1977

A serious, intricate line through the overhanging wall and bulges left of *Tophet Wall*. Start at a shallow groove 8 metres left of *Tophet Wall*.

1 25m (5c). Climb the groove, moving right at the top onto the wall and protection. Move up and make a difficult pull left onto the rib, which is followed to a large ledge and pinnacle. Belay at its right-hand end.

2 32m (6a). Climb the steep wall above to a bulge and poor protection, then traverse the hanging slab on the left to a steep groove which is climbed boldly to a good spike and resting place. Step right and climb a rib and groove that lead to good holds on the *Great Slab* above. Step left and climb the slab until an easy traverse can be made leftwards to a spike belay.

3 25m (5b). Climb the rib directly above the belay to a ledge on the right, then up the mossy slab on the left to a sloping ledge. Traverse right along the ledge than move up and right round the rib to better holds. Easy climbing up a wall and short groove lead to the top.

3 **The Vikings**	57m	E3+

A McHardy, P Braithwaite – June 1969

A superb route of magnetic attraction which climbs the obvious overhanging crackline towards the left side of an impressive overhanging wall. Start about 15 metres left of *Tophet Wall* at an upstanding block directly below the crack.

1 15m (5b). Climb the crack until it steepens, then step right into another crack, which is followed to a stance and belay on the left.

2 27m (5c). The extremely strenuous and overhanging crack above is climbed passing an awkward flared niche at the top. Easier ground is followed to a large pedestal belay.

3 15m (4b). Continue up the crack and groove above to the top.

4 **Tophet Grooves Direct**	75m	HVS+

P1: **P L Fearnehough, J E Howard** – June 1968 P2: **R J Birkett, V Veevers** – Oct 1940
(Straightened out by **J Grinbergs, A Davis** – June 1989) P3: **S H J Reid, J Grinbergs** – July 1991

Strenuous and technical climbing but with all the difficulties short and well protected. Rather slow to dry. Start about 13 metres left of the *Vikings* at a prominent steep groove.

Left: Tom Foster, on the crux moves of the *Vikings* (E3+), Tophet Wall, Great Gable.
Photo: Phil Rigby

1 18m (5b). Climb the groove, which is hard to start, to a ledge below a groove.
2 18m (5b). Climb the scoop above, passing a doubtful block, to the overhang; then traverse right a metre and climb directly over the mossy bulge to a stance.
3 24m (5b). From the stance, step right and climb the mossy wall to a good ledge. Move left and climb leftwards back into the main groove. Climb the overhanging cleft through the roof (with some puzzlement!) and follow the easier groove above to a large grass ledge.
4 15m. Finish up the sharp arête.

5 **Tophet Bastion**	66m	VD

H M Kelly, E H Pryor, A R Thomson, Mrs Kelly, G C Crawford – June 1919

Pleasant but polished climbing up the left arête of the ***Tophet Wall*** area. A good, all weather route. Start at the bottom of a broken arête around to the left of the steep Tophet face.
1 20m. Easily up the arête to a grass ledge, then climb the steep corner on the right to a rocky platform. It is possible to avoid the corner by the steep wall on the right, followed by easier ground to the rocky platform.
2 17m. Climb the slab above for 8 metres to a ledge, then step left round the corner and up the arête to a stance.
3 12m. Step right and climb straight up to the bottom of a groove at 7 metres. The groove above leads direct to the top or can be avoided by the easier crack on the left. From the belay, scramble up steep grass to the obvious feature of the ***Shark's Fin*** high on the left.
4 17m. Starting from the right, climb the edge of the rib to the foot of a crack, which is climbed on its left wall, exiting left at its top.

Napes Needle

This detached pinnacle of unique character is one of the most recognizable features in the Lake District and justifiably attracts many climbers. The routes are now very polished, with the section from the shoulder to the top requiring particular care and setting the grade for the routes.

Right: Napes Needle, the *Wasdale Crack* (HS), the epitome of Lakeland climbing
Photo: Phil Rigby

The Napes

	Route	Grade
6	The Wasdale Crack	HS
7	The Arête	HS
8	Needle Ridge	VD
9	Amos Moses	E1+
10	Crocodile Crack	HVS+
11	The Cayman	E2
12	Eagle's Nest Ridge Direct	MVS
13	Eagle's Nest Ordinary Route	D
14	Abbey Buttress	VD
15	Arrowhead Ridge Direct	VD

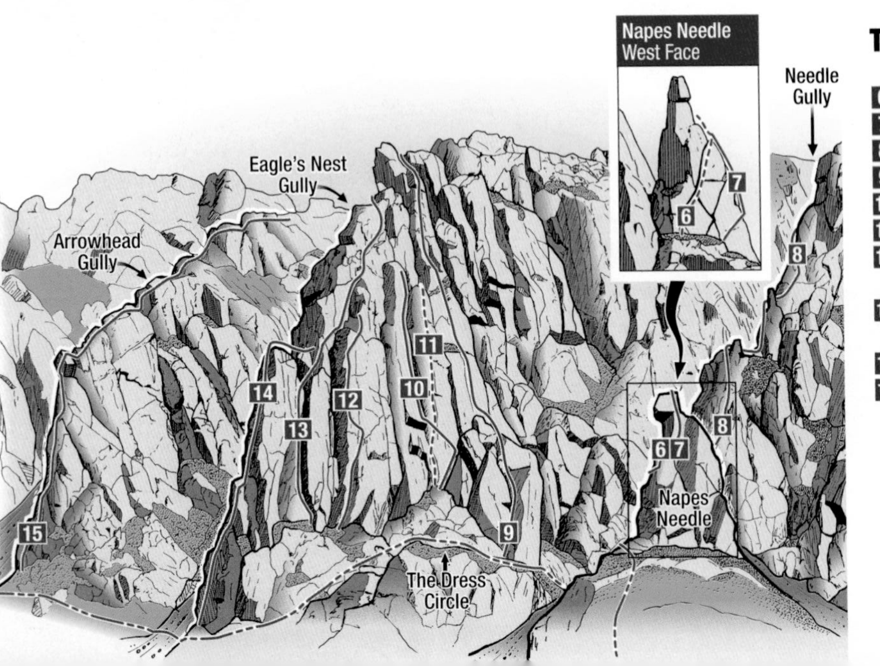

Descent: it is recommended that the leader, having lowered the second back to the ground, downclimbs whilst safeguarded by the runners placed on the ascent and left for this purpose. There have been several accidents amongst parties attempting to abseil from the summit.

6 **The Wasdale Crack**	17m	HS
W P Haskett-Smith (solo) – June 1886		

The most popular way to the top, with contrasting pitches, both very polished. The climb starts from the ledge just right of the gap.

1 13m. Climb the crack, left, then right to its finish; then ascend an easy slab to the shoulder.

2 4m. The highly polished and notorious top block (crux). Mantelshelf onto the ledge below the top block. (It is easier from the right-hand corner but it can be climbed by the left-hand corner.) Traverse left onto the face of the top block and up to the top. Belay round and under the overhanging nose of the top block.

7 **The Arête**	20m	HS
W H Fowler – Sept 1894		

Start at the bottom of the *Wasdale Crack*.

1 16m. Traverse delicately right until a pull round onto the arête can be made. Climb the arête to the shoulder.

2 4m. Pitch 2 of the *Wasdale Crack*.

8 **Needle Ridge**	99m	VD
W P Haskett-Smith (solo) – Sept 1884		

Excellent, safe climbing in superb surroundings on good though polished rock. Start from the gap directly behind the *Needle*.

1 12m. Climb the very polished slab above to a chimney that trends left to a stance below a steep wall.

2 15m. The steep wall above, followed by easier rocks, leads to a broken wall. Climb the wall, then traverse 7 metres right to the rib.

3 25m. Follow the rib above, then easy rocks to a corner, which is climbed on the right.

4 12m. Climb the groove on the left. Alternatively, climb the groove for 3 metres, then traverse right, under the overhang and finish straight up.

5 35m. Easy scrambling to the top.

Eagle's Nest Ridge Area

Up to the left of the gully beyond *Napes Needle* is a ledge level with the base of the *Needle* called the *Dress Circle*. This flat area of ground offers a convenient place for changing when climbing in this area and also provides a comfortable sunbathing and lunch platform with fine views of *Napes Needle*.

The *Ordinary Route* can be used as a descent from the harder climbs in this area.

9 **Amos Moses**	60m	E1+

P Long, T Parker – June 1987

An excellent climb taking a direct line up the buttress facing across the gully towards *Napes Needle*. Start at the bottom of the large subsidiary buttress below the right-hand end of the *Dress Circle*.

1 25m (5a). The buttress is split by a corner crack. Enter this from the left using a small rib, and climb the corner past two bulges to a slab. Climb up to grass ledges and the top of the pinnacle.

2 35m (5b). The wall above is split by a prominent thin crack. Climb the crack to a small ledge, then move up and left to the foot of an obvious groove in the wall above. Enter this and climb it to a junction with the upper section of *Eagle's Nest Ridge*. (This pitch can be split at the top of the thin crack at 15 metres.)

10 **Crocodile Crack**	58m	HVS+

G Oliver, G Arkless, P Ross, N Brown – April 1960

Directly above the *Dress Circle* is an obvious crackline running through an overhang to the top of the buttress. The climbing is good, hard and sustained. Start at the bottom of a flake-crack to the right of the main crack above.

1 43m (5a). Climb the flake-crack for 8 metres (protection), then make a long step left into the main crack, which is climbed to an overhang at 15 metres. Continue up the widening crack, past a small ledge on the left. Up the crack to a large grass ledge.

2 15m. The grassy chimney on the right is followed by a similar chimney to the ridge.

11 **The Cayman**	60m	E2
P Whillance, D Armstrong – Aug 1977		

An eliminate line up the centre of the slender face right of *Crocodile Crack* producing one of the best pitches on the *Napes*. Start just left of *Crocodile Crack* below an overhang.

1 45m (5b). Climb the overhang and crack above to where *Crocodile Crack* crosses the face. Step right, then follow the wall above to an overhang which is climbed via a thin crack above. Continue up the wall above to the next overhang, pull over, then move up and right to a ledge on the arête. Climb the arête to the top of the pinnacle.

2 15m. Pitch 2 of *Crocodile Crack*.

12 **Eagle's Nest Ridge Direct**	37m	MVS
G A Solly, W C Slingsby, G P Baker, W A Brigg (using combined tactics) – April 1892		

Delightful open and delicate climbing up the steep arête at the left end of the *Dress Circle*. Small wires have made all the difference to this once, very bold lead. Start directly below the arête.

(4b). Steep rocks with good holds are climbed, bearing right, to a ledge overlooking the *Dress Circle*. Climb up and left to the arête, using two parallel cracks, then step up to a small platform (*The Eagle's Nest*), followed by another platform (*The Crow's Nest*) after a further 5 metres. Delicate moves, on sloping and polished holds, are made from the platform onto the slab above, which leads to *Eagle's Nest Ordinary Route* (top of Pitch 3).

13 **Eagle's Nest Ordinary Route**	107m	D
G A Solly, M Schintz – April 1892		

A fine, old, traditional route that is now very polished. Start at the bottom of the obvious wide chimney 15 metres left of the *Dress Circle*.

1 30m. Easy rocks lead to the bottom of the chimney, which is climbed either by bridging or by the right wall.

2 12m. Climb up and right through a crevasse then go up a smooth slab to a belay in the corner.

3 12m. The easy chimney above is followed by a slab with polished holds.

4 18m. A chimney on the left is followed by easy scrambling up broken rocks.

5 35m. Following the scratches, scramble along the ridge.

To the left of ***Eagle's Nest Ordinary Route*** the ground falls away steeply to the foot of ***Abbey Buttress***, which is reached by carefully descending this steep and loose section of the path.

14 Abbey Buttress	58m	VD

F Botterill, J de V Hazard – April 1909

Good climbing with a devious and intimidating second pitch. Start from the foot of the buttress in a squeeze chimney (***Fat Man's Agony***) formed by a large detached flake.

1 20m. Climb the chimney and up to a ledge, step right and follow a steep crack to a ledge.
2 20m. Ascend the steep rock above to a wide ledge at 5 metres. Traverse left for 5 metres, then go straight up for 8 metres, where a traverse back right below an overhang can be made onto an arête that leads on good holds to a large ledge.
3 18m. The crack on the left followed by the left corner of the buttress are climbed to a junction with ***Eagle's Nest Ordinary Route***.

Left of ***Abbey Buttress***, a steep awkward descent gives access to ***Eagle's Nest Gully*** and thence more easily to the foot of ***Arrowhead Ridge***.

15 Arrowhead Ridge Direct	80m	VD

A G Topham, H Walker, W C Slingsby – March 1896

An excellent and exposed climb, characterized by the distinctive ***Arrowhead*** at the top of the steep section. Start at the left side of the lowest point of the next major ridge, which is found left of the gully left of ***Abbey Buttress***.

1 15m. Easy rocks followed by steeper climbing leads to a ledge.
2 25m. The steep ridge ahead is climbed either direct or round the corner on the right to the top of a small pinnacle. Step off the pinnacle onto the slab, ascend to the base of the ***Arrowhead*** then make an exposed move on good holds to the top.
3 10m. Stride across the gap and pass along a horizontal section of the ridge.
4 30m. Scramble along the ridge, passing the ***Strid*** en route.

Left: John Ramsden and Alan Stuart (with a combined age of over 150) climbing *Eagle's Nest Ridge Direct* (MVS) **Photo:** Stephen Reid

Ennerdale

by Stephen Reid

This heavily forested valley in the far west of the Lake District possesses several uninspiring crags and one magnificent venue – ***Pillar Rock***.

There are few facilities in this valley. The most convenient campsites are at Buttermere or Wasdale. There is a youth hostel at Gillerthwaite (handy for climbers) and another at Black Sail near the head of the valley.

Pillar Rock

Grid reference: 172 125
Altitude: 600m
Faces: North, East & West
Rock type: Borrowdale Volcanic
Approach time: 1½–2 hrs

Pillar Rock forms the central feature of the rugged north face of Pillar Mountain, and its summit was the focal point for the earliest pioneers of rock climbing in the Lakes. It is an imposing, atmospheric venue offering superb climbs at all grades on impeccable rock.

Pillar Rock is accessible from Ennerdale, Wasdale and Buttermere

Ennerdale – This is the normal access route to the Rock for those having use of mountain bikes as vehicles are not allowed past the Forestry car park at Bowness Knott (109 153). Cycling reduces the 2 hour walk-in by ½ hour.

Follow the main valley road for 7.5 kilometres, crossing the River Liza via a concrete bridge, until the Memorial Footbridge can be seen down to the left and a junction with the upper forest road. Turn right up this and continue another 400 metres to a signed path. Leave bicycles here and take the pleasant path through the forest to follow a stream into the combe. If walking, 50 metres past the concrete bridge a cairn marks the start of a good path which eventually joins the previous route.

Wasdale – The traditional approach. From Wasdale Head (186 088) take the path to Black Sail Pass. Head north-west for 1 kilometre, past Looking Stead, to pick up the well-marked track known as the **High Level Route**, which contours the northern slopes of Pillar Mountain. Follow this route to Robinson's Cairn where the magnificent eastern profile of *Pillar Rock* can be seen.

Buttermere – From Gatesgarth Farm, (194 150) follow the path to Scarth Gap. Do not descend to Black Sail YHA, but follow a path which starts a short distance down on the Ennerdale side and heads diagonally down in a westerly direction to reach the valley bottom at the Memorial Footbridge and a junction with the Ennerdale approach.

Pillar Rock is practically conical in appearance. In fact there are two cones stuck together, forming the summits of *High Man* and *Low Man*. *High Man* the highest point of the crag, is only accessible by climbing, which makes for difficult descents from some routes.

Looking from the north, on the left of the main crag is the *Shamrock*, a wide buttress of ribs and grooves which has a conspicuous heathery ledge running diagonally across its centre. Separating the *Shamrock* from *Pillar Rock* is *Walker's Gully*. To the right of *Walker's Gully* is the *North Face of Low Man*, which rises vertically from the gully initially, then further right it becomes more broken in structure, the home for routes such as *North Climb*. The *North Face* increases in size moving rightwards, until it forms an arête (the *Bounding Buttress*) at the junction with the *West Face of Low Man*. At the base of the *West Face* is a deeply-cut gully known as the *Waterfall* which marks the right-hand extremity of the crag as seen from the valley. The *North* and *West Faces* of this lower part of *Pillar* rise up to form a rounded dome, *Low Man*.

Above *Low Man*, the upper cone rises to form the summit of *Pillar* called *High Man*. On the right of this is the clean *West Face of High Man*, which is an upper extension to the *West Face of Low Man*, the two being separated by a series of grassy shelves which form the lower part of the *Old West Route*, a useful descent.

The 'uphill' side of the *West Face* ends abruptly at a deep chimney which forms a pronounced notch behind the *High Man* called *Jordan Gap*, which separates the summit of *Pillar Rock* from *Pisgah*, the truncated pinnacle which rises out of the main mountainside to the south. *Jordan Gap* forms the short southern face of *Pillar Rock*. Continuing around the summit of *High Man*, the *East* and *North*

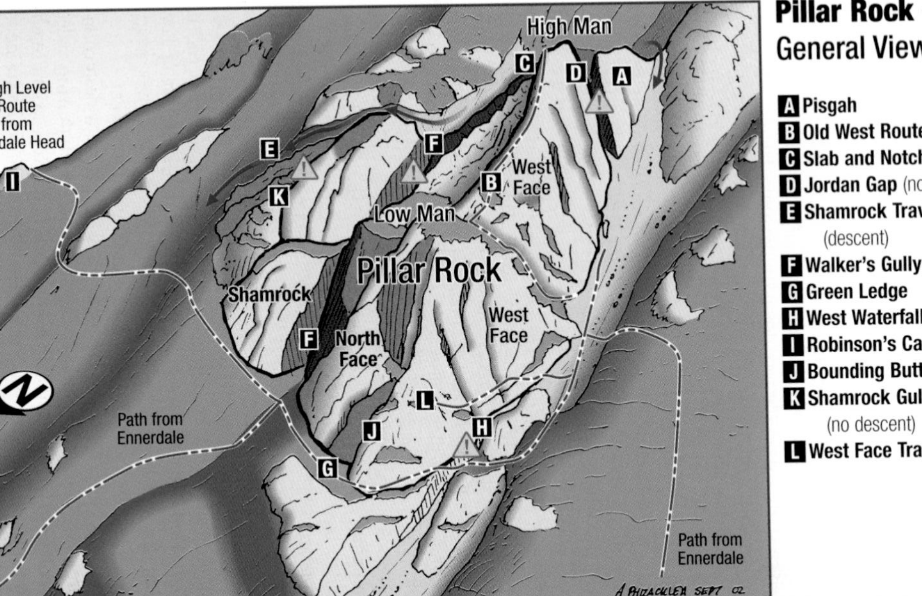

Pillar Rock – General View

- **A Pisgah**
- **B Old West Route** (descent)
- **C Slab and Notch** (descent)
- **D Jordan Gap** (no descent)
- **E Shamrock Traverse** (descent)
- **F Walker's Gully** (no descent)
- **G Green Ledge**
- **H West Waterfall** (no descent)
- **I Robinson's Cairn**
- **J Bounding Buttress**
- **K Shamrock Gully** (no descent)
- **L West Face Traverse**

Faces form steep, rough ground unsuitable for continuous climbing, but it provides an excellent venue for scrambling. One classic scramble, the ***Slab and Notch Route***, is the easiest ascent and descent from ***High Man*** (see Route **26**).

Shamrock

Above: Jim Fairey on the second pitch of *Eros* (E2–) **Photo:** Stephen Reid

A large rambling crag with several long and interesting routes, in the main on excellent rock. There is, unfortunately, an excess of grassy ledges, and dry conditions are therefore desirable. The ***Shamrock*** is split by the ***Great Heather Shelf***, which runs diagonally across its centre and is reached by easy scrambling, starting just right of a huge, prominent overhanging wall.

Descent: the easiest descent from the summit of ***Shamrock***, and indeed from the ***Slab and Notch*** area of ***Pillar***, is to gain the hillside above the head of ***Shamrock Gully***, and above the top of the scree funnel leading into ***Walker's Gully*** (this is at a similar level to the summit of ***Pisgah***). This is the start of an exposed sloping diagonal rake lying above the crag, called the ***Shamrock Traverse***. This is well marked and leads down to the open fellside on the left.

1 **Photon**	147m	MVS+

W A Barnes, A Jackman, J C Eilbeck, D A Elliott – Sept 1967

A long and varied climb of a mountaineering character. The stances are large and the protection good. Start by scrambling 60 metres up the ***Great Heather Shelf*** to the foot of a cleaned groove on the left. Alternatively reach the same point by climbing ***Thanatos*** (HVS) and descending down the ***Great Heather Shelf***.

1 25m (4b). Climb the steepening groove.
2 30m (4c). Move right, and go up a slabby corner to the foot of the groove. Ascend the steep corner to a bulge and climb this using the steep crack on the right. Continue up the crack to reach a good ledge on the left.
3 37m. Climb the corner above and continue past a huge chockstone to a good ledge. Climb the mossy slab on the left to finish on a ledge overlooking *Shamrock Gully*.
4 25m (4b). Climb up a couple of metres to the left of the steep wall of the final tower, then traverse 3 metres left along a grass ledge under a shallow groove to climb up into a broken groove, which is followed to the crest of the ridge.
5 30m. Easier climbing along the ridge to the *Tea Table*.

2 Eros	152m	E2–
W S Lounds, J C Eilbeck – May 1968		

An extremely good climb, taking the bold ribs starting to the right of *Photon*. Start on the immediate right of the first groove of *Photon*.
1 25m (5a). Climb the rib direct to a mossy slab, which leads to a good ledge at the foot of a sharp arête. A bold pitch.
2 30m (5b). Gain the steep rib above, which is climbed on its right side for 18 metres. Continue up the slab above to a ledge, then traverse left to a grassy corner – a fine and even bolder pitch.
3 22m (5b). Climb the corner-groove above (the right edge of the diamond-shaped wall) with difficulty, using the rib on the right as necessary.
4 20m (4a). Continue to a ledge on the right. Step left across the groove and climb the left edge of a slab to a ridge, which leads to beneath the final tower.
5 25m (4b). As for *Photon*. Climb up a couple of metres to the left of the steep wall of the final tower, then traverse 3 metres left along a grass ledge, under a shallow groove, to climb up into a broken groove, which is followed to the crest of the ridge.
6 30m. Easier climbing along the ridge to the *Tea Table*.

3 Thanatos/Electron	158m	HVS
W S Lounds, J C Eilbeck – May 1968	**A G Cram, J C Eilbeck** – Sept 1966	

One of the best outings at its grade on the crag. Start just right of the lowest part of the crag, beneath the large corner. Pitch 4 is slow to dry.

Pillar Rock – Shamrock

1 Photon	MVS+	**3 Thanatos/Electron**	HVS
2 Eros	E2–	**4 Walker's Gully**	MVS+

1 18m (4b). **Thanatos**. Climb a slab and vegetation to a corner. Go up this for a couple of metres, then move left onto the steep slab, which leads to a bilberry ledge. Continue to the base of the corner to belay.

2 30m (5a). An excellent, well protected pitch. Climb the corner to some jammed blocks below the first overhang. Traverse left onto a rib, and enter a groove below the second overhang. Make difficult moves on the left to reach a good ledge.

3 10m. An easy groove leads to the *Great Heather Shelf* just right of the big corner of *Electron*. Belay under a short hourglass-shaped chimney.

4 25m (5a). **Electron**. Climb the right-angled corner on the left to a chockstone at 6 metres. Continue over an awkward bulge, up the corner, with another awkward move higher up. Belay on a large grass ledge.

5 25m (4b). Continue up the groove for 12 metres, then cross the small grass ledge and ascend the wall at the back to belay on a large block just below and to the left of a prominent crack.

6 20m (4c). The imposing crack, with resting places and protection en route.

7 30m (4b). Move right and go up the grey arête to a cairn. Move 6 metres right and ascend a second arête on good holds to the *Tea Table*.

4 **Walker's Gully**	125m	MVS+

O G Jones, G D Abraham, A E Field – Jan 1899

One of the few good gully climbs of the district; it follows the deep cleft separating *Shamrock* from the *North Face of Low Man*. The pitches may be split if necessary. Helmets are strongly advised as there is much loose scree above the gully. The last pitch may be found harder by short people.

1 27m. Climb a short chimney, easily, followed by scree, to the foot of a high, green chimney. Climb the right wall of the chimney and gain a sloping terrace.

2 40m (4a). An exposed groove, with poor holds, is climbed until it is possible to step on to the first chockstone in the chimney. Another chockstone just above is easily surmounted, followed by scrambling up the bed of the gully for 30 metres.

3 18m (4b). Climb rocks on the left of a chimney to a cave, which is usually wet. Climb up behind, then over, a chockstone; then bridge the gully until a sloping chockstone is reached. Another chockstone is very awkward.

4 25m. A short scree slope leads to a cave formed by a large chockstone. The through route is strenuous but short. It can be avoided by climbing the left wall, outside the cave. A further through route leads to a wet cave.

5 15m (4c). More large chockstones are encountered until the cave below the crux is reached. Here, a thread runner may be found

high up in the recess between the capstone and the exit wall, but it is awkward to fix. Move across the right wall on sloping holds to a recess under the final capstone. The tall can then back-up – back on the left wall. Otherwise continue climbing strenuously up the right wall.

Low Man

Above: Bob Wightman on *Tapestry* (E4)
Photo: Al Phizacklea

North Face of Low Man

The *North Face* is a large crag, up to 130 metres high, which offers a good variety of worthwhile climbs. On the left a steep white wall rises out of *Walker's Gully*, while on the centre and right-hand side, Difficults and Extremes lie side by side, many of which are among the best in the district. Virtually all the routes become very unpleasant in wet conditions. Just right of *Walker's Gully* there is a short step up in the path which brings one to the left-hand end of *Green Ledge*, a wide terrace running under the *North Face*. Towards the far end of *Green Ledge* is *Bounding Buttress*, a curved flying buttress of rock rising almost half the height of the crag. Just beyond *Bounding Buttress*, *Green Ledge* peters out, but an easy scramble leads down into the bed of the *Waterfall* under the *West Face* from where it is possible to reach the *West Face* (to the left is D, to the right is M).

Descent: the quickest descent for the first three routes described is to scramble across leftwards to reach the amphitheatre above *Walker's Gully*, where a scree slope leads diagonally leftwards to reach the top of *Shamrock Traverse*. The easiest descent to regain the foot of the *North Face* for the routes to the right of *North Climb* is to ascend to the summit of *High Man* by a well marked moderate scramble up the wall behind the summit of the *Low Man*, and then to descend *Slab and Notch* (see Route 26) and the *Shamrock Traverse*. To gain the *West Face*, descend the *Old West Route*, the steep scramble descent which leads rightwards (looking in) from the summit of the *Low Man*. This is not easy to locate from above on first acquaintance.

5 **Grooved Wall**	99m	VS+

H M Kelly, H G Knight, W G Standing – April 1928

A good climb, despite the first pitch, taking the prominent series of difficult grooves running up the right wall of *Walker's Gully*. Start immediately right of the foot of the gully and scramble 15 metres up grass. All difficulties are well protected.

1 30m. High grassy ledges lead up to a wide broken chimney composed of a great flake for one of its sides. The chimney is followed to its top.

2 25m (5a). The first groove above is followed and a ledge attained. Above is an overhang, which is the crux of the climb. Gain the groove above and continue up it to a good spike belay.

3 20m (4b). Continue up the sustained groove to belay by a corner on the side of the groove.

4 24m (4c). The final groove above is not without interest, but ends after 12 metres. Continue up ledges and grass to a rock gateway which opens onto the scree just above *Walker's Gully*.

6 **Tapestry**	70m	E4

A Stephenson, C Sice, W Young, R G Wilson – April 1980

Fit to hang on any wall! Excellent climbing in good situations but with a serious second pitch. Scramble 12 metres up from *Walker's Gully* to start at the foot of its steep right-bounding wall.

1 25m (5b). Climb the centre of a huge pinnacle to finish by its left edge (junction with *Grooved Wall*), and belay beneath the overhang on the crux pitch of that climb.

2 20m (6a). Climb the overhang of *Grooved Wall* and immediately step right to a shallow corner. Follow this almost to the top, then gain the wall on its left and climb it, moving right to finish on the belay ledge.

3 25m (5b). Another very fine pitch. From the right-hand end of the ledge, a groove in the arête leads to a soaring, leftward hand-traverse. Follow this and then climb a crack back right to finish.

7 Sheol/Cunning Stunts/Tapestry Connection | 67m | E2

P1: **A G Cram, T Martin** – April 1965 P2: **A Stephenson, W Young** – April 1981 P3: as above

A excellent combination. Start by scrambling up grass to start at the foot of the impressive, jagged soaring crack in the wall immediately right of the start of *Grooved Wall*.

1 22m (5b). The strenuous crack, which is nearly vertical and tilts slightly to one side, is followed in its entirety to a good stance and chockstone belay.

2 20m (5c). Climb up leftwards to a higher ledge and then step left across the overhanging wall to gain a flake-crack on the arête. Levitate strenuously onto the exposed ledge and up twin jamming cracks to a belay below the final pitch of *Tapestry*. (This pitch can be omitted by easier climbing (5a) up right and then back left from the stance, lowering the standard to E2–.)

3 25m (5b). Pitch 3 of *Tapestry*.

8 North Climb | 96m | S

W P Haskett-Smith, G Hastings, W C Slingsby – July 1891

The route is a superb, classic 'Difficult' with an awkward finish, which has been the scene of many epics. Start from the very left end of *Green Ledge* where a short wall leads to a square platform.

1 10m. An easy mantelshelf and short slab lead to a large ledge at the foot of a broken groove. This groove is the lower section of **Savage Gully** (MVS, 1901).

2 20m. The groove leads to a recess. A wall on the right is followed by a chimney in the gully and then a groove to a small grassy bay. On the left, the smooth double groove of *Savage Gully* continues in a soaring line. On the right is a deep twisting chimney.

3 34m. Climb the chimney and then trend leftwards up an open groove. Scramble up to a belay on a small ledge at the meeting of two narrow chimneys.

4 9m. The *Stomach Traverse*. Climb the right-hand chimney which curves to its right in the upper half.

5 18m. The be-chockstoned corner is climbed via a capstone followed by a walk of 6 metres to the *Split Blocks*. These are climbed by the obvious chimney. Traverse to the left, crossing the *Strid*, to a ledge below and right of the *Nose*.

6 5m. The *Nose*. From the corner, work out left to stand on the tip of the projecting flake. Hard moves up and left gain better holds

High Man
Low Man
5
8
4
9
6 7
Savage Gully
Shamrock Buttress
6
5
7
4

Pillar Rock – North Face

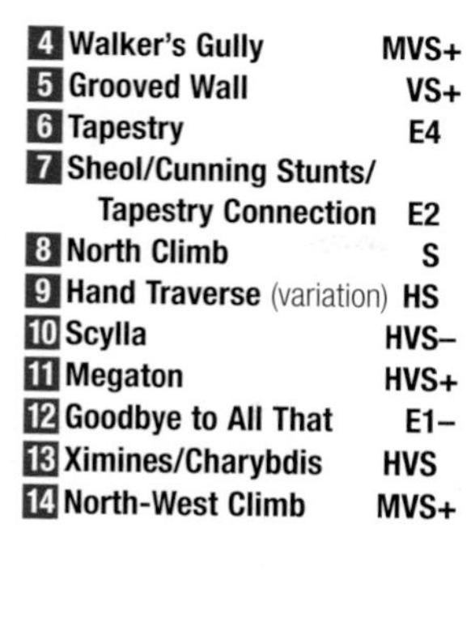

- **4** Walker's Gully — MVS+
- **5** Grooved Wall — VS+
- **6** Tapestry — E4
- **7** Sheol/Cunning Stunts/ Tapestry Connection — E2
- **8** North Climb — S
- **9** Hand Traverse (variation) — HS
- **10** Scylla — HVS–
- **11** Megaton — HVS+
- **12** Goodbye to All That — E1–
- **13** Ximines/Charybdis — HVS
- **14** North-West Climb — MVS+

and a belay just above. (The grassy gully leads in 60 metres to the summit of *Low Man*.)

9 The Hand Traverse (Variation) | 8m | HS

G A Solly, G Hastings, H A Gwynne, E Greenwood, W C Slingsby – Feb 1892

An excellent alternative finish, particularly when the *Nose* is wet.

6. From the right end of the ledge below the *Nose*, climb the steep wall for about 3 metres on tremendous holds until the sharp edge of a flake is reached. Traverse boldly left to the top of the *Nose*.

Fifty metres along ***Green Ledge*** is the start of a steep grassy bay guarded by a short wall. Thirty metres further right, this bay is bounded on the right by a great flying buttress of rock, the ***Bounding Buttress***, which descends all the way to the path. The next three routes start up the grassy bay to gain cleaner rock above.

10 Scylla | 123m | HVS–

A G Cram, W Young – June 1963

A good route of a mountaineering character, which climbs the crack in the centre of the huge upper wall on the *North Face of Low Man*. Start at the left side of the grassy bay, just right of a short impending band of rock. When looking up, high on the crag will be seen a blank wall with a crack in it. Below the wall is a square chimney which forms the second pitch of *Scylla*. If you can see this chimney then you are in the right area. Start up left a few metres at a grassy groove.

1 25m. Scramble into the corner to a small groove. Follow the groove, move right and go over grass ledges and a large chockstone to the foot of the very large square chimney, directly below the centre of the huge wall.

2 25m. Climb the chimney to belay below the wall.

3 30m (4c). Climb the wall by a crack in the centre, which becomes a chimney-groove at 12 metres. Avoid a large loose block on the left and continue up the easier groove to belay on the highest ledge.

4 25m (5a). From the left end of the ledge, pull up an overhanging wall. Traverse left to the foot of a narrow crack, which is climbed to the top of a pinnacle, from where a swing right leads to easier ground. Scramble right to a stance.

5 18m (4c). Climb the arête on the right of a wide, dirty gully to the summit of *Low Man*.

11 **Megaton**	120m	HVS+
W Young, W A Barnes – May 1972		

A varied and interesting route which is sustained at a good level and contains a bold slab pitch. Start towards the right-hand side of ***Green Ledge*** some 7 metres left of the ***Bounding Buttress*** below the steep grassy bay.

1 18m. Climb a 3 metre rib/spike to grass. Make the best of the rock rib above to a rightward-rising grass ramp under a steep slab. It is best to follow this rightwards to belay under the steep wall of the ***Bounding Buttress***.

2 26m (5a). From the lower end of the grass ramp, starting some 5 metres from the ***Bounding Buttress*** wall on the right, climb boldly up the slab above for 9 metres before moving left to gain a vague rightward-curving fault which is followed to easier ground. Follow the general line back leftwards and take a belay well up on the left by a pile of blocks on a ledge under an impressive overhung deep V-groove (this is the main pitch of **Caucus Race**, E3 (6a), 1993). A better protected alternative is to climb the thin crackline 2 metres to the right which is quitted at two-thirds height for a rising traverse leftwards to the belay.

3 36m (5a). Step off the pile of blocks, and traverse to the right along two rock ledges to a groove. Climb this for 2 metres then leave it to move leftwards up a gangway to a thin corner crack which is followed until the angle eases. Climb up rightwards for 12 metres or so to a recess with a dubious spike and a loose pebble thread in a corner.

4 20m (4c). Pull directly over the bulge above into a groove and follow it to a huge shallow niche. Continue in the same line to easier ground under a steep crack. (There is a similar crack some 7 metres to the right which is ***Oppenheimer's Chimney*** on ***North-West Climb***).

5 20m (4c). Climb the crack (not as bad as it looks!) to the top of ***Low Man***.

12 **Goodbye to All That**	124m	E1–
S J H Reid, S Stout – Sept 1996		

A direct line on excellent rock taking in the prominent, ragged crack right of the main pitch of ***Megaton*** and culminating in a sensational top pitch. Start as for ***Megaton***, 7 metres left of the ***Bounding Buttress***.

1 18m. As for ***Megaton***, climb a 3 metre wall to heather and then a vague rock rib to a rightward-slanting grass ledge under slabs. Belay under the bounding wall on the right at the foot of a slab.

2 26m (4c). Two metres left of the ***Bounding Buttress*** wall is a thin crack in the slab. Climb this direct to a narrow bilberry ledge and huge flake belay.

3 36m (5b). Climb up into an overhung scoop just left of the belay and pull out awkwardly onto a small ledge on the left. Climb directly up to join ***Megaton*** at the right-hand end of its traverse and continue straight up the crack directly above (***Megaton*** goes left along a narrow ramp into a narrow corner), pulling out rightwards to easier ground. Climb directly up over bulges and slabby rock to belay as for ***Megaton*** and *North-West Climb* in a recess with a dubious spike and a loose pebble thread in a corner.

4 20m (5a). Pull directly over the bulge above into a groove (part of Pitch 4 of ***Megaton***) and follow the groove for 3 metres until it is possible to traverse right along a narrow footledge and pull out diagonally rightwards to emerge into a huge shallow niche. Climb the wall on the right to a square pocket and traverse right to a flake on the arête. Go straight up to easy ground below a deep chimney/crack (***Oppenheimer's Chimney***). The best belay is well below the chimney on a small quartz ledge on a superbly exposed rib out on the extreme right.

5 24m (5b). A bold pitch. Climb up to the base of ***Oppenheimer's Chimney*** and fix some good runners! Traverse horizontally leftwards on blocks to some tiny footholds on a rib and make a long reach up and left for a jug. (The technical standard now drops to 4c.) Climb directly up the wall above in an exposed position on good holds but with no further protection until eventually a runner can be placed under a chockstone on the left in the final crack of ***Megaton***. Further juggy climbing, slightly rightwards, leads up a rib to easy ground and the top.

13 **Ximenes/Charybdis**	138m	HVS

P1–2: **A G Cram, W Young** – April 1968 P3–5: **A G Cram, W Young** – Sept 1964

A long and varied outing. Start 2 metres right of the left edge of the ***Bounding Buttress*** at an overhung recess below a crack. This is just left of the initial gangway of *North-West Climb*.

1 18m (5a). **Ximines**. Gain the crack from the recess, and follow it strenuously to an easing. Move left and climb the slab to the foot

of the crack in the prow of the buttress, just left of the wide chimney on *North-West Climb*.

2 33m (5b). Climb the crack, which is awkward and strenuous but well protected, to a ledge (possible belay) and continue up easy slabs to the *Terrace* at the left-hand end of the *West Wall Traverse*.

3 35m (5a). **Charybdis**. Above is a deep overhanging groove with a large flake on its left wall. (To the right of this is a much wider open book corner which is the first pitch of *Goth*.) Climb up the glacis and steepening grassy rock into the base of the overhung groove. Descend a little and surmount the left wall by laybacking up the flake. Return rightwards along an awkward gangway and move up to belay on a sloping ledge.

4 30m (5a). Climb the cracked green groove above moving left at the top to a ledge. Climb up to the roof and pull out rightwards to gain the superb arête which is followed boldly to a belay on a small quartz ledge.

5 22m (5a). The obvious deep cleft up on the left is *Oppenheimer's Chimney* which is the final pitch of *North-West Climb*, and the curving crack on the right is the final pitch of *Goth*. In between the two, and directly above, is a shallow groove. Climb this to a bulge and pull out rightwards to gain a left-slanting crack which is followed to the top.

(The original start for *Charybdis* is much easier than *Ximenes* and followed the gangway start of *North-West Climb*, but, where that climb moves left, continues in two or three pitches (4c) in a direct line via a chimney and a cracked wall to the *Terrace*.)

14 **North-West Climb**	130m	MVS+

F W Botterill, L J Oppenheimer, A Botterill, J H Taylor – June 1906

A fine route, giving varied climbing and good situations. Start at the right-hand end of *Green Ledge*, underneath the *Bounding Buttress*, at an obvious rightwards-slanting, short gangway.

1 20m. Climb the gangway to a ledge, and follow a chimney for 10 metres to a slab. Avoid the continuation chimney by traversing left across the slab to belay at the foot of a much wider chimney.

2 36m (4a). The wide chimney is taken direct to finish on a grassy slab in a corner (possible belay). Avoid the chimney crack ahead by climbing up a short crack onto the crest of the buttress on the left and follow another crack up this until the angle eases at the

Terrace. Cross the large platform rightwards 9 metres to belay at the base of a smooth easy-angled slab.

3 25m (4b). Ascend the slab and a short grassy corner to a grassy ledge under a prominent steep V-groove. Avoid this by traversing the ledge leftwards around a rib and climb up into the first of a series of three recesses. Carry on up into a second recess which at its farther end contains a dubious pointed spike, a solid blunt spike and a loose but threadable pebble in a short corner.

4 25m (4b). The undercut groove directly above the belay is part of ***Megaton***. To the left of this groove are three other vague grooves, the first of which is known as ***Lamb's Chimney***. To gain this, traverse left to a nose and ascend this to a ledge containing a large block. Climb the groove above, mainly on the left, and pulling out left at its top. Stride immediately back right and go up to a belay below the impending crack above which is the final pitch of ***Megaton***.

5 24m (4b). Traverse rightwards under bulges and go up to the foot of another impending crack (***Oppenheimer's Chimney***). After an awkward start it becomes more reasonable and easy scrambling then leads to the top of ***Low Man***.

West Face of Low Man

This is one of the best faces of ***Pillar Rock*** with excellent rock that dries quickly after rain and catches the afternoon sun. This face is reached from below the ***North Face*** by following the ***Green Ledge*** rightwards to where it drops away into a wide, wet gully. This cuts deeply into the hillside below the ***West Face of Low Man***, and is known as the ***Waterfall***. An awkward scramble leads down and onto the scree on the other side of the ***Waterfall***, where a path leads up below the ***West Face of Pillar***. When approaching this face from Buttermere or Ennerdale, the waterfall crossing is avoided by ascending the fellside to the right of the ***Waterfall***.

The climbs are reached by following the ***West Face Traverse***, a slightly worn scramble that starts some 10 metres up the scree from the head of the ***Waterfall***. This point is also about 40 metres down the scree from the start of the ***Old West*** and opposite the lower approach path that ends on the other side of the scree. A vague path traverses more or less horizontally, passing under a long, low smooth wall and then rising slightly to the huge block at the foot of ***Appian Way***. A slight descent from here leads round the edge of the crag to the ***Terrace*** half way up the ***North Face*** at the top of the ***Bounding***

Pillar Rock – Low Man West Face

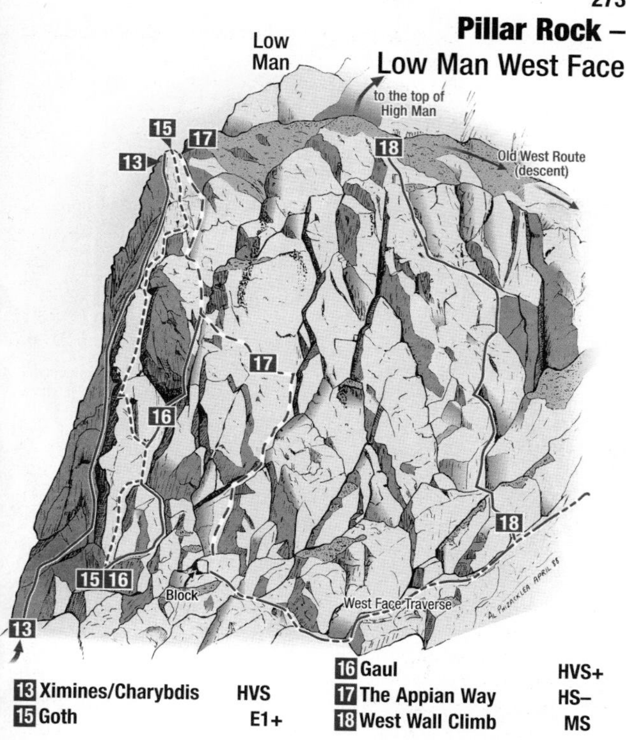

13 Ximines/Charybdis	**HVS**	**16 Gaul**	**HVS+**
15 Goth	**E1+**	**17 The Appian Way**	**HS–**
		18 West Wall Climb	**MS**

Buttress, and the start of *Goth*. All the routes end on the summit of *Low Man* from whence the lower section of the *Old West* makes a good **descent**: from just below the summit of *Low Man*, scramble rightwards down a well marked way to an exit onto scree near the foot of *Rib and Slab Climb*.

The climbs are described from **left** to **right**.

15 **Goth**	75m	E1+

M de St Jorre, N Hannaby – July 1959

The route follows the huge open curving groove at the junction of the *North* and *West Faces* of *Low Man*. A fine climb with a well positioned but intimidating crux that requires very small wires for protection

and probably warrants E2 if you are short. Follow the ***West Wall Traverse*** leftwards to a huge block on a grass ledge at the start of ***Appian Way***. Scramble down and left, passing a smaller block, to another grass ledge at the foot of an open book corner with an undercut arête on its left (left again is the deep overhanging groove of ***Charybdis*** with a large flake on its left wall). A blunt spike belay will be found at this point. A good alternative approach is to climb ***Ximines*** from *Green Ledge* to the *Terrace*.

1 20m (4c). Climb the vague open groove to a hanging stance in the V-groove beneath the overhang.

2 35m (5b). Traverse left for 2 metres to the foot of a groove leading up to the roof of the overhang. This is climbed until a dubious block in the roof of a small overhang is reached; then break out left across a small slab to an arête and runners. Climb the poorly protected overhanging wall above to a narrow sloping ledge and hand-traverse strenuously to the corner on the right. Continue up this until a small overhang bars the way. Traverse left across the wall to a stance on a quartz ledge.

3 20m (4a). Climb up to a short curving crack on the right. Ascend this and finish up rough slabs.

16 Gaul	73m	HVS+
J D Wilson, T Martin – June 1974		

An excellent main pitch, at the upper limit of the grade, makes this a route not to be missed. Start as for ***Goth*** at the blunt spike belay.

1 20m (4b). Cross grass rightwards to a short shallow greasy chimney. Climb this and leftwards up the slab above to a grass ledge on *Goth*.

2 35m (5a). Climb onto the slab on the right and cross it to a groove. Follow this and the wall above with difficulty, to an easier groove (*Appian Way*) which leads to a grass terrace. A good pitch.

3 18m (4a). Ascend the crack on the left as for *Appian Way*.

17 The Appian Way	65m	HS–
H M Kelly, R E W Pritchard – 1923		

A very pleasant and exposed route with delicate wall climbing and good situations. Follow the ***West Wall Traverse*** leftwards some 70 metres to a huge block on a grass ledge.

1 20m. Avoid the mossy open chimney by climbing up on the left for 4 metres and traversing to the right across the top of the chimney; then go up the corner to a stance with a flake belay.

2 15m. Climb the thin crack in the corner and, from the top of this, traverse delicately left across the imposing wall to a spike of rock on the skyline. Stance and belay on spike.

3 12m. Move left and ascend a series of steep ledges straight ahead to a grassy terrace, where will be found a large block leaning against the wall. Thread belay.

4 18m. The slightly overhanging crack on the left of the block is followed by slabs.

18 West Wall Climb	65m	MS

H M Kelly, C F Holland, C G Crawford – July 1919

An excellent route of continuous interest. Follow the ***West Wall Traverse*** a few metres to a platform below a 3 metre wall.

1 15m. A short crack leads to a grass rake. Cross this and make a hard start up a V-groove until it is possible to pull out left to a sloping ledge and flake belay.

2 15m. Step right: steep rocks then lead to a rock glacis. A superb crack in the wall on the right leads to a small sloping ledge some 3 metres below the end of the crack.

3 15m. Make an awkward traverse leftwards, crossing a huge scoop, to belay at the base of a cracked pinnacle.

4 20m. From the top of the pinnacle climb a short awkward groove, or the wall on its left, and then easier rock to the top of ***Low Man***.

High Man

West Face of High Man

The most impressive face of ***Pillar Rock*** and also the quickest to dry. The notes on the ***West Face of Low Man*** provide the approach details for this area.

The climbs are reached from the Western Scree or by scrambling up the ***Old West Route***. The routes are described from **left** to **right**. **Descents:** *Slab and Notch Climb* (Route 26) followed by the Western Scree provides the easiest descent. Care is needed not to dislodge scree whilst descending ***Western Gully***, which starts where the separate pinnacle of ***Pisgah*** merges in with the main mountainside. An alternative descent is provided by the ***Old West Route***, which follows the rounded ridge down from the summit of ***High Man*** to the top of ***Low Man***, where the descent from ***Low Man*** can be followed. Don't try to descend ***West Jordan Gully*** from the ***Jordan Gap*** as it's a loose Severe.

19 **Gondor**	70m	E2
A G Cram, K Robson (one point of aid) – April 1967 FFA: **G Tinnings** – 1978		

An impressive and exposed climb, which is both strenuous and delicate. The route follows the bulging arête on the left of the prominent groove of *Gomorrah*.

1 25m. Pitch 1 of *Gomorrah*.
2 18m (5b). Climb the groove in the arête to the bulge. Above on the left is a large triangular hold. Pull up, and move boldly up right until the angle eases. Belay in a small corner below a grass ledge.
3 27m (5c). Climb down from the stance for 2 metres and traverse delicately right, round the nose onto the wall. Climb up and left to easier climbing, following a groove to a large ledge and block belay. An alternative way to start this pitch (the original route) is to climb the overhanging arête on the right wall for 2 metres (very bold), then move onto the wall and continue up as above.

20 **Gomorrah**	80m	VS–
H M Kelly, C F Holland – Aug 1919		

A superb climb which ascends the big groove on the left side of the ***West Face of High Man***. Start on a small grass ledge, well below and left of the huge triangular roof, reached by scrambling up the ***Old West*** some 40 metres to a belay on a spike just left of a rough rib.

1 25m (4a). Follow the rib to a green ledge on the left. A wall and slab lead to huge block belays.
2 20m (4b). Step up right and traverse round the rib and across the corner to a chimney on the right below the big groove. This is climbed to a stance below a small roof.
3 35m (4b). Continue up the groove, overcoming a bulge, to the top.

Pillar Rock –
High Man West Face

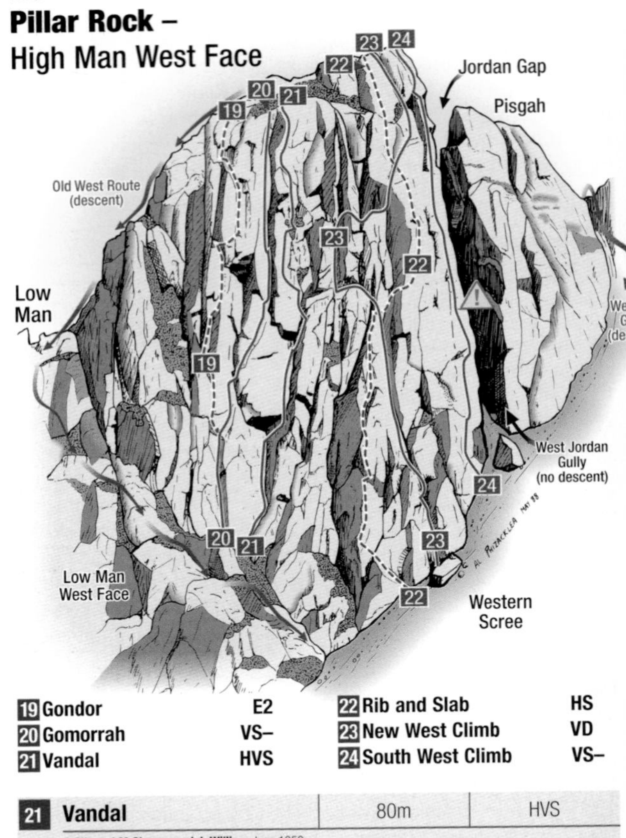

19	Gondor	E2	22	Rib and Slab	HS
20	Gomorrah	VS–	23	New West Climb	VD
21	Vandal	HVS	24	South West Climb	VS–

21 **Vandal**	80m	HVS

G Oliver, J M Cheesmond, L Willis – June 1959

A fine route, steep and well protected in its lower half, but becoming rather worrying with height. It takes the grooveline arising from the large triangular overhang of the *West Face*. Start directly below the triangular roof.

1 25m (4c). Climb the grassy corner to about 5 metres below the roof, where a line up the wall on the right leads with a difficult move to a small ledge. The short curving crack on the right is followed to a good stance.

2 35m (5a). A fine pitch. Climb the main crack, passing a large overhang on the left to a small overhang at 12 metres. Move left round this and either traverse left to the left arête, or move up and traverse left a few metres higher. Climb boldly up the slab above until it is possible to traverse right into an easier slabby amphitheatre and eventually to find a runner. Climb up leftwards to a flake belay on a ledge at the foot of a flaky rib.

3 20m (4a). Climb the hollow rib to the top. Alternatively, go back down into the amphitheatre and traverse rightwards through a gap in the jagged arête to climb up the final few metres of the chimney of **Sodom** (VS, 1919) – this was the original finish.

22 **Rib and Slab Climb**	90m	HS

C F Holland, H M Kelly, C G Crawford – July 1919

At its grade, one of the best climbs in the Lakes, and an extremely enjoyable way to the summit of ***Pillar Rock***. Start at an area of white rock 2 metres below the large embedded block which is at the foot of *New West Climb*.

1 26m. Traverse left along a footledge and continue leftwards to a steep rib with a groove. Climb this to break out left at a small ledge. Climb the slab right of the groove, or the rib on its right, to a ledge. A bold pitch.

2 20m. The groove above is hard to start (crux) but the difficulties soon ease. Climb the steep rib on the left of the groove of *New West Climb* to a stance at the top.

3 20m. Traverse right and upwards onto a superb rough slab; climb it, rising rightwards to a rib which is followed to the belay blocks of *New West Climb*.

4 24m. Follow the crack of *New West Climb* for about 3 metres then traverse leftwards via a block. Climb the blistered slab and rib above directly to the top.

23 **New West Climb**	87m	VD

G D Abraham, A P Abraham, C W Barton, J H Wigner – May 1901

A fine climb, which finds its way through areas of rock usually reserved for harder things. The situations are superb, making it one of the best routes of this standard in the Lake District. Start just above a big embedded block, 25 metres or so down the scree from *West Jordan Gully*.

1 20m. Follow easy rocks in a shallow chimney, trending slightly to the left, to a rib which leads to a small corner. Follow a steep staircase to belay on a good ledge.
2 10m. Climb a wide, shallow chimney which leads to a small platform, and traverse horizontally left for 4 metres to a good belay.
3 17m. Climb the obvious groove to ledges and make an awkward traverse left to the foot of a chimney.
4 20m. The imposing chimney above is climbed or thrutched, depending on ability and girth, to an obvious chockstone at 9 metres (possible belay). Avoid the chimney above by traversing horizontally right and around a rib to surmount a pile of blocks which form a magnificent belay.
5 20m. Climb the crack up the slab above to a small ledge. Finish via a block-filled grassy groove on the right or the slab on the left.

24 **South-West Climb**	70m	VS–

H R Pope, W B Brunskill (finishing via New West Climb) – Sept 1911
Route as described: **H M Kelly, C F Holland, C G Crawford, N E Odell** – July 1919

Delectable climbing on small but positive holds. A justly popular route. The start is 1 metre left of the entrance to ***West Jordan Gully***.
1 30m (4b). Easy climbing up a short groove leads to a grassy ledge on the left of a slab. Climb the slab to a deep-cut hold. Move awkwardly right and continue up the slab to where it steepens. Good holds lead to a small ledge. Continue up the slab on the edge of the gully to a second ledge.
2 22m (4b). Traverse left for 4 metres, then climb the slab, keeping to the right. Traverse right towards ***Jordan Gap***, under a large block, to a stance. A bold pitch.
3 18m (4b). Return under the block and climb up a steep rib, to the summit of ***High Man***.

East Face of High Man

25 **Slab and Notch Climb**	50m	M

J W E Conybeare, A J Butler, E Leeke, J C Leeke, T R C Campbell, J D Poyer, J W Pratt – Aug 1863

One of the easiest routes of ascent and descent on the Rock; it is described in both directions. Numerous belay possibilities exist en route. Start at the foot of ***East Jordan Gully***.

Climb up on to a large easy-angled slab on the right, traverse easily across its base and climb a steep corner to the ***Notch***

Pillar Rock – High Man East Face

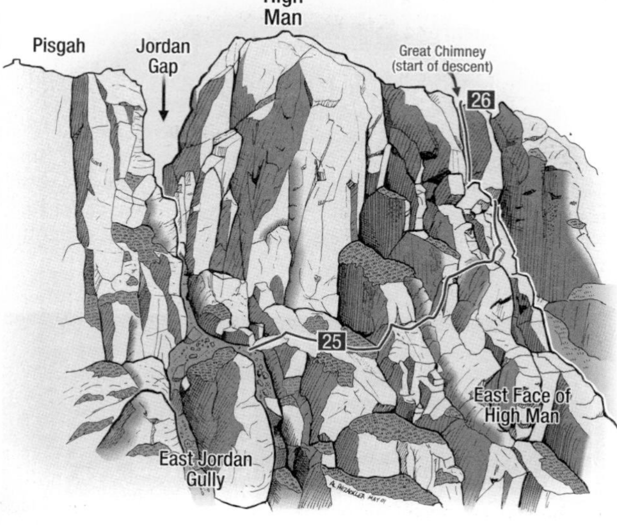

25 Slab and Notch M **26 Slab and Notch** (descent) M

(20 metres). Move right along a ledge for 4 metres and then climb the arête direct to another ledge. Move right and climb slabs on the left of a large gully (*Great Chimney*) until it is possible to step right into the upper section of *Great Chimney*, up which the climb finishes.

26	**Slab and Notch** (in descent)	50m	M

From the summit of ***High Man*** move north for 10 metres to an obvious cleft and chimney (***Great Chimney***) splitting the ***East Face of High Man***. Descend the chimney, easily, for a few metres, move left (facing in) onto a stepped slab, and descend this to a good ledge which leads left, to a short, steep arête. Descend the arête for 5 metres to another ledge. From the ledge move left (facing in) to the ***Notch*** and descend the corner beyond to gain the ***Slab***. Traverse the ***Slab*** leftwards (facing in) and climb into the foot of ***East Jordan Gully***.

Buttermere

by Rick Graham and Colin Read

Buttermere is an idyllic but oft-forgotten valley on the north-west side of the Lake District about 15 kilometres south of Cockermouth. Access is easy from the west, but seems remote from the east or south. Even the short trip from Borrowdale over Honister Pass is not often taken by climbers. The valley is easily reached from Keswick over one of three passes – Whinlatter Pass, Newlands Pass or Honister Pass – and climbing in this delightful valley is highly recommended.

Yew Crags

Grid reference:	**220 147**
Altitude:	**350m**
Faces:	**South-West**
Rock type:	**Natural Slate**
Approach time:	**20 mins**

This cluster of small cliffs is the first climbable rock on the left when ascending Honister Pass from Buttermere village.

The main feature of the crag is *Yew Crag Gully*, a direct ascent from the road to its foot being the best approach (20mins).

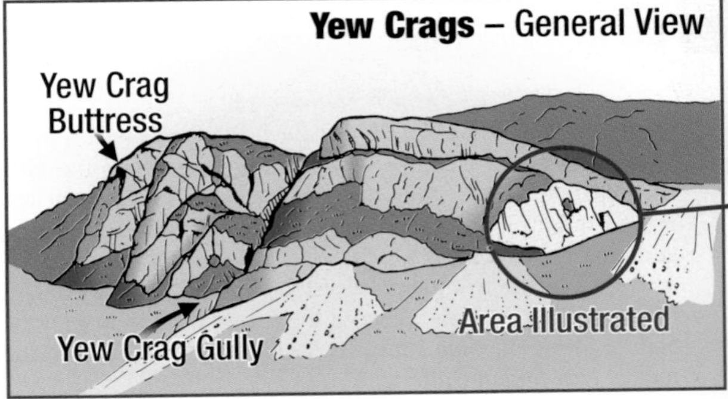

	Route	Grade
1	Face the Music	E1
2	Substitute	E1+
3	Eternal Spring	E1–
4	Hearth Direct	E1

About 200 metres to the right of *Yew Crag Gully* is a steep compact buttress where the following routes tackle the highest, most continuous area of rock.

Descent: is straightforward and obvious, down to the right.

The routes are described from **left** to **right**.

1 Face the Music	35m	E1
C Downer, T Rogers, R E Wightman – April 1987		

Good climbing up the prominent twin grooves on the left. Start directly below the main corner of *Substitute*.

(5b). Climb leftwards to climb the left-hand of the twin grooves to a good ledge. Finish up another groove above.

2 Substitute	40m	E1+
A Greig, J Moore (finishing via Eternal Spring) – Aug 1977	**R O Graham, T W Birkett** – March 1981	

Steep, well protected climbing up the main corner on the left side of the buttress.

(5b). Gain the corner via a ramp from the right and climb it until a glacis on the right can be gained with difficulty. Continue up the steep corner above on excellent holds.

3 Eternal Spring	40m	E1–
T W Birkett, K Forsythe, W Peascod – March 1981		

Takes the groove to the right of a small square overhang and the overhanging chimney above.

1 22m (5b). Up to a thorn bush. Move up and gain the groove via a large detached flake. Up the groove and exit right to a tree belay.

2 18m (5a). Step left, then straight up the wall to gain the chimney. Up this to the top.

Further right below the main arête are two well defined corners.

4 Hearth Direct	30m	E1
R O Graham, T W Birkett – March 1981		

A sustained pitch with an exhilarating bulge.

(5b). Climb the right-hand corner, then continue straight over the overhang on big flat holds. A wall and short groove above on the right lead to the top.

Buckstone How

Grid reference: **223 143**
Altitude: **400m**
Faces: **South-West**
Rock type: **Natural Slate**
Approach time: **10 mins**

Shown as ***Yew Crag Quarries*** on OS Maps. A popular crag despite some routes being fairly awkward for their grade. Most routes are now comfortably sound and the south-west aspect and lack of drainage help the crag to dry out readily. It can be quickly reached from the road by taking the old quarry track which forks left from the north side of the summit of Honister Pass, then crossing slate spoil on a descending traverse.

Descent: the best way down, though awkward, is by a series of scree-littered slabs that slant from near the crown of the crag to its right-hand bottom corner (near *Groove Two*).

The routes are described from **left** to **right**.

1	**Sinister Grooves**	80m	VS+

W Peascod, S B Beck – March 1946

A climb of unforgettable character. Start 10 metres left of the large block beneath an open groove. (It lies 30 metres right of the left extremity of the climbable rock.)

1 25m (4a). Climb the groove beside a heathery central crackline, move up the open groove, and step right to a stance below the deep V-groove.

2 25m (4c). Climb the groove to its top, step right round the arête, and climb a shallow corner until it is possible to traverse left round a rib into a bay below a long crack.

3 30m (4c). Climb the crack and then the chimney to the top.

2 **Honister Wall**	95m	HS+

W Peascod, S B Beck – May 1946

A fine series of typical ***Buckstone How*** pitches. Start right of the block.
1 20m. Climb the wall to a stance below the overhangs.
2 13m. Traverse left and climb a steep arête to a niche behind a small oak.
3 14m. From the bollard on the right climb a short wall and groove to a large grassy corner.
4 13m. The ***Black Wall***. Traverse diagonally right, then climb the rib.
5 20m. Traverse diagonally left across a slab and under a small overhang before moving up to a ledge.
6 15m. Climb the short wall on the right and scramble to the top of the crag.

3 **Alexas**	64m	HVS+

B Ingle, P Crew – Sept 1962

Interesting throughout with a fine second pitch. Start 8 metres right of the block.
1 12m (4c). Climb the shallow groove in the front of the lower buttress and move up to a shattered ledge.
2 26m (5a). Traverse right below the overhangs to a perch at the foot of an undercut groove. Climb the groove, steeply, to a ledge on the right below the overhangs, then climb diagonally left until it is possible to move up right to a ledge.
3 26m (4b). Move right to gain a bottomless groove, then climb its left wall and its continuation to the top of the crag.

4 **Cleopatra**	71m	HVS–

W Peascod, B Blake – May 1951

The classic climb of the crag. An ingenious and airy way through the layers of overhangs. Start below the smooth, brown-stained wall (Cleopatra's 'tawny front'), 7 metres right of ***Alexas***.
1 25m (4c). Climb onto a pillar then move rightwards over a bulge to a gangway. Follow this up leftwards to a crack and climb this for 3 metres. Traverse the wall on the right to gain a large ledge.
2 20m (5a). Move delicately up the rib on the left then traverse left to the left-hand of two grooves. Climb this and step left to good belays but a poor stance.

Buckstone How

3 **26m (4b).** Move right to gain a bottomless groove, then climb the left wall. (Pitch 3 *Alexas*.)

5 **Groove Two**	48m	HVS–

W Peascod, S B Beck, G Rushworth – July 1947

A classic pitch, made formidable by the stone-ground smoothness of its walls. Start to the right of a broken buttress with a birch, 20 metres left of the right extremity of the crag.

1 **20m.** Scramble up to a worn chimney-groove and climb it to a stance beside the birch.

2 **28m (5a).** Move right and climb the main groove. (The very steep entrance can be avoided by the polished black groove on the left, which is a grade easier.)

High Crag

Grid reference: **183 145**
Altitude: **450m**
Faces: **North-East**
Rock type: **Borrowdale Volcanic**
Approach time: **45 mins**

Shown as ***High Crag Buttress*** on OS Maps. On the north-eastern flank of High Crag overlooking Buttermere Lake, this sweep of excellent rock yields some of the most enjoyable routes in the valley, and is well worth an early start to make the most of the morning sun. The main buttress is characterized by the twin caves of *High Crag Buttress*, the *Goblin's Eyes.*

The quickest approach is from Gatesgarth Farm, following a faint track to the right of the wall leading up to the crag after the initial zig-zags of the Scarth Gap path, or, less energetic, follow the main path leftwards before cutting back right to the crag.

Descent: from the top of the main buttress descend well to the left (east). It starts as a well-defined path. A short steep corner (easier than it looks from above) gives access to a long clean groove leading back under *Rock Table Ledge*.

About 100 metres to the left of the main crag a 20-metre wall gives the following excellent pitches.

1 **Wishful Thinking**	20m	VS+
C Downer, R Royce, C Bacon – June 1986		

(5a). The left-hand groove is climbed to the overhang. Traverse right on undercuts to the steep crack which is followed in a fine position on good holds.

2 **Felony**	20m	HVS–
T Rogers, I Gray – April 1986		

(5a). The corner to the right gives a good pitch.

3 **Indecent Obsession**	20m	E2+
C Downer, M Scott – May 1986		

Start 4 metres right again. Sustained. A good test of technique and footwork.

(6a). Climb the wall to a small overlap. Move left, then back right above it to a small ledge. Finish up the thin crack, hard at first.

4 **Foul Play**	20m	HVS+
S Swindells, P Read – April 1986		

(5b). Fine climbing up the central crack in the main slab.

High Crag Main Buttress

The main buttress has the obvious sloping ***Rock Table Ledge***, up on a ledge, at its left side. Fifteen metres further right and under the blunt arête of ***Philistine*** is the ***Gearing Up Stone***, another flat boulder. **12 Gatesgarth Chimney** (VD, 1913) is the deep chimney on the right.

5 **Resurrection Route**	75m	VS
W Peascod, E Banner-Mendus, A Barton – Sept 1941		

This climb gives a satisfying route up the left-hand corner of the upper wall. Start below and to the right of ***Rock Table Ledge***.

1 25m. Ascend a short corner to the ***Table***. From the blocks step onto the rib on the right. Ascend the rib to a large glacis below an imposing corner crack.

2 15m (4b). The crack.

3 20m (4b). Step down and onto the right wall along a short ledge. Make an exposed move into a mossy crack. Climb this to ledges and continue to a block belay below a rough slab.

4 15m. The pleasant slab is climbed to the top.

The following three routes start from a large sloping platform which is easily reached by scrambling up leftwards from the ***Gearing Up Stone***.

6	**Samson**	33m	HVS+
	L Kendall, A Clarkson (some aid – now free) – May 1963		

A fine pitch up the centre of the smooth east wall. Start below the left-hand side of the prominent overhang.

(5b). Make an ascending traverse right, above the overhang, to gain the crack in the centre of the wall. Climb the crack which eases as height is gained.

7	**The Philistine**	35m	E1
	E Cleasby, T W Birkett – June 1975		

A great climb up the blunt arête. Protection is only good when it is most needed. Start below the large overhang, 3 metres left of the arête.

(5b). Climb to the overhang and traverse right to a good foothold on the arête. Climb the crack past the overhang to a poor resting place; then step delicately down and left to gain the left side of the rib. Continue up the arête in a superb situation to the top.

8	**Lost Colonies**	46m	E3
	P Livesey, J Sheard – July 1976	Direct Start: **J Lamb, J Taylor, P Botterill** – May 1978	

Excellent climbing. Start 4 metres right of the arête of *Philistine*.

(6a). Delicate moves lead diagonally right to a good runner in a shallow corner. Traverse left onto the centre of the wall and straight up this to a thread runner in a diagonal crack. Move right and climb another superb crack to a horizontal break. Continue up the wall above to gain easy slabs and the top.

9	**High Crag Buttress**	55m	HVS
	J J S Allison, L Kendall (1 point of aid) – Sept 1962	FFA: **P Nunn, P Fearnehough**	

A direct line up the main face, passing between the caves. Start beneath the right-hand cave.

1 15m (4c). A short corner crack on the right leads to a grass ledge, then an awkward wall crack gives access to the two caves. Belay in the left cave.

2 15m (4c). Pass the overhangs by using the rib between the caves. Continue up the chimney-crack above to a small square cave.

	Route	Grade
1	Wishful Thinking	VS+
2	Felony	HVS–
3	Indecent Obsession	E2+
4	Foul Play	HVS+
5	Resurrection Route	VS
6	Samson	HVS+
7	The Philistine	E1
8	Lost Colonies	E3
9	High Crag Buttress	HVS
10	Gethsemane	E1–
11	Delilah	VS–
12	Gatesgarth Chimney	VD

High Crag

3 25m (5a). Climb the rib on the right of the cave to a thread. Make a delicate traverse up to a slab on the right. Ascend easy grooves to a grassy shoulder at the top of the crag.

10	**Gethsemane**	47m	E1–

J A Gosling, J A Brooder (some aid) – May 1970 FFA: **C Read, J Adams** – 1972

The prominent crackline in the centre of the right-hand wall. Start just left of **12 Gatesgarth Chimney**.

1 9m. A short wall to a grass ledge; move left to belay.

2 38m (5b). Take the main crackline direct to a resting place below an overhang. Pull onto a hanging block in the overhang, then swing left to a groove which leads to the top.

11	**Delilah**	50m	VS–

W Peascod, B Blake – Aug 1951

Sustained and delectable climbing, the upper section taking the fine groove. Start from the top of a large chockstone at the foot of ***Gatesgarth Chimney***.

1 18m (4a). Move left onto the grass ledge, then gain a narrow rock ledge just above. Traverse this back right to an excellent crack. Climb this to a stance and belay in the chimney.

2 32m (4c). Ascend leftward into the groove and climb it direct, exiting right just below the top.

Left: Pete Greening in the classic position on the *Philistine* (E1) **Photo:** Ron Kenyon

Birkness Combe

On the opposite side of the lake from the road is the large hanging valley of Birkness Combe, (Burtness Combe on OS Maps), the spiritual heart of Buttermere climbing. ***Eagle Crag*** looms darkly at the back, and the dry, welcoming faces of ***Grey Crag*** look down from the right. The floor is studded with moraines and boulders, but the close-cropped turf beside the beck provides perfect small camp-sites.

From Gatesgarth, follow the track across the valley floor but quit the Scarth Gap path a few metres up the hillside for a narrow track that slants rightwards across the hillside under some vegetated outcrops to enter the base of the combe.

Eagle Crag

Grid reference:	**172 145**
Altitude:	**600m**
Faces:	**North**
Rock type:	**Borrowdale Volcanic**
Approach time:	**1 hr 15 mins**

Eagle Crag is the magnificent buttress which dominates the upper combe. All the routes described justify the haul up from the valley. Standards rise dramatically in less than perfect conditions due to the algae and lichen on the rock, but over-optimistic climbers can easily alternate to ***Grey Crag*** or ***High Crag***.

The two main chimneys provide prominent landmarks, **Central Chimney** (VS, 1948) is obviously situated, and **Birkness Chimney** (HS, 1903) lies to the left above broken ground.
Descent: the loose scree gully on the right of the crag.
The routes are described from **left** to **right**.

1	**Easter Buttress**	70m	VS

F Graham, M Wood, J Hirst, J F Burton – April 1925

A fine classic with three magnificently varied pitches. Scramble up to start from the grass terrace half-way up the crag, which leads right

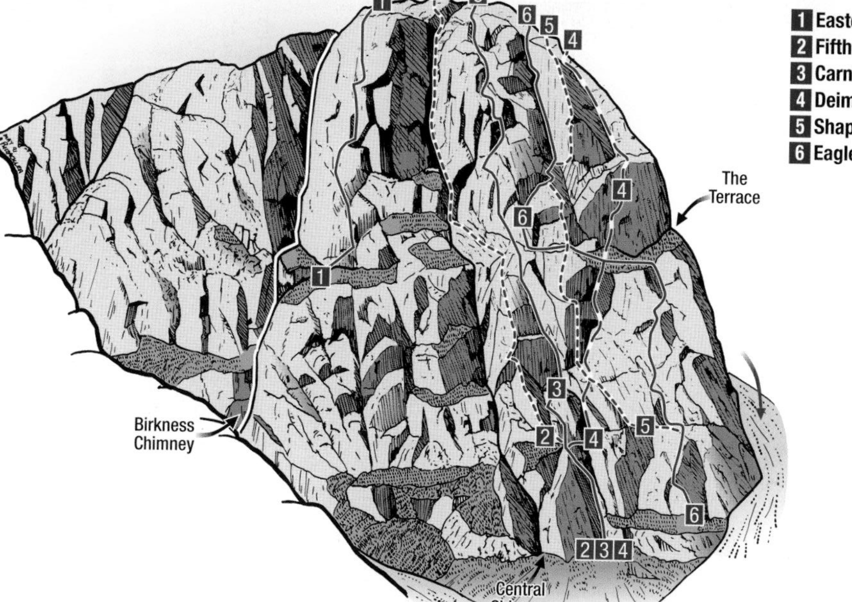

	Route	Grade
1	Easter Buttress	VS
2	Fifth Avenue/Central Chimney	VS+
3	Carnival	E1–
4	Deimos	E3
5	Shape of Things to Come	E3–
6	Eagle Front	VS

from *Birkness Chimney*. Start at the lowest point of the rock ribs, just right of the chimney.

1 30m (4b). Easy rocks lead up to below a steep groove. Bridge up the groove on small holds to a ledge. Climb to a flake and go right to a turfy ledge.
2 8m. Traverse right to an overhung platform.
3 14m (4c). Step round right, enter an undercut crack (crux), and jam it to an unstable flake. Climb past it up slabby rock to a roomy niche.
4 18m (4a). Traverse left on a ledge and climb the steep crack to the top of the crag.

The next three routes start in the vicinity of an alcove about 5 metres right of *Central Chimney*.

2 **Fifth Avenue/Central Chimney**	150m	VS+

P1–2: **W Peascod, S B Beck, J F Monkhouse** – July 1940
P3–6: **W Peascod, S B Beck, G Rushforth** – May 1948

A long, delicate pitch with adequate protection, leads up to the impressive upper pitches of *Central Chimney*. Start below an alcove, about 5 metres right of the foot of *Central Chimney*.

1 30m. Climb up to the right-hand side of the alcove via steep grassy cracks and corners.
2 42m (4c). From the alcove, move left and make a difficult move up the wall. Trend rightwards to an open groove; delectable climbing up this to the *Terrace* and a junction with *Eagle Front*.
3 16m (4b). Traverse left into *Central Chimney*.
4 27m (4c). Climb the intimidating cleft above.
5 25m (4c). Another steep chimney.
6 10m (4a). More easily to the top.

3 **Carnival**	146m	E1–

I Roper, J A Austin, N J Soper – July 1965

An enjoyable and varied route at the lower limit of its grade. One of the quickest-drying routes on the crag.

1 30m. As for *Fifth Avenue/Central Chimney*, climb up to the right-hand side of the alcove via steep grassy cracks and corners.
2 35m (5b). The steep crack at the back of the recess leads to a ledge and possible belay. Move right across a little slab to another steep crack which leads to a V-groove and the *Terrace*.

3 12m (4b). Traverse left to a stance in a grassy bay.
4 27m (5a). A spooky pitch. Climb the shallow grooves above on the left, then move right to a small ledge. Move up and traverse right to a groove and belay on a ledge above.
5 27m. The cracked rib and easier rock above.
6 15m. Even easier, a grassy trench.

4	**Deimos**	134m	E3

C Read, J Adams (4 points of aid on a more direct line) – Oct 1972 FFA: **P Whillance** – May 1975

A sustained expedition. Solid climbing all the way from the alcove to the top.
1 30m. As Pitch 1 of ***Fifth Avenue/Central Chimney***, climb up to the right-hand side of the alcove via steep grassy cracks and corners.
2 10m (4c). Go round to the right and up a shallow groove to a small ledge.
3 36m (5c). Climb up into the corner below the overhangs slanting away to the right. A few delicate moves up the slab gains the line of undercuts and layaways; follow these rightwards to below a bulging groove with an excellent jug on the smooth left wall. Climb the groove with a hard exit (crux) to the *Terrace*. (Continuing the traverse to ***Eagle Front*** reduces the overall grade to E2.)
4 25m (5b). Up on the right is a rightward-slanting groove. Enter this from the left and climb it to a ledge on the right. Climb the steep wall above on good holds to a good ledge.
5 33m (5b). The bulging crack and groove above lead, without loss of interest, to the top.

5	**Shape of Things to Come**	97m	E3–

S J H Reid, T W Birkett – Sept 1986

An excellent way up the crag finishing on the superb arête right of ***Eagle Front's*** crack. Start at a blunt spike below mossy slabs that descend from the overlap on the crux pitch of ***Deimos***. Reach this by traversing left for 6 metres from the top of ***Eagle Front*** Pitch 1.
1 12m (5a). A knobbly ramp leads left. Climb a groove above and step left to the belay of ***Deimos*** (top of Pitch 2).
2 30m (5c). Climb the overhanging groove above direct to a resting place (***Deimos*** quits this groove after a few metres). Move left to a sloping ledge and climb the bold wall above to the *Terrace*.

3 25m (5a). Climb onto a large detached flake and up the bubbly groove above to a scoop. Continue delicately to the traverse on *Eagle Front* and follow it rightwards and up to the foot of that climb's final crack.

4 30m (5b). Climb the right wall to a niche in the arête. Move back onto the wall and make delicate moves out onto a small ledge above the overhang. Climb the arête, awkward at first.

6 **Eagle Front**	150m	VS

W Peascod, S B Beck – June 1940

An exhilarating route taking the line of least resistance up the front of the buttress. It strings together a succession of excellent pitches on good rock. Start up an obvious rib about 20 metres left of the corner (obvious profile) of the crag.

1 18m. Climb the rib and traverse right to a nook and belay.

2 28m (4c). Climb into the steep groove above, then escape right to the base of a ramp sloping back to the left. Follow this to a peg runner and steep shallow groove (the ***Difficult Bit***). Reach a small ledge, swing up right to a higher ledge, then traverse back left across a sweep of awkward slabs. Flake handholds lead to a ledge up on the right.

3 20m (4c). Pull up into the shallow groove above, step right around a rib to a grass ledge and ascend easily to the ***Terrace***.

4 22m. The ***Long Green Traverse*** left, crossing a mossy slab at 15 metres, leads to a small rock ledge up to the left with peg belay usually in place.

5 14m (4c). Climb the steep wall, trending slightly left, before stepping back right across a delicate slab into a groove. Climb this to *Nail Ledge*.

6 20m (4b). Traverse right, crossing several exposed ribs to the waterworn slab. Climb this to a large stance below a fine corner crack.

7 18m (4b). Climb the crack, finally stepping right to a belvedere.

8 10m. Easy climbing leads to the top of the buttress.

Grey Crag

Grid reference: **171 148**
Altitude: **660m**
Faces: **South-East**
Rock type: **Borrowdale Volcanic**
Approach time: **1 hr 25 mins**

Grey Crag comprises a quartet of short buttresses superbly positioned in three tiers high above Birkness Combe. It takes no drainage and the clean, rough rock dries rapidly. It is worth working out sequences of routes that travel up the whole crag.

The crag can be reached by the path up from Gatesgarth, as for *Eagle Crag*, then leaving it to strike straight up the scree on the right. **Descents:** are obvious and take the rather skinned scree-chutes to either side of the buttresses.

The routes are described from **left** to **right**.

Harrow Buttress

This forms the lowest point of the crags, the usual point of arrival.

1 **Harrow Buttress**	45m	D–

W Bishop, W A Woodsend – 1912

A good climb with a steep start just left of the toe of the buttress.
1 10m. Climb the corner or the arête on the right to a roomy ledge.
2 13m. Climb the chimney above the corner, then traverse 3 metres left to a ledge below a broken groove.
3 22m. Climb the groove and scramble up to an overhung corner. Pull up left and climb to the top of the buttress.

2 **Spider Wall**	40m	VS–

W Peascod, G G Macphee – Aug 1945

An ingenious way up the front of the buttress with two good main pitches, one strenuous and the other delicate.
1 8m. Climb the steep vegetated groove 4 metres right of *Harrow Buttress* to a ledge below an overhanging crack.
2 19m (4c). Climb the crack to gain a prominent loose but apparently mechanically safe hold on the right wall. Move right and

up and cross back left to a platform. Pull up into a shallow groove on the right and climb it.

3 13m (4b). Traverse the steep wall diagonally right to a small bracket in the middle (poorly protected). Climb directly to the top.

Mitre Buttress

The left-hand buttress of the lower crag.

3 **Mitre Buttress Direct**	80m	MS

A C Pigou and party – July 1915

A varied route which explores the whole front of the buttress. Start at its lowest point, just left of the short scree chute which separates *Harrow* and *Mitre Buttresses*.

1 13m. Climb the wall leftwards to a ledge.

2 15m. Climb a short wall and walk right to the steep east face of the buttress.

3 15m. Climb the wall on its left side, make a mantelshelf onto a narrow ledge on the right and follow it left to the edge of the buttress.

4 22m. Climb directly up the steep exposed wall above, just left of the edge of the east face, to a ledge. Alternatively climb the scoop round to the left which leads to a cave, then move right to regain the steep wall. Another short wall leads to a ledge and belays.

5 15m. Easy climbing above gains the top, but more interesting, and traditional, is to traverse left to a steep chimney/crack and climb it to the top.

Chockstone Buttress

This buttress lies above and right of *Mitre* and *Harrow Buttresses*.

4 **Slabs West Route**	55m	HS+

W Peascod, A Barton – Sept 1942

A fine, open climb. Start up the gully 9 metres below and right of a small grassy bay which bounds the left side of the slabs, at the start of the traverse line of *Slabs Ordinary*.

Grey Crag

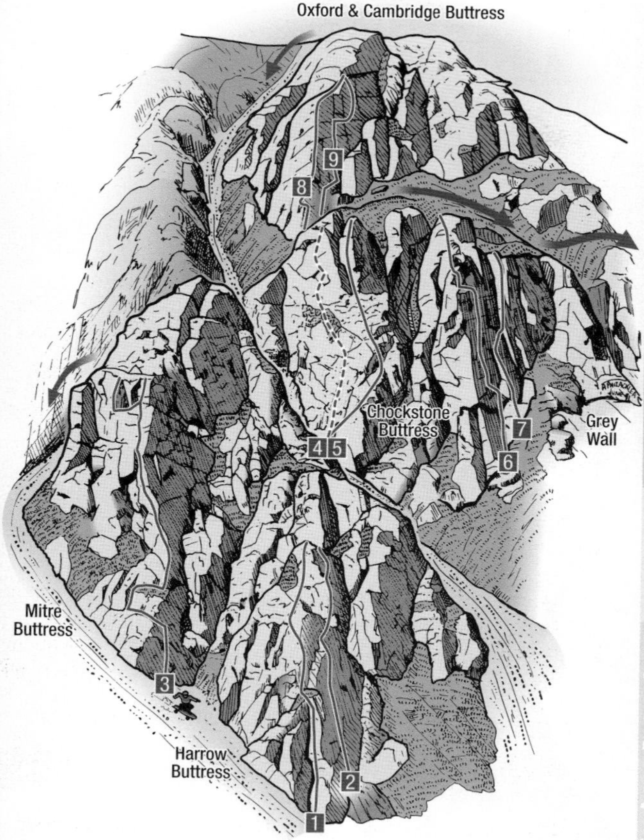

1 Harrow Buttress	D–	6 Suaviter	S
2 Spider Wall	VS–	7 Fortiter	MVS
3 Mitre Buttress Direct	MS	8 Oxford and Cambridge Direct Route	MS
4 Slabs West Route	HS+	9 Dexter Wall	VS+
5 Slabs Ordinary	VD–		

1 32m. Ascend a thin crack in the slab for 5 metres to where it steepens. Climb the wall to the left, where the crack fades out, and move up right to a ledge. Slant up left, then climb straight up the slab to a ledge below a pile of blocks under a jutting nose.
2 23m. Climb left to a niche; step right above the nose, climb up (crux), step left, and finish straight up the slabby wall.

5 **Slabs Ordinary**	61m	VD–
H Bishop, W A Woodsend – Aug 1913 P2: Reclimbed after rockfall **W F Hurford** – Sept 2000		

Pleasant and varied climbing up the right side of the slabs. Start several metres up the gully left of the toe of the slabs, at a traverse line, which ascends in steps to the right.
1 18m. Make the ascending traverse to blocks at the top. Climb over them and up to the left side of a large sloping ledge. Belay either just before the ledge, or at its right-hand end at a spike.
2 23m. From the left-hand end of the sloping ledge go up easy-angled rock to a crack. Follow this and the clean slab above to the foot of a right-facing corner/groove.
3 20m. Climb the corner on good holds to the top.

Grey Wall

The next two routes are on *Grey Wall*, the fine wall marked by horizontal striations and continuous cracks, 30 metres horizontally right of *Chockstone Buttress*.

6 **Suaviter**	45m	S
W Peascod, S B Beck – July 1941		

A delightfully exposed second pitch.
1 7m. From a bollard in a shallow corner, climb the corner, move right, and then up to a long ledge; or climb the crack on the right of the bollard (harder).
2 16m. Step down from the left end of the ledge, traverse delicately to a crack, and climb it to a ledge with doubtful blocks. Climb past them to a roomy ledge on the left.
3 22m. Climb the ridge above to a triangular turfy ledge and climb a chimney to the top of the buttress.

Left: Anne McDonald and Colwyn Jones enjoying a tremendous mountain atmosphere on *Mitre Buttress Direct* (MS) **Photo:** Stephen Reid

7 Fortiter	38m	MVS
W Peascod, S B Beck – July 1941		

A good climb up the prominent crackline right of centre, clean and direct. Start 3 metres right of *Suaviter*.

1 7m. Climb a crack and blocks to the right end of the long ledge.
2 23m (4b). Move up to the small ledge on the right, step left into the crack, and follow it to an overhang. Pull over this (crux) and move right to a further crack. Climb it to a narrow ledge below a flake in a corner.
3 8m. Climb the crack in the corner to a ledge and finish up an arête to the top of the wall.

Oxford and Cambridge Buttress

The upper buttress of the crags.

8 Oxford and Cambridge Direct Route	42m	MS
H V Reade – Sept 1914		

An exposed line on immaculate rock, up the main arête of the buttress. Start at the junction of the left and right-hand faces.

1 15m. Climb the arête, first on the right, then on the left, before pulling steeply onto the crest and climbing it to a ledge.
2 27m. Move up left and climb a short, bulging crack, then move back right to a ledge. Follow the right edge over another bulge to the top.

9 Dexter Wall	42m	VS+
W Peascod, S B Beck – March 1941		

Fine open wall climbing. The comfortable steps of the first pitch lead out onto a sheer wall just off vertical, split by a crack, whose widely-spaced holds are nicely sufficient.

1 24m (4a). Five metres right of the arête, climb a crack to a V-niche just left of an overhang; step right below it, and climb a crack to a narrow ledge. Traverse right to a slim corner, climb it to a niche, and move right to a roomy ledge.
2 18m (4c). Move right to the thin crack and climb it to the top.

St Bees

by Bill Young & Bill Hannah

Above: Sven Rowan *Dreaming of Red Rocks* (F7a+) **Photo:** David Kells

St Bees Head, situated 5 kilometres south-west of the town of Whitehaven, is the most westerly point of the Cumbrian coastline. The cliffs face west and catch a great deal of sun from mid-day onwards. The rock is well-weathered sandstone and provides good friction. It also dries very quickly after rain though some routes can be affected by seepage.

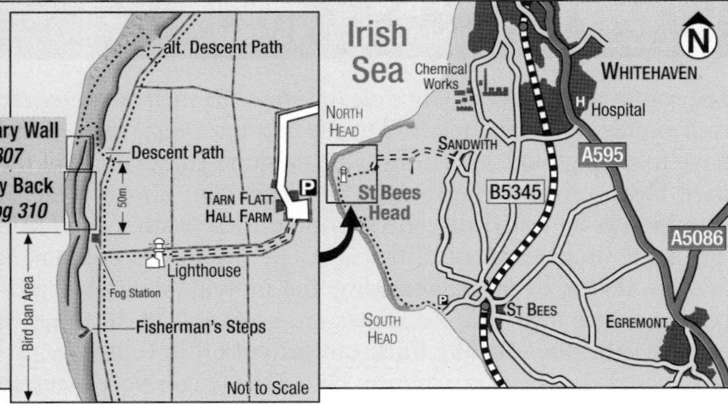

The best approach is from Whitehaven. Drive to the village of Sandwith. In the centre of the village is a narrow private road leading to the lighthouse. Follow this road up over the hill for 2 kilometres to Tarn Flatt Hall Farm. The farmer currently allows parking for £1 a day - please pay at the farm. There is a camping barn at the farm too (01946 692 162) **Please do not obstruct access to gates and please use only the following approach to the cliff and do not cross fences except at the stiles.** From the farmyard, follow the continuation road on foot to the lighthouse. Carry straight on down a concrete path to the foghorn station. Turn north (right-facing out) and follow the fence for 50 metres to a stile. Cross this and follow a path down a short gully then under a small crag, heading north until it starts to descend steeply towards the sea. Follow this down (at the time of writing there were short sections of knotted fixed rope on the steeper sections). This section ends on a ledge denuded of grass. The first route starts 15 metres along this. This is the upper left area of *Apiary Wall*, the main part of which is just to the right and at a lower level. Immediately right of this and at a slightly higher level is *Scabby Back* which is accessed via the short easy-angled *Access Groove*, which is (at the time of writing) equipped with a fixed chain.

St Bees – North Head

Grid reference: **939 145**
Altitude: **5m**
Faces: **West**
Rock type: **Sandstone**
Approach time: **15 mins**

The routes described rise to a maximum of 25 metres. Many are well bolted, and on the whole only require quickdraws. Most have fixed 'pig's tail' lower offs which require competence of the user. Please do not climb onto the vegetation above these. It should also be noted that in describing these routes, the FRCC has made no assessment of the safety of any in situ equipment and, as always in mountaineering, the individual climber proceeds at their own risk. All routes are accessible at all times in calm weather, but ***Scabby Back*** can get cut off in rough weather at high tide. The rock platform below the crag is very green in many places and can be extremely slippery when damp. The boulders on this platform provide some of the best and sunniest bouldering in the county – bouldering mat strongly advised. The ***Main Cliff*** further south (right), rises to about 100 metres and contains bands of soft rock, which are not as pleasant to climb on – no routes are described in this area.

Bird Restriction: St Bees Head is an extremely important area for nesting seabirds, and large numbers of gulls, guillemots, razorbills, fulmars and kittiwakes and even a few puffins can be seen there. It is a Site of Special Scientific Interest and is owned by the Royal Society for the Protection of Birds (RSPB). Please respect this unique environment. **The RSPB have stipulated no climbing or access to the area south (right) of Army Screamers between 1st February and 31st July** – this ban does not apply to any of the routes described below which are available all year round.

Apiary Wall

1 Blooming Marvellous

F6c (E3 6a)

I Williamson – Nov 1993

5 bolts

The square arête with a sting in the tail.

2 Ancient Mariner

F5+ (E1 5b)

J Wilson – 1993

5 bolts

The corner crack.

Apiary Wall – Left Hand

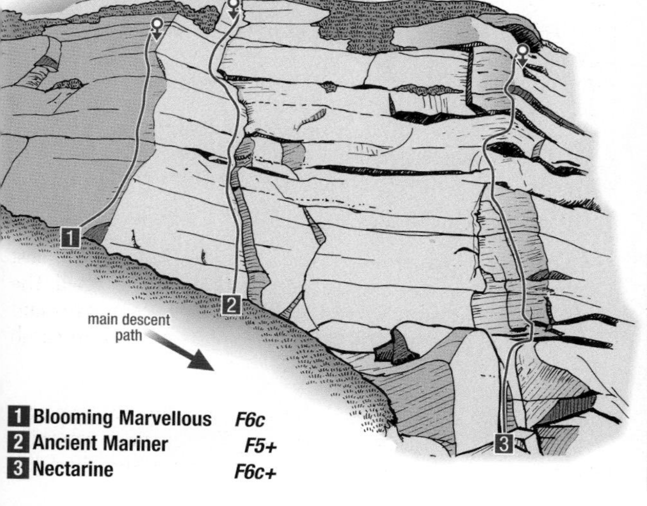

3 Nectarine F6c+
4 Drone F7a+
5 The Apiarist F6b+

Left: Nick Wharton bouldering below the Apiary Wall, St Bees Photo: Liam Grant

3	**Nectarine**	*F6c+*	(E4 6a)
	J Adams, S Scott – April 1994		**7 bolts**

The impressive left arête of the big wall.

4	**Drone**	*F7a+*	(E5 6b)
	A Jones – 1989		**8 bolts**

Starts in a leftward-facing corner.

5	**The Apiarist**	*F6b+*	(E3 5c)
	A Jones and party – 1989		**8 bolts**

Starts just right of a low level roof and climbs a series of grooves and corners.

Scabby Back

6	**Toxic Rock**	*F7a*	(E5 6a)
	S Miller – Oct 1993		**4 bolts**

Start immediately above the chain in the easy-angled *Access Groove* and climb the bubbly arête.

Scabby Back – Left Hand

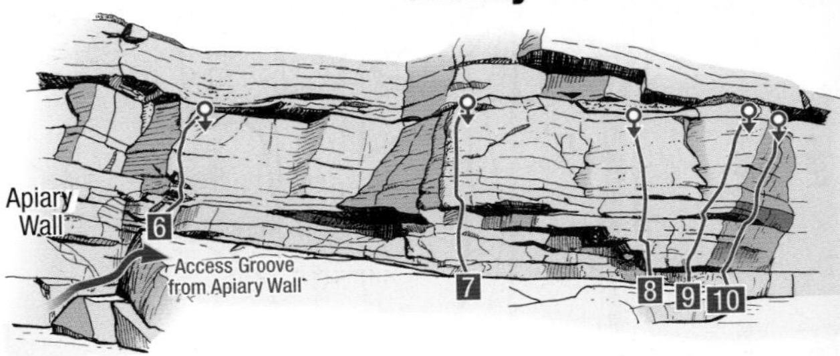

6 Toxic Rock	*F7a*	9 Megadrive	*F6b+*
7 Andy's Route	*F6b*	10 Dreaming of Red Rocks	*F7a+*
8 Feeling Groovy	*F6c*		

7 Andy's Route

F6b (E2 5c)

A Jones and party – 1989

4 bolts

Starts 20 metres right of the *Access Groove* chain.

8 Feeling Groovy

F6c (E3 6b)

S Wood – 1992

3 bolts

The central line on the slab has a balancy crux.

9 Megadrive

F6b+ (E3 6a)

J Adams, S Scott – May 1994

5 bolts

Climb the left side of the leaning arête.

10 Dreaming of Red Rocks

F7a+ (E5 6a)

A Hyslop – 1992

5 bolts

A stunning route up the overhanging right side of the arête.

11 Driller Killer

F6a (E1 5b)

J Adams, B Davison, A King – Nov 1993

2 bolts

The right-hand crackline.

12 Pieces of Eight

F6a (E2 5c)

J Hughes – 1993

3 bolts

A left-slanting line up the slab left of the overhang.

13 Northern Lights

F6b+ (E3 6a)

C Sice, A Stephenson – 1993

3 bolts

The overhanging crack left of the prominent *Nose*.

14 Legend's Friend

F7a (E4 6a)

C Johnson – Oct 1993

4 bolts

Starts below a hanging corner right of the *Nose*. Difficult moves gain access to the corner and thence the top.

Scabby Back – Central (above) & Right Hand (below)

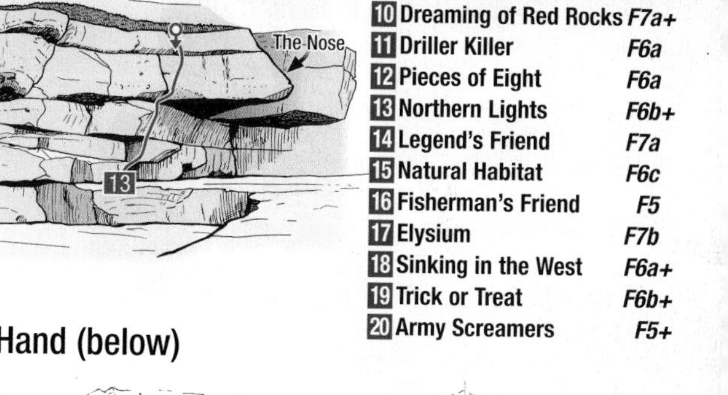

No.	Route	Grade
10	Dreaming of Red Rocks	F7a+
11	Driller Killer	F6a
12	Pieces of Eight	F6a
13	Northern Lights	F6b+
14	Legend's Friend	F7a
15	Natural Habitat	F6c
16	Fisherman's Friend	F5
17	Elysium	F7b
18	Sinking in the West	F6a+
19	Trick or Treat	F6b+
20	Army Screamers	F5+

The Nose
14 15 16 17 18 19 20

Left: Crispin Waddy surrounded by awesome sandstone on *Dreaming of Red Rocks* (*F7a+*)
Photo: Ron Kenyon

15 Natural Habitat — F6c (E3 6a)

C Cunningham – 1999 — **4 bolts**

A line up the wall right of ***Legend's Friend***. Climb to ledge then left under the roof (1 bolt – when the second bolt has been clipped, unclip the first to avoid rope drag). Up the wall via two small finger pockets.

16 Fisherman's Friend — F5 (HVS 5a)

G Bowen – 1993 — **3 bolts**

The flake and crack right of the corner.

17 Elysium — F7b (E4 6c)

S Wood – Sept 1998 — **3 bolts**

Move up to the obvious pocket to the right of ***Fisherman's Friend*** (bolt). Step in the pocket and make a difficult, balancy move to a sloping break. Straight up the pocketed wall above to the lower-off. Magnificent.

18 Sinking in the West — F6a+ (E2 5c)

J Adams, W Young – Oct 1993 — **3 bolts**

Climb up to the overhang and make awkward moves round the left of this to get established on the wall.

19 Trick or Treat — F6b+ (E2 6a)

J Adams, A King, B Davison – Nov 1993 — **3 bolts**

The awkward left-slanting slabby groove.

20 Army Screamers — F5+ (E1 5b)

J Adams, A King, B Davison – Nov 1993 — **2 bolts**

The crack.

Left: Sven Rowan preparing to make the desperate move from the pocket up to the rounded break on *Elysium* (*F7b*) **Photo:** David Kells

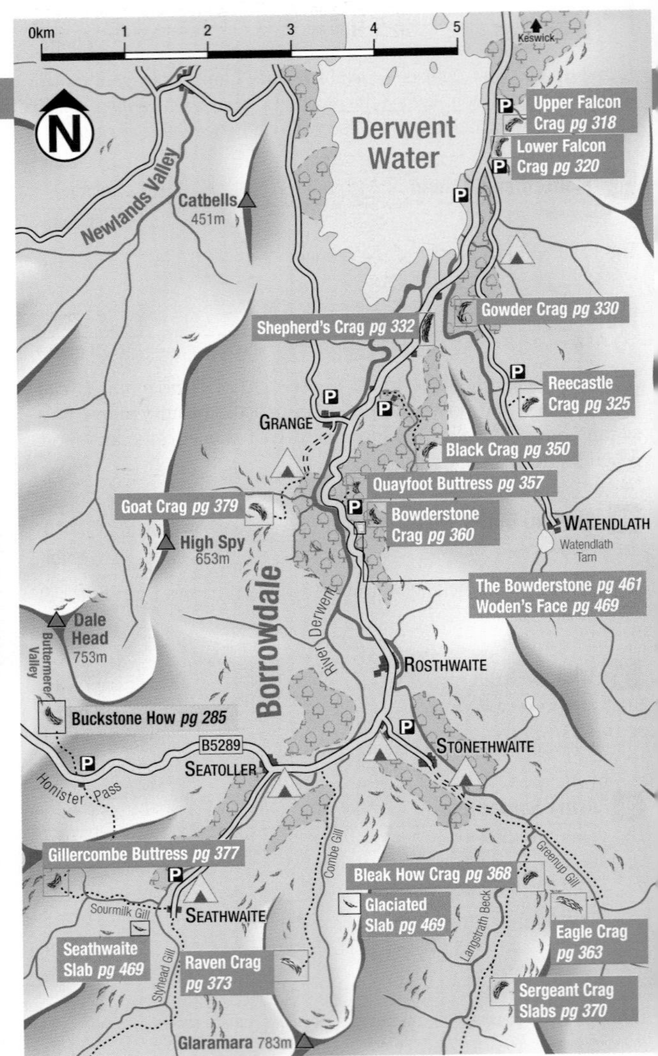
0km
1
2
3
4
5
N
Keswick
Derwent Water
Upper Falcon Crag pg 318
Lower Falcon Crag pg 320
Newlands Valley
Catbells
451m
Gowder Crag pg 330
Shepherd's Crag pg 332
Reecastle Crag pg 325
GRANGE
Black Crag pg 350
Quayfoot Buttress pg 357
Goat Crag pg 379
Bowderstone Crag pg 360
WATENDLATH
Watendlath Tarn
High Spy
653m
The Bowderstone pg 461
Woden's Face pg 469
Borrowdale
River Derwent
Dale Head
753m
Buttermere Valley
ROSTHWAITE
Buckstone How pg 285
B5289
STONETHWAITE
SEATOLLER
Honister Pass
Gillercombe Buttress pg 377
Combe Gill
Greenup Gill
Bleak How Crag pg 368
Glaciated Slab pg 469
Sourmilk Gill
SEATHWAITE
Langstrath Beck
Eagle Crag pg 363
Seathwaite Slab pg 469
Raven Crag pg 373
Styhead Gill
Sergeant Crag Slabs pg 370
Glaramara 783m

Left: Stephen and Jilly Reid on the final pitch of *Little Chamonix* (VD)

Borrowdale

by Gary Baum and Alan Hewison

The Borrowdale Valley is one of the most popular venues for climbing in the Lake District, due to the ease of access and the abundance of low level, fast drying crags along its length. It runs from north to south with Keswick at the northern end and Seathwaite at the other. The B5289 road connects the two, running along the eastern side of Derwentwater, with a bus service travelling via Grange and Rosthwaite to Seatoller. For the motorist, parking can be found at the various car parks along the valley. These should be used to avoid obstructing the roads and footpaths, and aggravating the local constabulary.

The crags are described in a clockwise sequence around the valley, starting from Keswick, proceeding southwards along the east side of the valley and then returning up the western flank.

More details on approaches are included under the heading for each crag, though all can be reached in under 60mins assuming a normal walking pace.

The Falcon Crags

The two **Falcon Crags** dominate the hillside about three kilometres south of Keswick. The upper crag, a 70 metre dome in a magnificent situation, is characterized by a large smooth wall in the upper left corner. This wall is bounded on its right by a prominent corner up which *Route 1* finishes.

To the right of and below the upper crag is **Lower Falcon Crag**. This is a compact crag about 50 metres high, extending some 200 metres and abounding in overhangs. There is still some loose rock on the lower crag, due to the blocky, slaty nature of the rock, however no widespread friability occurs as on parts of the upper crag. The climbing is rather serious for a small crag. At every point of the crag there is an overhang at some height; all the routes are in the Very Severe category or above and some are not easy to protect even with modern devices.

The approach to the crag is easy, taking but a few minutes from either the lay-by in the main road below the upper crag or from a car park a few metres up the Watendlath road.

There may be a **Bird Restriction** on one or both *Falcon Crags* from 1st March to 30th June or part thereof. Signs at the crag should inform you, but if in doubt contact details for further information are given in **Access and Conservation**.

Upper Falcon Crag

Grid reference: **271 205**
Altitude: **240m**
Faces: **West**
Rock type: **Borrowdale Volcanic**
Approach time: **10 mins**

Descent: to the left of the crag, down the ridge and loose scree slope.

The climbs are described from **left** to **right**.

1 Dry Grasp	60m	E4–

P Livesey Solo with back rope – June 1974

The friable groove to the left of *Route 1* leads to an excellent sustained pitch up the centre of the headwall. Start above an ash tree on a grassy hump below the centre of the crag.

Upper Falcon Crag

Bird restrictions possible between 1st March and 30th June

1 Dry Grasp E4–
2 Route 1 E3–

1 22m (4a). Climb the broken groove, past an old oak tree, until a move right and a short right-slanting groove lead to a ledge. Belay below the groove on the left.

2 20m (5b). Climb the groove, over a bulge, and up to a second bulge. Pull over this and go up leftwards to an easy groove leading to a stance at the foot of the headwall (peg belay).

3 18m (6a). Climb the crack going diagonally left (peg runner). When the crack closes, use sloping ramp holds on the wall above to gain a small ledge and in-situ thread runner. Move up to good holds leading leftwards to another ledge, then follow a break up and rightwards to a crack. Climb this and finish by stepping left.

2 Route 1	60m	E3–
P Ross, P Lockey (4 points of aid) – May 1958	FFA: **A Parkin, P Clarke** – May 1975	

A stunning route finishing up the impressive corner on the right of the headwall. Start as for *Dry Grasp*.

1 20m (4a). Pitch 1 of *Dry Grasp*. Belay at the right-hand end of the ledge below a short wall.

2 22m (5b). Climb the wall for 6 metres (peg runner). Move diagonally up left, then climb an overhanging crack (peg runner just right of an ivy mass). Continue straight up, then left, to a peg belay below the corner.

3 18m (5c). Climb the corner direct. The final groove is entered with difficulty, then followed more easily to the top.

Lower Falcon Crag

Grid reference: **270 204**
Altitude: **180m**
Faces: **West**
Rock type: **Borrowdale Volcanic**
Approach time: **10 mins**

Reasonably quick drying though winter seepage can be a problem (particularly on ***Illusion***). Allow one dry day .
Descent: down the scree slide on the left side of the crag.

The climbs are described from **left** to **right**.

1 Spinup	45m	VS+
P Ross, D Sewell – May 1957		

A very popular and exciting climb, starting at the back left corner of a grassy bay, reached by scrambling up and right from the large ash tree below the left-bounding rib of the crag.

1 20m (4c). Follow a small slab leftwards then step left around a rib to a ledge. Climb straight up from the left end to a gangway leading left for 3 metres, then up right to a small stance just left of a black groove. A bold pitch.

2 25m (4c). Move up slightly, step right and climb the black groove for about 5 metres. Step right and down to gain an exposed traverse line above the overhangs. Follow this to its end then climb

up to a pillar of rock. Step left onto a narrow slab and climb an airy and fingery wall to the top.

2 **Hedera Grooves**	40m	MVS+

P Ross, P Lockey – Aug 1956

The easiest route here, giving a good introduction to the crag. It takes the groove with a holly tree, above the left edge of an ivy mass. Start in a small bay, left of the ivy, 15 metres left of the *Niche*.

1 24m (4a). Gain a grass ledge, then climb the short groove above to a niche. A traverse line leading rightwards is followed to a groove. Climb this, then step left to the holly tree.

2 16m (4b). Climb the groove above the holly, then follow the ramp leading leftwards to the top of the crag. A brilliant pitch.

3 **The Niche**	60m	E2

A Liddell, R McHaffie (3 points of aid – now free) – Aug 1962

A classic route, giving good, sustained climbing in excellent positions. Start in the centre of the crag, directly below the obvious *Niche* which is 20 metres above the ground.

1 26m (5c). Climb the bulging wall for 10 metres, step left onto a rib and climb to a peg runner 3 metres left of the *Niche*. Traverse right with difficulty and pull up to a peg belay in the *Niche*.

2 12m (5b). Climb the back of the niche and exit on the right. Traverse right to a break in the overhang. Pull over this into a short groove, then step right to a small ledge and belay.

3 22m (4c). Step back left and climb the gangway/groove. Pull over a slight bulge on the right and finish up the slabby wall.

4 **Interloper**	50m	E1+

A Liddell, R McHaffie (4 points of aid) – July 1962 FFA: **C Read, J Adams** – June 1971

An enjoyable route which takes the steep grooveline starting 6 metres right of the *Niche*.

1 29m (5c). Climb easily up to a ledge with a small tree on the right, then go left for 5 metres to a sloping ledge. Step right and ascend to a large ledge. On the left is the steep groove. After an awkward start, continue on good holds past two peg runners to a small stance and peg belay on the left (top of Pitch 2 of the *Niche*).

2 21m (4c). Climb the bulge above the belay and follow the gangway/slab leftwards to a bulge (junction with the *Niche*). Move right and climb up the slabby wall to the top.

5 **Dedication**	48m	E1–

P Ross, E Metcalf – May 1957

A fine popular climb. Start as for ***Interloper***.

1 18m (4a). Follow ***Interloper*** to a ledge then go up right to another ledge and easily to a large ledge and block belay.

2 30m (5a). Pull over a small overhang and enter an open groove. Climb it on rickety holds, now either step right onto the edge, go up a metre, and step left, or climb directly (harder) into a fine slanting corner, which is followed until it is possible to traverse left. Finish up the groove on the left.

6 **Kidnapped**	42m	E2+

P Botterill, J Lamb – April 1978

Tremendous and sustained climbing. Start below a groove behind and between two large trees.

(5c). Climb the groove and continue to reach some small spikes on ***Dedication*** after 16 metres. Climb into the overhung niche (junction with ***Plagiarism***). Move up to the roof (peg runner), traverse left to the arête and follow the groove above to the top.

The next three routes start just to the right of the pair of large trees, 5 metres to the right of ***Kidnapped***. The trees lie below and to the left of the large overhang, beneath which ***Illusion*** crosses.

7 **Plagiarism**	48m	E2

P Nunn, O Woolcock (2 points of aid – now free) – Aug 1962

A justifiably popular route up the rust-coloured groove just left of ***Illusion***.

1 8m (4b). Climb straight up to a stance at a large block on the right.

2 30m (5c). Move left and climb the slanting groove, finishing up its left rib to gain a small ledge. Traverse left across a steep wall (peg runner) to a shallow groove, which is followed up to a roof (peg runner). Surmount this on the right and move left to reach a small stance and peg belay in a groove.

No.	Route	Grade
1	Spinup	VS+
2	Hedera Grooves	MVS+
3	The Niche	E2
4	Interloper	E1+
5	Dedication	E1–
6	Kidnapped	E2+
7	Plagiarism	E2
8	Usurper	E1
9	Illusion	HVS
10	Lamplighter	VS+

3 10m. The groove above is followed to the top.

8	**Usurper**	50m	E1
	P Gomersall, N Bulmer – June 1975		

Enjoyable steep climbing with fine, open and improbable positions. Care required with some hollow flakes near the top of Pitch 2. Everything rattles!!

1 8m (4b). Climb straight up to a stance at a large block on the right, as for ***Plagiarism***.
2 26m (5a). Continue up ***Illusion*** until it moves to the right. Move left on a steep gangway to a ledge on the left (peg runner). Move right and up to a roof, then pull up round the rib on the right to a small niche. Up left through the overhang onto the wall above and continue up rightwards to a tree belay.
3 16m. Follow the groove above to the top.

9	**Illusion**	44m	HVS
	P Lockey, P Ross – June 1956		

Pleasant climbing across the wall below the large overhang at the right-hand end of the crag.

1 8m (4b). Climb straight up to a stance at a large block on the right, as for ***Plagiarism***.
2 30m (5a). Climb the steep groove above until it is possible to gain a large flake on the right. Traverse to the right, past several grooves, into the corner groove. Go up this for a couple of metres; then swing out right round the arête and move up to a ledge.
3 6m. Climb up the wall above to finish beside a holly.

10	**Lamplighter**	40m	VS+
	L Hewitt, S Glass – May 1964		

An interesting route up an obvious slanting groove. Start just right of ivy and thorns, 15 metres right of ***Illusion***, at a short crack.

1 16m (4b). Ascend the short steep crack past a vegetated niche on the right and pull up into a short, steep groove above. Step left and go up to a stance at the foot of a left-slanting groove.

2 18m (4c). Follow the groove to a small ledge at 8 metres. Continue straight up the groove with a smooth slab on the left to join *Illusion*. Follow this to the top of Pitch 2.

3 6m. Climb up the wall above to finish beside a holly.

Reecastle Crag

Grid reference: **273 176**
Altitude: **300m**
Faces: **North-West**
Rock type: **Borrowdale Volcanic**
Approach time: **10 minutes**

Above: Typical fingery climbing at Reecastle
Photo: John Fletcher

A superb crag of good rock in the delightful valley of Watendlath. Three kilometres south of Keswick, take the signed left fork to Ashness Bridge and Watendlath. After 3 kilometres, the road leaves the woods and the crag appears on the left. It can be reached in a few minutes from the road. The left half of the crag is smooth and barrel-shaped; the right is split by slim grooves and ramps. The rock is of good quality and fairly clean. All the routes are strenuous. An excellent crag in the modern idiom.

The most obvious faultline in the centre of the crag is taken by *Rack Direct*. *White Noise* follows the leftwards-slanting crack just to its left.

Descent: can be made at either end. Please do not abseil from the tree at the top of the main wall as further damage could kill it.

The routes are described from **left** to **right**.

1 The Torture Board	26m	E7
P Cornforth – May 1987		

A desperate modern testpiece. Start on grass ledges below twin cracks 2 metres to the right of the overhanging flake-crack behind the obvious ash tree.

(6c). Climb the steep rock to gain the base of the twin cracks (peg runner). Make hard moves up the crack to the horizontal break. Continue directly up the steep wall with less difficulty.

2 Penal Servitude	30m	E5
D Armstrong, P Whillance – May 1981		

Brilliant climbing up the overhanging wall, starting 5 metres left of *White Noise* below three horizontal quartz breaks.

(6b). Climb up rightwards to a peg runner in the top break. Pull up right to a crucial RP, then go leftwards on tiny finger pockets and move up to a resting place. Step left into a slight groove and follow it more easily to the top.

3 White Noise	30m	E3
J Lamb, R McHaffie – Aug 1978		

Superb climbing up the left-slanting crack immediately left of ***Rack Direct***. Start at the right-hand end of a ledge running below the left side of the crag.

(5c). Climb up to a small overhang. Pull up left to gain the crack and follow this up the wall to a bulge. Go over this to a nut belay at the top.

4 Rack Direct	30m	E2
S Miller, R Parker – Sept 1977		

A very direct route up the obvious faultline in the centre of the crag. Poorly protected initially but the difficulties soon diminish.

(5b). Climb up the steep wall to a break in the bulges. Pull over and climb the crack, as for the ***Rack***, to the top.

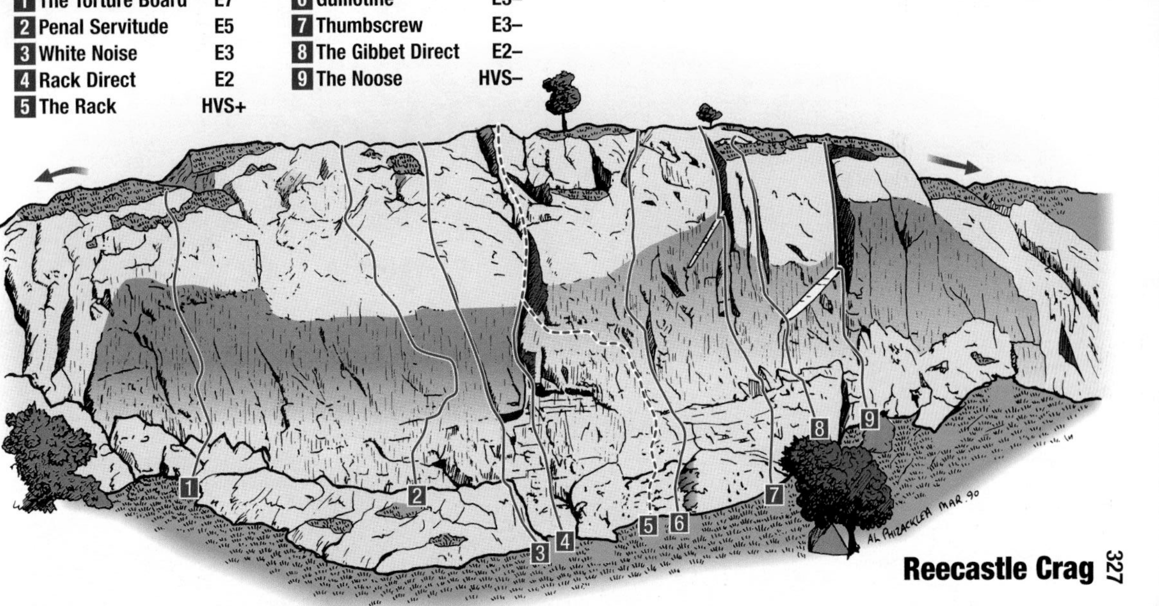
1 The Torture Board E7
2 Penal Servitude E5
3 White Noise E3
4 Rack Direct E2
5 The Rack HVS+
6 Guillotine E3–
7 Thumbscrew E3–
8 The Gibbet Direct E2–
9 The Noose HVS–
1
2
3
4
5
6
7
8
9
AL PHIZACKLEA MAR. 90

5 The Rack	40m	HVS+
R McHaffie, B Mallaghan – Oct 1973		

A good route which gains the classic central crack from the steep walls on its right. Start 6 metres right of ***Rack Direct*** in a small grassy bay below a short bulging wall.

(5a). Climb a short wall, past a sloping ledge, to a better ledge on the right. Climb the wall to a resting place on the left. Move up left to a sloping ledge. Descend and traverse left boldly to the obvious crack. Go up this, and a short groove, to a flake and ledge on the right. A rib leads to a tree belay.

6 Guillotine	30m	E3–
J Lamb – Sept 1978		

A superb route giving sustained climbing on small holds. Start 2 metres right of the ***Rack*** below a bulging black wall.

(5c). Climb the black wall to a ledge. Continue up a thin groove to a bulge, and pull over to a thin hollow flake on the wall. Step right and up to a second bulge. Surmount this, step left, and continue to the top.

7 Thumbscrew	30m	E3–
J Lamb, D Cherry – Aug 1978		

A fine steep route, fingery and sustained, up the bubbly wall. Start behind the sprawling silver birch below the right-hand half of the crag.

(5c). Take the easy wall to a ledge. Go up the steep wall to a flat hold below a tiny overhang, between two parallel cracks. Climb the left-hand crack and groove above direct.

8 The Gibbet Direct	30m	E2–
C Downer, R McHaffie – July 1984		

Fine fingery climbing. The problem is staying on line! Start behind the silver birch.

(5c). Climb diagonally left, then right to below the short wall at the foot of the gangway. Gain the gangway then pull out steeply

Left: Leo Houlding climbs the fingery crux of *Penal Servitude* (E5) **Photo:** Phil Rigby

left onto the wall. Climb this and the central crack above, just right of *Thumbscrew*, to the top.

9 The Noose	30m	HVS–

R McHaffie and chums – April 1972

Follows the prominent crack and corner right of and behind the silver birch.

(4c). Easy slabs lead up rightwards to a short corner. Climb the corner crack above to a junction with the top of the gangway crossed by ***Gibbet Direct***. Take the steep groove above which is climbed until it is possible to move out right and up to the top.

Gowder Crag

Grid reference: **266 187**
Altitude: **200m**
Faces: **West**
Rock type: **Borrowdale Volcanic**
Approach time: **10 mins**

Above: Stephen Reid on *Fool's Paradise* (VS–) **Photo:** Jill Reid

This is the steep imposing buttress rising out of the trees on the east bank of Lodore Falls, behind the Lodore Hotel.

The crag can be approached by a footpath starting at a small lay-by at a bend in the road 200 metres north of the hotel. The nearest car park is Kettlewell, one kilometre to the north on the lakeside. The crag dries quickly after rain and is only a few minutes walk from the road. **Descent:** can be made either well along to the right of the right-hand buttress or by the open wooded gully to its left.

Gowder Crag

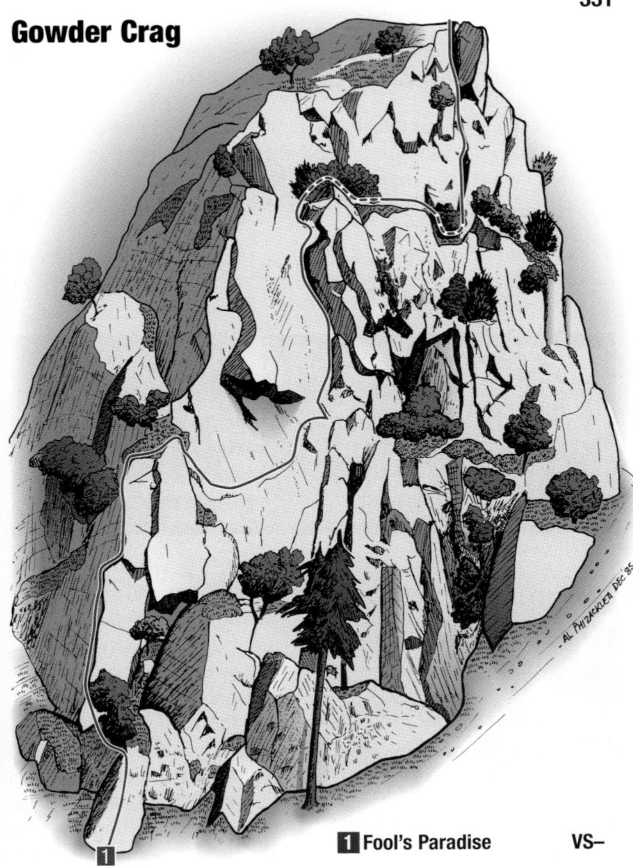

1	**Fool's Paradise**	113m	VS–

P W Vaughan, J D J Wildridge – April 1951

A varied climb and one of the most popular in the valley. Start at the toe of the main buttress, just above the path.

1 **15m.** Climb the short buttress, past a tree, and go up ledges to a tree at the foot of the clean buttress.

2 24m (4c). Gain the groove just above the tree, move left onto the arête and reach a hidden hold. Climb up just left of the arête to a tree belay.
3 22m (4c). Descend the groove on the right for 5 metres and traverse right to a small tree. Climb up, then move right, awkwardly, to belay beside a large block of doubtful stability.
4 22m (4b). Move back left and climb a steep groove, leaning left slightly, to a stance.
5 10m. Traverse easily right to a large yew below a deep chimney.
6 20m (4b). Climb the chimney direct to the top.

Shepherd's Crag

Grid reference: **263 185**
Altitude: **140m**
Faces: **West**
Rock type: **Borrowdale Volcanic**
Approach time: **5–20 mins**

Above: Ryan Dempsey and Neil Carnegie on *Black Icicle* (E1–) **Photo:** Nick Wharton

Situated 5 kilometres from Keswick between the Lodore and Borrowdale Hotels, this crag is one of the most accessible in the valley and can be approached in a few minutes from the road. Unfortunately, cars may not be parked on the roadside below the crag. The nearest car-park lies 1½ kilometres on the Keswick side of the crag; perhaps it is better to get a bus or a launch to the Lodore Hotel from Keswick. Refreshments are available at Shepherd's Café, High Lodore Farm, just south of ***Shepherd's Crag***.

The crag runs roughly north to south and is bounded at each end by stone walls extending from the road to the foot of the cliff. Working

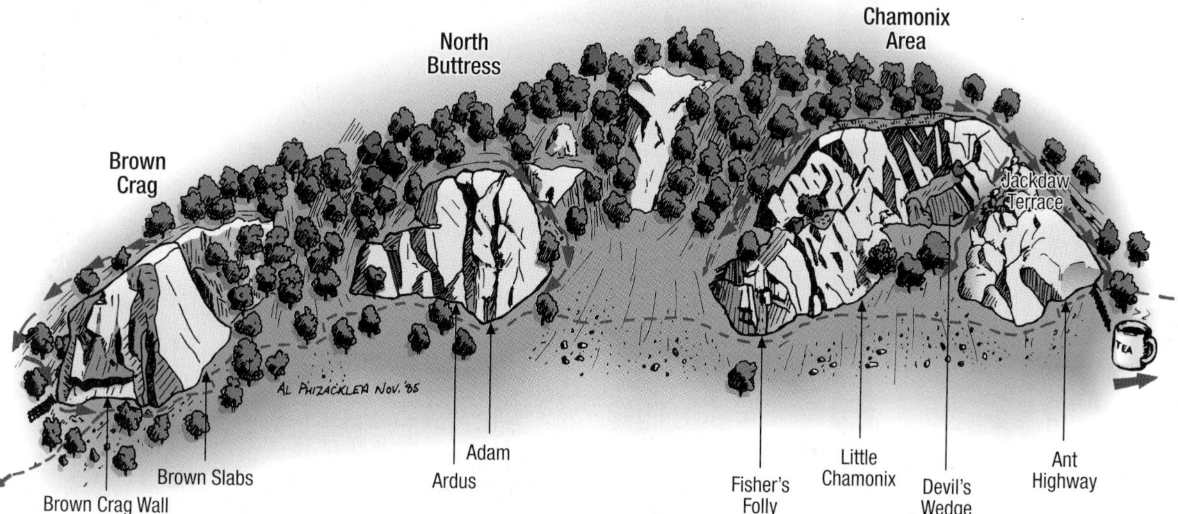

Shepherd's Crag – General View

from the south, or right-hand end, the crag can be divided into three main sections: ***Chamonix Area***, ***North Buttress Area*** and ***Brown Crag***.

The crag has gained popularity due mainly to the ease of access, but also by the quick drying nature of the rock. This is generally clean, but is also polished on many trade routes.

The crag is described from **south** to **north**, as if approaching from High Lodore Farm.

Chamonix Area

This is the first area of crag reached when crossing the stile on the path from High Lodore Farm. It extends from the boundary wall to the steep ***Fisher's Folly Buttress*** (containing the prominent feature of ***Kransic Crack***) 100 metres to the north. Nearly all the climbs end on the ***Belvedere***, the flat, platform-like top of the crag.

Descent: from the ***Belvedere***, traverse rightwards (looking in), descend slightly into the top of a gully (this gully is a possible but unpleasant descent), and reascend the other side to a good path that leads back down to the stile. Alternatively, locate the top of the easy variation of ***Donkey's Ears*** and scramble down it to the ledge.

1 **Jackdaw Ridge**	76m	D
B Beetham – Aug 1946		

Start 10 metres left of the dry stone boundary wall at a prominent rib.

1 26m. Climb the rib for 10 metres. Traverse 3 metres right to an oak, ascend a scoop and then move left to a ridge, belaying above. Alternatively continue above the lower rib passing a yew stump to reach the belay.

2 24m. Continue directly to a ledge then climb a short rib and awkward corner to ***Jackdaw Terrace***.

3 26m. Easy rocks lead up to the ***Belvedere*** along the crest of the ridge.

2 **Ant Highway**	48m	MVS–
B Beetham – Sept 1947		

An intriguing little route with an awkward start. Start 5 metres up and left of the toe of the buttress behind a large tree on a ledge below a wall featuring a rightward-rising crackline.

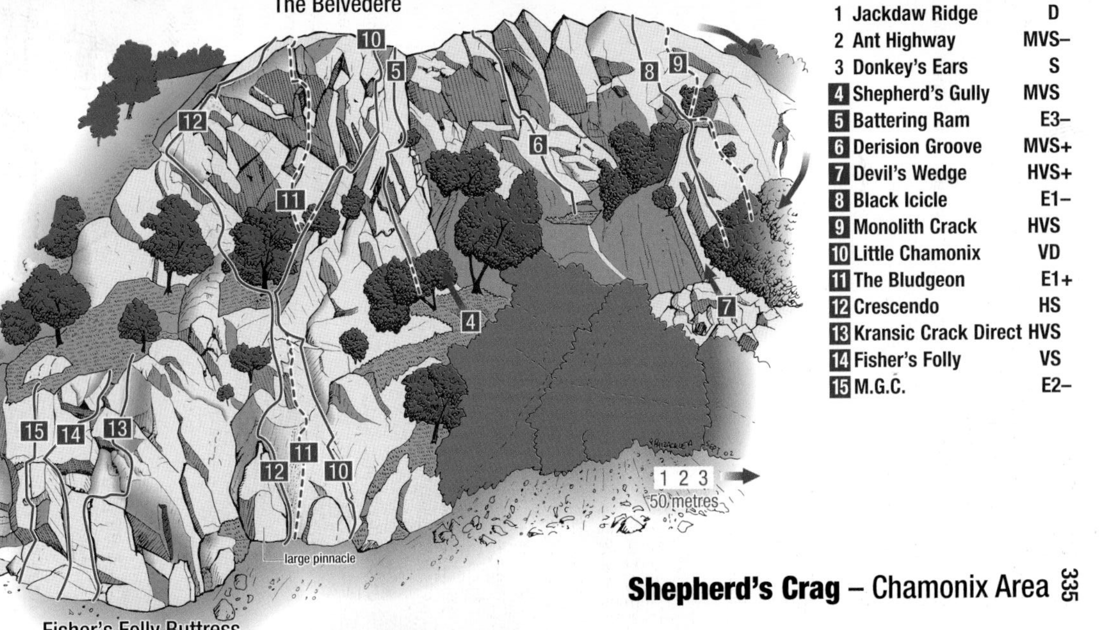

No.	Route	Grade
1	Jackdaw Ridge	D
2	Ant Highway	MVS–
3	Donkey's Ears	S
4	Shepherd's Gully	MVS
5	Battering Ram	E3–
6	Derision Groove	MVS+
7	Devil's Wedge	HVS+
8	Black Icicle	E1–
9	Monolith Crack	HVS
10	Little Chamonix	VD
11	The Bludgeon	E1+
12	Crescendo	HS
13	Kransic Crack Direct	HVS
14	Fisher's Folly	VS
15	M.G.C.	E2–

Shepherd's Crag – Chamonix Area

1 26m (4b). Climb the wall to gain a rightward-slanting gangway on the right. Climb this until a move can be made to the left. Go up to a belay.
2 22m. Climb easily up to a tree ledge then move left to ascend the left-hand of two sharp ridges to gain *Jackdaw Terrace*. Either continue up ***Jackdaw Ridge*** or descend to the left.

3 **Donkey's Ears**	80m	S
B Beetham – April 1947	(VD if Pitch 4 is omitted)	

A popular climb. This starts at an obvious but small flake resting against an ash tree, 40 metres round to the left of the drystone boundary wall and stile. This is 5 metres left of a chimney.
1 28m. An easy wall leads to a short chimney which is ascended. Walk 6 metres left to a small cave below a cannon stone.
2 8m. Crawl into the cave and climb up onto an outward-pointing spike. Either hand-traverse left and go up to a ledge, or fight up between the two ***Ears*** to the ledge.
3 22m. Ascend rightwards up the pile of blocks above (at the right side of *Jackdaw Terrace*) to below an overhanging block. There is a tree belay midway up and on the right of the wall.
4 16m. Traverse left into a corner and along an obvious traverse line to V-cracks. Climb these precariously and continue up right to an oak. (Alternatively, to reduce the standard to VD, follow the jumbled ridge to the top.)
5 6m. Continue up to the *Belvedere*.

The crag now forms a tree-filled bay above a cone of scree. Follow the base of the crag for about 35 metres up and left until scrambling leads you to the high point of the bay below a smooth, gently overhanging orange/brown wall. The prominent dirty gully you see over to the left behind the large tree is **4 Shepherd's Gully** (MVS).

The routes in this bay are described from **left** to **right**. The first route starts just to the left of *Shepherd's Gully*.

5 **Battering Ram**	33m	E3–
R Smith, J Earl – May 1984		

An eliminate up the right side of the arching overhang, finishing up a fine steep finger crack. Start to the left of *Shepherd's Gully* directly below the upper pitch of ***Little Chamonix***, below a large flake.

1 18m (5c). From the flake, climb directly up the wall to the right end of the overhang. Follow the overhanging diagonal groove above the overhang to a ledge and traverse right to belay at an oak tree.

2 15m (5c). Climb the right-hand crack directly behind the oak to a groove, which is followed to the top.

6 **Derision Groove**	32m	MVS+

J Wood, P Ross – Feb 1955

A popular route with some tricky moves which follows the obvious gangway 8 metres right of ***Shepherd's Gully***. Its first pitch, illogically, ascends the diagonal flaw to the right of the stepped corner.

1 8m (4a). Ascend the flaw to belay below the upper gangway.

2 24m (4b). Continue up the steep gangway until a traverse left can be made to the ***Belvedere***.

8 **The Black Icicle**	30m	E1–

D Fielding – 1958

Although well protected, the blocks at the foot of this climb give this route a serious feel. It is reached by scrambling up and right over sharp blocks to below an obvious left-slanting V-cleft (**7 Devil's Wedge**, a fearsome HVS+). The route starts at the large spikes just to the right.

1 14m (5b). Climb the thin, black quartz crack running up the steep wall and move up to a yew tree belay.

2 16m (5a). With or without the use of the tree, gain and climb the blunt arête above. Finish airily up the wall above, slightly on the left, using a good but suspect hold.

9 **Monolith Crack**	32m	HVS

B Beetham – July 1947

An interesting and popular route up the centre of the wall. Start below the oak stump sporting a single branch. A tricky and poorly protected first pitch leads to an awkward finishing crack.

1 12m (4c). Gain a small slanting niche at 3 metres and then move up using a small slanting foot-ledge on the left. Pass the oak stump and gain the ledge above, with interest, and ascend a short chimney to a tree belay.

2 20m (4b). To the left is the ***Monolith***. Climb the crack, just to its right, then ascend a short corner and finish up the wall above.

Following the crag 40 metres or so down to the left leads you out of the trees to the final, more open section of the *Chamonix Area*.

It is the most extensive but also the most broken area of the crag, characterized by its spiky, aiguille-like nature. The crag consists of many small buttresses interlinked with large boulders and tree covered ledges. It is topped by a series of impressive overhanging walls below the flat top area of the ***Belvedere***.

Descents: can be made either down the path on the extreme right of the crag, the gully just right of ***Jackdaw Ridge***, or the sloping shelf of *Jackdaw Terrace*. All are gained from the right end of the ***Belvedere***. Alternatively, it is possible to descend to the left of the crag by a steep path heading from just left of the finish of ***Crescendo*** to just above the finish of ***Kransic Crack***, traversing to the left behind a large block to gain the scree on the left of the crag.

The right-hand end is marked by a prominent outcrop sporting two stunted trees and at the far northern end, beyond the very large central pinnacle, lies ***Fisher's Folly Buttress***.

The routes are again described from **right** to **left**.

10 Little Chamonix | 71m | VD

B Beetham – May 1946

A well photographed final pitch has made this a justifiably popular route. Start below a polished open groove just left of the outcrop in a small bay with a crack on its left side. This is 5 metres to the right of the large pinnacle that forms the left side of the chimney of *Crescendo*.

1 30m. Climb the crack and continue upwards and slightly rightwards into a groove slanting up to the left. Follow this, finishing up the flake-crack on the left to gain a tree root belay.

2 12m. Scramble up right through a wood to below the left-hand of two conspicuous V-corners.

3 16m. Ascend the left-hand corner to an overhang. Use the block under the overhang (best done sitting down) to gain and cross the slab on the right. Climb its right arête to a belay on the ***Saddle***.

Left: Bob Murdoch sliding off the block on the third pitch of *Little Chamonix* (VD)
Photo: Dave Willis

4 13m. Ascend to the pinnacle above. Step right and continue directly to the top in a superb position.

11 **The Bludgeon**	54m	E1+
P Ross, P Lockey – April 1957		

A strenuous and spectacular final pitch up the steep wall below the left side of the ***Belvedere***. Start just right of the chimney of ***Crescendo*** behind the large pinnacle.

1 30m (4c). Climb the blunt arête to a ledge and go straight up the wall above, just left of a large spike on ***Little Chamonix***. Scramble up to belay at a three-stemmed oak tree on the right-hand side of the large tree covered terrace.

2 24m (5b). Move left and climb the easy-angled rib up the right side of the large dirty central groove. Swing right, then go up a short groove to its top, below and right of a large overhanging pinnacle. Climb the crack on the right of the pinnacle and swing left onto its top. Finish up the crack in the overhang above, direct, or quit it for flake holds on the right wall.

12 **Crescendo**	66m	HS
B Beetham – Aug 1948		

A good route starting just right of the large pinnacle at a short chimney/crack.

1 26m. Climb the chimney to a platform behind the pinnacle. Climb boldly up the polished wall on the right and exit to the tree covered ledge using cracks on the left.

2 40m. Scramble directly up to a large triangular block below a small ridge. Ascend the ridge, or the rock to its left, and then move left to an oak. Climb easily up the ridge on the right to the ***Belvedere***.

Right: James McHaffie on *The Bludgeon* (E1+) with one eye on the welcoming Shepherd's Café in the background **Photo:** Dave Willis

Fisher's Folly Buttress

Down and left of the pinnacle is a small compact buttress containing a prominent wide crack in its centre (*Kransic Crack*) and a rightward-facing corner just to its left (*Fisher's Folly*). This is *Fisher's Folly Buttress*. **Descent:** is easy from this crag and takes less time than rigging up an abseil: traverse horizontally leftwards and then scramble up slightly to a notch from whence a path leads down to the foot of the crag. Please do not abseil off, or top rope directly from the trees! They are required for belays and have suffered from needless abuse in recent years.

The routes are described from **right** to **left**.

13 **Kransic Crack Direct**	20m	HVS

D Peel – 1956

A popular direct route, which starts up the prominent crack forming the left side of a huge flake, and finishes on superb holds in a fine position.

(5a). Struggle up the crack to the top of the huge flake. Traverse along the top of the flake. Move right off the flake, below a bulge, for a metre or so. Climb up and leftwards until excellent holds are gained to finish up the wall above.

14 **Fisher's Folly**	24m	VS

M Thompson, P Nichol – Easter 1955

A fine little climb starting at the obvious corner, just left of *Kransic Crack Direct*.

1 12m (4c). Climb the corner to a ledge on the left.

2 12m (4b). Move delicately rightwards for 5 metres. Climb up to the overhang, pass it on the right and continue to the top.

15 **M.G.C.**	20m	E2–

FFA: **B Robert, G West** – 1958

A technical problem attracting many failures. To the left of the corner of *Fisher's Folly* is a steep wall split by a thin peg-scarred crack. Hard for the short.

(5c). Ascend the overhung base and the short crack to gain a flake. Attack the crack on the left to gain a ledge. Have a rest, then continue up the wall above.

North Buttress

This buttress is encountered when traversing horizontally across the scree from the base of *Fisher's Folly Buttress* (about 100 metres to the left). It contains a host of justifiably popular routes.

Descents: are possible to the left or the right of the crag – both require care, particularly the one down *North Gully* to the right where a greasy holdless slab must be down-climbed and a large dubious block circumnavigated. **A much better and safer descent that is very quick is to walk up the hill behind the crag a few metres to a path that leads leftwards to the top of *Brown Slabs* from where an easy descent can be made to the left.** Due to the

Shepherd's Crag – North Buttress

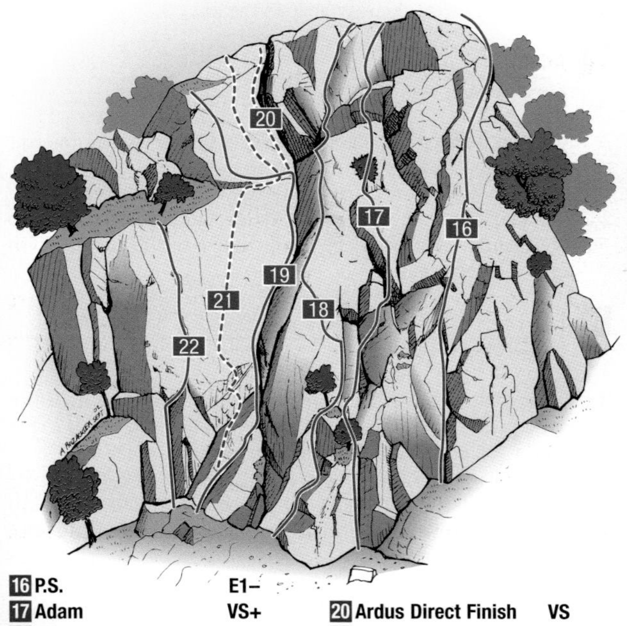

16 P.S.	E1–		
17 Adam	VS+	20 Ardus Direct Finish	VS
18 Eve	VS	21 Aaros	E1
19 Ardus	MVS	22 Finale	HVS++!

dangerous state of *North Gully*, many parties have been tempted into abseiling down the crag over the years and this has resulted in damage to the trees which are often an important part of the belays. There have also been numerous incidents of climbers at the base of the crag or on routes, being hit by dislodged stones and/or thrown ropes. **Please do not abseil from this crag**.

The routes are described from **right** to **left**.

16 **P.S.**	38m	E1–
P Ross, W Aughton – April 1959		

An awkward climb starting just right of a large flake at a left-facing corner/groove on the right-hand side of the buttress.

1 18m (5a). Climb the groove to a stance.
2 20m (5b). Continue up the fault above then swing right, with difficulty, and follow the easy arête to the top.

17 **Adam**	40m	VS+
P Ross, B Wilkinson – Aug 1955		

A varied and harder companion to *Eve*. Start in the corner immediately right of the lowest point of the crag.

1 12m (4c). Ascend the corner to a ledge shared with *Eve*.
2 28m (5a). Climb up right then back left and up a short crack to a holly tree. Climb the slab above the tree moving left to finish up a fine steep wall.

18 **Eve**	50m	VS
W Peascod, B Blake – Aug 1951		

A popular route which weaves up the buttress. Start 8 metres left of the lowest point of the crag behind a large ash tree and beside a split block. Poor protection for both leader and second on Pitch 2.

1 13m (4b). Climb the short slab and steep crack to a ledge.
2 22m (4c). Ascend the groove for a metre or so and step left to gain a slab. Work across the slab then go straight up to a stance overlooking *Ardus*.
3 15m (4b). Climb the short rib above until it abuts the overhang. Move right onto the face and continue to the top, using a good crack.

Right: The delightful *Brown Slabs Arête* (D) **Photo:** Nick Wharton

19 Ardus	42m	MVS
V Veevers, H Westmorland, P Holt – May 1946		

A varied and very popular climb up the slabby recessed corner. Start by the line of four large trees at the foot of slabby rocks leading right to the central corner.

1 18m (4a). Ascend rightwards and up to a block belay at the foot of the main corner.

2 12m (4a). Ascend the block and the corner above to a ledge with a block belay. (Above is the chimney of **20 Ardus Direct Finish** – VS 4c.)

3 12m (4b). Traverse left across the exposed slab for 5 metres and climb a crack to the top. Another crack, 3 metres left, is slightly easier.

21 Aaros	40m	E1
R O Graham, R McHaffie, T W Birkett, K Forsythe – Oct 1978		

Fine, fingery climbing up the steep wall with the crux saved until the end. Initially poorly protected. Start as for *Ardus*.

(5b). Move up the ramp for 3 metres then follow the narrow right-slanting gangway, just left of *Ardus*, for about 4 metres. Gain a shallow V-shaped sentry box in the wall on the left. Climb straight up the steep wall on the right to a ledge on the left. Move back right and climb the wall, which leads to the traverse of *Ardus*. Follow this right (*Ardus* in reverse) and finish up a thin slanting crack in the headwall, 2 metres left of the corner of *Ardus Direct Finish*.

22 Finale	40m	HVS++!
T Savage, P Ross (1 point of aid – now free) – July 1965		

A good route at the very top end of the grade giving strenuous and sustained climbing. Protection is good but only if you can hang around to place it. Start just left of *Ardus* at a steep groove.

1 24m (5a). Climb the groove for 6 metres then step right and climb the bulge and crack above to a tree belay.

2 16m (4a). Move right and finish up the open groove and crack in the slab on the right.

Brown Crag

The most northerly crag; it lies only a few metres through the trees from the top of a rise in the road, 100 metres south of the Lodore Hotel. A steep rock wall, ***Brown Crag Wall***, facing west through the trees, is bounded on the right by a slabby area of rock rising from a tree-filled bay. This is the ***Brown Slabs*** area.

Descent: is to the left of the crag. **Please do not abseil directly from the trees**.

The routes are described from **right** to **left**.

23 **Brown Slabs Crack**	30m	VS
B Beetham – April 1947		

Start on the right of the main slab.

1 **20m (4c).** Climb the corner/groove which leads, in 10 metres, to a tree stump. Ascend the gleaming corner above, with difficulty, to a tree belay.

2 **10m.** Either move left onto the slab and follow it to the top, or climb the corner direct.

24 **Brown Slabs**	36m	D
B Beetham – April 1946		

The climb takes the well worn faultline 5 metres left of ***Brown Slabs Crack***. Start just left of ***Brown Slabs Crack*** and move up and left to an oak. Alternatively climb directly to the oak. From here follow the obvious line to the top. A belay is possible on a second oak just to the left of the faultline.

25 **Brown Slabs Direct**	38m	VD
B Beetham – April 1948		

A popular and now well worn route. Start about halfway between two obvious trees at the base of the slabs where a smooth line leads diagonally left.

1 **26m.** Climb straight up then rightwards and ascend a scoop to a good tree belay.

2 **12m.** Climb the wall above, moving left slightly to finish.

Shepherd's Crag – Brown Crag

	Route	Grade
23	Brown Slabs Crack	VS
24	Brown Slabs	D
25	Brown Slabs Direct	VD
26	Brown Slabs Arête	D
27	Conclusion	E1–
28	Brown Crag Wall	VS–
29	Brown Crag Grooves	E1+

26 Brown Slabs Arête	44m	D
C D Frankland, B Beetham – 1922		

A very popular route. Start as for *Brown Slabs Direct*.

1 16m. Ascend the scratched line to a conspicuous notch in the arête.
2 10m. Climb the crest of the arête.
3 18m. Continue up the pleasantly exposed ridge.

Just down and left of *Brown Slabs* lies the right-facing corner of *Conclusion*.

27 Conclusion	42m	E1–
P Ross, P Whitwell – Oct 1955		

A striking and strenuous route up the prominent right-facing corner. Low in the grade.

1 24m (5b). Climb the steep corner over a small bulge. Follow the corner above until it curves right and then gain an easier V-groove, which is followed more easily to its top.
2 18m. Climb easily up slabs above.

28 Brown Crag Wall	45m	VS–
R Wilkinson, K C Ogilvie, J D J Wildridge – April 1950		

A classic route, varied and interesting, though it is now rather polished, especially on the first pitch. Start at a weakness in the wall at a twin-stemmed oak 8 metres left of *Conclusion*.

1 15m (4b). Gain and climb the scoop for 3 metres and step right onto an arête. Move up boldly into a corner and onto a ledge.
2 15m (4a). Move up, traverse left for 3 metres and ascend the slab to a sloping ledge. Continue up the slab and scoop then traverse right to a tree belay.
3 15m (4a). Climb straight up a shallow corner and continue to the top.

29 Brown Crag Grooves	57m	E1+
F Crosby, P Muscroft – Sept 1959		

A fine climb taking the grooveline just right of the undercut wall with two crux sections on Pitch 1. The pegs are old but can be backed up with good gear. Start at a smooth corner just left of the twin-stemmed oak at the foot of *Brown Crag Wall*.

1 24m (5b). Climb the steep wall for 3 metres, then move right and ascend a steep corner leftwards to the wall above. Move left to the base of the upper groove and climb this with interest to a ledge.

2 33m (4b). Climb delicately onto the block above and move left to climb a groove for 10 metres. Finish up to the right.

Black Crag

Grid reference: 263 172
Altitude: 260m
Faces: West to North
Rock type: Borrowdale Volcanic
Approach time: 20 mins

One of the most impressive crags in Borrowdale, with something for everyone on clean sound rock. Protection is generally good, the climbing is delightful and the situations are excellent.

The crag dominates the small valley of Troutdale and is easily visible from the road after passing *Shepherd's Crag* and the Borrowdale Hotel. Parking is found ½ kilometre further on, in two small areas just past the Derwent Hotel where the road enters a series of sharp bends. From here, walk back 100 metres and take a narrow lane (no vehicles or parking) opposite the hotel. This leads past several cottages to an open grassy meadow. *Black Crag* is now obvious! Follow the track and stream until the valley narrows where an improved path zig-zags up the hill to the crag.

The cliff has two distinct halves, split by a vegetated gully just to the left of the lowest part of the crag, which is also the point of arrival. The best climbs are found either side of this feature as things tend to deteriorate where the crag merges into the fellside. To the left is a steep central wall topped by overhangs which eases in angle towards the summit. To the right of the gully is a series of grooves and corners, further right is *Troutdale Pinnacle*, directly above the lowest part of the crag and usually waymarked by climbers!

The point of arrival and gearing up spot is also the lowest point of the crag; an old fallen tree marks the start of the *Pinnacle* routes,

above and left is the grassy gully. The *Pinnacle* itself is now obvious high on the crag and straight above the toe of the buttress.
Descent: walk right across the plateau to a gully to where a stile crosses a stone wall.

The climbs are described from **right** to **left**.

1 **Raindrop**	90m	E1

P Livesey, J Sheard – June 1973

A very direct route up to the *Pinnacle*. Start at a thin left-slanting crack 3 metres right of the fallen tree and just right of a wide crack.
1 15m (5b). Climb the crack to a ledge. Climb the slab behind, trending left to break through the moustache of heather at the left end.
2 27m (5a). Climb straight up to the left end of a small overhang, then move left along a diagonal crack to below a shallow scoop which is followed to a stance.
3 33m (5b). Climb the wall on flakes, 2 metres right of the crack of *Troutdale Pinnacle Superdirect* to a good foothold on the right. Move left for 2 metres to the crack, then go straight up to gain a rightward-slanting groove. Climb this and the arête on the right to the top of the *Pinnacle*. A sustained pitch.
4 15m (4c). Climb a little way up the groove, taken by pitch 6 of *Troutdale Pinnacle*. Then swing round the arête to the left and move up to the top. Alternatively, like most people, finish up *Troutdale Pinnacle.*

2 **Troutdale Pinnacle**	105m	S

F Mallinson, R Mayson – May 1914

Originally known as *Black Crag Buttress*, this magnificent route fully deserves its 'classic' status. Start at the lowest point of the crag behind an old fallen tree at a short, wide, broken crack.
1 21m. Climb the crack, past a tree stump, to a ledge. Move to a birch tree at the right end of the ledge. Climb the wall behind for 6 metres to another ledge and continue up a broken groove to a large block belay.
2 28m. Follow a groove on the right onto slabs. Climb these rightwards to a large ledge below a shattered corner.
3 10m. Ascend the steep corner on good holds, then step left to a small stance on the right extremity of a sweep of slabs.

4 21m. Traverse left and down the slabs below a steep wall to a corner. Swing across the steep left wall on polished holds and pull up to some ledges.
5 12m. Continue easily up to the top of the *Pinnacle* to an exposed belay.
6 13m. Climb the steep, exposed groove above until it abuts a steeper wall. Pull up left across this then go more easily up the rocks above to finish.

3 Troutdale Pinnacle Superdirect | 95m | HVS

P Ross, D Oliver – Aug 1954

An enjoyable and varied route with both delicate and strenuous climbing. Start at a slab behind the fallen tree.
1 24m (4b). Climb the steep slab to a ledge. Go up the large flake/corner crack to another ledge and traverse right along a narrow ledge, and then go up to a block belay at the top of Pitch 1 of *Troutdale Pinnacle*.
2 24m (4c). Move left a little and climb the wall direct for 10 metres. Step left and continue more easily to a small ledge.
3 24m (5a). Climb the steep crack, just left of the stance, and pull out left at the top to a ledge.
4 10m (5a). Move into a broken groove and make an awkward move to gain the *Finger Traverse* (5b for fat fingers!) which leads rightwards. Continue up an easier groove to the top of the pinnacle.
5 13m. The final pitch of *Troutdale Pinnacle*.

4 The Mortician | 89m | HVS+

B Thompson, W A Barnes – Aug 1969

A very good route up a clean groove and jamming crack. Start as for the *Superdirect*.
1 30m (4b). Climb the steep slab to a ledge beside a wide flake-crack. Climb the wall on the left to a ledge. Move left and ascend a vegetated corner to a belay just below and right of a birch tree.
2 36m (5a). Step up right, and enter an obvious clean-cut groove with difficulty. Climb this and the crack above to belay below the *Finger Traverse* of *Troutdale Pinnacle Superdirect*.

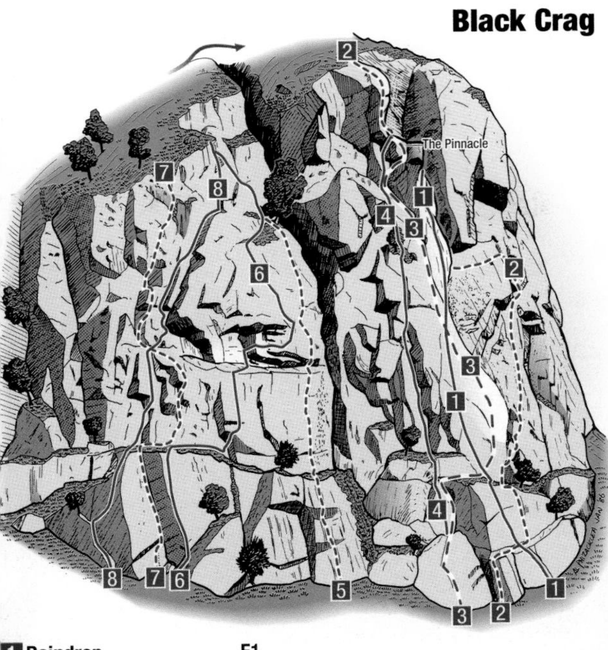

	Route	Grade
1	Raindrop	E1
2	Troutdale Pinnacle	S
3	Troutdale Pinnacle Superdirect	HVS
4	The Mortician	HVS+
5	Prana	E3
6	Grand Alliance	E4–
7	The Shroud	VS
8	Jubilee Grooves	E1–

3 10m (4c). Move into a broken groove and continue directly to the top of the pinnacle on *Troutdale Pinnacle*.

4 13m. The final pitch of *Troutdale Pinnacle*.

The crag is now split by a dirty vegetated gully.

To the left of the gully lies the superb steep wall containing the next two routes. They are both amongst the best in the valley.

5 Prana	72m	E3

P Gomersall – Sept 1977

A brilliant route with good holds and reasonable protection up the wall left of the vegetated gully. Start at the foot of the easy-angled and often wet slab below and left of the gully.

1 12m (4b). Climb the fault leftwards up the slabs to a tree belay below the wall.

2 42m (5c). Move right and climb up the wall, 3 metres left of the gully, pulling up left onto the slab below the overhangs of the half-way break. Pull over on small holds, usually climbed by an easier alternative 2 metres right. Climb the wall until a step left can be made to a ledge (junction with *Grand Alliance*). Climb the bulging wall above to where the angle eases and continue to a large ledge.

3 18m. Scramble up easier rocks on the left to the top.

Another 30 metres along the crag you will arrive at a distinctive and very symmetrically split oak tree just below the open corner of the *Shroud*, with the blunt arête of *Grand Alliance* bounding its right side.

6 Grand Alliance	70m	E4–

R Matheson, E Cleasby – July 1976

A superb climb, varied and delicate, and full of character. It is even considered by some to be a soft touch at E4, but as a wise old man once said, "that means it's very hard E3!" Start at the arête on the right of the corner of the *Shroud*.

1 10m (4c). Climb the blunt arête to a ledge.

2 15m (5b). Traverse right to twin blocks on the ledge. Climb into the overhung corner above. Pull out right and climb the wall above to a slab and belay.

3 32m (6a). Go up right, across the slab, to the left end of a long overhang. Mantelshelf onto a ledge on the wall above and traverse delicately right between the overhangs. Ascend with less difficulty to small ledges. Now go up the wall, trending left to some small undercuts. Step right, and make some difficult moves up the wall to better holds. Easier climbing leads to the large ledge.

4 13m. Easy scrambling up the rib above to the top.

Left: Jon Sparks and James Griffiths on the superbly positioned final pitch of *Troutdale Pinnacle* (S) **Photo:** Al Phizacklea

7 The Shroud | 72m | VS

P Ross, P Lockey – June 1958

A good and varied route of great interest, starting up the aforementioned corner by the split oak tree.

1 12m (4b). Ascend the corner to a stance on the right.
2 15m (4c). Climb the groove to a peg runner under the overhang. Reach right (for the tall) or teeter right (for the short) and then enjoy steep jug-pulling to easier ground. Peg belay below the overhang.
3 21m (4c). Cross the slab on the left for about 7 metres and then climb up left and up a short groove on the left of a nose. Continue up to the right to another small overhang which is passed on its left. Go up the short groove above and step left to a ledge.
4 24m (4a). Move onto a rib on the right and climb a series of mossy slabs and grooves towards bulging rock up on the right. Move right at the bulge, then climb up easily to the top.

8 Jubilee Grooves | 114m | E1–

W Freelands, R McHaffie – June 1977

Enjoyable and varied climbing requiring a bold approach on Pitch 1. Start just left of the left arête of the corner of the *Shroud*.

1 21m (5a). Climb straight up a scoop in the wall to a ledge. Step right and move boldly up to a heather ledge. Traverse 5 metres right to belay on the *Shroud* – as no good belay can be found in the line of the route. A serious pitch.
2 33m (4c). Move back left for 5 metres, ascend a short wall and continue up a groove on the left. At the top, climb back right and down the slab to a peg belay below the overhang.
3 36m (5b). Climb back left for 3 metres to a groove at the end of the overhang. Surmount this, moving out right at the top. Continue up the slabby groove to a heather ledge. Walk right to a large block belay.
4 24m (4a). Go back left to the top of the groove. Climb directly up a rib and continue to a tree belay.

Quayfoot Buttress

Grid reference: **254 167**
Altitude: **135m**
Faces: **North-West and North**
Rock type: **Borrowdale Volcanic**
Approach time: **5 mins**

Locally pronounced "Whyfoot" (but not by climbers). This is the obvious buttress above the Bowderstone Quarry car-park which gives good, very accessible and popular climbs on compact rock. It can be reached, in a few minutes, by going over a stile and striking directly up to the crag.

Descent: can be on either side of the crag.

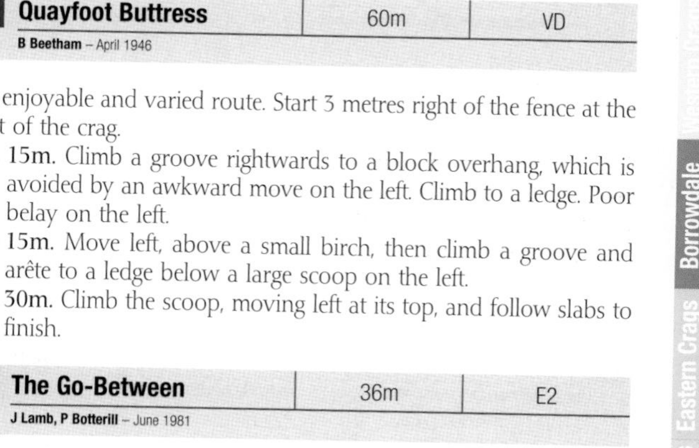

1	**Quayfoot Buttress**	60m	VD

B Beetham – April 1946

An enjoyable and varied route. Start 3 metres right of the fence at the foot of the crag.

1 15m. Climb a groove rightwards to a block overhang, which is avoided by an awkward move on the left. Climb to a ledge. Poor belay on the left.

2 15m. Move left, above a small birch, then climb a groove and arête to a ledge below a large scoop on the left.

3 30m. Climb the scoop, moving left at its top, and follow slabs to finish.

2	**The Go-Between**	36m	E2

J Lamb, P Botterill – June 1981

An enjoyable route giving delicate climbing up the wall left of *Mandrake*. Start on a ledge, left of *Mandrake*, at a short crack in a steep little wall.

1 20m (5b). Pull up the crack and continue more easily up grooves above to a large ledge, 5 metres right of a birch tree. If the lower crack is wet it is possible to gain the large ledge by climbing directly up to the birch tree.

2 16m (5c). Climb up onto the wall above and follow a vague crackline in the middle of the wall to a horizontal break. Continue directly up the wall above to the top.

3 Aberration	38m	MVS+
O Woolcock, P Nunn – May 1965		

A pleasant route with good positions. Start below the obtuse-angled corner in the centre of the buttress.

1 20m (4a). Gain the corner and climb it and the chimney above to a ledge on the right.

2 18m (4c). Move left with difficulty, and then up a steep slab, crossing *Mandrake*, to a chimney/groove which is climbed past a tree to the top.

4 Mandrake	44m	HVS
A Liddell, M Burbage (1 point of aid – now free) – July 1964		

A superb and popular climb. Start as for ***Aberration***, below the obtuse-angled corner in the centre of the crag.

1 20m (4c). Gain the corner, step up, and immediately follow the obvious hand-traverse leftwards for 3 metres before climbing up to a large sloping ledge.

2 24m (5a). Climb a crack to the bottom of the chimney/groove on *Aberration*. Move right for 6 metres to another crack and climb this to an overhang. Surmount this and continue to the top, in a fine position.

5 Irony	40m	HVS–
R Beldon (with aid) – 1961	FFA: **A Liddell, R McHaffie** – 1961	

A good climb with sustained interest on each pitch. Start to the right of ***Aberration*** below a short groove.

1 18m (4c). Climb the groove to a grass ledge. Follow a groove and slab on the left. Move slightly rightwards to a crack which is climbed to a ledge.

2 12m (4c). Surmount the broken overhang and the thin crack above. A swing right at the top leads to a ledge and peg belay.

3 10m (5a). Move up left under the overhang (gnarled peg) then pull over it with great difficulty and continue to the top.

Quayfoot Buttress

	Route	Grade
1	Quayfoot Buttress	VD
2	The Go-Between	E2
3	Aberration	MVS+
4	Mandrake	HVS
5	Irony	HVS–

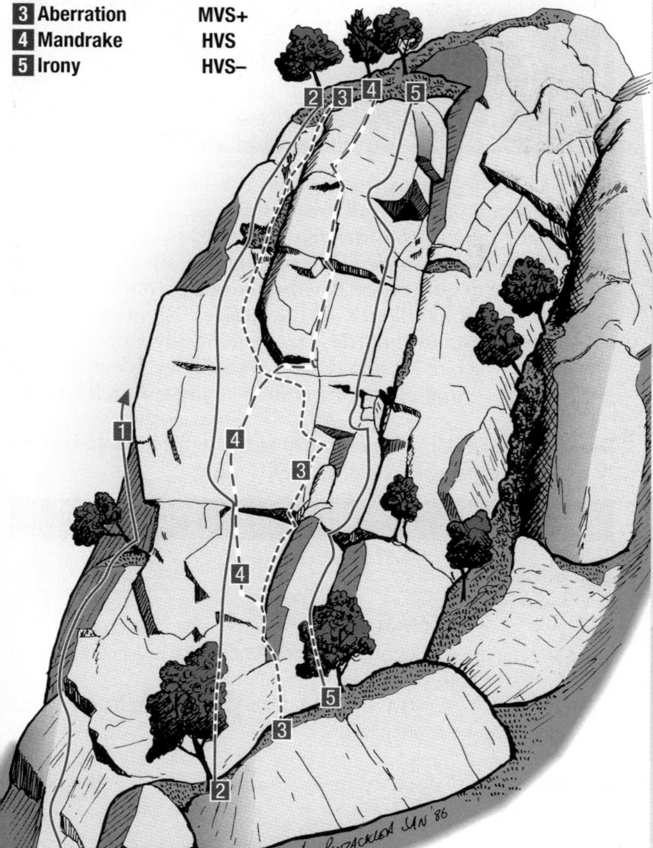

Bowderstone Crag

Grid reference: **256 165**
Altitude: **220m**
Faces: **South-West**
Rock type: **Borrowdale Volcanic**
Approach time: **20 mins**

The following routes are fine examples of the modern testpieces to be found at the ***Hell's Wall Area*** of this crag. The routes are best approached from the ***Bowderstone Quarry*** car park from where a track leads to the ***Bowderstone***, passing beneath ***Woden's Face***. About 100 metres before the ***Bowderstone*** take a track on the left heading more or less directly up the hillside. The prominent feature of ***Bowderstone Pinnacle*** is reached initially. From here follow a path which rises up to the left. Where it levels out you will see 15 metres ahead of you the prominent arête of ***Hell's Wall***.

Descent: scramble down the gully/ramp system on the left of the buttress.

The routes are described from **left** to **right**.

Hell's Wall

1	**Bleed in Hell**	30m	E8
	D Birkett – May 1992		

The stunning arête gives an intense route that could leave you with less finger skin than you started with.

(6c). Start as for *Hell's Wall* but, instead of climbing its crux crack, follow the arête throughout.

2	**Hell's Wall**	30m	E6
	S Clarke, B Henderson (with aid) – Feb 1964	FFA: **R Fawcett, C Gibb** – 1979	

The original testpiece. Previously an old artificial route, it now gives an excellent, technically very hard and sustained free climb. Well protected by in-situ pegs. Start at the wide crack left of the arête.

(6c). Climb the wide crack to a ledge then go up right to a ledge on the arête. Move up and right to gain a crack. Go up this then move out right and climb up rightwards to below a curving groove. This is followed boldly to the top.

Bowderstone Crag – Hell's Wall

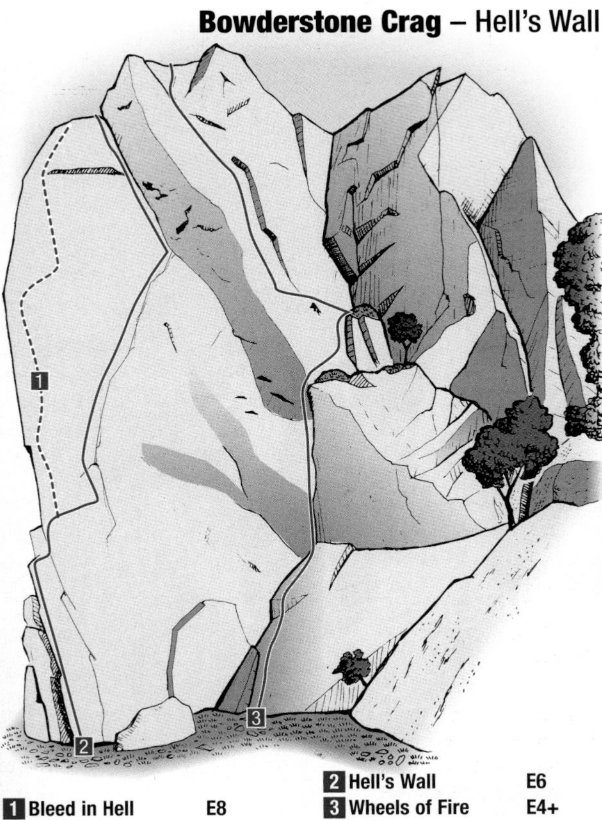

1 Bleed in Hell **E8**
2 Hell's Wall **E6**
3 Wheels of Fire **E4+**

3	**Wheels of Fire**	35m	E4+

P Whillance, D Armstrong – April 1979

Start at the corner at the right-hand side of ***Hell's Wall***.

The awkward first corner leads to a very good top pitch above the impressive wall. Start in the slabby corner at the right-hand side of the wall, behind a large block.

1 15m (6a). Ascend the corner to a ledge. Climb directly up the steep corner and crack above to a tree belay.

2 20m (6a). Traverse diagonally left along the lip of the overhang. Pull up (long reach) then finish up the short wall and groove on the left.

Greenup & Langstrath

The head of the valley south of Rosthwaite divides into two subsidiary valleys. As you travel south down Borrowdale, the left-hand valley of Stonethwaite, which sub-divides again into Greenup and Langstrath, contains ***Eagle Crag***, ***Bleak How*** and ***Sergeant Crag***. The steep profile of ***Eagle Crag*** is very prominent from the road junction. The road terminates at Stonethwaite, where limited parking and a campsite are situated.

Eagle Crag

Grid reference: **277 122**
Altitude: **500m**
Faces: **East-North-East**
Rock type: **Borrowdale Volcanic**
Approach time: **35 mins**

The bold nose of ***Eagle Crag*** is a familiar landmark. It is situated on the spur between Greenup and Langstrath, facing east across Greenup Gill towards Ullscarf.

It is best approached by following the path up Greenup Gill to a point where a wall runs up the fellside towards the lower crag. Cross the stream above a small waterfall and ascend beside the wall, up the gully to the left side of the main crag.

This wide grassy gully splits the *Lower Crag* from the *Main Crag* and is the usual **descent** route from both crags.

The *Main Crag* belies its image from Stonethwaite by its rectangular structure. A series of ledges divides the *Main Crag*, which is about 50 metres high, from some very steep and unpleasant vegetated rock below.

The most prominent feature of the *Main Crag* is the overhanging corner-crack high on its right side; this is *Post Mortem*. To the left of

Right: Chris Gore powers up the fingery crack of *Hell's Wall* (E6) **Photo:** Al Phizacklea

this, green streaked walls are cut by various corner and groovelines. Towards its left side, a series of ledges cuts into the crag between steep walls. These become more pronounced towards the end, giving the cliff a less impressive appearance.

The rock is generally good, though it tends to be rather green and lichenous and can be slow to dry after rain.

There may be a **Bird Restriction** on part or all of *Eagle Crag* from 1st March to 30th June or part thereof. Signs at the crag should inform you, but if in doubt contact details for further information are given in the **Access and Conservation** section.

The routes are described from **left** to **right**: the first lies on the smaller, left-hand buttress, separated from the main part of the crag by a dirty cleft.

1	**Flying Circus**	40m	E5
	P Whillance, D Armstrong – July 1981		

Fine bold climbing up an impending grey wall. Start at the foot of a slab.

1 22m (5b). Climb the right-hand side of the slab, move left a metre or so and up a green crack, rightwards, to a good ledge. Pull up left over a slight bulge, then up to a narrow ledge and poor belay.

2 18m (6b). Follow the thin left-trending crack and finish on the left.

At the southern end of the main crag a short rake ascends from left to right giving easy access to ledges below the crag. The next climb starts from just above the rake.

2	**The Squawk**	54m	E2–
	B Henderson, K Moseley (2 points of aid) – June 1965 FFA: **R Bennett, G Edwards** – April 1978		

A sustained route starting behind a large detached flake below the undercut wall.

1 15m (5b). From the flake, ascend the hollow flakes and the thin crack above the small overhang. Enter the corner and go up this to a ledge and belay.

2 16m (5a). From the left-hand end of the ledge, climb a corner for 2 metres then move left to a ledge and quartz break. Traverse right and go up just left of *Falconer's Crack*.

3 23m (5b). Move left round a corner and climb up doubtful blocks to a steep groove, which is followed to the top.

Bird restrictions possible between
1st March and 30th June
1 Flying Circus E5
2 The Squawk E2–
3 Where Eagles Dare E2
4 Falconer's Crack VS+
5 The Cleft Direct E3
6 Post Mortem E3–
7 Autopsy E1
8 Postern Rib VS
7 8 around the corner
steep approach scramble

3 Where Eagles Dare | 51m | E2

P Whillance, S Clegg – Aug 1975

A superb and soaring classic which climbs the steep groove immediately right of the *Squawk*. Start as for the *Squawk*.

1 15m (5c). Step right, then climb the jamming crack and the absorbing groove above, moving up right to belay in the corner.

2 36m (5b). Start up the obvious scoop, then move left to a thin crack. Pull up and swing left round a rib on good holds to gain a ledge. Follow the rib steeply for 5 metres to a welcome peg runner. Step right, and continue up to a ledge below the final rib of *Falconer's Crack* which is followed to the top.

4 Falconer's Crack | 58m | VS+

W Peascod, S B Beck – June 1946

A classic route, alternating strenuous crack climbing with delicate and quite bold, face climbing. Start on a ledge below and just left of the prominent overhang, 8 metres right of *Where Eagles Dare*, at a good crack.

1 18m (4c). Climb the crack, passing an awkward bulge, to a ledge. Continue up the groove above, past a small sapling, and move left to belay in a corner.

2 18m (4c). Move 5 metres left to a rib, teeter up the wall beyond, then easier ledges lead left to a belay below a chimney.

3 22m (4b). Move to the rib right of the chimney, and climb it pleasantly to the top.

5 The Cleft Direct | 45m | E3

P Botterill, S Clegg – June 1975

A good strenuous route up the obvious steep groove in the centre of the crag. Start at the foot of the steep corner below a groove.

1 12m (5c). Climb the strenuous corner crack to a large ledge.

2 15m (5c). Ascend the corner until moves can be made out left to a sloping ledge and large flake. Continue up the groove above, then move rightwards to a ledge.

3 18m (5b). Step left and climb the steep wall, leftwards, to a small ledge below a faint groove that is followed to the top.

Follow grass ledges round to the right to where the obvious overhanging corner of the next route dominates the crag. Start on a grass ledge a little to the left of the line of this corner.

6 Post Mortem	42m	E3–
P Ross, P Lockey – May 1956		

A crack of unusual character provides the final decisive pitch. A classic of its type!

1 24m (5a). A flake-crack is followed diagonally rightwards to a dirty vegetated crack, which is followed direct to the ledge below the wide crack.

2 18m (5c). Climb the crack over a bulge and continue to the top with less difficulty.

The next routes are at the right-hand end of the crag. These are best reached by descending rightwards from the top of the rake giving access to the crag and following the grass ledges to the gully at the right end of the crag. Scramble up this to a good grass ledge on the left.

7 Autopsy	30m	E1
S Clegg, P Botterill – Aug 1975		

A hidden gem. Start on a ledge with an ash tree below a 'Damoclean flake'.

(5b). Gain and climb the left side of the flake. At its top, move left round the rib to below a shallow groove, which is climbed until a hand-traverse can be made onto the arête. An awkward move up leads to easier climbing and the top.

8 Postern Rib	42m	VS
P Whillance (solo) – July 1981		

Takes the clean rib to the right of *Autopsy*. A good little route with immaculate rock on Pitch 2. Start in the corner 3 metres right of *Autopsy*, below a silver birch.

1 12m (4a). Climb the wall on the left to a ledge.

2 30m (4c). Traverse right past a large silver birch to a ledge on the rib. Follow the rib in a fine position to the top.

Bleak How

Grid reference: **273 124**
Altitude: **270m**
Faces: **North-West**
Rock type: **Borrowdale Volcanic**
Approach time: **30 mins**

The crag is situated a hundred metres up the hillside above the footbridge crossing the lower reaches of Langstrath Beck. The best approach is to bypass the lower rock and scrub on the left and follow a path rightwards below the crag.

Descent: tree belays which abound on the top can be used for abseil descent, though some are rather loose. Alternatively, walk off round to the left.

The routes are described from **left** to **right**.

1 **Brush Off**	30m	HVS

C Downer, C Bacon, S Kysow – May 1984

A featureless but extremely good bold route up the white slabs on the left side of the crag. Start 5 metres left of the corner on the right of the slabs.

(4c). Climb the slabs until forced left at 8 metres to a shallow triangular pocket. Move back right, and then go directly up to a ledge just left of a fallen tree. Finish up the short wall above.

2 **Fancy Free**	30m	E1–

C Downer, S Kysow, C Bacon – May 1984

A striking route up the curving arête right of the slabs. Start below the right-hand side.

(5a). Climb the arête, with a short deviation to the left at half height, to a small overhang. Pull over on good holds, then follow the edge of a narrow white slab up rightwards to a tree belay.

Bleak How

1 Brush Off	**HVS**	**3 Bleak How Buttress**	**E2–**
2 Fancy Free	**E1–**	**4 The Reiver**	**HVS**

3 **Bleak How Buttress**	36m	E2–

D Hellier – Nov 1983

A first class route up the left-hand side of the main buttress. Start at the lowest point of the buttress below an oval slab.

(5c). A short groove gives access to the oval slab. Climb precariously up and leftwards to a spike runner at its top. Start up a short groove until a swing left can be made on a huge jug. Mantelshelf onto this and follow a series of easier grooves above to a tree belay.

4 The Reiver	36m	HVS

C Downer – June 1984

A compelling climb taking the right-hand side of the main buttress. Interesting throughout.

(5a). Follow ***Bleak How Buttress*** for 6 metres. Step right and climb a rib and reddish wall to a ledge. Where the wall steepens, climb slightly leftwards on good holds, then go directly to the top.

The north-west facing very prominent crag overlooking Langstrath is *Sergeant Crag*. Its most obvious feature is the striking **Sergeant Crag Gully** (S, 1893). This provides a memorable outing whether on a wet summer's day, or in a hard winter.

A few hundred metres further along the valley lies one of the more recently discovered jewels of Borrowdale.

Sergeant Crag Slabs

Grid reference: **271 113**
Altitude: **400m**
Faces: **West**
Rock type: **Borrowdale Volcanic**
Approach time: **45 mins**

These fine slabs are slightly below and to the right of ***Sergeant Crag*** and can be reached in 45mins from Stonethwaite. Approach as for **Bleak How** but continue along the path to ***Gash Rock*** (a large boulder by the beck) and then strike directly up the hillside. The routes are on excellent rock and receive the afternoon and evening sun. The foot of the slab is gained by scrambling up to a narrow earthy ledge from the left. The excellent ***Lakeland Cragsman*** takes the most obvious crack to the left of centre of the main slab.

Descent: It is best to scramble up to the top and then descend to the right. (NB. The main abseil tree above *Lakeland Cragsman*, mentioned in the Borrowdale guide, has been cut down due to rottenness.)

The routes are described from **left** to **right**.

Sergeant Crag Slabs

	Route	Grade
1	Revelation	VS–
2	Endurance	HVS
3	Between the Lines	E1–
4	Lakeland Cragsman	HVS–
5	Terminator 2	HVS
6	Aphasia	E2
7	Holly Tree Crack	E1

1 **Revelation**	45m	VS–
R McHaffie, J Bosher – July 1991		

Start at the left-hand side of the main slab.

(4c). Climb leftwards towards a block step in the overhang. Step up right and swing left to surmount this. Follow the crack above until it peters out then move right and up to a groove. Follow this to a belay. Scrambling remains.

The next crack to the right is **2 Endurance** (HVS 5a).

3 **Between the Lines**	45m	E1–
J Campbell, S J H Reid – May 1995		

This takes the slab between the cracks of ***Endurance*** and ***Lakeland Cragsman***.

(5b). Start up ***Lakeland Cragsman*** for a few metres then step left and climb the slabs between it and ***Endurance***, without recourse to either. Finish up the pebbly pillar to the belay ledge. Scrambling remains.

4 **Lakeland Cragsman**	45m	HVS–
R McHaffie, J Bosher – July 1991		

The slightly wider crackline 3 metres right of ***Revelation***. Well protected and low in the grade.

(5a). Climb the slab and then the crack formed by large jammed blocks (easier on the left) to the overlap. Surmount this and follow the crack past two more overlaps to an easier corner and the belay ledge. Scrambling remains.

5 **Terminator 2**	45m	HVS
R McHaffie, J Bosher – Sept 1991		

Start 2 metres right of ***Lakeland Cragsman***.

(5a). Climb the thin crack right of ***Lakeland Cragsman*** through the left-hand of three breaks in the overhang. Thin moves lead up and left until a rightward-slanting ramp/groove can be followed to a narrow ledge. Pull into a corner on the right and hand-traverse the horizontal crack leftwards to pull out left. Follow easier ground to a tree belay.

6 **Aphasia**	45m	E2

C Downer, C Bacon, R McHaffie – June 1992

One of the best slab pitches in the Lakes! A fine, sustained pitch with reasonable protection. Simply brilliant! Start at the centre of the main slab, just left of a crack containing a holly (**7 Holly Tree Crack** E1 5b, 1991).

(5b). Climb a short steep slab to a good hold below the right-hand break in the overlap. Pull up right onto the slab and then go straight up to a bulge. A hard move over the bulge leads to a good hold. Continue up until moves right lead to a crack. Follow this to a narrow ledge. Pull up into the slight corner via a horizontal crack and climb the wall above directly to the top.

Combe Ghyll

This heavily glaciated valley abounds in outcrops of good rock. The valley is accessible within 60mins from the lane running from Mountain View Cottages, about 1½ kilometres east of Seatoller, to Thornythwaite Farm. Parking is available about 500 metres along the lane on the right on the grassy area next to the river. Follow a path over a stile, on the left, just before the parking area, which leads up to a gate in a wall at the entrance to the combe. Across the river and up the hill at this point can be seen the fine south-facing **Glaciated Slab** (254 128) which has numerous lines between M and VD and is popular with beginners. *Raven Crag* will be seen dominating the head of the Combe.

Raven Crag

Grid reference: **248 114**
Altitude: **360m**
Faces: **North-East**
Rock type: **Borrowdale Volcanic**
Approach time: **1 hr**

This large broken crag lies on the south-west side of Combe Ghyll and provides long routes. The most obvious feature is the central gully of ***Raven Crag Gully*** with a shallower gully, **Tyro's Gully** (M), to its left. ***Corvus***, one of the best routes of its standard in the valley takes the buttress on the left of ***Tyro's Gully***.

Descent: Walk around to the left of the crag.

1 **Pedestal Wall**	13m	S
B Beetham – Aug 1940		

A pleasant little climb. Start at the small buttress of rock to the left of the main crag.

Climb the centre of the face of the small buttress, trending right up a crack near the top.

2 **Crystal Slab**	94m	MVS
P Hirst, E Hirst – June 1985		

This excellent route takes the light-coloured slabby rock to the right of an obvious dark overhung recess. Start at a groove below the slab.

1 45m (4b). Start up a spiky groove and continue up a shallow scoop onto a light-coloured slab below a wall. Step up at the right-hand side of the wall, traverse left to a jug, move up and continue easily to the tree at the top of the slab above.

2 16m. Climb the gangway leftwards. Go up a groove on the right to below a crack in a groove.

3 33m. Climb the crack and the groove above.

3 **Raven Crag Buttress**	112m	VD
B Beetham and party – Sept 1939		

This pleasant route is often overlooked in favour of ***Corvus***. Start from the left end of the grassy shelf above the crag foot.

1 33m. Climb the chimney/groove and ledges above to a good ledge.

2 26m. Bear slightly left and climb up to a ledge overlooking the gully on the left. Continue past a projecting flake to a ledge.

3 30m. Climb up a groove, and either continue up the groove above, or move left and climb the groove overlooking the gully, until exposed moves up a short corner lead up to a large bilberry ledge.

4 23m. Climb the easy rocks above.

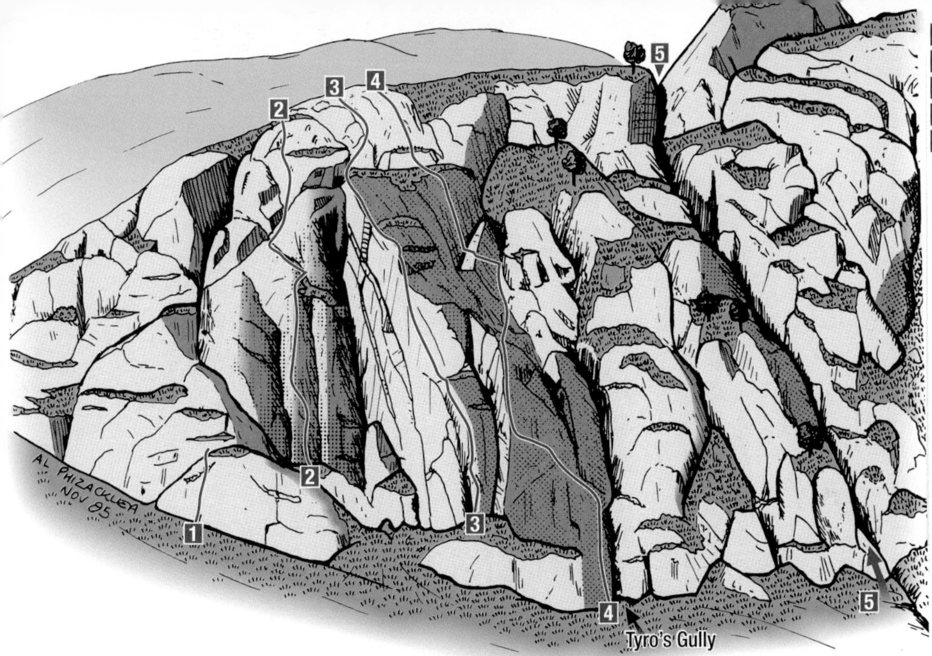

	Route	Grade
1	Pedestal Wall	S
2	Crystal Slab	MVS
3	Raven Crag Buttress	VD
4	Corvus	D
5	Raven Crag Gully	VD

4 **Corvus**	157m	D
B Beetham – June 1950		

'A route for all seasons'. An exceedingly popular climb, starting just left of ***Tyro's Gully*** on the grey slabs.

1 20m. Start up the slabs and move right at the top to a ledge in the gully.
2 16m. Climb the first V-cleft in the left wall of the gully to a ledge.
3 10m. Traverse left along a series of ledges to below a corner.
4 26m. Climb the corner, which deepens into a chimney, and a slabby scoop above to a good stance.
5 35m. Move right for 5 metres to the foot of a rib, which is enjoyed to gain a steep slabby wall. Belay on the right.
6 10m. Move up right to gain a line of flake handholds (the ***Hand Traverse***) and follow these left across the wall to a recess.
7 25m. Climb up to a large ledge and continue up a rib to below a scoop.
8 15m. Gain the scoop via a large flake and continue to the top.

5 **Raven Crag Gully**	178m	VD
W A Wilson, J W Robinson – Sept 1893		

The obvious gully in the centre of the crag gives a good route, which can also provide an excellent winter climb. Start with easy scrambling for 25 metres to a cave formed by a chockstone.

1 23m. Climb the groove on the right side of the gully. Traverse across to the gully bed to a belay.
2 30m. Climb the groove on the right. Avoid a cave by easy climbing on the left.
3 15m. Scramble up the gully.
4 23m. Climb the rib on the right and turn a cave at 12 metres on the right.
5 60m. Continue up the gully bed to where it steepens.
6 16m. Climb up the right of the gully past a chockstone and move right to a belay.
7 11m. Move up a short way, then traverse across the gully, below the capstone which is passed on the left.

Gillercombe

The hanging valley of Gillercombe lies above and west of Seathwaite Farm. It can be approached from Seathwaite by following the path from the farm up the hillside just left of Sourmilk Gill. A quicker approach is from the top of Honister, by following an indefinite path diagonally left to a col on the skyline ridge.

Gillercombe

Grid reference: **223 124**
Altitude: **480m**
Faces: **South-East**
Rock type: **Borrowdale Volcanic**
Approach time: **35–50 mins**

This large but rather broken crag lies on the south-east face of Grey Knotts, towering above the valley. It is called ***Raven Crag*** on O.S. maps. If following the Sourmilk Gill approach, the crag will be seen ahead as you enter the combe. If approaching from Honister, it comes into sight upon reaching the col.

Descent: Cross the fence just to the right (north) of the finish of *Gillercombe Buttress* and descend the wide gully.

1 Gillercombe Buttress	195m	S

H B Lyon, W A Woodsend – May 1912

A justly popular route, starting at the foot of the buttress just left of the rocky ramp on the right of **Gillercombe Gully** (VD, 1913), the forked gully that splits the left side of the crag.

1 15m. Climb up slabby rocks then move up left to a square recess on the right of the gully. Climb the recess to a stance.
2 15m. Ascend right past a flake to the upper ramp. Follow this rightwards to a stance.
3 40m. Move up right and traverse back left for 7 metres to an awkward exit. Go up easy rock to a possible belay. Scramble up for 25 metres and move left to a platform below a corner crack.
4 20m. Climb the crack, or the broken groove and arête on the right. Move up right to a stance.

1 Gillercombe Buttress S

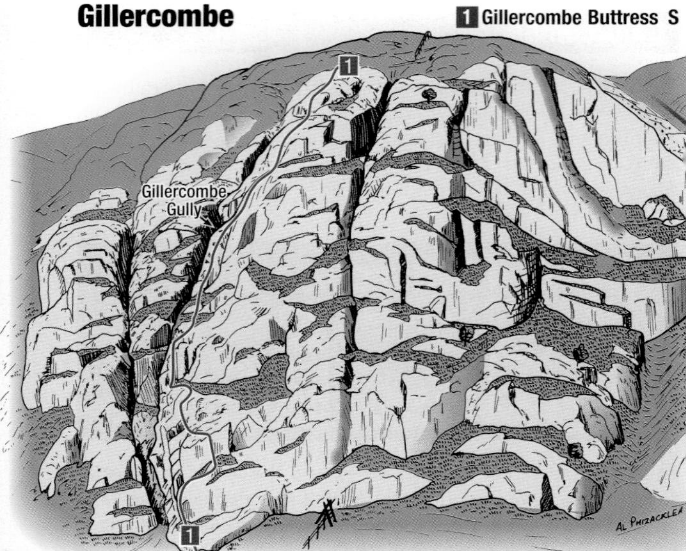

5 **40m.** Climb a short steep scoop/corner on the right to a large ledge and possible belay and scramble up an open corner to a large ledge.

6 **40m.** Step left from a flake of rock and climb a groove to a ledge (possible belay on the left). Continue up slabs passing a V-groove, on the right, to easier ground.

7 **25m.** Scramble to the top.

Borrowdale West

On the whole, the crags on the western side of Borrowdale offer rather poorer fare than their cousins on the east side. There is, however, one exception.

Goat Crag

Grid reference: **245 165**
Altitude: **350m**
Faces: **North-East**
Rock type: **Borrowdale Volcanic**
Approach time: **30 mins**

Above: Brian Davison on *Bitter Oasis* (E4–)
Photo: Nick Wharton

Goat Crag lies on the right of the valley as you drive into Borrowdale, and is found 1 kilometre south-west of Grange-in-Borrowdale. Much of the crag is heavily vegetated, but the main buttress is sound and clean, providing steep and impressive routes which have become favourites for hard climbers. Most of the routes dry quickly, but the vegetation above the crags usually seeps drainage down the upper slabs for some time after rain.

Parking is available in Grange village. A track signposted Honister, Seatoller and Rosthwaite leaves Grange just right of a tea shop (GR 252 174). Follow this for about 800 metres until you reach a small metal ladder over the wall on your left. At this point turn off right and continue past a camping area where a stile leads to the open fell. The path trends leftwards, above the woods, until it runs up to the lower left end of the crag (15mins from leaving the track). The path continues right under the crag. An awkward step leads to a rocky rake directly below the crag; this terminates at a prominent shoulder.

Descent: from all routes is usually effected by careful abseils from a variety of trees. Otherwise, an unpleasant scramble up left leads to the ridge above the crag. A long loose descent down a gully to the south is made before contouring back round under various buttresses.

The routes are described from **left** to **right**.

1 **The Peeler**	53m	VS
B Henderson, D McDonald, J Cook – Nov 1965		

A popular climb which takes the crack and its continuation groove starting behind a yew tree and large embedded flake found on the left, halfway up the rocky rake.

1 30m (4b). Move left from the tree, and climb the crack in its entirety to a good stance and oak stump belay.

2 23m (4c). Ascend the corner-groove on the left, and step left to gain an arête which leads to a holly. It is usual to abseil from this point, although the poor corner above can be climbed.

2 **Manpower**	75m	E2
C Downer, A Hall – May 1983		

An excellent route with some bold, thin climbing. Protection on Pitch 1 is only as good as the state of the in-situ peg! Start 5 metres right of the embedded flake of the *Peeler*, below a crack leading to a corner-groove below the left side of some overhangs.

1 36m (5c). Climb the crack, over a bulge, and follow a narrow ramp up the corner to below the overhangs at its top. Pull left across the overhangs, and go up a short groove to a corner. Climb this, and pull up to a grassy ledge and thread belay.

2 26m (5b). Follow the slab above to a steep headwall. Move right and climb the wall to a ledge.

3 13m (5a). Cross the wall on the right, firstly up a little bit, then back left into a corner. Follow this to a ledge and tree belays.

3 **Alone in Space**	100m	E1
T Stephenson, C Sice, R Parker – Sept 1977		

This excellent route has a well protected crux but do not underestimate the first and last pitches, both of which can feel distinctly exciting. Start by traversing left 14 metres from the prominent shoulder below the crag, to reach a clean slab, just left of a pile of perched flakes on the rocky rake.

1 26m (5a). Climb the flake and slab, until it is possible to move left to gain a short crack in a bulge. Go up this, then move right to a ledge and peg belay.

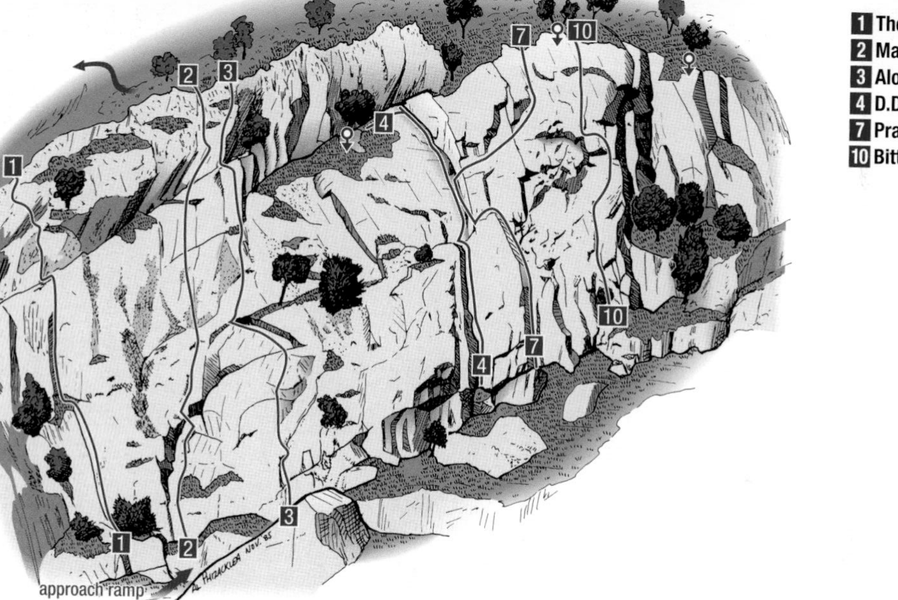

1	The Peeler	VS
2	Manpower	E2
3	Alone in Space	E1
4	D.D.T.	HVS+
7	Praying Mantis	E1–
10	Bitter Oasis	E4–

2 28m (5b). Step up right to a thin crack below a break in the bulge above. Pull up, step left and ascend the slab and corner to a thread belay below an overhang.
3 15m (5a). Climb the overhang and continuation groove. Step right to a grass ledge below a green wall.
4 31m (5a). From the right side of the ledge, make an ascending traverse left to a tree. Climb the jamming crack above and swing left onto an arête. Easier climbing leads to tree belays.

4	**D.D.T.**	70m	HVS+
	J Lee, A Jackman, P Ross (3 points of aid) – Oct 1965 FFA: **A Liddell**		

An impressive route with a bold entry up the first major corner to the right of the prominent shoulder below the crag. Start by a holly tree below the corner.
1 40m (5a). Climb the corner avoiding a bulge on its right wall. Step back left into the corner and climb it, and the crack above, to a ledge and tree belay.
2 30m (4c). A short wall on the right leads to a V-groove (***Praying Mantis*** shares this groove for 5 metres). Climb the groove, past an awkward steepening, onto an upper slab. Traverse off diagonally leftwards to a tree belay.

5	**The Voyage**	83m	E3+
	S Clegg, P Botterill – July 1976		

A magnificent trip, being a rising traverse of the impressive North Buttress. Sustained and always interesting. Start as for ***D.D.T.***
1 30m (5c). Climb ***D.D.T.*** for 10 metres, then step right to a junction with ***Tumbleweed Connection*** below a bulge. Go straight up to a peg runner, traverse right to a groove in the arête and follow this to a tree belay shared with ***Praying Mantis***.
2 30m (5c). Step down and traverse right below an overlap. Step up right precariously and then follow a rightwards-rising line to a cluster of pegs. Traverse down rightwards onto ***Bitter Oasis*** and follow this up an easy slab to a ledge.
3 23m (5c). Step left to a pedestal, then pull straight up and follow the flake-crack over a bulge to a foothold below a corner. Climb the corner and wall above to a tree belay at the top.

4 D.D.T.	HVS+	7 Praying Mantis	E1–
5 The Voyage	E3+	8 Footless Crow	E6
6 Tumbleweed Connection	E2+	9 Mirage	E5
		10 Bitter Oasis	E4–

6 Tumbleweed Connection | 56m | E2+

P Botterill, D Rawcliffe – July 1976

A tremendous route with varied and interesting climbing up the buttress between *D.D.T.* and ***Praying Mantis***. Start on a ledge at the foot of the corner of ***Praying Mantis***.

1 26m (5c). Follow the prominent hand-traverse line left to the arête. Pull up into a slight scoop. Traverse left to the foot of twin, thin cracks. Continue traversing leftwards for 3 metres. Move up to a bulge and straight up to a peg runner. Traverse delicately right for 3 metres to a groove in the arête, which is followed to the tree belay at the top of Pitch 1 of ***Praying Mantis***.

2 30m (5b). Follow the ramp on the left to a steep wall and climb the prominent groove above. Continue in the same line, crossing the traverse of Pitch 3 of ***Praying Mantis*** until a pull up left can be made across the undercut arête onto the slab above. Climb more easily up the slab to the top.

7 Praying Mantis | 85m | E1–

L Brown, S Bradshaw (1 point of aid – now free) – May 1965

The original and classic route of the crag, which is one of the best routes of its grade in the valley. Whether you overcome the crux crack with elegance, or with brute force and ignorance, this is a route that you will not forget. The final pitches are easier but the interest is maintained throughout. Start below the second prominent large corner, 15 metres right of *D.D.T.* and left of the beetling, yellow overhangs.

1 25m (5b). Climb the square-cut groove, past a large flake, then the rather polished crack to a niche. Step left to a slabby wall, attain the groove above by stepping up to the right, and move up to a tree belay.

2 16m (4c). Follow a ramp up to the left, and then traverse left across a smooth wall to a V-groove. Climb the groove for 5 metres until a step up right leads to a small stance below block overhangs.

3 8m (4c). Traverse horizontally right to a small stance in a very exposed position.

4 36m (4c). Ascend the wall on the right to a depression in the buttress above. Climb this, until a step left gains a final slab leading to a heathery finish.

Six metres to the right of *Praying Mantis* is the start of **8 Footless Crow** (E6 6c, 1974) – a route that is now harder and more serious since the loss of a crucial undercut.

A further 3 metres right is found the start of the now more popular *Mirage* and up to its right the excellent and slightly more amenable *Bitter Oasis*.

9	**Mirage**	60m	E5

P1: **R O Graham, D Lyle** – April 1981 P2: **P Botterill, M Berzins** – June 1981

At first delicate and bold, then very steep and strenuous, this route gives excellent climbing. Start 9 metres right of ***Praying Mantis***.

1 30m (6b). Climb the groove and go up to the obvious undercuts. Follow these up leftwards, then climb a thin crack to an awkward pull up right. Pull straight up to a large flat hold, stand on it, and step right, round a rib. Go up rightwards to a pocket some 2 metres to the left of ***Bitter Oasis***. Traverse left from the pocket to a slight rib and then go straight up to the bolt and peg belay.

2 30m (6a). Climb up rightwards, past an old bolt runner and move straight up to beneath a bulge (old bolt runner on the left). Step left and climb the weakness through the bulges to a thread. Pull into the scoop above, beneath the downward-pointing spike of ***Bitter Oasis***, which is then followed to the top.

10	**Bitter Oasis**	54m	E4–

P Livesey, J Sheard – May 1974

A magnificent route made more serious by the relatively recent loss of the peg at the start of Pitch 2. Start at a birch tree 5 metres up a vegetated crack, about 10 metres right of ***Praying Mantis***. This is reached by scrambling from the right.

1 28m (5c). Climb up leftwards from the tree, then step right into the groove and climb it to a bulge. Pull over this to a slab (the ***Oasis***), and follow this diagonally rightwards. Move up to a ledge.

2 26m (5c). Step up left to a pedestal, gain the wall above and traverse leftwards, to a small foothold below a hanging spike. Climb the left side of the spike, then move left where an old bolt runner used to be. Go straight up the wall on finger pockets to a ledge and climb more easily up leftwards to twin birch trees.

Eastern Crags Area Map

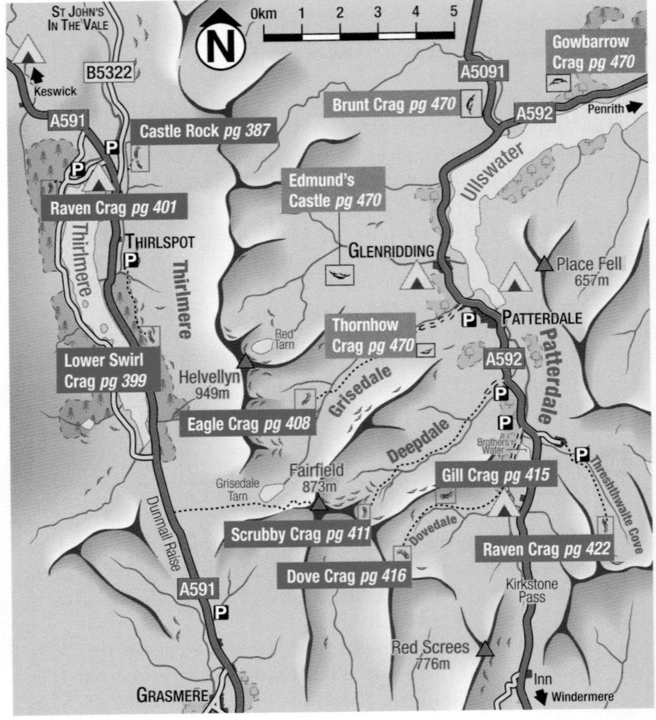

Eastern Crags

Thirlmere, Patterdale & Swindale

Left: Helen Davies on *Gangway Climb* (VD+) **Photo:** Nick Wharton

Thirlmere

by Al Davis

The Thirlmere valley provides the line of the A591 road, which is the main thoroughfare between the north and the south Lakes. As such it is a place that people generally pass through rather than visit. It does however contain some of the finest roadside crags in the Lake District which provide popular and sheltered climbing.

Castle Rock of Triermain

Grid reference: **322 197**
Altitude: **275m**
Faces: **West to South Facing**
Rock type: **Borrowdale Volcanic**
Approach time: **10 mins**

Castle Rock is situated in St John's Vale and overlooks the northern end of Thirlmere. The crag has two distinct areas. On the left,

North Crag is an impressively steep wall breached in the centre by the deep V-groove of ***May Day Cracks***. It is 75 metres high at its higher left-hand end and wooded along its base. To the right of ***North Crag*** is an area of steep broken ground before ***South Crag*** is reached, which is a clean compact dome almost 40 metres high.

A convenient car park is situated directly beneath the crag. From here a footpath crosses the road and leads into a field. To reach *North Crag*, follow the track which heads up to the top left corner of the field, cross the culvert and scramble up the wooded boulder slope alongside the wall. To reach *South Crag*, follow the track and break off right up to the top right corner of the field, cross the culvert and follow a path through the wood to the crag.

North Crag

The *North Crag of Castle Rock* provides some of the finest middle grade climbing in the area. The rock is steep and tends to incut holds but protection can be sparse and many routes call for a bold approach.

Descent: Over the top of *South Crag* to the right and down the stone staircase. *North Gully* on the left provides a shorter but serious and dirty descent.

A stone wall bounding the wood meets the crag near its left end and provides a convenient reference point. The climbs are described from **left** to **right**.

1 The Watchtower | 60m | E2

S Miller, P Andrews – May 1990

An interesting and worthwhile route with a very exposed finish. After a poor start the climbing improves rapidly. Start from the small tree 10 metres left of the stone wall at the left end of the crag.

1 30m (5a). Climb the short wall rightwards to gain a dirty gangway. Starting from the left, boldly climb the rib above trending right to the slab on *North Crag Eliminate*. Continue straight up over a bulge and slab to a perched block and belay.

2 30m (5b). A superb pitch, but the upper section is serious. Climb past two bushes to below an overhanging corner just right of the

Castle Rock – North Crag

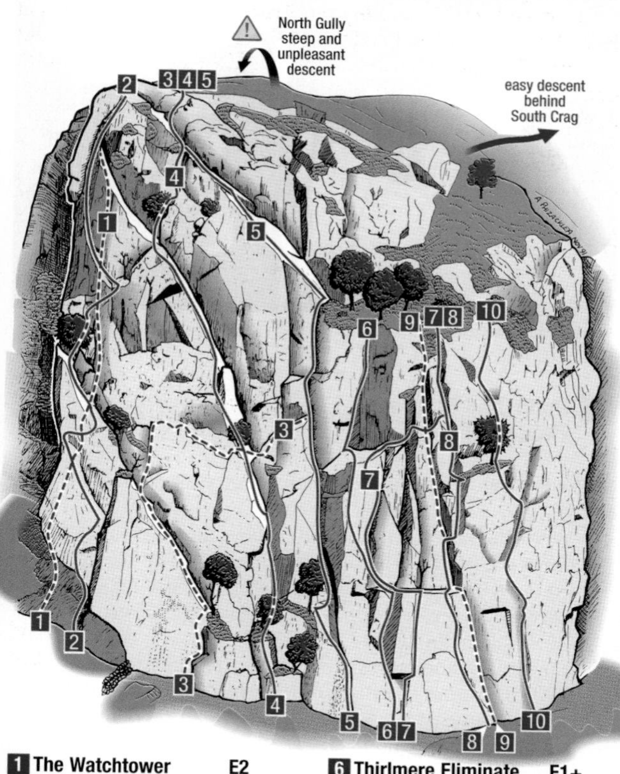

1	**The Watchtower**	**E2**
2	**North Crag Eliminate**	**E1**
3	**Zig Zag**	**MVS+**
4	**Overhanging Bastion**	**VS+**
5	**May Day Cracks**	**VS+**
6	**Thirlmere Eliminate**	**E1+**
7	**Rigor Mortis**	**E2+**
8	**Harlot Face**	**E1**
9	**Trierman Eliminate**	**E2**
10	**Ted Cheasby**	**E2+**

yew tree on *North Crag Eliminate*. Layback up this strenuously and continue in the same line crossing the gangway of *North Crag Eliminate* to gain the top of a flake. From the right end of the flake climb straight up on worrying holds, then move left to good finishing holds in the shallow chimney.

Above: Richard Tolley tackles the yew on Pitch 3 of *North Crag Eliminate* (E1)
Photo: Stephen Reid

2 **North Crag Eliminate**	75m	E1
H Drasdo, D D Gray – Sept 1952		

A classic and popular route. Start at the large ash just left of the stone wall.

1 33m (4b). Enter the corner groove above the tree from the left (or direct – 5b) and climb it until it steepens. Follow the slab on the left up to its edge, then step up and move slightly right to reach a terrace. The corner groove can be climbed direct with little increase in difficulty.
2 9m. Step left and bushwhack behind a pinnacle to a yew tree.
3 9m (5a). Ape precariously up the much abused yew to gain holds above the overhang and swing across to the top of the gangway on the right. Move up to a balcony and tree belays.
4 24m (5b). Climb the narrowing gangway on the left and make a blind move left to reach a flake-crack and resting place at its top. Traverse left round the exposed corner into a niche. Pull awkwardly out right to reach easier ground.

3 **Zig Zag**	100m	MVS+
R J Birkett, C R Wilson, L Muscroft – April 1939		

This interesting, varied and well protected route is the best introduction to the *North Crag*. Start at a pointed pedestal 10 metres right of the stone wall.

1 **37m** (4b). Climb easily to an ash at the base of a slanting gangway cutting across the steep wall on the left. Follow the gangway to a large terrace.
2 **15m.** Walk to the right, descending slightly, and traverse a big flake to an ash.
3 **24m** (4b). Ascend the slab on the right and climb two successive cracks to a large ledge.
4 **24m.** Climb the big slab on the left.

4 **Overhanging Bastion**	78m	VS+

R J Birkett, C R Wilson, L Muscroft – April 1939

The classic route of the crag, taking the gangway which cuts the *North Crag* in such an obvious and exposed manner. The crux move is at the top of its grade. Start 15 metres right of the stone wall at the lowest point of the crag where an easy-angled mossy slab leads to a steep wall with a clean crack on the left.
1 **15m** (4b). Climb the slab and crack on the left. Belay beneath a steep corner on the right.
2 **18m** (4b). Ascend the wall for 5 metres and climb the corner to a leftward-slanting gangway which leads to an ash.
3 **32m** (5a). Ascend the slab on the left to the pinnacle. From the top of the pinnacle make an awkward step onto the gangway and follow it to its top. Traverse leftwards onto the exposed face and climb the steep wall on large holds (some are suspect) to a recess with a yew.
4 **13m.** Climb out of the recess on the right and continue easily to the top, or follow the continuation gangway leftwards.

5 **May Day Cracks**	70m	VS+

R J Birkett, L Muscroft – May 1947

This fine climb takes a series of cracks which divide the high left part of the crag from the lower right-hand section. Although the start of the second pitch is often wet the climb is sustained and very worthwhile. Start at a shallow groove, 5 metres right of *Overhanging Bastion*, which leads to a vegetated ledge. There is an obvious deep V-groove above.
1 **10m.** Ascend the groove to the ash tree.
2 **36m** (5a). Climb the chimney and V-groove. Continue to the large ledges.

3 24m. Climb the big slab on the left.

6	**Thirlmere Eliminate**	55m	E1+

P Ross, P J Greenwood (1 point of aid – now free) – June 1955

An enjoyable and sustained climb up the ribs and corners to the right of *May Day Cracks*. Protection is only adequate. Start below a 2 metre high perched flake, 4 metres right of *May Day Cracks*.

1 15m (4c). Climb up onto the flake and continue up a corner to the left end of a long narrow ledge.
2 22m (4c). Traverse diagonally left into a corner and pull onto the arête. Follow the arête to a sloping ledge in an overhanging bay.
3 18m (5b). Climb the steep corner, moving onto the right wall at the top.

7	**Rigor Mortis**	57m	E2+

P Ross, B W Aughton (5 points of aid) – April 1959 FFA: **M Boysen**

A good and varied climb; the second pitch is bold and technical and the third pitch is very exposed. Start at a shallow corner, just right of the perched flake of *Thirlmere Eliminate*.

1 15m (4c). Climb the wall to a small overhang in the corner. Swing right onto the front, and follow a steep crack to the long narrow ledge.
2 20m (5c). A thin corner which peters out into a crack rises from the left end of the ledge. Climb the corner and crack to the top of the *White Cone*. Step up and traverse the steep little wall leftwards into a shallow scoop. Climb the scoop and belay in the bay of *Thirlmere Eliminate*.
3 22m (5a). Round the corner on the right a line of interrupted gangways provides a sensational passage, ending with a swing round a rib into the final chimney of *Harlot Face*.

Left: Tony Lywood makes his way up the ramp on *Overhanging Bastion* (VS+)
Photo: Stephen Reid

8	**Harlot Face**	50m	E1
	R J Birkett, L Muscroft – June 1949		

A good climb with a well protected crux. Start 10 metres right of the high perched flake of ***Thirlmere Eliminate*** at a line of shallow, interrupted corners rising to the left.

1 15m (4c). Climb the line of corners to the long narrow ledge.
2 15m (5b). Climb a short way up the overhanging corner at the right end of the ledge as for ***Triermain Eliminate*** until an escape can be made round the rib on the right. Continue steeply to a good resting place, then up an awkward corner to a tree covered ledge.
3 20m (4c). Bridge up the open groove above.

9	**Triermain Eliminate**	49m	E2
	D D Whillans, J Brown, D Cowan – March 1953		

The main pitch provides strenuous but well protected climbing. Start at a crack just right of the line of shallow, interrupted corners rising to the left which are taken by ***Harlot Face***.

1 16m (5a). Climb to a small ledge and go up a corner above to the long narrow ledge.
2 15m (5b). Ascend the overhanging corner at the right end of the ledge to a little chimney. Move up to a tree-covered ledge.
3 18m. Finish by the shallow groove above.

10	**Ted Cheasby**	45m	E2+
	P Gomersall – April 1977		

A very strenuous and sustained crack and groove in the left side of the blunt rib at the right side of the crag. Start just to the left of the rib.

1 30m (5c). Climb directly up the thin crack past peg runners and the groove above until a step right can be made above the bulge. Move back left and climb a shallow groove to a belay.
2 15m. Climb the wall above.

South Crag

An open sunny aspect and good clean rock ensure the popularity of the *South Crag*.

Although there is a good selection of routes in the easier grades, protection is not always easy to arrange and it is not an ideal place for beginners. Particular care is required on selecting belays at the top of routes.

A stone wall runs up to the centre of the crag and this provides a convenient reference point for identifying the start of routes.

Descent: is to the right down the constructed path.

Routes are described from **left** to **right**.

11 Gazebo	38m	HVS–
G Lee, C Downer – 1971		

Pleasant climbing on good holds with spaced protection. Start at the foot of a big groove 5 metres left of the stone wall.

1 9m (4b). Climb the groove and exit right.

2 29m (5a). Climb the centre of the wall, in between the cracks of *Via Media* and the *Direct Route*, direct to the top.

12 Via Media	38m	S
G F Parkinson, W Rae – May 1945		

A fine steep route with a hard crux. Start as for *Gazebo* at the foot of the big groove 5 metres left of the stone wall.

1 12m. Cross the right wall of the groove to the rib. Climb the rib and belay on the slabs above.

2 26m. Climb the slabs and then the obvious crack on the left side of the steep wall. The crack is hard to enter.

13 Direct Route	36m	VS–
A T Hargreaves, G G Macphee – May 1930		

A very good climb with an intimidating and serious start. It begins 3 metres right of the stone wall.

1 27m (4b). Climb the steep wall boldly for 6 metres and move leftwards and up to ledges. Climb the wall to a sentry box and follow the crack to a ledge.

2 9m. Climb the bulge and slab above.

14 Kleine Rinne	36m	VS
J J S Allison – April 1963		

An excellent route. Start at the foot of a steep groove, 5 metres right of the stone wall.

	Route	Grade
11	Gazebo	HVS–
12	Via Media	S
13	Direct Route	VS–
14	Kleine Rinne	VS
15	Yew Tree Climb	VD
16	Gangway Climb	VD+
17	Slab Climb	S+

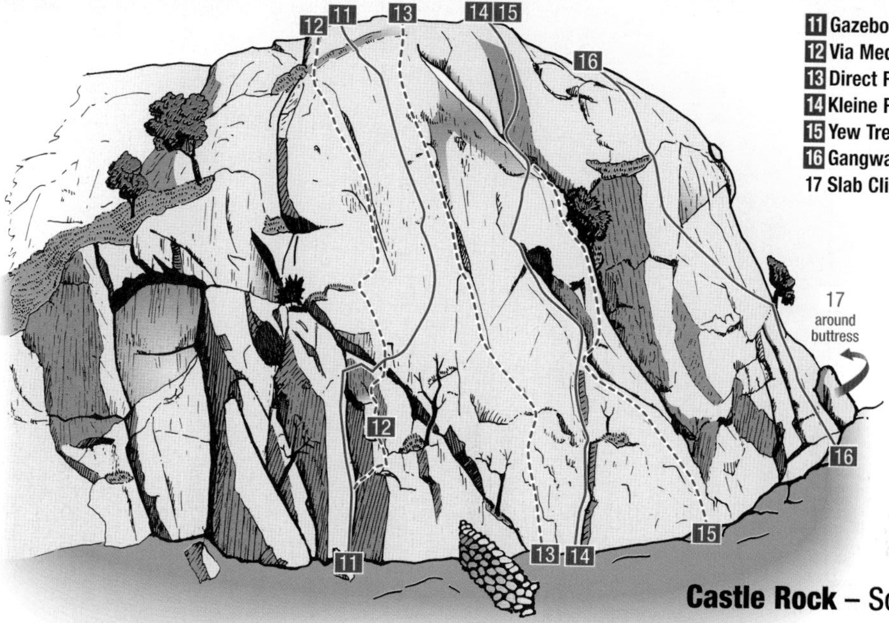

17 around buttress

Left: Minty Sainsbury relaxed and enjoying the position on *Slab Climb* (S+)
Photo: Nick Wharton

(4b). Climb the groove, passing a small tree on its left. Climb the slab to its left edge below a steep groove in the wall above. Pull up into the groove and continue up the exposed wall to easier ground.

15 **Yew Tree Climb**	38m	VD

G G Macphee, M M Barker – March 1928

Start at the corner of the buttress, just next to a large flat gearing-up boulder and 12 metres right of the stone wall, at the obvious wide slabby ramp that slants up leftwards under a heathery groove.

1 26m. Climb the slab/ramp leftwards to its end just below an overhung corner. Traverse right on to the broken rib and go up to a ledge and yew tree, then move left and up the slab to ledges below a wall.

2 12m. Either climb the wall to the right of the crack and the slabs above, or finish up the crack.

16 **Gangway Climb**	34m	VD+

G G Macphee, J W Baxter – May 1928

A superb but serious second pitch with very poor protection where it matters. Start just up and right of *Yew Tree Climb* at the foot of a rib, 3 metres to the left of the large blocks not far above the right-hand corner of the crag.

1 9m. Climb on to the ledge on the left and ascend the rib to a stance on the right.

2 25m. Climb the slim 8 metre gangway on the left and continue up the slab above.

17 **Slab Climb**	25m	S+

M M Barker, G G Macphee – July 1928

A pleasant climb though the corner is bold and reachy. Start 5 metres up right from the right-hand corner of the crag at an obvious slab with a holly tree to its right.

Climb the slab to the foot of a short steep corner which is climbed direct. Easy slabs lead to the top. The steep corner may be avoided on the right.

Lower Swirl Crag

Grid reference: **321 159**
Altitude: **330m**
Faces: **South-West**
Rock type: **Borrowdale Volcanic**
Approach time: **40 mins**

On first appearance this crag appears to be a rather insignificant large boulder. This impression is correct. However, the routes combine quality with brevity. The left-hand side is vegetated but the right-hand side presents a steep wall with a prominent grooveline on the front.

Approach from the car park for Swirl Forest National Trail (about 1 kilometre south of the King's Head, Thirlspot). Follow the footpath, as for Helvellyn, cross a footbridge and go through a gate onto the open hillside. From the gate follow the wall south along the hillside just above the forest and under several broken crags. After 1½ kilometres, the wall turns into a fence and drops down under the crag. **Descent:** is to the right.

The climbs are described from **left** to **right**.

1 Burger	24m	E1–

D Armstrong – May 1984

The right-hand side of the obvious corner at the left of the crag. The long reach to enter the corner is hard for short climbers.

(5b). Climb the slab to below the corner and then follow the corner to the top.

2 American Pie	24m	E2+

D Armstrong, P Whillance – April 1984

The thin crack in the wall right of ***Burger***. Serious to start the crack.

(5c). Up an easy groove on the right of the slab to the crack. Follow the crack to join the rib; up this to the top.

Lower Swirl Crag

	Route	Grade
1	Burger	E1–
2	American Pie	E2+
3	Frank	HVS+
4	Californian Weirdo	E2

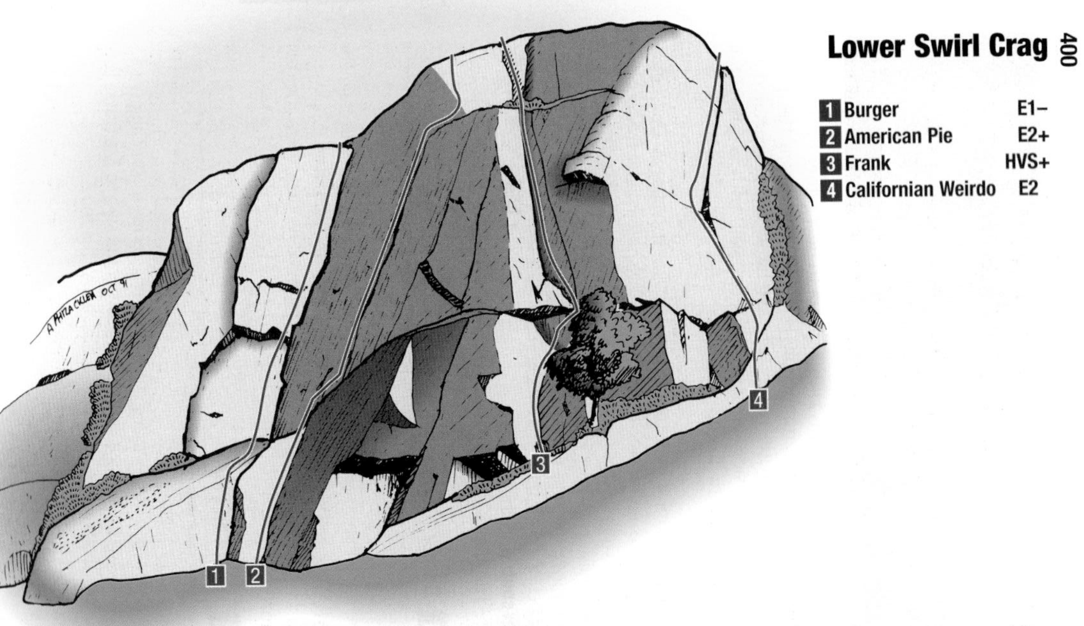

3 **Frank**	21m	HVS+

D Bowen, R J Kenyon, C King – June 1983

Start to the right of the prominent groove at a short slab, below a groove with a holly tree in it.

(5a). Climb up to the groove, which is ascended past the holly. Surmount a small overlap to gain a small ledge. Move up and left with difficulty and follow the ribbed slab to the top.

4 **Californian Weirdo**	15m	E2

R J Kenyon, C King, D Bowen – June 1983

Small but perfectly formed. Steep and strenuous climbing.

(5c). The right-hand wall is split by a prominent crack. Start at the foot of the crack and move up left into a small pod. Leave the pod with difficulty and continue up the crack above on excellent holds.

Raven Crag

Grid reference: **304 188**
Altitude: **300m**
Faces: **East**
Rock type: **Borrowdale Volcanic**
Approach time: **20 mins**

Raven Crag faces east on the afforested hillside overlooking the Thirlmere Dam. It is about 100 metres high and is steep and impressive. Although it provides one or two very good middle grade climbs, its main attraction is the number of excellent hard routes. The most striking feature of the crag is a huge depression, the ***Cave***, in the centre of the main face. To the right of the ***Cave*** there is an obvious right-angled corner with, on its right, a subsidiary buttress consisting of a series of walls. The rock on the main pitches is sound but the lower pitches of some routes and the access to the ***Cave*** have some poor rock and require care. In view of this it is advisable to leave rucksacks at either side of the crag. In wet conditions it all becomes quite intimidating.

Cars can either be parked at the road junction where the road over the dam meets the road down the west side of the lake or at a lay-by 100 metres north. Between the two parking places there is a public footpath which is followed up through the trees to a forestry track, which is in turn followed leftwards to a right-angled bend, from where the crag is best viewed. Continue some 20 metres further up this track until a vague path off left contours beneath the crag. Approximately 15mins from the road.

Descent: the only safe descent is on the right of the crag.

The climbs are described from **right** to **left**.

1 **Anarchist**	77m	HS
P J Greenwood, R Miller – June 1953		

An excellent climb with a mountaineering feel about it. It starts up the subsidiary right-hand buttress and finishes up the prominent right-angled corner to its left. Start 6 metres right of a dead larch tree at a little bulge directly beneath a square-cut overhang.

1 30m. Climb the grassy left-hand groove to the square-cut overhang. Move right and follow the groove and crack to a recess. Ascend the corner-crack and move out on the right wall to reach a ledge.

2 12m. Boldly climb the steep wall, starting just left of the highest point of the ledge. Bushwhack left to a large oak tree.

3 35m. Climb the groove and corner-crack above. Start up the left-hand side of the groove. A superb pitch. Traverse off right to descend.

2 **Creation**	33m	E5
P Botterill, S Clegg – Sept 1976		

A fine pitch, both hard and serious. Start at the oak tree at the top of Pitch 2 of *Anarchist*. The oak tree may be reached via a direct ascent, but this is best avoided.

1 24m (6a). Climb the left side of the arête to a groove (poor in-situ peg runner out left) which is followed to the small overhang. Hard moves right and over the small overhang; then up the wall to the belay at the top of *Anarchist*.

2 9m (6a). An awkward move up the wall above leads to the final crack of *Totalitarian*.

	Route	Grade
1	Anarchist	HS
2	Creation	E5
3	Empire	E3
4	Totalitarian	E1+
5	Communist Convert	VS
6	Blitzkrieg	E4
7	The Gates of Delirium	E4+
8	The Medlar	E3+
9	Peels of Laughter	E5

3 **Empire**	63m	E3
K Myhill, K Jones (2 points of aid) – Sept 1973 FFA: **J Lamb** – 1974		

An excellent route up the wall left of *Anarchist*. Start as for *Totalitarian*.

1 18m (5a). Move right and climb directly into a shallow groove. Continue straight up to the ledge system and belay on the right.

2 33m (5c). Go left into the niche and make an awkward move out of its right-hand side. Follow the ramp rightwards and climb up to a small ledge. Continue up the slab above to the obvious steep groove. Climb this, move left to cross *Communist Convert* and continue up to belay as for *Totalitarian*.

3 12m (6a). Climb up to the overlap and pull awkwardly onto the wall above (peg runner) and then up to the top.

4 **Totalitarian**	78m	E1+
C J S Bonington, M Thompson (1 point of aid) – Sept 1964 FFA: **E Grindley**		

A magnificent climb crossing the smooth buttress right of the *Cave*. It is the outstanding route of its grade in the area. Above the usual arrival point at the crag is a shallow grassy bowl. Start at the top of this at a large block. This is directly below the right-hand corner of the *Cave*.

1 18m (5a). A bold and grassy pitch. From the block, move left round a rib and climb a shallow corner on the right. Step down to the left across a steep wall and climb up to a niche. Move up and right on good holds and continue to a good ledge and belay below an open groove to the right of the rib flanking the *Cave*.

2 20m (5b). Climb the groove. At the top, step up right and continue slightly rightwards to the belay below Pitch 2 of *Communist Convert*.

3 22m (4b). Move diagonally right to an open groove; mantelshelf onto a small ledge and continue rightwards to a small rock ledge (all as for *Communist Convert* Pitch 2). Mount the block above, step right and pull up to a good stance below the roof.

4 18m (5c). Climb the corner on the right (peg runner) leading up to the roof and pull out right to the edge. Climb the crack above to the top.

The following routes start from a ledge below the *Cave*. This is reached by scrambling up from the left, starting from behind a large flake and tree.

5 **Communist Convert**	42m	VS

A R Dolphin, D Hopkin, M Dwyer, J Ramsden – May 1953

The route runs diagonally from left to right across the *Totalitarian Buttress*. A popular climb, exposed and delicate on sound rock; a sheep among wolves. Protection is not easy to arrange and the crux is slow to dry. Start at the right-hand side of the short wall below the *Cave*.

1 15m (4a). Climb the slabs and move right onto the nose.
2 27m (4b). Move diagonally right to an open groove, mantelshelf onto a small ledge and continue rightwards to a small rock ledge. Traverse right and upwards, step down into the crack of *Anarchist* and move up to the top. Traverse off right to descend.

6 **Blitzkrieg**	58m	E4

FFA: **P Gomersall, P Livesey** – July 1977 Supercedes ***Blitz*** climbed by **R Matheson, J Poole** in 1971

A fine, strenuous assault on the *Cave* headwall. The climbing is well-protected with a short technical crux section. Start in the back of the *Cave*, right of the medlar tree.

1 19m (5b). Climb the groove to a hole below the roof, swing right and traverse strenuously rightwards (peg runner) to a recess.
2 24m (6a). Traverse back left to a niche and climb the obvious flake to the overhang. Move left and up to the break through the overhang; pull over this with difficulty to belay below the chimney.
3 15m (5c). Climb the chimney and exit left. Move up and follow a line of flakes out left onto the wall. Follow this to the top.

7 **The Gates of Delirium**	60m	E4+

P Botterill, S Clegg – Aug 1976

This brilliant classic takes the back of the *Cave* and then the groove system right of the *Medlar*. Start in the back of the *Cave*, right of the medlar tree.

1 18m (6a). Climb the groove to a hole below the roof. Make a spectacular bunched-up traverse left past 2 old peg runners then up leftwards to a foothold stance and hanging belay in a groove.
2 21m (6a). Step up and right to attain a standing position in the groove above. Climb the groove, pulling out left with difficulty and passing a sloping ledge to gain another ledge. Step right, back

above the groove, and climb the wall above moving right to a grass stance.

3 21m (4b). Scramble up left to the corner-crack of the ***Medlar*** and finish up this.

8	**The Medlar**	51m	E3+

M Boysen, C J S Bonington (3 points of aid) – Aug 1964 FFA: **C Jones** – 1976

An excellent route with a very technical section up the open-book corner rising from the left side of the ***Cave***. Start at the medlar tree at the left side of the ***Cave***.

1 27m (6a). Climb the curving grey-green wall immediately left of the tree to the overhang. Move left round the nose and pull up to a ledge at the foot of the corner. Bridge up the corner (awkward protection now the pegs have gone) and make a hard move left to a jug. Continue traversing and then climb up to a good ledge.

2 24m (4b). Ascend to the recess and climb to a grass ledge. Climb the corner-crack to the top.

9	**Peels of Laughter**	60m	E5

P Livesey, P Gomersall – June 1977

A superb route combining thin wall climbing with a brutal roof. To the left of the ***Medlar*** is a steep wall capped by a large overhang. Start directly below the middle of this wall, 3 metres left of a sycamore.

1 36m (6b). Climb a very shallow, loose groove to a large break. Pull leftwards off a block onto the steep wall, using small holds, step back right to the shallow scoop which is climbed to beneath the roof. Traverse left and surmount the roof with difficulty at the obvious weakness to a good hold. Continue more easily up the groove above to a block belay.

2 24m (4c). Climb the shallow depression above, exit right and up grass to a groove. Finish up this.

Left: 'Jungle' Hollows makes the mantelshelf move on *Totalitarian* (E1+) to join his father, Dave **Photo:** Nick Wharton

Patterdale

by Al Davis

This area stretches from Kirkstone Pass to the south end of Ullswater. The A592 Ambleside to Penrith road runs the length of the valley and ensures easy access. As the road runs south towards Ambleside, the valley produces four major side valleys which contain the climbing areas. These valleys are described in an anti-clockwise order.

Grisedale

Grisedale descends to the north-east from the tarn below Fairfield to the Patterdale valley. It is about 6 kilometres long and contains one major climbing ground, ***Eagle Crag***.

A good track runs all the way up the valley, starting as a metalled road, from the Grisedale Bridge at Patterdale. There is no parking in the valley and cars should be left at the bridge or in the lakeside car park towards Glenridding. Using a mountain bike can knock an hour off the approach.

Eagle Crag

Grid reference: **357 143**
Altitude: **400m**
Faces: **East**
Rock type: **Borrowdale Volcanic**
Approach time: **1 hr 20 mins**

Eagle Crag stands at the base of the east ridge of Nethermost Pike, about 4 kilometres from Patterdale. There are some old mine workings just below the crag. From the valley approach, two sections may be seen: The ***North Crag***, which is damp, vegetated and neglected lies to the right. All the routes described are on the ***South Crag*** on the left, which is clean, quick-drying and popular. The most popular routes are on the left-hand side of the ***South Crag*** which receives most sunshine. The rock is sound but protection can be sparse on the slabs.

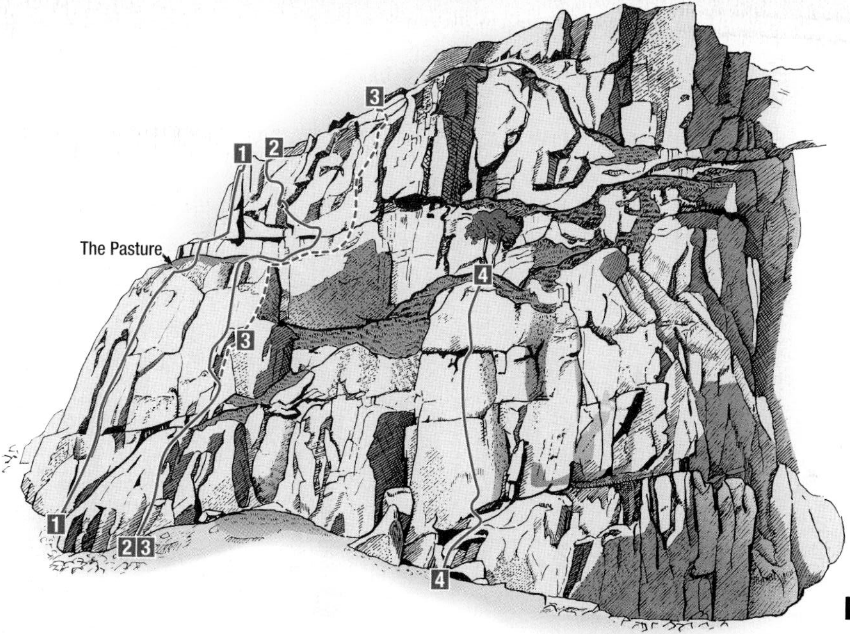

	Route	Grade
1	Kestrel Wall	S
2	Sobrenada	VS
3	Soliloquy	E2–
4	Morning Slab	HVS

The Pasture

1 2 3 3 4 4 2 3 1

Eagle Crag, Grisedale

Descent: to the left.

The routes are described from **left** to **right**.

1 **Kestrel Wall**	45m	S
R J Birkett, A H Griffin – July 1954		

A superb climb which starts up and left of the 15 metre slab which lies at the foot of the buttress. There is a prominent flake-crack above.

1 18m. Climb to the rock ledge and ascend the crack, moving left at the top to a stance behind a perched block.

2 9m. Continue directly to the *Pasture*.

3 18m. Climb the steep slab, 8 metres right of the stone wall, to the upper ledge. Climb into the scoop above the right end of the ledge, move right to the rib and up to the top.

2 **Sobrenada**	59m	VS
M A James, G A Leaver, K A Brookes – June 1957		

An excellent climb, starting at the foot of the 15 metre slab beneath the buttress, below and to the right of *Kestrel Wall*.

1 36m (4b). Climb the slab. Move up into the cave, pull out to the left and ascend the corner. Move right to the nose, climb the short wall and follow the sharp rib to the *Pasture*.

2 23m (4c). Starting to the right of the piled blocks, traverse 5 metres right to below a flat-topped spike. Up to this and traverse back left until it is possible to gain the large shallow chimney. Ascend the chimney with interest to a slab and move left to a second slab. Climb this to the top.

3 **Soliloquy**	76m	E2–
N Allinson, C Greenhow – June 1975		

The second pitch is superb though very poorly protected. Start as for *Sobrenada*.

1 36m (4b). Climb to the cave, as for *Sobrenada*. Mantelshelf out onto the right-hand rib. Pull out of the groove and, keeping to the edge of the rib, ascend to the *Pasture*.

2 40m (5b). Follow the ascending traverse of *Sobrenada* to its end below the prominent rib. Climb up to an obvious flat hold and, using the groove on the left, ascend to a ledge leading back to the rib. Continue up the rib and then slabs to the top.

4 **Morning Slab**	37m	HVS

R G Hutchinson, C Fuller – April 1976

A fine climb taking the faint grooveline in the slab; not well protected. Start at a large flake 18 metres right of ***Sobrenda***.

(4c). Traverse easily for 5 metres along the gangway to the undercut slab. Pull onto the slab and continue more delicately up the groove to a ledge. Climb the continuation groove above to a crack in the slabs. Continue up this to the ash tree.

Deepdale

Deepdale lies to the south-east of Grisedale, joining the Patterdale valley at Bridgend (limited parking) about 1½ kilometres south of Patterdale Village. It is a long valley with Fairfield standing at the head. The spur of Greenhow End splits the upper valley into two parts: Sleet Cove on the right, and Link Cove is the left-hand hanging valley.

Scrubby Crag

Grid reference: **367 116**
Altitude: **710m**
Faces: **South-East**
Rock type: **Borrowdale Volcanic**
Approach time: **1 hr 30 mins**

Scrubby Crag stands at the top of Link Cove, its southern end almost reaches Link Hause, the shallow col between Fairfield and Hart Crag. It is about 60 metres high, a very steep wall cut by vertical corners and grooves, and provides some very exposed climbing outside these features. The rock is sound and the holds tend to be good.

The three routes described give an outstanding day's climbing in a remote and impressive setting.

The crag is usually approached from Bridgend, following a walled track past a farm from where a path is followed along the northern side of the beck as far as the drumlins below Greenhow

End. Deepdale Beck is now crossed and a steep diagonal walk leftwards leads into Link Cove and up to the crag. An alternative, more pleasant route follows the Hartsop above How ridge on the left of Deepdale. A marginally shorter third alternative is from the top of Dunmail Raise via Grisedale Tarn and the summit of Fairfield.

Descent: is on the left, towards Link Hause.

The climbs start on a grassy ledge above the main descent path. They are described from **left** to **right**.

1 **Beowulf**	54m	VS

N J Soper, P E Brown – Sept 1959

This good line takes the wall and crack to the right of a large mossy right-angled corner near the left of the crag. Pitch 1 is poorly protected.

1 27m (4c). Climb a short wall to a grassy ledge. Climb the wall above on small holds, first trending right to surmount a slight bulge; then make an ascending traverse to the left into and across a shallow groove. A mantelshelf leads to a stance with a flake belay 5 metres up on the right.

2 27m (4b). Ascend past the belay to a prominent overhang, which is reached at its left end. Climb the overhang on good flake holds and continue up the curved crack to a flake. Traverse to the right for about 5 metres and ascend to the top of the crag.

2 **Grendel**	67m	MVS

H Drasdo, G Batty – June 1956

An excellent route which takes the left-hand of two grooves in the centre of the crag. It is slow to dry but climbable when damp. Scramble across to the start, below and slightly left of the main groove.

1 9m. Climb up to the right to a stance by a big flake below the main groove.

2 30m (4b). Climb onto the flake, traverse left across the groove and move up to a ledge on the left. Re-enter the groove and climb to *Long Ledge*, using the right wall as necessary.

3 28m (4a). Climb the right-hand corner of the big recess, passing a pedestal, and move rightwards over poised blocks to an area of ledges.

Scrubby Crag

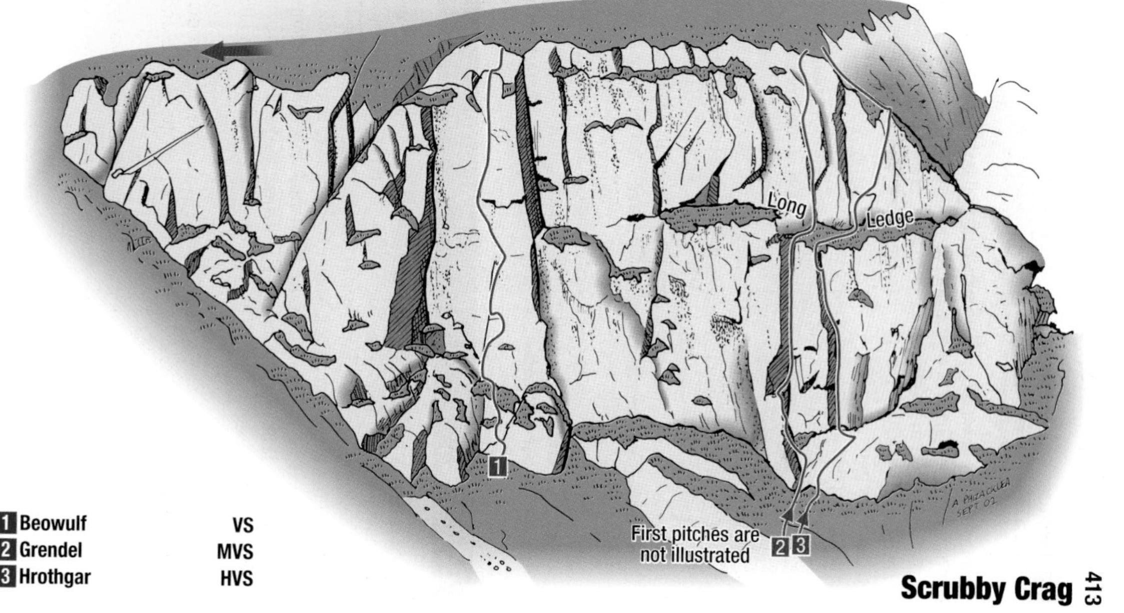

1	Beowulf	VS
2	Grendel	MVS
3	Hrothgar	HVS

3 Hrothgar | 84m | HVS

P1–2: **N J Soper, D McE Dixon, C D Curtis** – April 1960
P3: **N J Soper, L J Griffin, O Woolcock** (1 point of aid – now free) – May 1962

An impressive and excellent climb which takes the steep open groove to the right of ***Grendel***. Below the groove there is a vegetated amphitheatre. The first ramp on the left simply leads back to the start of ***Grendel***. Scramble up into a damp bay below and slightly right of a second ramp.

1 17m. Step left and go up the grass ramp to the foot of a rock corner. Climb this, exit left and then traverse right to a good stance and belay below the groove. In damp conditions it is much more pleasant to traverse right from Pitch 1 of ***Grendel*** to reach the same stance (4a).

2 37m (5a). Move easily rightwards then go back left up an awkward gangway to the foot of the groove. Climb the groove to where it steepens, move onto the left wall and make an exposed mantelshelf, and continue up to ***Long Ledge***. Walk 11 metres right to a flake belay.

3 30m (4c). Climb up above the belay to a bilberry ledge. Work right and surmount a bulge on flaky holds. Continue up with decreasing difficulty and scramble to a good belay. A serious pitch.

Dovedale

Dovedale lies to the south of Deepdale. It is about 3 kilometres long and runs north-east to join the main valley to the south of Brothers Water. The Patterdale–Kirkstone road crosses the main beck just north of the tarn (parking), and a track leads into Dovedale from this point. Alternatively, from the Brotherswater Hotel walk through the campsite to Hartsop Hall. Just beyond the Hall, follow the right-hand path ascending the hillside.

Gill Crag

Grid reference: **387 119** Altitude: **490m**
Faces: **South** Rock type: **Borrowdale Volcanic**
Approach time: **45 mins**

Gill Crag (sometimes called ***Dovedale Slabs***) lies high on the hillside on the right as the gate through the wall 1 km above the farm is passed. A lower 15 metre wall is separated from the main slabs by a grassy terrace called ***Bird-Cage Walk***.

The crag can be approached directly from the gate on the track up Dovedale or, when walking along the ridge to or from Hart Crag, by descending to the *Perch*, a 3 metre pinnacle which lies just above the slabs about 50 metres to the south of the ridge (45mins).

The rock is uniformly excellent and the climbs are great fun; variation is possible almost anywhere but the routes listed take the best lines.

Descent: to the right.

The climbs are described from **left** to **right**.

1	**Flake Buttress**	53m	D

M M Barker, B G S Wood, C R Wilson, N E G Ridyard – June 1937

Start 12 metres right of the lowest part of the crag, at the centre of the lower wall.

1 **15m.** Climb the clean rib to *Bird-Cage Walk*.
2 **15m.** Climb the flake at the back of the *Walk* by its face, by a through route, or as a chimney, and continue to the foot of the next pitch.
3 **18m.** Climb the slab to a stance on the left edge and scramble up into a grassy recess.
4 **5m.** Climb the steep corner or the nose on its right. Scramble to the top.

2	**Main Slab Route to the Perch**	47m	VD

B G S Wood, C R Wilson, M M Barker, N E G Ridyard – June 1937

Start 12 metres right of ***Flake Buttress*** at a boulder by the right end of the crag. Bold for the grade.

1 14m. Climb the wall to *Bird-Cage Walk*.
2 33m. Climb the main slab directly to the top. Superb, but no protection. Scrambling leads to the *Perch*.

3 **Right Ridge**	28m	HS–
First ascentionist unknown		

Start at the right-hand end of *Bird-Cage Walk* at a steep rib leaning towards the main slab. Two pleasant little pitches, but no protection.
1 15m. Ascend 2 metres to a juniper ledge and continue up the south-east-facing slab to the arête above the rib which is followed until it joins the main face.
2 13m. Traverse 5 metres left across the little gully and climb the steep wall.

Dove Crag

Grid reference: **375 109**
Altitude: **580m**
Faces: **North-East**
Rock type: **Borrowdale Volcanic**
Approach time: **1 hr 15 mins**

This magnificent crag is one of the most impressive pieces of rock in the district, its central and right-hand sections being sheer or overhanging for most of their height. The main face consists of two buttresses separated by a triangle of slabs leading up to steep corners and overhangs. The right-hand or **North Buttress**, about 60 metres in height, is a sustained overhang with excellent rock; the left-hand, about 90 metres at the highest point, is almost vertical. From the southern end of this face a sharp ridge, ***Westmorland's Route***, descends forming the lower part of the wall of **South Gully**, the left-hand limit of the crag.

The crag is approached by following the path from Dovedale.
Descent: Move back from the top of the crag and descend on the right side of the crag.

The climbs are described from **right** to **left**.

1 **Fast and Furious**	45m	E5–

R O Graham, D Lyle, T W Birkett – May 1982

A bold and sustained climb of great quality which takes the shallow groove and headwall directly above the starting flake. Several longish narrow tapes are useful for the small spikes encountered on the wall. Start at a flake-crack above large blocks at the right end of the crag.

(6a). Layback to the top of the flake then climb the short bold rib to the base of a smooth wall guarding entry to the groove. Neatly avoid this obstacle with a step up to the right before hand-traversing back left to an old peg at the base of the groove. Layback boldly up the groove to better holds and runners, then trend rightwards passing a tiny spike to a long reach (crux) to gain a superb hidden jug on top of a short rib. The wall above is climbed, first right, then left, then straight up aiming for the obvious finishing chimney. Belay above this or continue to better nuts further up to the left.

2 **Bucket City**	45m	E6

M Berzins, N Foster – May 1988

A tremendous pitch taking the obvious diagonal crack to the left of ***Fast and Furious*** and an intricate line up the superb headwall.

(6b). Layback the starting flake of ***Fast and Furious*** but step left into a shallow cave. Pull over the bulge and climb up to the break. Step left round the rib to the base of a thin diagonal crack sporting several old pegs. Fight the stubborn crack to a rest in the niche (***Fear and Fascination*** gains this point from the left), then climb up and rightwards, as for ***Fear and Fascination***, passing an obvious spike to gain the right end of the obvious ledge system and a good rest. Make a couple of moves up the groove above before breaking out left via a line of holds on the lip of an overlap. These lead to an obvious slot from which a line of reasonable holds, breaks and ledges lead directly up the wall, passing a peg runner just below the top.

3 **Fear and Fascination**	48m	E5+

R O Graham, T W Birkett – June 1980

A classic climb; bold, strenuous, intimidating and maintaining interest right to the top. Brilliant. Start 6 metres left of ***Fast and Furious*** behind the large block.

(6a). Climb the flake-crack to the rock shelf. Pull up the wall at the right end of the shelf to an old peg runner. Continue up the wall to a good flake and then less easily to a short crozzly crack (Hex 7 essential). Hand-traverse right and pull into a niche, then step right and up, passing an obvious spike to gain the right end of the ledge system and a good rest. Climb the fine grooveline above, making a sneaky step out right when all the holds seem to run out, and finishing via the obvious deep groove. A belay may be taken on the shelf at 6 metres to reduce the runout, though this is not normally necessary.

4 **Hangover**	72m	HVS

J W Haggas, J K Booth, R Clough – May 1939

A fine route. The upper part is exposed and some of the rock needs care. Start at the right side of the triangle of slabs, just left of a big boulder.

1 18m. Climb the grassy groove and then traverse right to a belay below the corner.

2 29m (5a). Climb the corner for 12 metres, then traverse left with difficulty for 3 metres; step up and re-enter the corner over a bulge. Move up and climb a small chimney, then step round the rib to a stance.

4 25m (4c). Traverse right along the shattered ledge and climb a pinnacle. Move up to a groove, step right across a rib into a corner and climb the V-chimney to the top.

5 **Extol**	75m	E2+

D D Whillans, C Mortlock – April 1960

A classic of the Sixties, taking an impressive line up the centre of the crag with some very exposed positions in its upper reaches. Start at the left end of the triangular slab. Scramble up broken rocks to some trees below a chimney.

	Route	Grade
1	Fast and Furious	E5–
2	Bucket City	E6
3	Fear and Fascination	E5+
4	Hangover	HVS
5	Extol	E2+
6	Phobos	E2
7	Dovedale Groove	E1+
8	Westmorland's Route	MS

1 30m (5a). Climb the unpleasant chimney to join ***Hangover*** at the top of Pitch 2 (or start up ***Hangover***).

2 45m (5b). The grassy, leftward-slanting line 6 metres left of the stance is the initial objective. Descend a little and swing left on a good jug to its foot. Climb this and the smooth groove at its top to a small grass ledge on the right. Climb the overhanging wall to the big overhang. Step right and pull into a bottomless groove which splits the overhang. Follow the groove until forced to move right to finish up the rib.

6 **Phobos**	69m	E2
C Read, J Adams (1 point of aid) – Aug 1972 FFA: **P Long, R Valentine** – 1974		

A steep climb up the fluted wall left of ***Extol***. Many slings recommended for runners - not less than six should suffice. Well left of ***Extol***, the path at the foot of the crag steepens to a scramble leading up to the obvious crack of ***Dovedale Groove***. Start at the foot of the scramble.

1 30m (5c). Climb vegetated rock to reach a clean crack on the left of an overhang. Follow this crack to an obvious traverse line and move up right to the highest of the flat rock ledges. Climb leftwards for 6 metres up the steep wall, then move right to a shallow niche. Step back left and climb the groove, stepping left below the bulge, to the overhang above. Turn this on the right and take a stance at the foot of the terrace.

2 15m (4b). Step right and climb leftwards to a gangway, parallel to the terrace. Ascend the gangway and the chimney above rightwards to a stance.

3 24m (5a). Climb the short corner and move right past a large spike to below a large corner. Ascend the corner and hand-traverse right along a thin crack below a roof, then move up to gain easier ground and the top.

7 **Dovedale Groove**	54m	E1+
D D Whillans, J Brown, D Cowan (1 point of aid – now free) – May 1953		

A classic product of the 'Rock and Ice' years which takes the obvious crackline towards the left side of the face. Start by scrambling up to the foot of the crack behind a large boulder.

1 15m (5b). From the top of the slab make an awkward move into the groove and continue by bridging and jamming to a stance below a conspicuous overhanging crack.
2 18m (5b). Climb the crack to a chockstone, then pull awkwardly out left onto a slab. Continue more easily up a groove and slab to a large grass ledge.
3 8m. Move up to a grass ledge below some overhangs.
4 13m (5a). Above a short slab is a gap in the overhangs. Climb through this and step left into the left-hand groove. Follow the groove to the top.

8 Westmorland's Route | 96m | MS

P5–6: **H Westmorland, J Mounsey, W A North** – Oct 1910
P1–4: **C R Wilson, M M Barker, D Tweddle, J Bell** – May 1937

An interesting mountaineering route which takes the ridge which bounds ***South Gully*** to its right and abuts against the left end of the main face. It becomes much harder in anything less than perfect conditions and should not be underestimated. Start at the foot of the ridge.
1 21m. From the broken rock move right and ascend the slabs, bearing slightly right. On reaching ledges return leftwards to the arête.
2 12m. Ascend the ridge to a sloping stance.
3 15m. Step left, climb a short difficult crack, and continue over rocks and grass to the wall above.
4 15m. Move round to the right and ascend the small leftward slanting slab.
5 21m. Climb the little wall, traverse up to the left to the end of the gangway and move up and back to the right along a grassy ledge.
6 12m. Climb the final wall.

Threshthwaite Cove

Raven Crag

Grid reference: **419 112**
Altitude: **450m**
Faces: **South-East**
Rock type: **Borrowdale Volcanic**
Approach time: **40 mins**

This excellent crag is situated in the lower part of Threshthwaite Cove. The best approach is from the Patterdale to Kirkstone road, turning off at the small hamlet of Hartsop. Continue through Hartsop to a large parking area at the end of the road and follow Pasture Beck up the valley. The crag can be seen on the right, slanting diagonally up the hillside. The rock on the main area of the crag is of a sound nature offering superb climbing in the Extreme grades.

The upper section of the crag is dominated by the huge *Shield* which offers exposed and technical climbing on perfect rock. The lower section gives some tremendous wall and crack climbing with its upper tier bounded by prominent grooves, which are deceptively steep. Most of the belays are spikes set well back from the crag. The climbs are described from **left** to **right**.

There may be a **Bird Restriction** on part or all of *Raven Crag* from 1st March to 30th June or part thereof. Signs at the crag should inform you, but if in doubt contact details for further information are given in the **Access and Conservation** section.

Descent: best on the right, or by abseil.

The routes are described from **left** to **right**.

1 **Grand Prix**	40m	E3–

P Whillance, R Berzins, P Botterill – Sept 1980

An interesting climb with a distinct crux at one third height. Up on the left-hand side of the crag are prominent twin corners; this fine climb takes the left-hand corner.

(5c). Climb the corner to the overhang at the break. Move right slightly and climb the overhang to the leftward-slanting ramp

Right: Steve Hubbard pulls on to the shield on *Grand Prix* (E3–) **Photo:** Nick Wharton

Raven Crag, Threshthwaite

	Route	Grade
1	Grand Prix	E3–
2	Internal Combustion	E6
3	Top Gear	E4
4	Redex	E2
5	G.T.X.	E3
6	High Performance	E5

Bird restrictions possible between 1st March and 30th June

which is followed to a short groove. Up this, and finish up the obvious crack system.

2	**Internal Combustion**	40m	E6
	R Smith, J W Earl – June 1986		

An excellent climb up the middle of the ***Shield***. Technically very demanding and finger testing.

1 8m (5a). Climb the groove a few metres right of ***Grand Prix*** to the break.

2 32m (6c). Climb the first overlap to the two downward-pointing spikes (peg runner on the right). Surmount the overhang and pull across leftwards to the obvious crack; step back right until above the peg. Climb across the wall to a short diagonal crack and follow this to ***Top Gear***. Climb the cracks above to a small overhang (peg runner on the right), and follow the crack to a good finger jug (peg runner of the left). Continue up the slab above to a short corner and the top.

3	**Top Gear**	40m	E4
	P Whillance, D Armstrong – May 1981		

A superb, bold climb taking a diagonal line across the great ***Shield***. Start mid-way between ***Grand Prix*** and ***Redex*** at the thin ragged crack.

(6a). Climb the crack, step right and up the groove to the break below the overhang. Move right and climb a short flake-crack until a pull up left can be made into a steep groove. Swing across left to gain a large sloping foothold on the bottom right-hand edge of the ***Shield***. Move up to the obvious line of holds trending leftwards across the ***Shield*** to reach a slight groove. Follow this, then traverse right and mantelshelf onto the glacis. Step right and climb the short corner to the top.

4	**Redex**	30m	E2
	C W Brown, T W Birkett – July 1976		

This classic line takes the prominent diagonal crack sweeping from left to right across the centre of the crag giving fine sustained climbing.

1 13m (5b). Climb the diagonal crack to the horizontal fault.

2 17m (5c). Follow the crack to the small tree. Step right into the steep groove and follow this to the top.

5	**G.T.X.**	40m	E3
	P Whillance, R Parker – May 1980		

An impressive and sustained route taking a direct line through ***Redex***. Start 5 metres right of ***Redex*** at a shallow groove.

(6a). Climb the groove rightwards to the scoop, step left and climb steeply to the horizontal fault. Follow ***Redex*** to the small tree, then climb left and up to the overhang. Pull over this into the groove and up to a second overhang. Climb this to a ledge and exit left.

6	**High Performance**	40m	E5
	P Botterill, J Lamb – May 1981		

A tremendous, aptly named route, giving very varied climbing. Start at the open scoop a few metres down from an obvious low arch and 8 metres left of the easy groove on the right of the crag.

1 25m (6b). Climb into the niche below and left of the crack. Follow the crack diagonally right until it stops at the base of the wall. Climb the thin crack in the wall moving right at its top. Continue with ease to the horizontal break and the large block belay.

2 15m (6a). Climb into the large groove above the belay. Move across right to a good jug on the arête and then step back left into the groove which is followed to the ledge above the capping roof. Finish up the wall above. Belay well back to the left on spikes.

Left: Keith Phizacklea demonstrating *High Performance* (E5) at Raven Crag, Threshthwaite **Photo:** Rob Matheson

Swindale

by Al Davis

This pleasant secluded valley lies on the eastern side of the Lake District, between Haweswater and the A6 Kendal–Penrith road over Shap Fell. The valley descends to the north-east, the lower part being about 3 kilometres west of Shap. The approach is by Askham and Bampton from Penrith; by Rosgill from Shap.

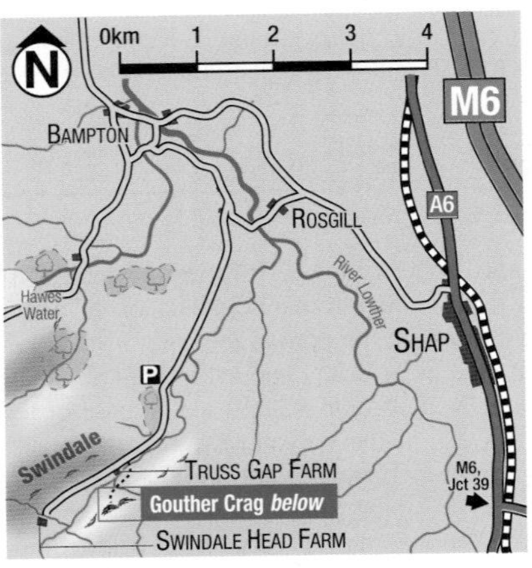

Gouther Crag

Grid reference: **515 127**
Altitude: **350m**
Faces: **North-West**
Rock type: **Borrowdale Volcanic**
Approach time: **20 mins**

The cliffs stand on the eastern side of the valley opposite Truss Gap Farm. The crag consists of four main buttresses – from left to right, ***North East Buttress***, ***Truss Buttress***, ***Fang Buttress*** and ***Nymph Buttress***, but climbs are described only on the central two.

The crags are not big but may be dry when the central Lakes areas are wet. The rock is clean and sound and provides excellent climbing at a variety of grades.

Park to the right of the road at Swindale Foot (signs advise). Walk for 1 km to just before Truss Gap Farm where the wall on the left stops. Cross the beck (stepping stones or footbridge) and follow the track by a wall up and right. After crossing a small beck, a small track leads steeply up by an old wall to the foot of ***Truss Buttress***. Fifty metres below the toe of the buttress, a faint track leads right over a small hummock and up to ***Fang Buttress***.

There may be a **Bird Restriction** on part or all of *Gouther Crag* from 1st March to 30th June or part thereof. Signs at the crag should inform you, but if in doubt contact details for further information are given in the **Access and Conservation** section.

Routes are described from **left** to **right**.

Truss Buttress

This is the right edge of the larger broken left-hand end of the crag. It is easily identified by its main feature, the stepped ridge of the original route, which rises above a dry-stone wall.

Descent: follow ridge upwards until tracks lead off right.

Thirty metres up to the left of the toe of the buttress is a steep, clean face.

1	**Castration Crack**	27m	E3

P Whillance, P Botterill – July 1980

A very good route with a short, sharp crux up the thin crackline in the centre of the face.

(6a). Climb the wall to gain the crack and follow it with increasing difficulty to a ledge. Continue in the same line to the top.

2	**Truss Buttress**	38m	VD

R H Fidler, C E Arnison – Aug 1933

A fine route on clean, sound rock taking the prominent ridge. Start just left of the foot of the ridge.

1 20m. Climb the slabs just left of the arête using thin cracks in the middle section to a point where the angle eases.

Gouther Crag – Truss Buttress

Bird restrictions possible between 1st March and 30th June

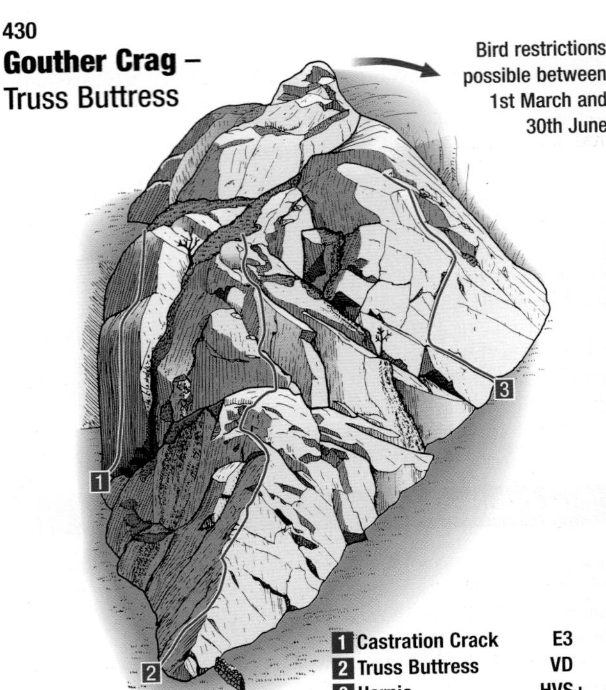

2 18m. Continue up a little slab to the left and ascend the rib above.

3 **Hernia**	22m	HVS+
B Rogers, W Day – 1976		

A strenuous and well protected route with some entertaining moves. Start at a huge flake which leans against the foot of the rounded buttress 30 metres above and right of ***Truss Buttress***.

(5a). Climb the flake by an easy gangway on its right and from its pointed top, climb steeply rightwards and round a bulge, then climb directly to the top.

Fang Buttress

This is the steep, clean buttress 200 metres to the right of *Truss Buttress* with a shallow 3 metre cave at its foot. It may be approached from *Truss Buttress* at the level of *Hernia*.

Descent: move right and scramble down the gully on the right of the slabs with great care or continue down the ridge overlooking the gully.

4 **Sostenuto**	36m	HVS–

H Drasdo, R B Evans, N J Soper, R P Harris – Aug 1958

A good, exposed climb up the front of the buttress. Just right of the 3 metre cave is an evil black crack. A grassy gangway leads up right for 7 metres. Start at the top of the gangway at a flake-crack.

1 28m (5a). Climb the flake-crack just left of a thin leftwards-slanting crack and then the steep wall to ledges below an impressive smooth pink groove. Move left along a crack to an easy rib which leads to a stance.

2 8m. The easy crack on the right is followed to the top.

5 **Fang Direct**	30m	HVS

R M Flood, J R Sutcliffe – July 1974

A very good route, though somewhat bold. Five metres to the right of *Sostenuto* the crag bends up and right. A blunt cracked arête leads up 3 metres left of a holly. Start at the foot of the arête to the left of the *Fang*.

(5a). Climb the crack past the overlap to the traverse of the *Fang*. Continue in the same line to boldly gain the shallow scoop to the right of the layback on the *Fang*, then exit rightwards. Finish up the *Fang*.

6 **The Fang**	40m	MVS–

J S Williams, C R Wilson, T Nicholson, R A Ewin – Oct 1946

A fine, steep climb. It is exposed and not always well protected. Start directly below a holly under an overhang at the right edge of the buttress.

1 20m (4a). Climb up to the holly and make a bold ascending traverse left to ledges on the front of the buttress. Ascend a steep, thin crack to a ledge on the right, on the edge of the face.

Gouther Crag –
Fang Buttress

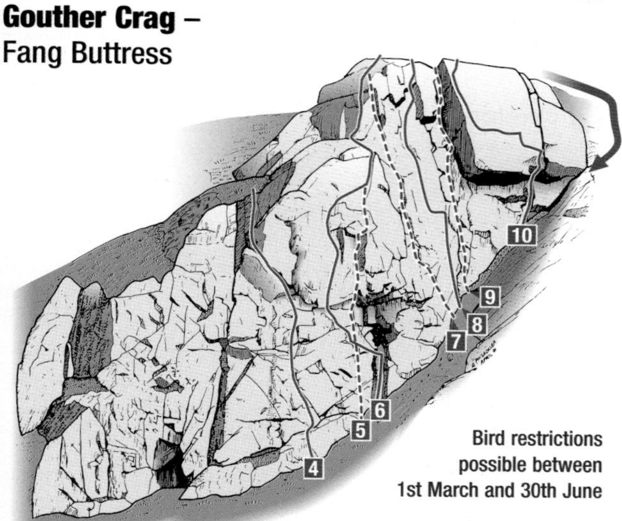

		7 Kennel Wall	**MS**
4 Sostenuto	**HVS–**	**8 Bloodhound**	**E2–**
5 Fang Direct	**HVS**	**9 Hindleg Crack**	**S**
6 The Fang	**MVS–**	**10 One Step Beyond**	**E3+**

2 10m. Ascend the steep arête at the right end of the ledge to a platform.
3 10m. Climb the blunt rib.

The crag now bends round to form the wall of a gully.

7	**Kennel Wall**	37m	MS

J S Williams, C R Wilson, T Nicholson, R A Ewin, G H Tyson – Oct 1946

This very good climb takes the middle of the large slabs rising out of the gully on the right. Start at the top of the gully scree fan.
1 26m. Climb the crack system to the right end of a narrow ledge. Ascend the wall and groove above to a platform.

Left: Tony Lywood on *Sostenuto* (HVS–) **Photo:** Stephen Reid

2 11m. Step right from the platform and ascend a crack and easier rocks.

8 **Bloodhound**	37m	E2–
R G Hutchinson, J W Earl – July 1978		

An excellent, sustained and quite bold route up the slabs between *Kennel Wall* and *Hindleg Crack*. Start in the centre of the slabs as for *Kennel Wall*.

(5b). Climb easily up right, then left with difficulty to gain an obvious flake in the middle of the slab. Continue directly upwards then move right to the base of an obvious groove in the top overhang. Climb the groove and the wall above.

9 **Hindleg Crack**	22m	S
J S Williams, C R Wilson, T Nicholson, R A Ewin, G H Tyson – Oct 1946		

The steep chimney right of the slab provides good strenuous climbing. Start as for *Kennel Wall*.

Move up and right easily then follow cracks and chimney, pulling up and left at the top of the chimney.

10 **One Step Beyond**	24m	E3+
I Williamson, J White – May 1980		

This superb climb crosses the hanging slab to the right of *Hindleg Crack*. Start to the right of the hanging slab at an obvious ragged crack.

(6a). Follow the crack to above the roof, then traverse down across the lip of the roof to a good hold and low peg runner. Up to another peg runner and then move down slightly to make a delicate series of moves to reach a resting foothold just right of the arête. Bold climbing just right of the arête on small holds leads to the top.

Right: Dominic Donnini stretches out for better holds on *Bloodhound* (E2–)
Photo: Ron Kenyon

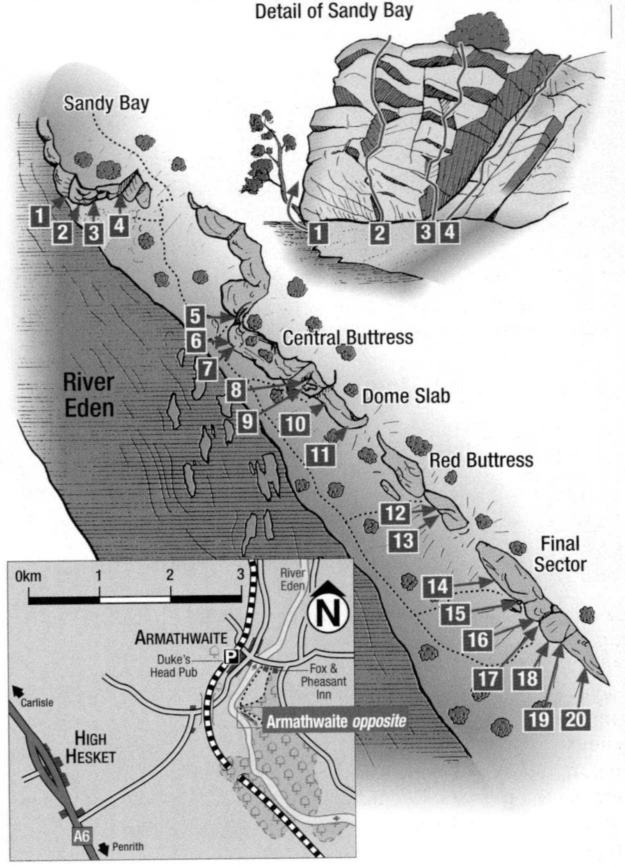
Detail of Sandy Bay
Sandy Bay
1
2
3
4
5
6
7
8
9
10
11
12
13
14
15
16
17
18
19
20
Central Buttress
Dome Slab
Red Buttress
Final Sector
River Eden
0km
1
2
3
River Eden
N
Armathwaite
P
Duke's Head Pub
Fox & Pheasant Inn
Carlisle
Armathwaite opposite
High Hesket
A6
Penrith

Outlying Areas

Eden Valley & South Lakes Limestone

Eden Valley

by Ron Kenyon

Lying to the east of the Lake District, the Eden Valley is considered by many to be Cumbria's best kept secret, an attractive area of rolling fields and pleasant villages with the Pennines as a backdrop. For those in the know, its sheltered and quick-drying crags have also rescued many a wet day in the Lakes.

Armathwaite

Grid reference: **505 452**
Altitude: **50m**
Faces: **South-West**
Rock type: **Sandstone**
Approach time: **10 mins**

Armathwaite Crags are situated in a delightful situation just upstream from the village of Armathwaite which lies some 16 kilometres equidistant between Carlisle and Penrith. These sandstone outcrops overlooking the River Eden are a suntrap and parts of the crag stay dry even in the rain. There are good climbs and some high quality bouldering, however the soft nature of the rock makes leading a serious business and climbs are often top-roped. Due to the softness of the rock wire brushes must not be used and top-ropers should make sure that their ropes are extended or well padded to stop the cutting of grooves in the top of the crag. The nature of the rock and the limited easy climbing available makes this venue unsuitable for groups.

The crags are situated on the east bank of the River Eden and approached from the bridge over the river in Armathwaite village. Parking is available beside the road between the bridge and the Fox and Pheasant Inn. Do not use the pub car park - unless permission is obtained and one intends to patronise the pub for a drink!

There are two paths to the crag:

1. On the east and downstream side of the bridge is a squeeze gate through which a path leads down and under the bridge to a very pleasant riverside path. Follow this path, past a river weir and above the left side of the crag to where a steep and slightly awkward descent leads to the riverside. To the left, looking in, is *Sandy Bay* and extending rightwards upstream are the other main climbing areas.
2. Past the front of the Fox and Pheasant, a track leads along a field, then through rough wooded ground to eventually join the riverside path mentioned above, near the weir.

The routes are described from **left** to **right**.

Sandy Bay

As one descends to the crag the overhanging wall above the beach of the *Sandy Bay* will be seen to the right. With its immaculate rock this has for long been one of the most popular areas here for bouldering. A number of quality routes also ascend this wall. A traverse left from the foot of *Kingfisher* is worth doing to view the 'Faces' and other rock carvings.

Descent: is via the approach path!

1 Kingfisher	16m	VD

S Wilson, A Yarrow – May 1973

Although short, this gives a good little adventure and has even been the scene of some unexpected soakings in the river below.

From the *Sandy Bay* move left along tree roots, just above the river, then behind the tree to follow an open groove. An easy corner is followed by a steeper one to gain the top.

2	**Time and Motion Man**	16m	E1+

R J Kenyon, S Wilson, T Dale – May 1973

The first route to breach the defences of the overhanging wall. The start has become harder as the ground has worn away, and though the interest is maintained throughout, the hardest technicalities are low down.

(5b). Start in the alcove at the base of the wall and move up leftwards, with much contortion, to gain the base of a groove/niche. Enter this, with some concern, and move up and out left to attain a good ledge. Above the right end of the ledge are two grooves – the left one is easier – finish awkwardly up the groove above.

3	**The Exorcist**	18m	E4

J Lamb – 1975

A strenuous testpiece.

(5c). Start at the base of ***Glenwillie Grooves*** directly below a prominent hanging rib. Climb steeply to a small ledge below the rib. Make a difficult move to reach a small pocket and hold in the rib (peg in corner). Pull up past the left side of the triangular roof on widely spaced holds, to reach a good ledge. Climb the short, steep groove above to the final overhang, which is turned on the left to a sloping finish.

4	**Glenwillie Grooves**	18m	HS

S Wilson, A Yarrow – May 1973

A very popular route taking the slanting corner just right of the overhanging wall.

(4b). Start just right of the corner crack and climb a wall to a ledge. Continue up the slab on the right and then up left to a good ledge below the final crucial corner. This corner, which does not yield too easily, leads to a slope which should be followed with care to a tree belay. The corner itself can be followed direct at MVS (4b).

Central Buttress

This is the large, complex buttress towering over the main path. Just above the river path, on the left of the buttress, is ***Hetherington's Bay***,

which is another fine and popular bouldering area. In the centre of the buttress is a rather vegetated slabby wall with a fine headwall and on the right are the grooves and corners of ***Flasherman*** and ***Erection***. **Descent:** can either be by following a track leftwards to join the approach path at the top of the descent near ***Sandy Bay*** or else rightwards, from above ***Flasherman***, above ***Dome Slab***, and down a steep path which cuts back below ***Dome Slab***.

5 **Cally Crack**	12m	E3
J Lamb – 1973		

An intimidating and bold route taking the steep crack above ***Hetherington's Bay***.

(5c). Climb the awkward corner at the back of the bay (***Joe Soap's Corner***) then up rightwards to the crack, which leads to the ***Heugh Chare Ledge***. Finish either up easier rock on the left or Pitch 2 of ***Monkeyhanger***.

6 **The Monkeyhanger**	35m	HVS
S Wilson, A Yarrow – 1973		

A varied route, weaving a way up the main buttress, with an airy and serious top pitch. Start just right of ***Hetherington's Bay*** below an overhanging nose.

1 16m (4a). Climb a slab up rightwards and continue upwards to the left end of long grassy ledge. Move right slightly and follow a fine crack to a belay on the ***Heugh Chare Ledge***.

2 19m (4c). Attain a shelf at the back of the bay and traverse right for 4 metres. Gain another slab above and continue up and rightwards in an exposed position.

7 **The Bullgine Run**	30m	VD+
S Wilson, A Yarrow – May 1973		

Named after one of the routes used by liners across the Atlantic – this interesting climb finds its way, at an easy grade, up the centre of the buttress. Start at the base of the buttress below rather dank mossy ledges underneath a large oak.

Left: Jilly Reid enjoying the jugs on the *Bullgine Run* (VD+) **Photo:** Stephen Reid

1 10m. Gain the ledges and move up rightwards and either ascend directly to the left of the oak or move further right then back left to attain and use the oak to gain the belay ledge above.
2 20m. Above looms the headwall of the buttress and below this is a juggy slab. Ascend this rightwards to a large horizontal block. Traverse across this block and continue rightwards to finish up an easy gully.

8 **Flasherman**	26m	VS
A Yarrow, S Wilson – May 1973		

A superb line, with an adventurous feel, on the right of the main buttress. The main line is the open corner guarded by an overhang at the base. Start on a rib, beneath the left side of the overhang.

(4b). Ascend a narrowing slab on the right and pull around the overhang to gain the ledge above. Continue up the corner above to a large flake. Move right and climb a shallow groove, with initial interest, to gain good holds which lead leftwards to a corner groove and finish up this.

9 **Erection**	26m	HVS+
J Lamb, A Liddell – Jan 1974		

An amazing and varied route taking the crack on the right of the distinctive block overhang.

(5a). Start up the awkward wall, just right of ***Flasherman***, to gain the crack. Ascend this with increasing interest to some wild moves around the tip of the block. Above a steep, shallow scoop leads to the top.

Dome Slab

Just to the right of ***Central Buttress*** is a buttress consisting of slabs and walls with an ascending series of dome-topped overhangs. It contains some fearsome lines.

Descent: is best made to the right.

10 **Close Encounters**	10m	E1+
R J Kenyon – April 1978		

Not quite 'of a Third Kind', but an intricate line weaving its way up the left side of the buttress.

(5b). Start at the left of the buttress below the lower barrier of overhangs and move up rightwards to a horizontal line of holds below the next barrier. Follow these leftwards with difficulty to near their left-hand end. A hard move leads up to a flake hold and finishing slab above. The left end of the traverse can also be gained directly from below at 5c.

11 **Dome Slab**	14m	E5
J Lamb – 1974		

A serious route that accepts the challenge of the widest and wildest part of the top overhang, above the slab on the right-hand side of the buttress.

(6a). Start directly below the widest point and ascend up the lower wall to just below the top overhang. Arrange what protection is possible and move rightwards to reach a horizontal crack. Follow this to gain the lip and make a desperate move onto the slab above.

Red Buttress and Final Sector

To the right, a series of shorter and more slabby buttresses give a number of routes which are often difficult to protect and are usually top-roped.

Towards the left of this area is ***Red Buttress*** and below the left-hand steep wall is the ***Split Boulder*** which is a useful landmark and a painful problem.

Descent: can made by the slope and short corner just right of ***Paper Moon***, the rake below ***Dome Slab*** or to the far right of the crag.

Just to the right is a slabby area with the following two routes.

12 **Wafer Thin**	12m	E5+
P Whillance, A Greig – Sept 1974		

A serious lead up the thin seam and rounded rib just left of the prominent overlap of ***Paper Moon***. Start just right of a heather-filled groove.

(6c). Climb up a short diagonal crack and levitate up the seam to gain the slab above. Continue up the seam leftwards to reach a small overlap and move right to finish.

13 **Paper Moon**	12m	E2+
J Lamb – 1974		

A superb but rather pokey lead up the prominent curving overlap.

(5b). Start below the overlap and attain its left side and follow it to a puzzling move to gain a ledge above its right-hand end.

To the right, a steep corner provides a useful **descent** before the ***Final Sector*** of the crag.

14 **Free and Easy**	12m	E4
P Whillance, A Greig – May 1974		

An outstanding route taking a fine direct line, up the left-hand end of the ***Final Sector*** of the crag, finishing up the prominent, final short curving crack near the top of the crag.

(6a). Start directly below this crack and climb the lower wall, through a bulge, to a delicate slab where a further difficult and committing move is made to gain the final crack. This is slightly easier but still hang on in there!

At the base of the crag, right of ***Free and Easy***, is a large boulder. Right again the crag is tree-shrouded and well worn along the base to the following routes. These routes can be dirty and dusty, especially early in the year, and cleaning may be essential (but only with a soft brush please!).

15 **Jelly Terror**	9m	E1
J Lamb, M Hetherington – 1974		

Directly above the large boulder is an obvious and protectable crack - start on the boulder.

(5b). Gain the slab and move up to gain and climb the crack, which eases after the initial bulge.

16 Y-Front	11m	E2+
P Botterill, M Hetherington – March 1974		

A bold lead starting as for *Barnacle Bill*.

(5b). Follow the corner to the overhang but, instead of moving right, step left and climb the cleft above, until near the top, where a move left leads to a finish up the arête.

17 Barnacle Bill	13m	E1
R J Kenyon, S Wilson (2 points of aid) – 1973	FFA: **J Lamb** – 1974	

Just right of the boulder is a prominent corner with a large slab on its right.

(5b). Climb the corner with increasing interest until blocked by a roof. Make worrying moves out right to gain and finish up the final corner.

19 Codpiece	12m	E2
A Yarrow, S Wilson, R May (2 points of aid) – 1973	FFA: **J Lamb** – 1974	

This is the prominent crack to the right of the thin slab (**18 Andy's Slab**, E3 6a, 1973) right of *Barnacle Bill*.

(5c). Climb the crack directly (without use of the ramp on the left) with increasing difficulty. Alternatively, a difficult step onto the ramp on the left leads to easier climbing to the top (5b).

20 Pickpocket	10m	E3
P Whillance – Sep 1974		

A sustained climb starting just right of *Codpiece*.

(5b). Pull up to a line of foot and hand pockets, which lead rightwards to a hand ledge and horizontal slot. Using this, gain and climb the wall above, via a prominent 'chickenhead'.

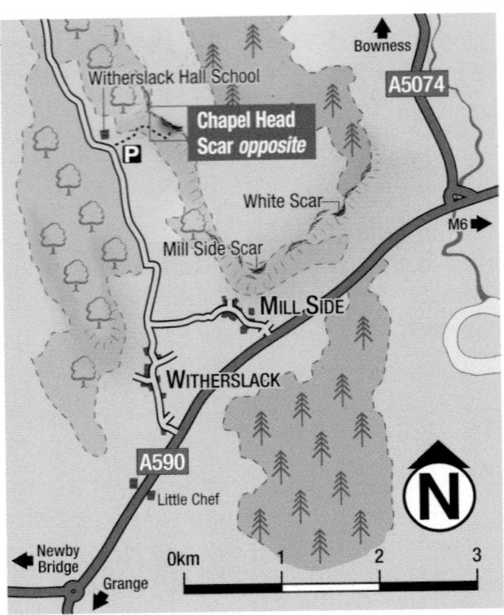

South Lakes Limestone

by Nick Wharton

Above: Chapel Head Scar from the car park
Photo: Nick Wharton

The limestone crags at the southern end of the Lake District provide a completely different type of climbing to any other part of the region. They are typically steep and compact, offering little in the way of natural protection and so are often bolt protected, yet the climbing is fantastic. There are several small crags: ***Scout Scar*** (487 916), ***Humphrey Head*** (390 739), ***Millside Scar*** (451 846), ***Farelton*** (539 797) and ***Hutton Roof*** (565 782); the last provides some excellent bouldering. There are also two larger crags: ***White Scar*** (459 853) and ***Chapel Head Scar***. The latter is by far the best and a selection of its finest routes is described here.

Chapel Head Scar

Grid reference:	**443 862**
Altitude:	**70m**
Faces:	**South-West**
Rock type:	**Limestone**
Approach time:	**15 mins**

Chapel Head Scar is a steep limestone crag on the west side of the Whitbarrow Escarpment in the Witherslack valley. The crag has a mixture of perfect, smooth grey limestone and rough tufas, pockets and other features. Throughout, the rock is compact offering little in the way of natural gear on most lines and this has resulted in the use of bolts for protection. The rock is generally sound and on most of the routes described here it is some of the best, unspoilt limestone to be found on any crag in Britain.

Due to the nature of the rock and the angle of the crag the routes available are hard. The selection given here is much harder than on any other crag in this book so it may not suit all climbers. Because of the difficulty of most of the routes many climbers will approach them in the European style – working the moves until they can be linked together in one successful 'red-point'. Routes that are entirely bolt protected have been given a French grade, whilst there are a few traditionally protected routes (***Moonchild***, ***Cyborg*** and ***Android***), which are given English grades.

The crag, while still within the boundaries of the Lake District National Park, lies at a low altitude, well to the south of the other Lakeland crags. Because of this, and with its steep nature, it is very often in good condition when all other venues are in the grip of bad weather. After prolonged rain the crag is prone to seepage, some parts being affected more than others. The crag also enjoys the advantage of any afternoon and evening sun, though in midsummer this can mean it is too hot, though trees do give some shade for belayers and dogs, and add to the beautiful ambience of the venue. Midges are rarely a problem but be aware of sheep ticks – they get into all sorts

Above: John Earl stepping off the *Android Tree* **Photo:** Nick Wharton

of warm, moist nooks and crannies!

The crag lies within an important nature reserve so access is delicate. There may be a **Bird Restriction** on all or part of *Chapel Head Scar* from March 1st to July 31st, though this end date is often brought forward. Information signs are posted at the car park and below the crag. If in doubt contact details for further information are given in the **Access & Conservation** section. In addition, certain rules apply to climbing at *Chapel Head*, which must be strictly observed if access is to be maintained.

1. There is no climbing allowed left of *Central Gully*.
2. Use only marked paths to and from the crag.
3. No gardening is allowed on or above the crag, and trees must not be damaged.
4. **Descent:** all routes finish at lower-off points. These must be used. Do not top-out from any route. (Because of this all descriptions are given as the routes should now be climbed, rather than as the first ascent was done).
5. Do not leave any litter including finger tape, chalk wrappers or packed lunches.
6. If you must relieve yourself – go well away from any path and leave as little evidence as possible.

The best approach is to leave the A590 dual carriageway at the Witherslack signs (not far from the Little Chef on both sides of the road). Drive through this lovely village until you reach Witherslack Hall School after about 3 miles. A short track on the right at a bend by the entrance to the Hall leads to a parking area. The crag can be seen above the woods across the field. An information board will be found here giving details of the access agreement. Follow the path across the field, passing a football pitch on your left. At the entrance to the woods follow the track up to the right for 200 metres until a path branches off to the left. Another information board will be found here. Follow the marked path through the woods, across a scree slope and up a short steep section to arrive at the crag between ***Moonchild*** (steep corner on right) and ***Phantom Zone*** (very steep wall on left).

Moonchild Buttress

Five metres left of where the path arrives at the crag is a right-facing corner flake. This is the line of **Sun God** (HVS) - now rather over-grown. Two metres left of this is a short, clean, pocketed wall with a vague crack/groove. This is the start of ***Interstellar Overdrive***. The routes are described from **left** to **right**, starting here.

1	**Interstellar Overdrive**	26m	*F6b* (E3 6a)
	D Cronshaw, D Knighton – July 1979		

One of the best of the 'easier' hard routes – a great introduction to the crag.

Climb the pocketed crack/groove until the old yew tree is reached. Stand on this to gain holds under the small roof, which lead rightwards round the flakeline and into the hanging groove. Follow the groove to the top.

An alternative, **2 Jelly Head** (*F7a+*), goes directly over the small roof and up the wall on the left.

3	**Phantom Zone**	15m	*F7c* (E6 6b)
	P Ingham – Aug 1986		

A tremendous hard route up the front of the buttress starting at the lowest point, just left of where the path arrives at the crag.

A short steep start enables a flake handrail to be reached. A high rock-over leads to a good hold on the right and a brief respite before moving up and left, then back right and straight up. Superb climbing! Either finish at the lower-off at the small ledge half way up the crag, or for the full experience move left to join the line of **4 Cement Head** (*F7b*). This climbs up to and over the small overlap and rightwards across the smooth, grey wall right of *Interstellar Overdrive*. The lower-off for this is a chain up and right.

5 **Moonchild**	24m	E4
R Fawcett, A Evans, D Parker – 1974		

Start at the steep groove just right of where the path arrives at the crag. (5c). Climb the groove, which is rather bold. From the top of the groove climb a blocky crack and series of short grooves to a yew tree.

An alternative, **6 The Moon-Loon Connection** (E4 5c), traverses right at the top of the initial groove across the wall past a ledge to another dead tree. It then climbs the lovely, clean groove above (finish of ***Lunatic***).

Another, very worthwhile alternative is **7 War Hero** (*F6c*). This starts 5 metres right of the ***Moonchild*** groove, behind a tree facing a slim groove. Climb this with a slight diversion to the left at the top of the groove before finishing up a line of bolts to the left of the final groove of ***Lunatic***.

Moving right past a vegetated gully, with the impressive **8 Maboulisme Merveilleux** (*F7c+*) on its steep left wall, the foot of a clean wall is reached. This is bounded on its left by a right-facing corner.

9 **Cyborg**	20m	E2
E Cleasby, M Lynch – March 1975		

(5c). Start up the corner, and then traverse right to a ledge. Keep moving up and right to reach flakes at the foot of a small tufa in the white streak. Climb the left side of this to a ledge and lower-off/belay.

10 **Route of All Evil**	30m	*F7a+* (E5 6b)
G Smith, A Phizacklea – Sept 1983		

A wandering line which moves back and forth across this superb wall. Start as for ***Cyborg*** but stay in the right-trending groove in the centre of the wall. Move left at the top of the groove to reach a large break (junction with ***Mid-Air Collision***). Climb up to another break, which is traversed left to a reasonable rest. Move back right and climb up to the belay.

Bird restrictions possible between 1st March and 30th June

← Central Gully 50m

Sun God (HVS)

No.	Route	Grade
1	Interstellar Overdrive	*F6b*
2	Jelly Head	*F7a+*
3	Phantom Zone	*F7c*
4	Cement Head	*F7b*
5	Moonchild	E4
6	Moon-Loon Connection	E4
7	War Hero	*F6c*
8	Maboulisme Merveilleux	*F7c+*
9	Cyborg	E2
10	Route of All Evil	*F7a+*
11	Eraser Head	*F7b*
12	Mid-Air Collision	*F7b*

There are two other excellent routes on this wall that take direct lines through the wanderings of *Route of All Evil*.

The first is **11 Eraser Head** (*F7b*), which includes the brilliant, original direct finish to *Route of All Evil*. From the initial traverse right, climb directly up the line of bolts on the left wall. Climb straight through the final break below the headwall. This is climbed using a small flake (Rock 4) and pockets.

The second alternative is **12 Mid-Air Collision** (*F7b*), another great route on superb rock with a spectacular finish up the headwall. Start up the wall to the right of *Cyborg* and climb a direct line up the wall to the start of the long traverse left on *Route of All Evil*. Move up and right to a seemingly difficult move. Up the headwall to the lower-off.

Twenty-five metres right of the start to the last routes, a large yew tree will be found growing out of the crag at 3 metres.

13 Up Town	22m	*F6c* (E3 5c)
G Gibson – 1984		

Climb the flake/groove up to the tree from where you can view the wall above. The wall sports three lines of bolts. *Up Town* steps up to the ledge on the right then takes the right-hand line of bolts up the wall behind the tree using some superb small tufas and other fine features until a delicate move onto a sloping ledge. A final hard move leads to the lower-off.

The central line to the left of *Up Town* is **14 Half Life** (*F6c*), which is also very worthwhile at about the same grade.

Great Buttress

Continuing along the path a large holly bush is reached which marks the start of the *Great Buttress*. Just to the left of the bush is the line of **15 Electric Warrior** (*F7b*).

To its right is the start of the best route of its grade at Chapel Head.

13 Up Town	*F6c*	18 Perverse Pepere	*F7a*	21 Super Duper Dupont	*F7b+*
14 Half Life	*F6c*	19 La Mangoustine Scatouflange	*F7a*	22 Super Dupont	*F7b*
15 Electric Warrior	*F7b*	20 A Song for Europe	*F7b+*	23 Tufa King Hard	*F6c+*
16 Wargames	*F7a+*				
17 Android	E4				

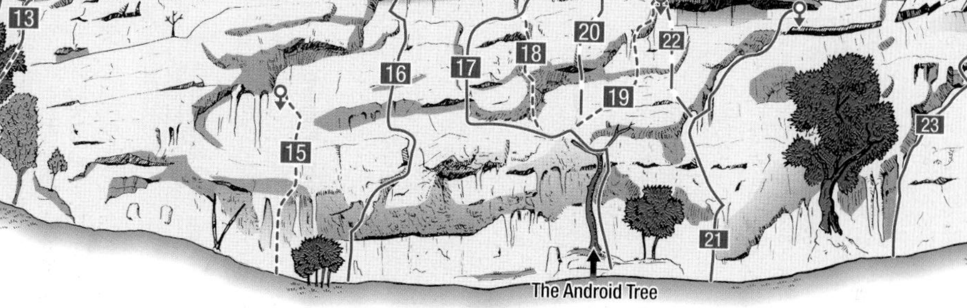

Chapel Head Scar – Great Buttress

16	**Wargames**	24m	*F7a+* (E5 6b)
	A Phizacklea – Oct 1985		

Start by climbing the short grey wall (sometimes seeping, but doesn't matter) to the stump of a small yew. From here go up and outwards, using tufas, sidepulls and pockets, until you are forced to make a long move right on undercuts to the base of a hanging groove. Climb the groove to reach the small ledge on the left then climb directly up the wall, all the way to the overlap at its top. Surmount this and trend rightwards up steep ground on good holds until the lower-off is reached. Magnificent!

Ten metres to the right is the infamous ***Android Tree***, which provides the start to a number of routes. Some find shinning up this and balancing out along the dodgy top branch the crux of the routes.

17	**Android**	29m	E4
	E Cleasby, P McVey (1 point of aid) – April 1979	FFA: **D Knighton** – 1979	

(5c). From the top of the tree, step onto the rock (now all bolt protected), and climb up into the scoop on the left. Move leftwards to a peg then step down before continuing the leftwards traverse to another peg. Climb up to a thin flake then move carefully rightwards to the base of a large hanging flake. Climb this moving right at its top to reach a lower-off belay.

A variation, **18 Perverse Pepere** (*F7a*) is a short cut from the first peg to the foot of the hanging flake. It climbs the steep bulge with a dynamic move for a huge hold.

19	**La Mangoustine Scatouflange**	22m	*F7a* (E4 6b)
	P Cornforth – Feb 1986		

Very good climbing with a short, hard section in the middle.

Climb the tree and up into the scoop as for ***Android*** but move up and right onto a small foot ledge below a small overlap. The smooth wall above is overcome by a hard move on tiny holds to reach a good ledge. Move up and left onto the superb, rough

Right: Richard Duffy prepares to do battle with the crux moves near the start of *Wargames* (E5) **Photo:** Nick Wharton

tufa flutings. Follow these until a step right leads to the lower-off at the roof.

An alternative is **20 A Song for Europe** (*F7b+*), which moves up and left from the scoop and climbs the parallel tufas, before following the right-trending flakeline to finish up the short headwall and over the small roof on the right. Lower off from the same point as ***Android***.

21 **Super Duper Dupont**	23m	*F7b+* (E6 6c)
P Cornforth – Nov 1985		

The English *6c* technical grade that this route earns is for the hard move near the start. The remainder is a magnificent, sustained pump up the right-trending weakness.

Start 4 metres right of the ***Android Tree*** to the right of a small, but useful holly tree. Step off the top of this holly, using several sidepulls and tufa flutings, heading left to a small ledge. Above the ledge is a tiny, sharp hold, which may be used to get stood on the ledge. Continue up into the scoop above then follow the right-rising grooveline to the small roof. Surmount this with a hard mantelshelf and finish more easily up and right.

Less sustained, but with the same crux is **22 Super Dupont** (*F7b*). This swings up and left at the start of the right-trending groove to stand on a good ledge. Some tricky moves get you off the ledge, followed by excellent, but run-out climbing to the same finishing point as ***Mangoustine***.

23 **Tufa King Hard**	12m	*F6c+* (E3 5c)
T Burnell – 1992		

At the right end of the crag, 5 metres right of ***Super Duper***, is a small grey wall. This final route climbs the groove at the left edge of this wall, just right of the large yew tree. Climb the tufas up into the groove then follow this on good holds to its top. One slightly harder move reaches the lower-off. A good route, despite being shorter than others.

Left: Bob Smith on the fingery crux of *La Mangoustine Scatouflange* (*F7a*)
Photo: Nick Wharton

Other Information

Left: Dominic Donnini at the Langdale Boulders
Photo: Nick Wharton

Bouldering in the Lake District

by Al Davis

The Lake District has a wealth of fine bouldering throughout the area. Two of the most popular and more highly developed locations are described in detail, whilst other good but lesser known spots are briefly outlined. As well as the handful of places described, the adventurous boulderer will find endless scope on the many tiny outcrops spread throughout the region. Sherman gradings are used.

Sherman Grading Guide

British	Sherman
5a/5b	V0 V0+
5b/5c	V1 V2
5c/6a	V2 V3 V4
6a/6b	V4 V5 V6 V7
6b/6c	V6 V7 V8 V8+ V9
6c/7a	V9 V10 V11 V12
7b/7b+	V12 V13 V14

Langdale Boulders (314 058)

One of the two most popular bouldering areas in the district. The routes are short but steep, on good rock, and generally have good landings. The principal problems lend themselves to topo description but there are lots of other possibilities for the enthusiast.

From Ambleside, take the road towards Langdale. Just past Chapel Stile, a large pocketed slab stands by the roadside on the right. Just beyond this, the two main ***Langdale Boulders*** can be seen standing in an open field on the left of the road. Limited parking is available on the right, just past the wicket gate which gives access to them. The boulders are on enclosed agricultural land and access is by kind consent of the farmer. Therefore, please ensure that the gate is shut, that no litter is left, and that walls are not damaged. Dogs should be kept on a lead at all times.

Please note that the ***Langdale Boulders*** have recently been designated by English Heritage as an ancient monument of national importance due to the discovery of prehistoric 'Cup & Ring' markings. These take the form of large dimples and shallow concentric circles and are thought to date from around 2,500 to 5,000 years ago. They are most noticeable on the ***East Face*** of the ***Bottom Boulder***, but exist elsewhere on the boulders as well. English Heritage have stated that they do not wish to instigate a ban on climbing at the boulders but ask that climbers voluntarily restrain from climbing in the areas containing these markings (this is highlighted on the topo).

Langdale Boulders

1 V1 (5b) Left crack, no break
2 V0 (5b) Slab without break
3 V5 (6b) Arête swinging left
4 V5 (6c) Wall and pocket
5 V7 (6c+) Wall and thin crack
6 V6 (6b) Wall, using sharp edge
7 V1 (5c) Crack
8 V5 (6b) Undercut wall, finishing left (sit start V7 (6c))
9 V9 (7a/b) **Stefan Grossman**. Rounded arête by the wall (sit start V11)
10 V0 (5b) Arête
11 V1 (5c) Wall (no big holds)

12 V0 (5a) Wall
13 V0 (4c) Crack
14 V1 (5c) To ledge
15 V5 (6b) Wall via undercut
16 V0 (5a) Crack
17 V0 (5b) Wall
18 V1 (5c) Arête (sit start V3 (6a))
19 V0 (4a) Wall
20 V2 (5c) Slab, no break
21 V5 (6b) Traverse low break
22 V4 (6b) High traverse to pocket
23 V2 (5c) Long traverse
24 V3 (5c) Lip traverse (both directions)
25 V4 (6a) Low traverse (both directions)
26 V3 (6a) Low traverse
27 V6 (6b+) **Full Monty**: *23, 24, 25, 15*

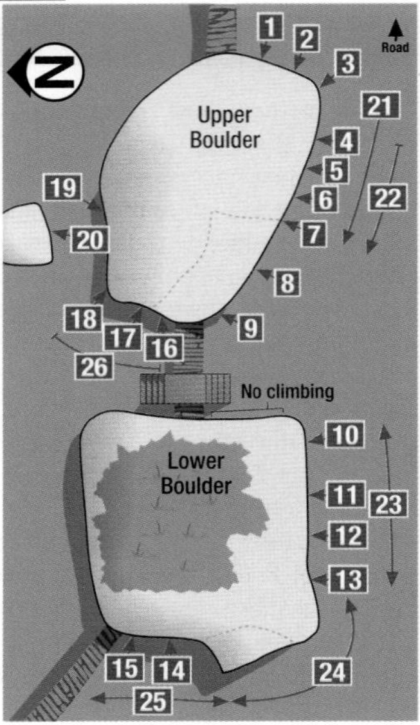

St Bees **(939 145)**

An idyllic location at its best on a clear evening with the sun setting over the Irish Sea. The rock is excellent quality sandstone with a surprising variety of problems giving the best mid-grade bouldering in the county. Landings on the flat wave-cut sandstone platform are generally good, though a crash mat is essential. In calm seas the area is non-tidal but beware of spring tides and a westerly gale. This is a very special area with its own unique ambience and is well worth a visit.

Approach as for *St Bees Crag* as described on page 305 There is a fine group of large boulders beneath *Apiary Wall*. More boulders will be found by walking south under the crag to the end of *Scabby Back Area* and scrambling up right.

Honister Boulders (217 144)

The major boulder offers a steep wall with excellent climbing at all standards mainly on juggy incuts of varied size. Traverses and eliminates abound.

From Keswick, drive down Borrowdale and over Honister Pass towards Buttermere. As the gradient starts to level off, the main boulder will be seen on the left, close to the road. Parking is in small lay-bys nearby. There are other boulders in the area but none approach the size and quality of the main boulder. Crash mat recommended.

The Bowderstone (254 164)

The ***Bowderstone*** has been a mecca for hard bouldering in the Lakes for several years. The challenge of the ***Ladder Wall*** was taken up in the early eighties and quite recently local climbers have added many new classic problems to this remarkable boulder. To reach it, take the Borrowdale road from Keswick, park in the National Trust car park beneath ***Quayfoot Buttress*** (described in the text on page 357), and follow the signed path past ***Woden's Face*** (5 minutes).

This is by no means an exhaustive guide; the local activists have many other variations which they will be happy to show you! What follows is a guide to the two main walls. There are more problems around the back but they are not as popular as the landings are not as good. The landings below the problems described are generally good and descent from the top is via a ladder. However, many problems on the ***Ladder Wall*** finish at the lip of the overhang, thus leaving the vegetation above undisturbed. The overhanging nature of the boulder ensures some dry rock even in the rain.

As to the ***Bowderstone's*** origin, there is still some doubt. Some say it is an erratic carried into place by ice and others that it fell from the hillside above. As the ***Bowderstone*** is 19 metres long, 11 metres high and weighs in at about 2,000 tonnes the latter event would have been worth watching!

The Problems

The most significant problems are described, starting from ***Ears of Perception*** at the southern end to the left of the ladder and working in an anti-clockwise direction around the block.

The Bowderstone

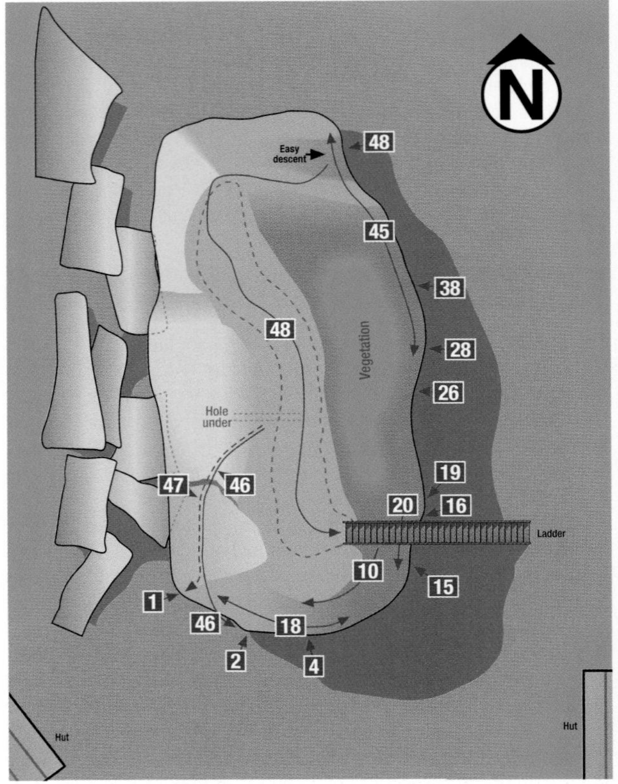

1 V8 (6c) **Ears of Perception**. Start in the recess of *The Crack* and climb leftwards across the prow for 4 metres, most of which utilises committing footjams to an easy but scary top-out.

2 V4 (6a) **The Crack**. The obvious classic crack!

3 V6 (6b) 1 and 2, up to 4 and up again.

4 V5 (6b) **The Crack Direct**. 3, 4, 5 and crack.

The Bowderstone – South Face

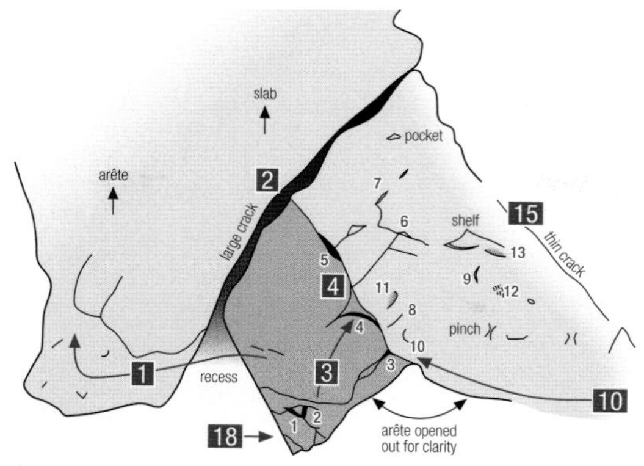

5 V6 (6b) **The Crack Superdirect**. 3, 4, 5, 6, 7, pocket and crack.

6 V7 (6b) 3, 8, 9, *Shelf*, 7, pocket and crack.

7 V10 (7a) 3 to 11 (poor sloper), *Shelf* by dyno or heel hooks, finish up arête. Variation (V8) 3 to 8 then *Shelf*.

8 V8 (6c) 3, 4, 6, 7, pocket and crack.

9 V8 (6c) 3, 11, 9 and *Shelf* (easy version of Problem 7).

10 V7 (6c) **Coming up for Air**. Start at slots below *Bowderiser*. Traverse left (low) to hold 3. Link to any of the above problems *4* to *8*.

11 V10 (6c) **Dave's Circuit**. Start with *Coming up for Air* then 10, 12 and 13 (slopers) to the *Jugs*. Down and right via 14 and 15 (pockets) to finish up *Inaudible Vaudeville* to ladder.

12 V9 (6c) Start on 3, slap up for sloper 12, heel hook 3 and reach *Shelf*.

13 V8 (6c) From *Pinch* up to 10, 12 and 13, *Shelf* and then *The Crack*.

14 V2 (5b) Jump off ground to *Shelf* and big holds to top of ladder.

15 V6 (6b) **Bowderiser**. The thin crack, painful! Finish on jugs.

16 V9 (6c) **Inaudible Vaudeville**. From small pinch 16 and sloper 17, launch up to 19 and 19a then 21 to the ladder. Or try the **Sit Down Start** (V9 (6c)): from start of *Coming Up for Air* to 16a, 17, 19a then as for *Inaudible Vaudeville*.

17 V10 (7a) **Frank**. Start as for *Inaudible Vaudeville* then move left to holds 14 and 15, then straight to the top.

The Bowderstone – Ladder Face

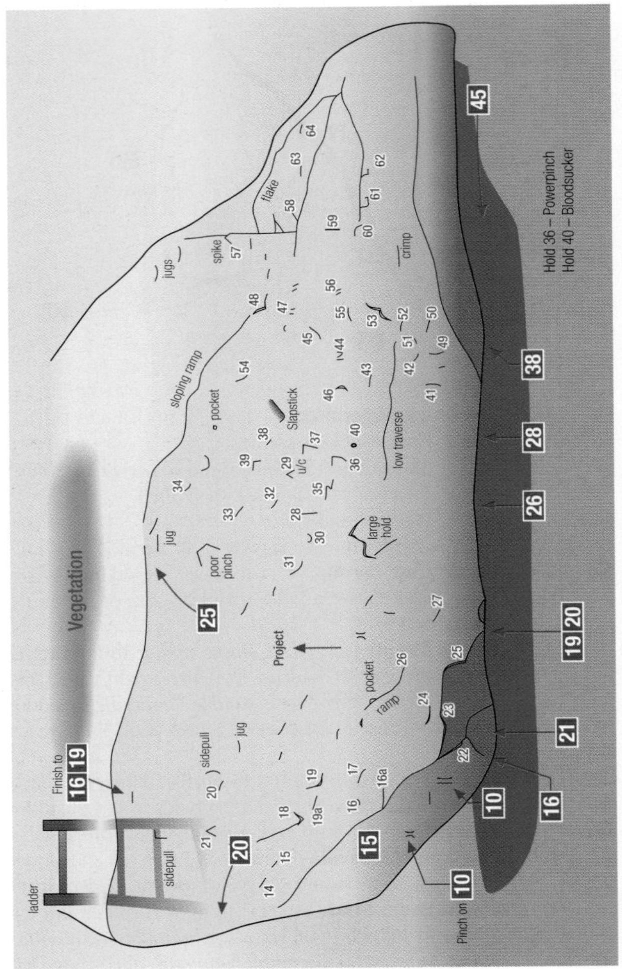

18 V7 (6c) **On the Rebound**. Start below *The Crack*, right to hold 3, link into problems *4* to *8*. Alternatively, start from hold 3 and reverse *Coming up for Air*.

19 V8+ (6c) **Picnic Sarcastic**. Best done with *Sit-Down Start* (Problem *22*) to the ramp and pocket, then up to the jug then left using sidepull, 20 and 21 to the ladder.

20 V9 (6c) **Hot Air**. Start of *Picnic Sarcastic* then left via pockets 14 and 15 to the jugs at the top of *Bowderiser*.

21 V10 (6c) **Sit-Down Start**. From undercut 22 and edge 24 into undercut 23 to gain *Ramp*, then *Picnic Sarcastic* or problem *23*.

22 V7 (6b) **Sit-Down Start**. From 25 and 27 long reach to 26 and *Picnic Sarcastic*.

23 V12 (7b) Problem 21 then *Picnic Sarcastic* to the large hold of *Impropa Opera* via a sharp flake and poor footholds.

24 V12 (7b) Continue problem 23 up *Impropa Opera*.

25 V9 (6c) **Grand Opera**. From large hold up left to edge and pinch and the top.

26 V8 (6c) **Impropa Opera**. A classic with many variations. From *Large Hold* to right 30 then edges 31, 32, 33 and 34 to jug and top.

V8+ (6c) *Variation* ***Large Hold*** to 35 (share) 30, 31, 32, 33 and 34, jug.

V9 (6c) *Variation* ***Large Hold*** to 35 (share) 32, 29, 33, 32, 34, jug.

V9 (6c) *Variation* ***Large Hold*** to 35 (share), 28, 32, 33, 34, jug.

27 V11 (7a) **The Sit-Down Start** to *Impropa Opera*.

28 V8+ (6c) **Power Pinch**. From the holds on the low traverse use 36 (the *Power Pinch*), then 37, 38 and 39 to pocket. Using 35 instead of 37 is (V8, 6c).

29 V10 (6c) **Bloodsucker**. As previous problem but use the painful pocket 40 instead of the *Power Pinch*.

30 V8 (6c) Use the holds on the *Low Traverse* and *Bloodsucker* pocket to gain the sloper of *Slapstick* and then edges and *Sloping Ramp*.

31 V10 (7a) Dyno from holds on low level traverse to *Slapstick*.

32 V7 (6c) Sit-down start 41, 42, 43, 44, 45 and *Rib*.

33 V9 (6c+) From holds on low traverse up to sloper 44, use 46 to udge up to *Slapstick* and up.

34 V10 (6c) **Adam's Problem**. Problem *35* to large slopers, then traverse the ramp left to top of *Impropa Opera*. The best line on the stone.

35 V7 (6b+) From holds on ***Low Traverse*** 44 for left hand then 47 and 48.

36 V7 (6c) Start at left end of ***Low Traverse***, into 44 with left hand then 45 out to 54 and ***Ramp***.

37 V9 (6c+) Sit down start to rib. Side pull and small edges 49, 50, 51, 52, 53, and 55 to 47 and 48.

38 V4 (6b) **The Rib**. Use everything to reach traverse line right to the ***Flake***.

39 V5 (6a) Use holds on the ***Rib*** to gain 48 then 57 to the ***Spike*** and ***Jugs*** to the top.

40 V8 (6c) From 53 to sloper 56, share on 47 and up to 48.

41 V7 (6c) Start below a triangular pod. Use large side hold and scar to reach pod and the ***Flake***.

42 V7 (6c) From 61 and 62 up to small edge 63 and the ***Flake***.

43 V8 (6c) Sit-down start to 42.

44 V4 (6a/b) Low start on slopers up and right to round hold (not flake), jump up right to below ***Flake***.

45 V8 (6c) **Lateral Gruntings**. Traverse from right to The Rib via 62, 61, 60, 59 and a sideways lunge. Continuation (V11, 7a). Carry on to the ***Low Traverse*** to finish up ***Impropa Opera*** or ***Grand Opera***.

46 V9 (6c) **The Bowels**. Start right of the handshake hole and make heinous moves right to finish up ***The Crack***.

47 V10 (6c) **Into the Light**. Link *46* to *1* – a superb problem.

48 **The Hopping Circuit**. Probably the greatest hopping problem in the world! Make a shin-grinding 'Techno-hop' on to the polished descent slab, which leads up to the top of the boulder and down the stairs. Only one leg to be used throughout, and no other body parts are to make contact with the rock.

Carrock Fell Boulders (357 330)

There is the huge boulder field on the eastern slopes of Carrock Fell just north of Mosedale village. The rock is gabbro and can be painfully rough – be prepared to shed skin. The bouldering is outstanding and is at its best on winter mornings or spring evenings before the midges start. The landings can be poor in places so a mat and a spotter are invaluable. The area of boulders is complex and the best climbing is not always obvious but the persistent will be rewarded.

From Keswick, take the A66 east for about 6 miles until a left turn leads north into Mungrisedale and on to Mosedale village. Just north of Mosedale the boulders appear to the left of the road at the foot of the East Face of Carrock Fell. The best climbing is at the northern end about three-quarters of a mile north of the village. Park on the right by a grit bin. Three obvious big boulders are directly above the road with loads of gems spaced throughout the boulder field further south, the best being generally close to the road.

Badger Rock (450 042)

A large solitary boulder in a lovely setting in a field near Kentmere Hall. The rock is good and clean giving traditional style bouldering with the great attraction of generally excellent landings. However some of the problems are disconcertingly high. From Staveley, a road leads up Kentmere to the Church. Park here and follow the track signed Garburn Pass which leads leftwards through a passage between the last buildings. After 200 metres ***Badger Rock*** will be seen in a field on the left. Access has been agreed with the farmer on condition that no dogs (even on leads) are allowed in the field.

Armathwaite (505 522)

Sandy Bay and Hetherington's Bay offer good sheltered sandstone bouldering with soft sandy landings – the saviour of many a wet day in the Lakes. Access is described on page 436.

Hutton Roof (565 782)

Excellent limestone bouldering, mainly in the easier grades, in an idyllic situation on the flat summit of Farleton Fell. Approach via the village of Hutton Roof, 1½ miles west of the A65 at Kirkby Lonsdale. A track opposite the Kirkby Lonsdale road is followed up the hill to the crags, which rise to a maximum height of 8 metres (15mins).

Crags Suitable for Groups

The following list of crags suitable for groups is given in the hope of spreading the load and to help stop congestion and wear and tear on the most popular crags.

Langdale

Copt Howe (316 058)
A popular group training area that has suffered badly from erosion in recent years.

Lower Scout Crag (298 069)
Described in the main text on page 26.

Long Scar (272 036)
Good easier short routes on excellent rock, 25 minutes from the Wrynose Pass. Described in the main text on page 103.

Duddon Valley

Wallowbarrow Crag (222 967)
Not really suitable - but used all the same. Described in the text on page 150.

Seathwaite Buttress (229 964)
To the left of the main crag, a 10 metre outcrop is particularly suitable for beginners.

Eskdale

Brantrake Crag (145 984)
Three granite outcrops close to the road. May be subject to **Bird Restrictions** from 1st March to 30th June.

Hare Crag (200 013)

Described in the main text on page 180.

Goat Crag (204 017)

Easy-angled granite slabs in a beautiful setting.

Ennerdale

Anglers' Crag (099 151)

The rather mossy and protectionless lower slab is sometimes used by groups.

Borrowdale

Castlehead (269 227)

Easily accessible with a number of short climbs. Not to be confused with the nearby quarry.

Shepherd's Crag (263 187)

Brown Slabs (described in the text on page 347) is a now rather over-used and worn introductory area of rock. There is another suitable area for instruction round and up the hill from the main crags (264 185).

Woden's Face (253 167)

A useful crag, though possibly rather long and now suffering from overuse. Approach described in the main text on page 360.

Glaciated Slab (254 128)

A pleasant south-facing slab in Combe Ghyll, with a number of easy routes. Approach described in the main text on page 373.

Seathwaite Slabs (234 123)

The lower boulders are handy for small groups and the upper slabs with their easy angle give suitable initiation and mountain atmosphere.

Eastern Crags

Castle Rock (322 197)

The South Crag has a number of short routes of varied grades but poor belays. Described in the text on page 387.

Carrock Fell (355 324)

Several outcrops scattered on the hillside.

Gowbarrow Crag (414 205)

Groups are restricted to the Lower Buttress and booking is administered by Ullswater Outward Bound School (01768 486 347)

Thornhow Crag (382 154)

Pleasant 25 metre routes.

Edmund's Castle (365 172)

A small crag of sound rough rock.

Brunt Crag (397 210)

A tiny crag just west of the A5091.

Far North Lakes

Head End Quarry (249 480)

Easily accessible south-facing 10 metre high limestone routes near Caldbeck. For access see page 467.

Far South Lakes

Hutton Roof (565 782)

West-facing limestone crags up to 8m high in an idyllic if rather isolated location.

Whitestone Crag (389 848)

Prominent slate crag on the hillside 2 Kilometres SE of Newby Bridge. Good routes from S to VS, but the steep ground requires care, so it is not suitable for beginners.

Climbing Walls

There is now a good range of climbing walls available to those living in or visiting the Lake District, of which the best, or most readily accessible, are described here for use on those occasional rainy days and dank evenings:

Ambleside: St Martin's College (ex-Charlotte Mason's College)
Low cost revamped wall at the college, with good bouldering but no leading. Open 13:30 to 21:30 Monday to Friday; 12:00 to 17:00 on Saturdays, but only during the term time. It may be open for reduced hours in the holidays. Not open on Sundays. Tickets available at the wall.
Access check – tel: 015394 30300

Barrow: Park Leisure Centre
Good access, low cost but limited climbing - rather compact with a tall narrow wall and a bouldering area. Excellent other facilities. Open all day until 21:45 weekdays; 10:00 to 18:00 weekends.
Access check – tel: 01229 871146

Carlisle: The Sands Centre
Reasonable, low cost, climbing facility in a large sports centre. Good bouldering and leading. Very good access and excellent general facilities. Open 09:30 to 22:30 seven days a week.
Access check – tel: 01228 625222

Carlisle: St Aidan's County High School
Good freeform featured leading wall open to the public. Bouldering may be possible but you might need your own mat. Open 17:00 to 21:00 Monday to Friday (last admission 20:00), 10:00 to 17:00 Saturday and Sunday (last admission 16:00).
Access check – tel: 01228 607469

Cockermouth: Leisure Centre
Varied bouldering with natural stonework and Bendcrete. Low cost and good access. Other sports facilities available. Open 08:00 to 22:00 Monday to Thursday; 08:00 to 21:30 Friday; 09:00 to 17:00 weekends.
Access check – tel: 01900 823596

Egremont: Wyndham Sports Centre

A good facility located in the centre of Egremont on the west coast, only half an hour from Wasdale Head. There are practice areas, bouldering, leading walls and a huge roof. Unfortunately no longer open to the public except on a club booking basis.

Access check – tel: 01946 820356

Ingleton: Inglesport Climbing Barn

Best of the small walls. Very good use of space with leading and bouldering. Regular innovations. Relaxed friendly atmosphere. Cafe and shop nearby. Open 09:00 to 22:00 Monday to Thursday; 09:00 to 17:30 Friday; 08:30 to 18:00 weekends.

Access check – tel: 015242 41146

Kendal: The Lakeland Climbing Centre

A magnificent indoor climbing facility with excellent bouldering and leading. Includes a very impressive 18 metre main wall (with fixed gear) and a huge roof. Located on the Lake District Business Park, across the A6 from Morrisons supermarket. Changing and shower facilities. Open Winter (September to April): 16:00 to 22:00 Monday; 10:00 to 22:00 Tuesday to Friday; 10:00 to 19:00 weekends and Bank Holidays. Summer (May to August): 10:00 to 22:00 Tuesday to Friday; 10:00 to 17:00 weekends and Bank Holidays.

Access check – tel: 01539 721766

Keswick: Keswick Climbing Wall and Activity Centre

Located on Southey Hill Industrial Estate, at the western end of the town. There is quite extensive bouldering, some leading and top-roping walls. Friendly atmosphere. Open 10:00 to 21:00 every day, with an extra hour (ie to 22:00), Tuesday to Thursday, from October to March.

Access check – tel: 017687 72000

Penrith: Penrith Leisure Centre – Eden Climbing Wall

An excellent wall adjoining the town's swimming pool. Good bouldering and leading walls. Open 10:00 to 21:30 weekdays; 10:00 to 21:00 weekends.

Access check – tel: 01768 863450

Bird Restrictions

by Kevin Howett & Peter Davies

As mentioned on page 19, several crags described in this guide carry Bird Restrictions in the Spring. The notes below have been drawn up jointly by the Lake District National Park Authority, the National Trust, the Cumbria Raptor Study Group, English Nature, The BMC Area Committee and the FRCC. They are only intended to cover the Lake District and outlying areas of Cumbria though they may be found useful elsewhere.

All birds, their eggs and nests, are protected by the Wildlife and Countryside Act 1981. Certain rare or more endangered species are further protected by increased penalties under the 1981 Act and must not be intentionally or recklessly disturbed when nesting. These birds are listed in the act and are referred to as *Schedule 1* species. Many are ground nesting or tree nesting birds, some are found on sea cliffs, but the *Schedule 1* bird species that climbers may most commonly encounter on crags in the Lake District is the peregrine falcon. Some agreed restrictions also apply to ravens (though these are not *Schedule 1*).

Peregrines

Peregrines are the largest falcons in the British Isles. They can be recognized by their distinctive profile, often sighted from the crag, as they plummet groundwards to seize some unsuspecting prey. Seen from below, they are pale coloured birds with dark tips to the tail and wings. Their call is a piercing shriek, once heard never forgotten, particularly if you are leading at the time! When disturbed this is uttered repeatedly for long periods. Peregrines hunt over a variety of habitats catching medium sized birds, mainly feral pigeons, by swooping at speeds of up to 200km an hour to seize them. The optimum and preferred nesting sites of peregrines in the United Kingdom are rocky coastal areas, cliffs and inland crags, but the actual nest site is not at all obvious, being just a shallow scrape in the soil. Some indication may be given by streaks of white guano (bird droppings) down an area of the crag, though this may merely be a roost site for the male rather than a nest. Peregrines are fairly common in the Lake District which is one of their most important European habitats, but they are rare elsewhere. In fact the United Kingdom supports approximately 14% of the European population. Of these, in Cumbria, there are usually about 85 nesting sites which hold one or more birds each year and approximately 65 pairs attempt to breed each season. This is 6% of the UK's total population and is considered to be the densest breeding population in the world. The Cumbrian birds are especially important because of the population numbers and productivity which is enabling the birds to spread and re-colonise other areas in the UK. They are particularly vulnerable to the weather, disturbance, poor food supply, and illegal activities such as shooting, poisoning, and egg and chick theft. In 2000 there were 83 occupied territories of which 46 pairs reared 111 young. However, in 2002 only 32 young were reared and this was the worst recorded breeding season for 30 years, predominantly due to appalling weather, but also to increased robberies. Climbers can assist here by reporting any suspicious characters they see near peregrine nest sites.

Ravens

Photo: Chris Gomersall/RSPB Images

Ravens are very large black birds, similar to a rook but a third bigger. They have distinctive deep "pruk-pruk" and "grok" calls and are great aerial acrobats that delight in soaring and tumbling. Ravens, while not protected in the same way as peregrines and eagles, are still under potential threat from increased disturbance, and there are some voluntary restrictions in the Lake District on their account. Their nests are very large piles of twigs.

Bird Restrictions

Bird Restrictions are agreed annually between the local BMC Area Committee, the National Park Authority and English Nature. The area of crag agreed to be avoided can vary depending upon various factors including the layout of the crag. Some pairs also vary their choice of nesting site each year either within a crag or between different crags and so agreements may change from year to year. In general, they only apply to the most popular crags but this does not mean that it is necessarily alright to climb on all other crags during this period; even where a crag is not subject to a restriction, if you suspect a bird (particularly a peregrine) is nesting on it, you should heed the advice below. Areas where birds are known to nest should be avoided for a period running from the **1st March to 30th June** in the case of the **peregrine**, and from **1st March to 31st May** for the **raven**.

How the law effects you

The law states that it is an offence to 'intentionally' or 'recklessly' disturb a *Schedule 1* bird 'at, on or near' the nest. It is also an offence to recklessly or intentionally disturb 'dependent' fledged young. These 'fledglings' are young birds that have just moved away from the nest but are still dependent to some extent on their parents for food and protection.

It is clear and unambiguous what 'at' and 'on' mean in this legislation, but the law does not stipulate a definition for 'near'. Nor does the law stipulate what constitutes 'disturbance'. It would be difficult to do this, as each bird species is different, and indeed individual birds are different. As a result, the prosecution would call upon expert witnesses to testify that disturbance occurred. It would also have to be shown that it was intentional or reckless.

Many peregrine falcon sites are monitored under licence by Raptor Study Groups, and it is important that climbers follow some basic guidance in order to minimise disturbance (and allow both birds and climbers to continue to coexist) as well as to make sure they are not breaking the law. Apart from possible prosecution, when arrested, police can confiscate your climbing equipment as evidence to present at the trial which may take a long time to come to court.

The following information will give a basic knowledge of *Schedule 1* bird behaviour for climbers to judge for themselves what action to take. It is not intended to be definitive, but to be a general guide.

Climbers visiting any crag in the Lake District should make efforts beforehand to find out if there are *Schedule 1* birds or ravens in residence on the crag they intend to visit. Usually restricted crags will be signed, but this may not always be the case and all climbers should acquaint themselves with the latest known details which can be found on the BMC website at www.thebmc.co.uk or on the FRCC website at www.frcc.co.uk. Where birds have not nested in any particular year, the ban may be lifted earlier. If there are birds nesting, and there is an agreed restriction, then please be prepared to change your plans according to the agreement. It may be that only some parts of the crag are restricted, so other routes can be climbed. If this is the case it will be indicated on the signs.

At the crag

If you visit a crag not listed as having an agreement, but then notice activity from a peregrine or other *Schedule 1* bird in the vicinity, then the guidance below will help you decide what to do. It can equally be used for some other nesting birds you may come across, such as ravens. Obviously, your choice of what can be done will depend on the extent of the crag and its topography as well as other factors outlined below.

As you walk into the crag keep a look out for peregrines and other birds. Peregrines in particular may be calling as they fly about the area. When you arrive they may be disturbed but this is quite normal intuitive disturbance. Try and move out of their line of sight as quickly as you can and then wait and see if they settle down and try to spot where they originate from. This will enable you to decide whether there is a nesting site that is being used near the climb that you are hoping to do, and to assess from the criteria below about disturbance, whether you feel your presence will be detrimental.

If the nest site is not directly beside where you are going to climb, the configuration of the crag means you can be separated from line of sight from the nest site to some extent, or the crucial period of egg incubation (see below) in cold weather is past, then you will probably find that the birds will have calmed down after the initial disturbance and climbing does not disturb them off the nest for long periods.

If the birds continue to appear aggressive and agitated and are staying away from the nest, then you should find another climb further away from the site, on another part of the crag, or indeed another crag, as to continue climbing could cause damaging disturbance by keeping the parents off the nest for too long.

How do you judge disturbance?

Most birds will act instinctively to protect their nest site when they perceive a threat. They will often make an initial reaction to human presence, calling, often repeatedly or aggressively. They will then either realise there is no threat and will settle down, or, if they continue and you then move away from them, they will then stop their instinctive behaviour.

It can be difficult for non-ornithologists to judge when a peregrine's call changes from normal activity to that of a protection call, but listen for a more aggressive tone. If the female then flies from the nest and stays away, then they have been disturbed and it becomes detrimental to breeding success.

How close is too close?

There are no hard and fast rules to determine when you might be too close as so much depends upon the tolerance of the individual bird. If the crag is very popular with climbers, then any nesting birds may be habituated to climbers' presence. Such peregrines may be able to accept climbing in quite close proximity, as long as it is around the other side of an arête or on a separate buttress. Of one thing you can be sure is that climbing very close or directly onto the nest will cause damaging disturbance. At crags in remote areas where there is little climbing activity, birds may be disturbed even at some distance. Of particular importance is the line of sight. If the bird can see you it is far more likely to be disturbed. The best policy is to err upon the side of caution and if in any doubt retreat.

The most important period of nesting

For most birds the most sensitive periods are up to egg-laying, and when they have just laid eggs; for peregrines this period can be from February to late April when the ambient air temperature is still low. A later sensitive period is when the chicks have just hatched (for peregrines, mid to end of May). If adults are repeatedly or continually kept off the nest by climbers, then the eggs or chicks will quickly cool and die, or become available to predation. Obviously there is an even greater risk in cold conditions, and the position of the nest (on a north or south-facing crag) and the time of day will also be important factors to take into account. For ravens, the period in mid-April to mid-May when they are feeding their chicks is critical as this process needs to be constant throughout the day or the chicks will starve.

Above: Herdwick sheep on Gable – the true locals **Photo:** Nick Wharton

What to do if challenged or arrested

Even with the best of intentions, it is possible that, having obeyed the above guidelines, you may be accused of disturbing a bird, or of climbing on a crag where you should not have done. If asked to leave, then please do so without fuss, but please ask and note the name of the person requesting you to leave, the organisation they represent, and the reason you have been asked to leave. If the worst happens and you are arrested, then as soon as possible make full notes of the circumstances leading up to your arrest with especial detail on the position of any nests vis-à-vis your climb and the behaviour of any birds. These notes will form vital evidence if the case goes to court, which may be months or even years after the event. In all circumstances please report the details to the BMC.

Useful Contacts

The telephone numbers and websites listed below were correct at time of going to press.

Climbing

British Mountaineering Council 0870 0104878 www.thebmc.co.uk
FRCC www.frcc.co.uk
National Mountaineering Exhibition, Rheged, Penrith 01768 868000 www.rheged.com

Lake District Weather

Fell Top Weather Forecast 017687 75757

Lake District National Park Authority

Head Office 01539 724555 www.lake-district.gov.uk
Bird Restrictions 017687 79633
Brockhole National Park Centre 015394 46601

Cumbria Tourist Board

Website www.golakes.co.uk

Lake District National Park and/or Cumbria Tourist Board Information Centres

Ambleside 015394 32582
Ambleside, Waterhead 015394 32729
Borrowdale, Seatoller 017687 77294
Bowness 015394 42895
Broughton in Furness 015242 62549
Coniston 015394 41533
Glenridding 017684 82414
Grasmere 015394 35245
Hawkshead 015394 36525
Egremont 01946 820693
Keswick 017687 72645
Kendal 01539 725758

Penrith 01768 867466
Camping Barns 017687 72645

Other Information
What's on in Cumbria 015394 46363
Cumbria County Council Journey Planner 01228 606000
www.cumbria.gov.uk

Above: The National Mountaineering Exhibition at the Rheged Centre near Penrith
Photo: NME

Campsites & Camping Barns

The list of Campsites and Camping Barns in the Lake District below is fairly comprehensive, but there are no doubt more, and fuller details will be available from the Tourist Information Offices. This information is current in 2002 but will almost certainly alter and it is probably best to make telephone contact before going to a particular site or barn.

Southern Lake District

Campsites	Grid Ref	Telephone
Coniston, Coniston Hall	304 962	015394 41223
Coniston, Crake	290 890	01229 885203
Coniston, Hoathwaite	297 949	015394 41349
Coniston, Park Coppice	297 957	015394 41555
Hawkshead, Hawkshead Hall	350 988	015394 36221
Hawkshead, Croft	353 982	015394 36374
Hawkshead, Low Wray	371 012	015394 32810
Skelwith, Tarn Foot	343 038	015394 32596
Langdale, National Trust	287 059	015394 37668
Langdale, Chapel Stile	315 052	015394 37615 or 37150
Windermere, Troutbeck, Limefitt Park	414 032	015394 32300
Camping Barns	**Grid Ref**	**Telephone**
Broughton in Furness, Fell End Farm	239 881	017687 72645
Langdale, Sticklebarn	295 064	015394 37356
Grasmere, Broadrayne Farm	337 094	015394 35055

Western Lake District

Campsites	Grid Ref	Telephone
Buttermere, Sykes Farm	173 171	017687 70222
Buttermere, Dalegarth	186 159	017687 70233
Buttermere, Gatesgarth	191 148	017687 70256
Lorton, Wheatsheaf Inn	155 259	01900 85268
Lorton, Whinfell Hall	150 254	01900 85260
St Bees, Seacote Park	962 120	01946 822777
Wasdale, Santon Bridge	111 017	019467 26286
Nether Wasdale, Church Stile	126 042	019467 26388
Wasdale Head	185 088	019467 26384
Wasdale Head – National Trust	185 073	019467 26220
Eskdale, Fisherground	152 001	019467 23319
Eskdale, Hollins Farm	178 010	019467 23253
Camping Barns	**Grid Ref**	**Telephone**
Buttermere, Crag Barn	174 172	017687 72645
Loweswater, Waterend Farm, Swallow Barn	116 226	017687 72645
Loweswater, Holme Wood Bothy	123 216	015394 63856
St Bees, Tarn Flatts Hall Farm	947 146	017687 72645
Ennerdale, High Gillerthwaite	142 141	017687 72645
Gosforth, Mill House Barn	800 044	017687 72645

Northern Lake District

Campsites	Grid Ref	Telephone
Threlkeld, Burns Farm	305 242	017687 79225
Threlkeld, Setmabanning	322 247	017687 79229
Thirlmere, Dale Bottom	295 220	017687 72176
Thirlmere, Bridge End Farm	315 192	017687 72166
Braithwaite, Scotgate	235 236	017687 78343
Keswick, Castlerigg Hall	280 225	017687 72437
Keswick, Castlerigg	283 223	017687 72479
Keswick, Derwentwater	260 232	017687 72392
Borrowdale, Ashness	192 271	017687 77361
Borrowdale, Grange, Hollows Farm	250 167	017687 77298
Borrowdale, Stonethwaite, Langstrath	268 133	017687 77234
Borrowdale, Stonethwaite, Chapel Farm	257 140	017687 77602
Borrowdale, Seatoller, Nichol Dub	245 139	017687 77232
Borrowdale, Seathwaite Farm	232 122	017687 77394
Camping Barns	**Grid Ref**	**Telephone**
Caldbeck – Hudscales	332 375	017687 72645
Mungrisdale, Blake Beck Farm	367 278	017687 72645
St Johns in the Vale, Low Bridge End	316 205	017687 79242
Thirlmere, Causeway Foot	294 218	017687 72290
Newlands, Catbells Barn	243 208	017687 72645
Rosthwaite, Dinah Hoggas Barn	259 151	017687 72645

Eastern Lake District

Campsites	Grid Ref	Telephone
Hartsop, Sykeside	401 120	017684 82239
Glenridding, Gillside	382 168	017684 82346
Patterdale, Side Farm	397 167	017684 82337
Watermillock, Cove Park	432 234	017684 86549
Watermillock, The Quiet Site	428 235	017684 86337
Watermillock, Ullswater	435 229	017684 86666
Pooley Bridge, Park Foot	470 235	017684 86309
Pooley Bridge, Waterside	463 231	017684 86332
Pooley Bridge, Roe Head	475 242	017684 86363
Penrith, Lowther	526 263	01768 863631
Troutbeck, Gillhead	364 270	017687 79652
Penruddock, Beckes	417 277	017684 83224
Berrier, Hopkinson Park	405 288	017684 83456
Bunkhouses	**Grid Ref**	**Telephone**
Glenridding, Gillside	382 168	017684 82346
Hartsop, Sykeside	401 120	017684 82239
Camping Barns	**Grid Ref**	**Telephone**
Greenside, Swirral Barn	364 174	017687 72645

Above: Mountain rescue team at work in White Ghyll **Photo:** Dave Willis

Mountain Accidents

by Dr John Ellerton (LDSAMRA)

Procedure for climbers in the Lake District

Mountain rescue in the Lake District is well served by 13 voluntary teams backed up by special search and cave/mine rescue units. They are equipped to a high standard and work closely with the RAF helicopters and Air Ambulance services. Consequently, only minor casualties should come within the scope of treatment and evacuation by the climber's companions. The rule for all other cases, is to make the casualty safe, to start first aid, and to send for a Mountain Rescue Team.

Sending for Help

A reliable member of the party, with full information about the nature of the injuries and the position of the incident (including, if possible, the map reference) should be sent to find the nearest telephone. He should dial 999, and ask for the Police, who will notify the appropriate team. The sender of the message should stay by the telephone until he receives instructions from the Team Leader. Mobile phones can save a considerable amount of time – please use them to call the Police. Have the mobile phone number handy and keep within reception range. Reception is often better on the tops or ridges of the mountains. Do not switch the phone off – the team leader will call back.

Lack of help

You have a difficult decision to make when the casualty is severely injured, possibly unconscious, and you are alone. You should try to summon help from nearby climbers or walkers by shouting, giving the distress call on a whistle (6 blasts repeated regularly), flashing a torch (6 flashes repeated regularly), or sending up a red flare. If there is no response then assess the relative dangers of leaving the casualty, or of failing to get help, and then act decisively in the interest of the casualty.

Emergency precautions and first aid

While waiting for the rescue team, you should check for further danger, and then carry out basic first-aid treatment.

Safety first

Are you and the casualty safe from further danger?
If not try and make yourselves safe: either by moving, or anchoring yourselves, or both. Is the casualty responsive?

Is the casualty's Airway open?

If necessary, open it by a simple jaw thrust or lift. If possible, avoid moving the neck after trauma. An open airway is essential if the casualty is unconscious or semi-conscious as reduced consciousness can cause death from asphyxia as the tongue falls back blocking the airway. The position of the casualty, in particular his head and tongue, should be adjusted to open the airway and continually reassessed.

Is the casualty Breathing?

Look, feel and listen for breathing. Basic Life Support should be started, if you are trained, when the casualty is unconscious and shows no signs of breathing, and it can be continued until help arrives and where there is a chance of recovery (lightning, drowning, heart attack). It is usually futile in casualties with internal injuries and is probably best to defer in cases of severe exposure/hypothermia until expert help is available. An unconscious and breathing casualty should be put in the Recovery Position if possible. Check the airway is still open.

Is the casualty's Circulation adequate

Stop any bleeding from wounds by elevation and direct pressure with dressings or clothing. The pressure needs to be applied continuously for at least 10 minutes. Raising the legs and/or lowering the head may be appropriate. Internal haemorrhage should be suspected if the casualty has sustained blows to the chest or abdomen or broken the femur (thigh bone). The condition often deteriorates and all steps should be taken to facilitate the rapid arrival of the Mountain Rescue Team and, if possible, a helicopter. A record of the pulse rate and consciousness level is very helpful.

Is the casualty Disabled due to damage to his head or spine?

Record the casualty's consciousness level – alert, responsive to voice, responsive to pain or unresponsive? Has the spine been damaged? If so, do not move the casualty unless essential for safety reasons. Maintain the head in the normal straight position using your hands.

Check the limbs for fractures

If present, immobilise the limb by the simplest method available. In the case of the arm, pad it and bandage it to the chest, and in the case of the leg, pad it and bandage it to the other leg.

Prevent hypothermia (exposure)

Shelter the casualty from wind and rain. Wrap them in as many layers of clothing as possible and encase them in a 'poly bag' or other impermeable barrier. Do not forget to insulate the head and underneath the casualty.

A **helicopter** may arrive before the mountain rescue team. Extinguish all flames and secure all equipment. The downdraught can knock you over, so get in a safe position. Do not approach the helicopter until clearly signalled to do so by the pilot.

Further Points to Consider

Large, **organised groups** should bear in mind that Mountain Rescue Teams are a finite resource and it is wrong to assume their availability.

The majority of climbers killed in the Lake District as a result of a climbing accident die from a head injury. A **helmet**, whilst not being 100% effective, can make the difference between living and dying.

Whilst **mobile phones** can be very useful in emergencies, any temptation to use them in the hills to call the emergency services in non-emergency circumstances should be resisted. If you are not sure whether it is an emergency or not, please investigate a little yourself first before reaching for your phone.

GPS systems, whilst also useful, are no substitute for carrying a **map** and **compass** and knowing how to use them.

The routine carrying of a suitable **head-torch** would save many needless call-outs.

Lake District Mountain Rescue Teams are made up of unpaid volunteers and rely on charitable contributions. Your consideration and a "Thank you" go a long way to ensure the service continues.

The Lake District Search and Mountain Rescue Association (LDSAMRA) acts as an umbrella body for the Lakeland Mountain Rescue Teams. It has a website at:
http://homepages.enterprise.net/ldsamra/
which gives contact details for the individual teams.

CRAG GUIDE Crag Name	Aspect	Alt (m)	Rock Type*	Drying Time‡	Route Lengths (m)	Approach Time (mins)	Total Routes 596	M D VD	MS S HS	MVS VS	HVS E1	E2 E3	E4+
Raven Crag, Walthwaite	S	180	*BV*	*F*	22–37	5	5		2	2	1		
Scout Crag	S	275	*BV*	*F*	11–55	10	7	4	2	1			
White Ghyll	W	400	*BV*	*F/M*	25–82	30	18		3	6	7	2	
Pavey Ark	SE/E	570	*BV*	*M/S*	46–112	55	22	3	3	2	7	4	3
Raven Crags, ODG	E/S/W	200	*BV*	*F*	18–90	15	19	2	5	4	6		2
Gimmer Crag	SE/S/NW	525	*BV*	*F/M*	31–97	55	22	3	5	5	6	3	
Neckband Crag	N	550	*BV*	*S*	33–40	75	7			1	3	3	
Flat Crag	ENE	750	*BV*	*M*	33–43	95	4		1		1	2	
Cambridge Crag	E	775	*BV*	*M*	77	100	1	1					
North Buttress	NE	785	*BV*	*S*	28–56	105	4				2	1	1
Bowfell	E/N	750	*BV*	*M*	60–112	105	4	2			1	1	
Black Crag, Wrynose	S/W	580	*BV*	*F*	12–16	25	8	1	1		3	3	
Long Scar	SW	560	*BV*	*F*	14–20	25	5	4	1				
Dow Crag	E	610	*BV*	*F/M*	25–115	65	30	4	6	4	7	4	5
Little How Crag	SE	550	*BV*	*F/M*	30–42	60	4	1	2	1			
Great How Crag	S/SE	540	*BV*	*M*	60–78	65	2	2					
Hodge Close Quarry	W	170	*Sl*	*F*	33–64	5	11				1	4	6
Cathedral Quarry	W/N	150	*Sl*	*F/M*	30–45	5–25	6				1	3	2
Wallowbarrow Crag	SW	210	*BV*	*F*	32–63	15	9	2	2	5			

* **Rock Type:** ***BV*** = *Borrowdale Volcanic*, ***Sa*** = *Sandstone*, ***Li*** = *Limestone*, ***Sl*** = *Slate*, ***Gr*** = *Granite*

‡ **Drying Time:** ***F*** = *Fast*, ***M*** = *Medium*, ***S*** = *Slow*

CRAG GUIDE Crag Name	Aspect	Alt (m)	Rock Type*	Drying Time‡	Route Lengths (m)	Approach Time (mins)	Total Routes 596	M D VD	MS S HS	MVS VS	HVS E1	E2 E3	E4+
Burnt Crag	S	350	*BV*	*F*	24–30	20	6					4	2
Esk Buttress	SE	490	*BV*	*F/M*	38–111	90	11		1	2	5	2	1
Hardknott Crag	W	440	*BV*	*F/M*	27–34	5	6				2	3	1
Bell Stand	S	210	*Gr*	*F*	12–17	15	6			2	2	2	
Hare Crag	SW	170	*Gr*	*F*	15–28	10	11	2	1	2	3	3	
Heron Crag	SE	250	*BV*	*F/M*	51–58	30	6			2	2	2	
Scafell Crag	N	790	*BV*	*M/S*	45–122	90	16	1	5	5	1	3	1
East Buttress	E/SE	750	*BV*	*M/S*	45–99	90	19			3	7	5	4
Pikes Crag	W	760	*BV*	*F/M*	75–129	80	5	2	1	1	1		
Buckbarrow, Wasdale	SE	350	*BV*	*F*	22–40	20	8			3	4	1	
Gable Crag	N	800	*BV*	*S*	45–75	75	8			2	2	4	
Kern Knotts	SW	520	*BV*	*F*	20–60	60–75	8		1	4	1	2	
The Napes	SE/SW	650	*BV*	*F*	17–107	75–90	15	5	3	1	3	2	1
Pillar Rock	N/S/E/W	600	*BV*	*M/S*	50–158	120	25	2	5	6	8	3	1
Yew Crags	SW	350	*Sl*	*F*	30–40	20	4				4		
Buckstone How	SW	400	*Sl*	*F*	48–95	10	5		1	1	3		
High Crag	NE	450	*BV*	*M*	20–75	45	12	1		3	6	2	
Eagle Crag	W/N	650	*BV*	*S*	70–150	75	6			3	1	2	
Grey Crag	SE	660	*BV*	*F*	38–80	85	9	2	4	3			

* **Rock Type:** ***BV*** = *Borrowdale Volcanic*, ***Sa*** = *Sandstone*, ***Li*** = *Limestone*, ***Sl*** = *Slate*, ***Gr*** = *Granite*

‡ **Drying Time:** ***F*** = *Fast*, ***M*** = *Medium*, ***S*** = *Slow*

CRAG GUIDE Crag Name	Aspect	Alt (m)	Rock Type*	Drying Time‡	Route Lengths (m)	Approach Time (mins)	Total Routes 596	M D VD	MS S HS	MVS VS	HVS E1	E2 E3	E4+
St Bees	W	5	*Sa*	*F*	<25	15	20				4	10	6
Falcon Crags	W	180	*BV*	*F*	40–60	10	12			3	4	4	1
Reecastle Crag	NW	300	*BV*	*M*	26–40	10	9				2	5	2
Gowder Crag	W	200	*BV*	*F/M*	113	10	1			1			
Shepherd's Crag	W	140	*BV*	*F*	20–80	5–20	29	5	2	10	10	2	
Black Crag, Borrowdale	W/N	260	*BV*	*M*	70–114	20	8		1	1	4	1	1
Quayfoot Buttress	NW/N	135	*BV*	*F/M*	36–60	5	5	1		1	2	1	
Bowderstone Crag	SW	220	*BV*	*F*	30–35	20	3						3
Eagle Crag, Langstrath	ENE	500	*BV*	*M/S*	30–58	35	8			2	1	4	1
Bleak How	NW	270	*BV*	*F*	30–36	30	4				3	1	
Sergeant Crag Slab	W	400	*BV*	*F/M*	45	45	7			1	5	1	
Raven Crag, Combe Ghyll	NE	360	*BV*	*M*	13–178	60	5	3	1	1			
Gillercombe	SE	480	*BV*	*F/M*	195	35–50	1		1				
Goat Crag	NE	350	*BV*	*M*	53–100	30	10			1	3	3	3
Castle Rock	W/S	275	*BV*	*F/M*	25–100	10	17	2	2	5	4	4	
Lower Swirl Crag	SW	330	*BV*	*F/M*	<25	40	4				2	2	
Raven Crag, Thirlmere	E	300	*BV*	*M*	42–78	20	9		1	1	1	2	4
Eagle Crag, Grisedale	E	400	*BV*	*F/M*	37–76	80	4		1	1	1	1	
Scrubby Crag	SE	710	*BV*	*M/S*	54–84	90	3			2	1		

* **Rock Type:** ***BV*** = *Borrowdale Volcanic*, ***Sa*** = *Sandstone*, ***Li*** = *Limestone*, ***Sl*** = *Slate*, ***Gr*** = *Granite*

‡ **Drying Time:** ***F*** = *Fast*, ***M*** = *Medium*, ***S*** = *Slow*

CRAG GUIDE Crag Name	Aspect	Alt (m)	Rock Type*	Drying Time‡	Route Lengths (m)	Approach Time (mins)	Total Routes 596	M D VD	MS S HS	MVS VS	HVS E1	E2 E3	E4+
Gill Crag	S	490	*BV*	*F*	28–53	45	3	2	1				
Dove Crag	NE	580	*BV*	*M/S*	45–96	75	8		1		2	2	3
Raven Crag, Threshthwaite	SE	450	*BV*	*M*	30–40	40	6					3	3
Gouther Crag	NW	350	*BV*	*F/M*	22–40	20	10	1	2	1	3	3	
Armathwaite	SW	50	*Sa*	*F*	9–35	10	20	2	1	1	6	6	4
Chapel Head Scar	SW	70	*Li*	*F*	12–30	15	23					6	17

* **Rock Type:** ***BV*** = *Borrowdale Volcanic*, ***Sa*** = *Sandstone*, ***Li*** = *Limestone*, ***Sl*** = *Slate*, ***Gr*** = *Granite*

‡ **Drying Time:** ***F*** = *Fast*, ***M*** = *Medium*, ***S*** = *Slow*

Index of Crags

Crag topos are shown in BOLD type

Index of Climbs

Geological Map
of the Lake District
Irish Sea
N
A596
MARYPORT
A595
A594
COCKERMOUTH
A66
WORKINGTON
A66
A595
A5086
Lowes-
water
Buttermere
Crummoc
Water
Ennerdale
Water
Ennerdale
WHITEHAVEN
A595
ENNERDALE
BRIDGE
Anglers
Crag pg 469
EGREMONT
St Bees Head pg 305
Wasdale
GOSFORTH
ESKDALE
GREEN
HOLMROOK
A595
Volcanic rock
Volcanic slate quarry
Granite
Limestone
Sandstone
Other sedimentary rock
This simplified geological map illustrates the various types
of rock which form the mountains of the Lake District.
It does not indicate the quality or the suitability of the rock
for climbing, as this varies greatly with each type of rock.